Introduction to Machine Learning with Python

A Guide for Data Scientists

Andreas C. Müller and Sarah Guido

Beijing • Boston • Farnham • Sebastopol • Tokyo O'REILLY®

Introduction to Machine Learning with Python

by Andreas C. Müller and Sarah Guido

Published by O'Reilly Media, Inc., 1005 Gravenstein Highway North, Sebastopol, CA 95472.

O'Reilly books may be purchased for educational, business, or sales promotional use. Online editions are also available for most titles (*http://oreilly.com/safari*). For more information, contact our corporate/institutional sales department: 800-998-9938 or *corporate@oreilly.com*.

Editor: Dawn Schanafelt
Production Editor: Kristen Brown
Copyeditor: Rachel Head
Proofreader: Jasmine Kwityn
Indexer: Judy McConville
Interior Designer: David Futato
Cover Designer: Karen Montgomery
Illustrator: Rebecca Demarest

October 2016: First Edition

Revision History for the First Edition

2016-09-22: First Release
2017-01-13: Second Release
2017-06-09: Third Release
2018-10-19: Fourth Release

See *http://oreilly.com/catalog/errata.csp?isbn=9781449369415* for release details.

978-1-449-36941-5

[LSI]

Table of Contents

Preface

Machine learning is an integral part of many commercial applications and research projects today, in areas ranging from medical diagnosis and treatment to finding your friends on social networks. Many people think that machine learning can only be applied by large companies with extensive research teams. In this book, we want to show you how easy it can be to build machine learning solutions yourself, and how to best go about it. With the knowledge in this book, you can build your own system for finding out how people feel on Twitter, or making predictions about global warming. The applications of machine learning are endless and, with the amount of data available today, mostly limited by your imagination.

Who Should Read This Book

This book is for current and aspiring machine learning practitioners looking to implement solutions to real-world machine learning problems. This is an introductory book requiring no previous knowledge of machine learning or artificial intelligence (AI). We focus on using Python and the `scikit-learn` library, and work through all the steps to create a successful machine learning application. The methods we introduce will be helpful for scientists and researchers, as well as data scientists working on commercial applications. You will get the most out of the book if you are somewhat familiar with Python and the NumPy and `matplotlib` libraries.

We made a conscious effort not to focus too much on the math, but rather on the practical aspects of using machine learning algorithms. As mathematics (probability theory, in particular) is the foundation upon which machine learning is built, we won't go into the analysis of the algorithms in great detail. If you are interested in the mathematics of machine learning algorithms, we recommend the book *The Elements of Statistical Learning* (Springer) by Trevor Hastie, Robert Tibshirani, and Jerome Friedman, which is available for free at the authors' website (*http://web.stanford.edu/~hastie/ElemStatLearn/*). We will also not describe how to write machine learning algorithms from scratch, and will instead focus on how to use the large array of models already implemented in `scikit-learn` and other libraries.

Why We Wrote This Book

There are many books on machine learning and AI. However, all of them are meant for graduate students or PhD students in computer science, and they're full of advanced mathematics. This is in stark contrast with how machine learning is being used, as a commodity tool in research and commercial applications. Today, applying machine learning does not require a PhD. However, there are few resources out there that fully cover all the important aspects of implementing machine learning in practice, without requiring you to take advanced math courses. We hope this book will help people who want to apply machine learning without reading up on years' worth of calculus, linear algebra, and probability theory.

Navigating This Book

This book is organized roughly as follows:

- Chapter 1 introduces the fundamental concepts of machine learning and its applications, and describes the setup we will be using throughout the book.
- Chapters 2 and 3 describe the actual machine learning algorithms that are most widely used in practice, and discuss their advantages and shortcomings.
- Chapter 4 discusses the importance of how we represent data that is processed by machine learning, and what aspects of the data to pay attention to.
- Chapter 5 covers advanced methods for model evaluation and parameter tuning, with a particular focus on cross-validation and grid search.
- Chapter 6 explains the concept of pipelines for chaining models and encapsulating your workflow.
- Chapter 7 shows how to apply the methods described in earlier chapters to text data, and introduces some text-specific processing techniques.
- Chapter 8 offers a high-level overview, and includes references to more advanced topics.

While Chapters 2 and 3 provide the actual algorithms, understanding all of these algorithms might not be necessary for a beginner. If you need to build a machine learning system ASAP, we suggest starting with Chapter 1 and the opening sections of Chapter 2, which introduce all the core concepts. You can then skip to Section 2.5 on page 129 in Chapter 2, which includes a list of all the supervised models that we cover. Choose the model that best fits your needs and flip back to read the section devoted to it for details. Then you can use the techniques in Chapter 5 to evaluate and tune your model.

Online Resources

While studying this book, definitely refer to the `scikit-learn` website (*http://scikit-learn.org*) for more in-depth documentation of the classes and functions, and many examples. There is also a video course created by Andreas Müller, "Advanced Machine Learning with scikit-learn," that supplements this book. You can find it at *http://bit.ly/advanced_machine_learning_scikit-learn*.

Conventions Used in This Book

The following typographical conventions are used in this book:

Italic
: Indicates new terms, URLs, email addresses, filenames, and file extensions.

`Constant width`
: Used for program listings, as well as within paragraphs to refer to program elements such as variable or function names, databases, data types, environment variables, statements, and keywords. Also used for commands and module and package names.

`Constant width bold`
: Shows commands or other text that should be typed literally by the user.

`Constant width italic`
: Shows text that should be replaced with user-supplied values or by values determined by context.

This element signifies a tip or suggestion.

This element signifies a general note.

This icon indicates a warning or caution.

Using Code Examples

Supplemental material (code examples, IPython notebooks, etc.) is available for download at *https://github.com/amueller/introduction_to_ml_with_python*.

This book is here to help you get your job done. In general, if example code is offered with this book, you may use it in your programs and documentation. You do not need to contact us for permission unless you're reproducing a significant portion of the code. For example, writing a program that uses several chunks of code from this book does not require permission. Selling or distributing a CD-ROM of examples from O'Reilly books does require permission. Answering a question by citing this book and quoting example code does not require permission. Incorporating a significant amount of example code from this book into your product's documentation does require permission.

We appreciate, but do not require, attribution. An attribution usually includes the title, author, publisher, and ISBN. For example: "*An Introduction to Machine Learning with Python* by Andreas C. Müller and Sarah Guido (O'Reilly). Copyright 2017 Sarah Guido and Andreas Müller, 978-1-449-36941-5."

If you feel your use of code examples falls outside fair use or the permission given above, feel free to contact us at *permissions@oreilly.com*.

O'Reilly Safari

Safari (formerly Safari Books Online) is a membership-based training and reference platform for enterprise, government, educators, and individuals.

Members have access to thousands of books, training videos, Learning Paths, interactive tutorials, and curated playlists from over 250 publishers, including O'Reilly Media, Harvard Business Review, Prentice Hall Professional, Addison-Wesley Professional, Microsoft Press, Sams, Que, Peachpit Press, Adobe, Focal Press, Cisco Press, John Wiley & Sons, Syngress, Morgan Kaufmann, IBM Redbooks, Packt, Adobe Press, FT Press, Apress, Manning, New Riders, McGraw-Hill, Jones & Bartlett, and Course Technology, among others.

For more information, please visit *http://oreilly.com/safari*.

How to Contact Us

Please address comments and questions concerning this book to the publisher:

O'Reilly Media, Inc.
1005 Gravenstein Highway North
Sebastopol, CA 95472
800-998-9938 (in the United States or Canada)
707-829-0515 (international or local)
707-829-0104 (fax)

We have a web page for this book, where we list errata, examples, and any additional information. You can access this page at *http://bit.ly/intro-machine-learning-python*.

To comment or ask technical questions about this book, send email to *bookquestions@oreilly.com*.

For more information about our books, courses, conferences, and news, see our website at *http://www.oreilly.com*.

Find us on Facebook: *http://facebook.com/oreilly*

Follow us on Twitter: *http://twitter.com/oreillymedia*

Watch us on YouTube: *http://www.youtube.com/oreillymedia*

Acknowledgments

From Andreas

Without the help and support of a large group of people, this book would never have existed.

I would like to thank the editors, Meghan Blanchette, Brian MacDonald, and in particular Dawn Schanafelt, for helping Sarah and me make this book a reality.

I want to thank my reviewers, Thomas Caswell, Olivier Grisel, Stefan van der Walt, and John Myles White, who took the time to read the early versions of this book and provided me with invaluable feedback—in addition to being some of the cornerstones of the scientific open source ecosystem.

I am forever thankful for the welcoming open source scientific Python community, especially the contributors to `scikit-learn`. Without the support and help from this community, in particular from Gael Varoquaux, Alex Gramfort, and Olivier Grisel, I would never have become a core contributor to `scikit-learn` or learned to understand this package as well as I do now. My thanks also go out to all the other contributors who donate their time to improve and maintain this package.

I'm also thankful for the discussions with many of my colleagues and peers that helped me understand the challenges of machine learning and gave me ideas for structuring a textbook. Among the people I talk to about machine learning, I specifically want to thank Brian McFee, Daniela Huttenkoppen, Joel Nothman, Gilles Louppe, Hugo Bowne-Anderson, Sven Kreis, Alice Zheng, Kyunghyun Cho, Pablo Baberas, and Dan Cervone.

My thanks also go out to Rachel Rakov, who was an eager beta tester and proofreader of an early version of this book, and helped me shape it in many ways.

On the personal side, I want to thank my parents, Harald and Margot, and my sister, Miriam, for their continuing support and encouragement. I also want to thank the many people in my life whose love and friendship gave me the energy and support to undertake such a challenging task.

From Sarah

I would like to thank Meg Blanchette, without whose help and guidance this project would not have even existed. Thanks to Celia La and Brian Carlson for reading in the early days. Thanks to the O'Reilly folks for their endless patience. And finally, thanks to DTS, for your everlasting and endless support.

CHAPTER 1
Introduction

Machine learning is about extracting knowledge from data. It is a research field at the intersection of statistics, artificial intelligence, and computer science and is also known as predictive analytics or statistical learning. The application of machine learning methods has in recent years become ubiquitous in everyday life. From automatic recommendations of which movies to watch, to what food to order or which products to buy, to personalized online radio and recognizing your friends in your photos, many modern websites and devices have machine learning algorithms at their core. When you look at a complex website like Facebook, Amazon, or Netflix, it is very likely that every part of the site contains multiple machine learning models.

Outside of commercial applications, machine learning has had a tremendous influence on the way data-driven research is done today. The tools introduced in this book have been applied to diverse scientific problems such as understanding stars, finding distant planets, discovering new particles, analyzing DNA sequences, and providing personalized cancer treatments.

Your application doesn't need to be as large-scale or world-changing as these examples in order to benefit from machine learning, though. In this chapter, we will explain why machine learning has become so popular, and discuss what kind of problem can be solved using machine learning. Then, we will show you how to build your first machine learning model, introducing important concepts along the way.

1.1 Why Machine Learning?

In the early days of "intelligent" applications, many systems used handcoded rules of "if" and "else" decisions to process data or adjust to user input. Think of a spam filter whose job is to move the appropriate incoming email messages to a spam folder. You could make up a blacklist of words that would result in an email being marked as spam. This would be an example of using an expert-designed rule system to design an "intelligent" application. Manually crafting decision rules is feasible for some applications, particularly those in which humans have a good understanding of the process to model. However, using handcoded rules to make decisions has two major disadvantages:

- The logic required to make a decision is specific to a single domain and task. Changing the task even slightly might require a rewrite of the whole system.
- Designing rules requires a deep understanding of how a decision should be made by a human expert.

One example of where this handcoded approach will fail is in detecting faces in images. Today, every smartphone can detect a face in an image. However, face detection was an unsolved problem until as recently as 2001. The main problem is that the way in which pixels (which make up an image in a computer) are "perceived" by the computer is very different from how humans perceive a face. This difference in representation makes it basically impossible for a human to come up with a good set of rules to describe what constitutes a face in a digital image.

Using machine learning, however, simply presenting a program with a large collection of images of faces is enough for an algorithm to determine what characteristics are needed to identify a face.

1.1.1 Problems Machine Learning Can Solve

The most successful kinds of machine learning algorithms are those that automate decision-making processes by generalizing from known examples. In this setting, which is known as *supervised learning*, the user provides the algorithm with pairs of inputs and desired outputs, and the algorithm finds a way to produce the desired output given an input. In particular, the algorithm is able to create an output for an input it has never seen before without any help from a human. Going back to our example of spam classification, using machine learning, the user provides the algorithm with a large number of emails (which are the input), together with information about whether any of these emails are spam (which is the desired output). Given a new email, the algorithm will then produce a prediction as to whether the new email is spam.

Machine learning algorithms that learn from input/output pairs are called supervised learning algorithms because a "teacher" provides supervision to the algorithms in the form of the desired outputs for each example that they learn from. While creating a dataset of inputs and outputs is often a laborious manual process, supervised learning algorithms are well understood and their performance is easy to measure. If your application can be formulated as a supervised learning problem, and you are able to create a dataset that includes the desired outcome, machine learning will likely be able to solve your problem.

Examples of supervised machine learning tasks include:

Identifying the zip code from handwritten digits on an envelope
: Here the input is a scan of the handwriting, and the desired output is the actual digits in the zip code. To create a dataset for building a machine learning model, you need to collect many envelopes. Then you can read the zip codes yourself and store the digits as your desired outcomes.

Determining whether a tumor is benign based on a medical image
: Here the input is the image, and the output is whether the tumor is benign. To create a dataset for building a model, you need a database of medical images. You also need an expert opinion, so a doctor needs to look at all of the images and decide which tumors are benign and which are not. It might even be necessary to do additional diagnosis beyond the content of the image to determine whether the tumor in the image is cancerous or not.

Detecting fraudulent activity in credit card transactions
: Here the input is a record of the credit card transaction, and the output is whether it is likely to be fraudulent or not. Assuming that you are the entity distributing the credit cards, collecting a dataset means storing all transactions and recording if a user reports any transaction as fraudulent.

An interesting thing to note about these examples is that although the inputs and outputs look fairly straightforward, the data collection process for these three tasks is vastly different. While reading envelopes is laborious, it is easy and cheap. Obtaining medical imaging and diagnoses, on the other hand, requires not only expensive machinery but also rare and expensive expert knowledge, not to mention the ethical concerns and privacy issues. In the example of detecting credit card fraud, data collection is much simpler. Your customers will provide you with the desired output, as they will report fraud. All you have to do to obtain the input/output pairs of fraudulent and nonfraudulent activity is wait.

Unsupervised algorithms are the other type of algorithm that we will cover in this book. In unsupervised learning, only the input data is known, and no known output data is given to the algorithm. While there are many successful applications of these methods, they are usually harder to understand and evaluate. Examples of unsupervised learning include:

Identifying topics in a set of blog posts
: If you have a large collection of text data, you might want to summarize it and find prevalent themes in it. You might not know beforehand what these topics are, or how many topics there might be. Therefore, there are no known outputs.

Segmenting customers into groups with similar preferences
Given a set of customer records, you might want to identify which customers are similar, and whether there are groups of customers with similar preferences. For a shopping site, these might be "parents," "bookworms," or "gamers." Because you don't know in advance what these groups might be, or even how many there are, you have no known outputs.

Detecting abnormal access patterns to a website
To identify abuse or bugs, it is often helpful to find access patterns that are different from the norm. Each abnormal pattern might be very different, and you might not have any recorded instances of abnormal behavior. Because in this example you only observe traffic, and you don't know what constitutes normal and abnormal behavior, this is an unsupervised problem.

For both supervised and unsupervised learning tasks, it is important to have a representation of your input data that a computer can understand. Often it is helpful to think of your data as a table. Each data point that you want to reason about (each email, each customer, each transaction) is a row, and each property that describes that data point (say, the age of a customer or the amount or location of a transaction) is a column. You might describe users by their age, their gender, when they created an account, and how often they have bought from your online shop. You might describe the image of a tumor by the grayscale values of each pixel, or maybe by using the size, shape, and color of the tumor.

Each entity or row here is known as a *sample* (or data point) in machine learning, while the columns—the properties that describe these entities—are called *features*.

Later in this book we will go into more detail on the topic of building a good representation of your data, which is called *feature extraction* or *feature engineering*. You should keep in mind, however, that no machine learning algorithm will be able to make a prediction on data for which it has no information. For example, if the only feature that you have for a patient is their last name, no algorithm will be able to predict their gender. This information is simply not contained in your data. If you add another feature that contains the patient's first name, you will have much better luck, as it is often possible to tell the gender by a person's first name.

1.1.2 Knowing Your Task and Knowing Your Data

Quite possibly the most important part in the machine learning process is understanding the data you are working with and how it relates to the task you want to solve. It will not be effective to randomly choose an algorithm and throw your data at it. It is necessary to understand what is going on in your dataset before you begin building a model. Each algorithm is different in terms of what kind of data and what problem setting it works best for. While you are building a machine learning solution, you should answer, or at least keep in mind, the following questions:

- What question(s) am I trying to answer? Do I think the data collected can answer that question?
- What is the best way to phrase my question(s) as a machine learning problem?
- Have I collected enough data to represent the problem I want to solve?
- What features of the data did I extract, and will these enable the right predictions?
- How will I measure success in my application?
- How will the machine learning solution interact with other parts of my research or business product?

In a larger context, the algorithms and methods in machine learning are only one part of a greater process to solve a particular problem, and it is good to keep the big picture in mind at all times. Many people spend a lot of time building complex machine learning solutions, only to find out they don't solve the right problem.

When going deep into the technical aspects of machine learning (as we will in this book), it is easy to lose sight of the ultimate goals. While we will not discuss the questions listed here in detail, we still encourage you to keep in mind all the assumptions that you might be making, explicitly or implicitly, when you start building machine learning models.

1.2 Why Python?

Python has become the lingua franca for many data science applications. It combines the power of general-purpose programming languages with the ease of use of domain-specific scripting languages like MATLAB or R. Python has libraries for data loading, visualization, statistics, natural language processing, image processing, and more. This vast toolbox provides data scientists with a large array of general- and special-purpose functionality. One of the main advantages of using Python is the ability to interact directly with the code, using a terminal or other tools like the Jupyter Notebook, which we'll look at shortly. Machine learning and data analysis are fundamentally iterative processes, in which the data drives the analysis. It is essential for these processes to have tools that allow quick iteration and easy interaction.

As a general-purpose programming language, Python also allows for the creation of complex graphical user interfaces (GUIs) and web services, and for integration into existing systems.

1.3 scikit-learn

`scikit-learn` is an open source project, meaning that it is free to use and distribute, and anyone can easily obtain the source code to see what is going on behind the scenes. The `scikit-learn` project is constantly being developed and improved, and it has a very active user community. It contains a number of state-of-the-art machine learning algorithms, as well as comprehensive documentation (*http://scikit-learn.org/stable/documentation*) about each algorithm. `scikit-learn` is a very popular tool, and the most prominent Python library for machine learning. It is widely used in industry and academia, and a wealth of tutorials and code snippets are available online. `scikit-learn` works well with a number of other scientific Python tools, which we will discuss later in this chapter.

While reading this, we recommend that you also browse the `scikit-learn` user guide (*http://scikit-learn.org/stable/user_guide.html*) and API documentation for additional details on and many more options for each algorithm. The online documentation is very thorough, and this book will provide you with all the prerequisites in machine learning to understand it in detail.

1.3.1 Installing scikit-learn

`scikit-learn` depends on two other Python packages, *NumPy* and *SciPy*. For plotting and interactive development, you should also install `matplotlib`, IPython, and the Jupyter Notebook. We recommend using one of the following prepackaged Python distributions, which will provide the necessary packages:

Anaconda (https://store.continuum.io/cshop/anaconda/)
: A Python distribution made for large-scale data processing, predictive analytics, and scientific computing. Anaconda comes with NumPy, SciPy, `matplotlib`, `pandas`, IPython, Jupyter Notebook, and `scikit-learn`. Available on Mac OS, Windows, and Linux, it is a very convenient solution and is the one we suggest for people without an existing installation of the scientific Python packages.

Enthought Canopy (https://www.enthought.com/products/canopy/)
: Another Python distribution for scientific computing. This comes with NumPy, SciPy, `matplotlib`, `pandas`, and IPython, but the free version does not come with `scikit-learn`. If you are part of an academic, degree-granting institution, you can request an academic license and get free access to the paid subscription version of Enthought Canopy. Enthought Canopy is available for Python 2.7.x, and works on Mac OS, Windows, and Linux.

Python(x,y) (http://python-xy.github.io/)
: A free Python distribution for scientific computing, specifically for Windows. Python(x,y) comes with NumPy, SciPy, `matplotlib`, `pandas`, IPython, and `scikit-learn`.

If you already have a Python installation set up, you can use `pip` to install all of these packages:

```
$ pip install numpy scipy matplotlib ipython scikit-learn pandas pillow
```

For the tree visualizations in Chapter 2, you also need the `graphviz` packages; see the accompanying code for instructions. For Chapter 7, you will also need the `nltk` and `spacy` libraries; see the instructions in that chapter.

1.4 Essential Libraries and Tools

Understanding what `scikit-learn` is and how to use it is important, but there are a few other libraries that will enhance your experience. `scikit-learn` is built on top of the NumPy and SciPy scientific Python libraries. In addition to NumPy and SciPy, we will be using `pandas` and `matplotlib`. We will also introduce the Jupyter Notebook, which is a browser-based interactive programming environment. Briefly, here is what you should know about these tools in order to get the most out of `scikit-learn`.[1]

1.4.1 Jupyter Notebook

The Jupyter Notebook is an interactive environment for running code in the browser. It is a great tool for exploratory data analysis and is widely used by data scientists. While the Jupyter Notebook supports many programming languages, we only need the Python support. The Jupyter Notebook makes it easy to incorporate code, text, and images, and all of this book was in fact written as a Jupyter Notebook. All of the code examples we include can be downloaded from *https://github.com/amueller/introduction_to_ml_with_python*.

1.4.2 NumPy

NumPy is one of the fundamental packages for scientific computing in Python. It contains functionality for multidimensional arrays, high-level mathematical functions such as linear algebra operations and the Fourier transform, and pseudorandom number generators.

1 If you are unfamiliar with NumPy or `matplotlib`, we recommend reading the first chapter of the SciPy Lecture Notes (*http://www.scipy-lectures.org/*).

In `scikit-learn`, the NumPy array is the fundamental data structure. `scikit-learn` takes in data in the form of NumPy arrays. Any data you're using will have to be converted to a NumPy array. The core functionality of NumPy is the `ndarray` class, a multidimensional (*n*-dimensional) array. All elements of the array must be of the same type. A NumPy array looks like this:

In[1]:

```
import numpy as np

x = np.array([[1, 2, 3], [4, 5, 6]])
print("x:\n{}".format(x))
```

Out[1]:

```
x:
[[1 2 3]
 [4 5 6]]
```

We will be using NumPy *a lot* in this book, and we will refer to objects of the NumPy `ndarray` class as "NumPy arrays" or just "arrays."

1.4.3 SciPy

SciPy is a collection of functions for scientific computing in Python. It provides, among other functionality, advanced linear algebra routines, mathematical function optimization, signal processing, special mathematical functions, and statistical distributions. `scikit-learn` draws from SciPy's collection of functions for implementing its algorithms. The most important part of SciPy for us is `scipy.sparse`: this provides *sparse matrices*, which are another representation that is used for data in `scikit-learn`. Sparse matrices are used whenever we want to store a 2D array that contains mostly zeros:

In[2]:

```
from scipy import sparse

# Create a 2D NumPy array with a diagonal of ones, and zeros everywhere else
eye = np.eye(4)
print("NumPy array:\n", eye)
```

Out[2]:

```
NumPy array:
[[1. 0. 0. 0.]
 [0. 1. 0. 0.]
 [0. 0. 1. 0.]
 [0. 0. 0. 1.]]
```

In[3]:

```
# Convert the NumPy array to a SciPy sparse matrix in CSR format
# Only the nonzero entries are stored
sparse_matrix = sparse.csr_matrix(eye)
print("\nSciPy sparse CSR matrix:\n", sparse_matrix)
```

Out[3]:

```
SciPy sparse CSR matrix:
  (0, 0)        1.0
  (1, 1)        1.0
  (2, 2)        1.0
  (3, 3)        1.0
```

Usually it is not possible to create dense representations of sparse data (as they would not fit into memory), so we need to create sparse representations directly. Here is a way to create the same sparse matrix as before, using the COO format:

In[4]:

```
data = np.ones(4)
row_indices = np.arange(4)
col_indices = np.arange(4)
eye_coo = sparse.coo_matrix((data, (row_indices, col_indices)))
print("COO representation:\n", eye_coo)
```

Out[4]:

```
COO representation:
  (0, 0)        1.0
  (1, 1)        1.0
  (2, 2)        1.0
  (3, 3)        1.0
```

More details on SciPy sparse matrices can be found in the SciPy Lecture Notes (*http://www.scipy-lectures.org/*).

1.4.4 matplotlib

`matplotlib` is the primary scientific plotting library in Python. It provides functions for making publication-quality visualizations such as line charts, histograms, scatter plots, and so on. Visualizing your data and different aspects of your analysis can give you important insights, and we will be using `matplotlib` for all our visualizations. When working inside the Jupyter Notebook, you can show figures directly in the browser by using the `%matplotlib notebook` and `%matplotlib inline` commands. We recommend using `%matplotlib notebook`, which provides an interactive environment (though we are using `%matplotlib inline` to produce this book). For example, this code produces the plot in Figure 1-1:

In[5]:

```
%matplotlib inline
import matplotlib.pyplot as plt
```

```
# Generate a sequence of numbers from -10 to 10 with 100 steps in between
x = np.linspace(-10, 10, 100)
# Create a second array using sine
y = np.sin(x)
# The plot function makes a line chart of one array against another
plt.plot(x, y, marker="x")
```

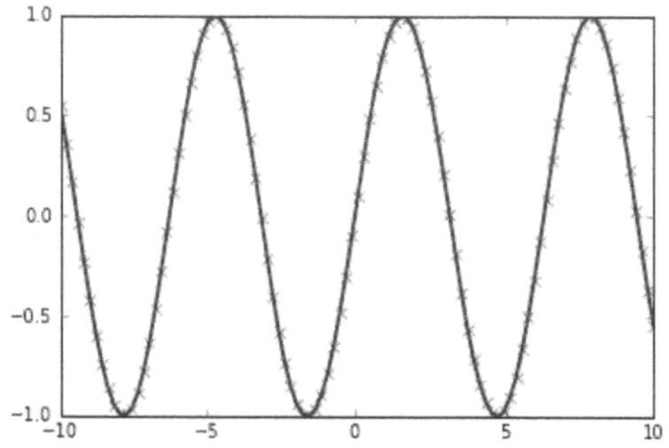

Figure 1-1. Simple line plot of the sine function using matplotlib

1.4.5 pandas

`pandas` is a Python library for data wrangling and analysis. It is built around a data structure called the `DataFrame` that is modeled after the R `DataFrame`. Simply put, a `pandas` `DataFrame` is a table, similar to an Excel spreadsheet. `pandas` provides a great range of methods to modify and operate on this table; in particular, it allows SQL-like queries and joins of tables. In contrast to NumPy, which requires that all entries in an array be of the same type, `pandas` allows each column to have a separate type (for example, integers, dates, floating-point numbers, and strings). Another valuable tool provided by `pandas` is its ability to ingest from a great variety of file formats and databases, like SQL, Excel files, and comma-separated values (CSV) files. Going into detail about the functionality of `pandas` is out of the scope of this book. However, *Python for Data Analysis* by Wes McKinney (O'Reilly, 2012) provides a great guide. Here is a small example of creating a `DataFrame` using a dictionary:

In[6]:

```
import pandas as pd

# create a simple dataset of people
data = {'Name': ["John", "Anna", "Peter", "Linda"],
        'Location' : ["New York", "Paris", "Berlin", "London"],
        'Age' : [24, 13, 53, 33]
       }

data_pandas = pd.DataFrame(data)
# IPython.display allows "pretty printing" of dataframes
```

```
# in the Jupyter notebook
display(data_pandas)
```

This produces the following output:

	Age	Location	Name
0	24	New York	John
1	13	Paris	Anna
2	53	Berlin	Peter
3	33	London	Linda

There are several possible ways to query this table. For example:

In[7]:

```
# Select all rows that have an age column greater than 30
display(data_pandas[data_pandas.Age > 30])
```

This produces the following result:

	Age	Location	Name
2	53	Berlin	Peter
3	33	London	Linda

1.4.6 mglearn

This book comes with accompanying code, which you can find on *https://github.com/amueller/introduction_to_ml_with_python*. The accompanying code includes not only all the examples shown in this book, but also the mglearn library. This is a library of utility functions we wrote for this book, so that we don't clutter up our code listings with details of plotting and data loading. If you're interested, you can look up all the functions in the repository, but the details of the `mglearn` module are not really important to the material in this book. If you see a call to `mglearn` in the code, it is usually a way to make a pretty picture quickly, or to get our hands on some interesting data. If you run the notebooks published on GitHub, the `mglearn` package is already in the right place and you don't have to worry about it. If you want to call `mglearn` functions from any other place, the easiest way to install it is by calling `pip install mglearn`.

Throughout the book we make ample use of NumPy, `matplotlib` and `pandas`. All the code will assume the following imports:

```
import numpy as np
import matplotlib.pyplot as plt
import pandas as pd
import mglearn
from IPython.display import display
```

We also assume that you will run the code in a Jupyter Notebook with the `%matplotlib notebook` or `%matplotlib inline` magic enabled to show plots. If you are not using the notebook or these magic commands, you will have to call `plt.show` to actually show any of the figures.

1.5 Python 2 Versus Python 3

There are two major versions of Python that are widely used at the moment: Python 2 (more precisely, 2.7) and Python 3 (with the latest release being 3.7 at the time of writing). This sometimes leads to some confusion. Python 2 is no longer actively developed, but because Python 3 contains major changes, Python 2 code usually does not run on Python 3. If you are new to Python, or are starting a new project from scratch, we highly recommend using the latest version of Python 3. If you have a large codebase that you rely on that is written for Python 2, you are excused from upgrading for now. However, you should try to migrate to Python 3 as soon as possible. When writing any new code, it is for the most part quite easy to write code that runs under Python 2 and Python 3. [2] If you don't have to interface with legacy software, you should definitely use Python 3. All the code in this book is written in a way that works for both versions. However, the exact output might differ slightly under Python 2. You should also note that many packages such as `matplotlib`, `numpy`, and `scikit-learn` are no longer releasing new features under Python 2.7; you need to upgrade to Python 3.7 to get the benefit of the improvements that come with newer versions.

1.6 Versions Used in this Book

We are using the following versions of the previously mentioned libraries in this book:

In[8]:

```
import sys
print("Python version:", sys.version)
```

2 The `six` package (*https://pypi.python.org/pypi/six*) can be very handy for that.

```
import pandas as pd
print("pandas version:", pd.__version__)

import matplotlib
print("matplotlib version:", matplotlib.__version__)

import numpy as np
print("NumPy version:", np.__version__)

import scipy as sp
print("SciPy version:", sp.__version__)

import IPython
print("IPython version:", IPython.__version__)

import sklearn
print("scikit-learn version:", sklearn.__version__)
```

Out[8]:

```
Python version: 3.7.0 (default, Jun 28 2018, 13:15:42)
[GCC 7.2.0]
pandas version: 0.23.4
matplotlib version: 3.0.0
NumPy version: 1.15.2
SciPy version: 1.1.0
IPython version: 6.4.0
scikit-learn version: 0.20.0
```

While it is not important to match these versions exactly, you should have a version of `scikit-learn` that is as least as recent as the one we used.

> When using the code in this book, you might sometimes see *DeprecationWarnings* or *FutureWarnings* from `scikit-learn`. These inform you about behavior in `scikit-learn` that will change in the future or will be removed. While going through this book, you can safely ignore these. If you are running a machine learning algorithm in production, you should carefully consider each warning, as they might inform you about functionality being removed in the future or outcomes of predictions changing.

Now that we have everything set up, let's dive into our first application of machine learning.

1.7 A First Application: Classifying Iris Species

In this section, we will go through a simple machine learning application and create our first model. In the process, we will introduce some core concepts and terms.

Let's assume that a hobby botanist is interested in distinguishing the species of some iris flowers that she has found. She has collected some measurements associated with each iris: the length and width of the petals and the length and width of the sepals, all measured in centimeters (see Figure 1-2).

She also has the measurements of some irises that have been previously identified by an expert botanist as belonging to the species *setosa*, *versicolor*, or *virginica*. For these measurements, she can be certain of which species each iris belongs to. Let's assume that these are the only species our hobby botanist will encounter in the wild.

Our goal is to build a machine learning model that can learn from the measurements of these irises whose species is known, so that we can predict the species for a new iris.

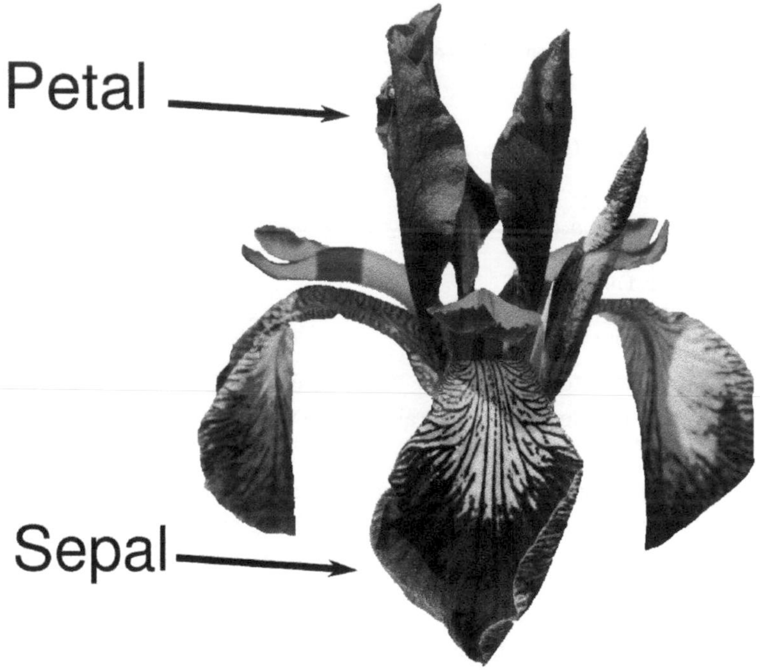

Figure 1-2. Parts of the iris flower

Because we have measurements for which we know the correct species of iris, this is a supervised learning problem. In this problem, we want to predict one of several options (the species of iris). This is an example of a *classification* problem. The possible outputs (different species of irises) are called *classes*. Every iris in the dataset belongs to one of three classes, so this problem is a three-class classification problem.

The desired output for a single data point (an iris) is the species of this flower. For a particular data point, the species it belongs to is called its *label*.

1.7.1 Meet the Data

The data we will use for this example is the Iris dataset, a classical dataset in machine learning and statistics. It is included in `scikit-learn` in the `dataset` module. We can load it by calling the `load_iris` function:

In[9]:

```
from sklearn.datasets import load_iris
iris_dataset = load_iris()
```

The iris object that is returned by `load_iris` is a `Bunch` object, which is very similar to a dictionary. It contains keys and values:

In[10]:

```
print("Keys of iris_dataset:\n", iris_dataset.keys())
```

Out[10]:

```
Keys of iris_dataset:
dict_keys(['data', 'target', 'target_names', 'DESCR', 'feature_names', 'filename'])
```

The value of the key `DESCR` is a short description of the dataset. We show the beginning of the description here (feel free to look up the rest yourself):

In[11]:

```
print(iris_dataset['DESCR'][:193] + "\n...")
```

Out[11]:

```
Iris Plants Database
====================

Notes
----
Data Set Characteristics:
    :Number of Instances: 150 (50 in each of three classes)
    :Number of Attributes: 4 numeric, predictive att
...
----
```

The value of the key `target_names` is an array of strings, containing the species of flower that we want to predict:

In[12]:

```
print("Target names:", iris_dataset['target_names'])
```

Out[12]:

```
Target names: ['setosa' 'versicolor' 'virginica']
```

The value of `feature_names` is a list of strings, giving the description of each feature:

In[13]:

```
print("Feature names:\n", iris_dataset['feature_names'])
```

Out[13]:

```
Feature names:
['sepal length (cm)', 'sepal width (cm)', 'petal length (cm)',
 'petal width (cm)']
```

The data itself is contained in the `target` and `data` fields. `data` contains the numeric measurements of sepal length, sepal width, petal length, and petal width in a NumPy array:

In[14]:

```
print("Type of data:", type(iris_dataset['data']))
```

Out[14]:

```
Type of data: <class 'numpy.ndarray'>
```

The rows in the `data` array correspond to flowers, while the columns represent the four measurements that were taken for each flower:

In[15]:

```
print("Shape of data:", iris_dataset['data'].shape)
```

Out[15]:

```
Shape of data: (150, 4)
```

We see that the array contains measurements for 150 different flowers. Remember that the individual items are called *samples* in machine learning, and their properties are called *features*. The *shape* of the `data` array is the number of samples times the number of features. This is a convention in `scikit-learn`, and your data will always be assumed to be in this shape. Here are the feature values for the first five samples:

In[16]:

```
print("First five rows of data:\n", iris_dataset['data'][:5])
```

Out[16]:

```
First five rows of data:
[[5.1 3.5 1.4 0.2]
 [4.9 3.  1.4 0.2]
 [4.7 3.2 1.3 0.2]
 [4.6 3.1 1.5 0.2]
 [5.  3.6 1.4 0.2]]
```

From this data, we can see that all of the first five flowers have a petal width of 0.2 cm and that the first flower has the longest sepal, at 5.1 cm.

The `target` array contains the species of each of the flowers that were measured, also as a NumPy array:

In[17]:

```
print("Type of target:", type(iris_dataset['target']))
```

Out[17]:

```
Type of target: <class 'numpy.ndarray'>
```

`target` is a one-dimensional array, with one entry per flower:

In[18]:

```
print("Shape of target:", iris_dataset['target'].shape)
```

Out[18]:

```
Shape of target: (150,)
```

The species are encoded as integers from 0 to 2:

In[19]:

```
print("Target:\n", iris_dataset['target'])
```

Out[19]:

```
Target:
[0 0 0 0 0 0 0 0 0 0 0 0 0 0 0 0 0 0 0 0 0 0 0 0 0 0 0 0 0 0 0 0 0 0 0 0 0
 0 0 0 0 0 0 0 0 0 0 0 0 0 1 1 1 1 1 1 1 1 1 1 1 1 1 1 1 1 1 1 1 1 1 1 1 1
 1 1 1 1 1 1 1 1 1 1 1 1 1 1 1 1 1 1 1 1 1 1 1 1 1 1 2 2 2 2 2 2 2 2 2 2 2
 2 2 2 2 2 2 2 2 2 2 2 2 2 2 2 2 2 2 2 2 2 2 2 2 2 2 2 2 2 2 2 2 2 2 2 2 2
 2 2]
```

The meanings of the numbers are given by the `iris['target_names']` array: 0 means *setosa*, 1 means *versicolor*, and 2 means *virginica*.

1.7.2 Measuring Success: Training and Testing Data

We want to build a machine learning model from this data that can predict the species of iris for a new set of measurements. But before we can apply our model to new measurements, we need to know whether it actually works—that is, whether we should trust its predictions.

Unfortunately, we cannot use the data we used to build the model to evaluate it. This is because our model can always simply remember the whole training set, and will therefore always predict the correct label for any point in the training set. This "remembering" does not indicate to us whether our model will *generalize* well (in other words, whether it will also perform well on new data).

To assess the model's performance, we show it new data (data that it hasn't seen before) for which we have labels. This is usually done by splitting the labeled data we have collected (here, our 150 flower measurements) into two parts. One part of the data is used to build our machine learning model, and is called the *training data* or *training set*. The rest of the data will be used to assess how well the model works; this is called the *test data*, *test set*, or *hold-out set*.

`scikit-learn` contains a function that shuffles the dataset and splits it for you: the `train_test_split` function. This function extracts 75% of the rows in the data as the training set, together with the corresponding labels for this data. The remaining 25% of the data, together with the remaining labels, is declared as the test set. Deciding how much data you want to put into the training and the test set respectively is somewhat arbitrary, but using a test set containing 25% of the data is a good rule of thumb.

In `scikit-learn`, data is usually denoted with a capital `X`, while labels are denoted by a lowercase `y`. This is inspired by the standard formulation $f(x)=y$ in mathematics, where x is the input to a function and y is the output. Following more conventions from mathematics, we use a capital `X` because the data is a two-dimensional array (a matrix) and a lowercase `y` because the target is a one-dimensional array (a vector).

Let's call `train_test_split` on our data and assign the outputs using this nomenclature:

In[20]:

```
from sklearn.model_selection import train_test_split
X_train, X_test, y_train, y_test = train_test_split(
    iris_dataset['data'], iris_dataset['target'], random_state=0)
```

Before making the split, the `train_test_split` function shuffles the dataset using a pseudorandom number generator. If we just took the last 25% of the data as a test set, all the data points would have the label `2`, as the data points are sorted by the label (see the output for `iris['target']` shown earlier). Using a test set containing only one of the three classes would not tell us much about how well our model generalizes, so we shuffle our data to make sure the test data contains data from all classes.

To make sure that we will get the same output if we run the same function several times, we provide the pseudorandom number generator with a fixed seed using the `random_state` parameter. This will make the outcome deterministic, so this line will always have the same outcome. We will always fix the `random_state` in this way when using randomized procedures in this book.

The output of the train_test_split function is X_train, X_test, y_train, and y_test, which are all NumPy arrays. X_train contains 75% of the rows of the dataset, and X_test contains the remaining 25%:

In[21]:

```
print("X_train shape:", X_train.shape)
print("y_train shape:", y_train.shape)
```

Out[21]:

```
X_train shape: (112, 4)
y_train shape: (112,)
```

In[22]:

```
print("X_test shape:", X_test.shape)
print("y_test shape:", y_test.shape)
```

Out[22]:

```
X_test shape: (38, 4)
y_test shape: (38,)
```

1.7.3 First Things First: Look at Your Data

Before building a machine learning model it is often a good idea to inspect the data, to see if the task is easily solvable without machine learning, or if the desired information might not be contained in the data.

Additionally, inspecting your data is a good way to find abnormalities and peculiarities. Maybe some of your irises were measured using inches and not centimeters, for example. In the real world, inconsistencies in the data and unexpected measurements are very common.

One of the best ways to inspect data is to visualize it. One way to do this is by using a *scatter plot*. A scatter plot of the data puts one feature along the x-axis and another along the y-axis, and draws a dot for each data point. Unfortunately, computer screens have only two dimensions, which allows us to plot only two (or maybe three) features at a time. It is difficult to plot datasets with more than three features this way. One way around this problem is to do a *pair plot*, which looks at all possible pairs of features. If you have a small number of features, such as the four we have here, this is quite reasonable. You should keep in mind, however, that a pair plot does not show the interaction of all of features at once, so some interesting aspects of the data may not be revealed when visualizing it this way.

Figure 1-3 is a pair plot of the features in the training set. The data points are colored according to the species the iris belongs to. To create the plot, we first convert the NumPy array into a pandas DataFrame. pandas has a function to create pair plots called scatter_matrix. The diagonal of this matrix is filled with histograms of each feature:

In[23]:

```
# create dataframe from data in X_train
# label the columns using the strings in iris_dataset.feature_names
iris_dataframe = pd.DataFrame(X_train, columns=iris_dataset.feature_names)
# create a scatter matrix from the dataframe, color by y_train
pd.plotting.scatter_matrix(iris_dataframe, c=y_train, figsize=(15, 15),
                           marker='o', hist_kwds={'bins': 20}, s=60,
                           alpha=.8, cmap=mglearn.cm3)
```

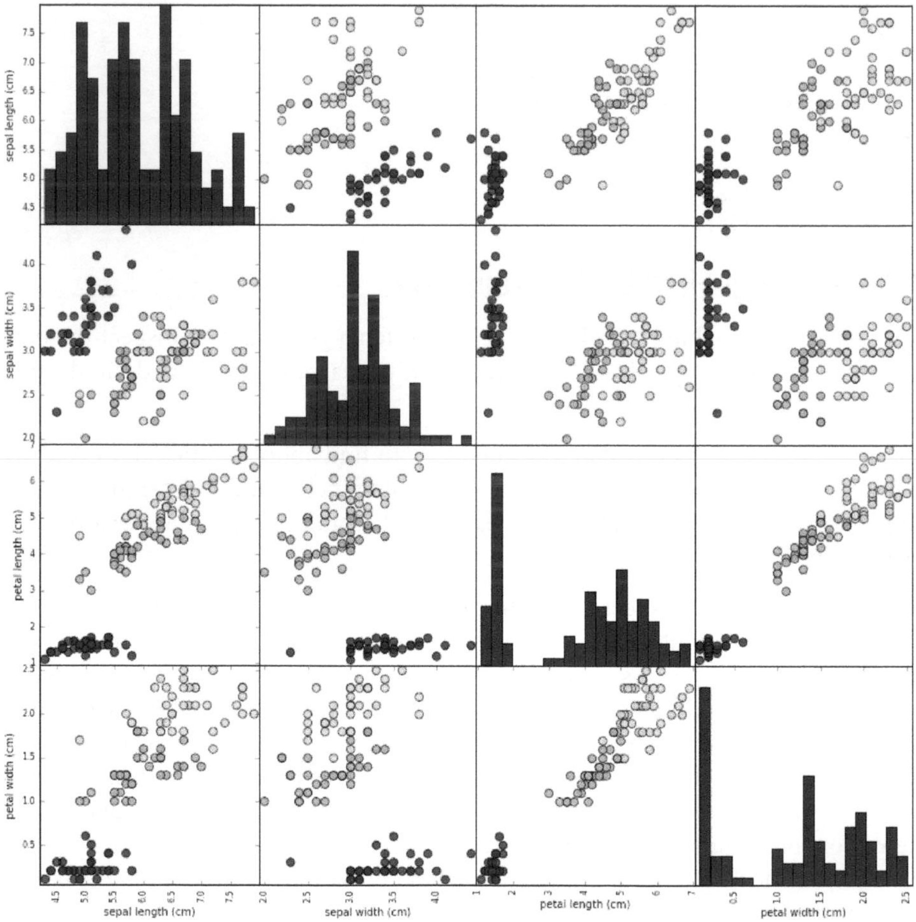

Figure 1-3. Pair plot of the Iris dataset, colored by class label

From the plots, we can see that the three classes seem to be relatively well separated using the sepal and petal measurements. This means that a machine learning model will likely be able to learn to separate them.

1.7.4 Building Your First Model: k-Nearest Neighbors

Now we can start building the actual machine learning model. There are many classification algorithms in `scikit-learn` that we could use. Here we will use a *k*-nearest neighbors classifier, which is easy to understand. Building this model only consists of storing the training set. To make a prediction for a new data point, the algorithm finds the point in the training set that is closest to the new point. Then it assigns the label of this training point to the new data point.

The *k* in *k*-nearest neighbors signifies that instead of using only the closest neighbor to the new data point, we can consider any fixed number k of neighbors in the training (for example, the closest three or five neighbors). Then, we can make a prediction using the majority class among these neighbors. We will go into more detail about this in Chapter 2; for now, we'll use only a single neighbor.

All machine learning models in `scikit-learn` are implemented in their own classes, which are called `Estimator` classes. The *k*-nearest neighbors classification algorithm is implemented in the `KNeighborsClassifier` class in the `neighbors` module. Before we can use the model, we need to instantiate the class into an object. This is when we will set any parameters of the model. The most important parameter of `KNeighborsClassifier` is the number of neighbors, which we will set to 1:

In[24]:

```
from sklearn.neighbors import KNeighborsClassifier
knn = KNeighborsClassifier(n_neighbors=1)
```

The `knn` object encapsulates the algorithm that will be used to build the model from the training data, as well the algorithm to make predictions on new data points. It will also hold the information that the algorithm has extracted from the training data. In the case of `KNeighborsClassifier`, it will just store the training set.

To build the model on the training set, we call the `fit` method of the `knn` object, which takes as arguments the NumPy array `X_train` containing the training data and the NumPy array `y_train` of the corresponding training labels:

In[25]:

```
knn.fit(X_train, y_train)
```

Out[25]:

```
KNeighborsClassifier(algorithm='auto', leaf_size=30, metric='minkowski',
           metric_params=None, n_jobs=None, n_neighbors=1, p=2,
           weights='uniform')
```

The `fit` method returns the knn object itself (and modifies it in place), so we get a string representation of our classifier. The representation shows us which parameters were used in creating the model. Nearly all of them are the default values, but you can also find `n_neighbors=1`, which is the parameter that we passed. Most models in `scikit-learn` have many parameters, but the majority of them are either speed optimizations or for very special use cases. You don't have to worry about the other parameters shown in this representation. Printing a `scikit-learn` model can yield very long strings, but don't be intimidated by these. We will cover all the important parameters in Chapter 2. In the remainder of this book, we will not usually show the output of `fit` because it doesn't contain any new information.

1.7.5 Making Predictions

We can now make predictions using this model on new data for which we might not know the correct labels. Imagine we found an iris in the wild with a sepal length of 5 cm, a sepal width of 2.9 cm, a petal length of 1 cm, and a petal width of 0.2 cm. What species of iris would this be? We can put this data into a NumPy array, again by calculating the shape—that is, the number of samples (1) multiplied by the number of features (4):

In[26]:

```
X_new = np.array([[5, 2.9, 1, 0.2]])
print("X_new.shape:", X_new.shape)
```

Out[26]:

```
X_new.shape: (1, 4)
```

Note that we made the measurements of this single flower into a row in a two-dimensional NumPy array, as `scikit-learn` always expects two-dimensional arrays for the data.

To make a prediction, we call the `predict` method of the knn object:

In[27]:

```
prediction = knn.predict(X_new)
print("Prediction:", prediction)
print("Predicted target name:",
       iris_dataset['target_names'][prediction])
```

Out[27]:

```
Prediction: [0]
Predicted target name: ['setosa']
```

Our model predicts that this new iris belongs to the class 0, meaning its species is *setosa*. But how do we know whether we can trust our model? We don't know the correct species of this sample, which is the whole point of building the model!

1.7.6 Evaluating the Model

This is where the test set that we created earlier comes in. This data was not used to build the model, but we do know what the correct species is for each iris in the test set.

Therefore, we can make a prediction for each iris in the test data and compare it against its label (the known species). We can measure how well the model works by computing the *accuracy*, which is the fraction of flowers for which the right species was predicted:

In[28]:

```
y_pred = knn.predict(X_test)
print("Test set predictions:\n", y_pred)
```

Out[28]:

```
Test set predictions:
 [2 1 0 2 0 2 0 1 1 1 2 1 1 1 1 0 1 1 0 0 2 1 0 0 2 0 0 1 1 0 2 1 0 2 2 1 0 2]
```

In[29]:

```
print("Test set score: {:.2f}".format(np.mean(y_pred == y_test)))
```

Out[29]:

```
Test set score: 0.97
```

We can also use the `score` method of the `knn` object, which will compute the test set accuracy for us:

In[30]:

```
print("Test set score: {:.2f}".format(knn.score(X_test, y_test)))
```

Out[30]:

```
Test set score: 0.97
```

For this model, the test set accuracy is about 0.97, which means we made the right prediction for 97% of the irises in the test set. Under some mathematical assumptions, this means that we can expect our model to be correct 97% of the time for new irises. For our hobby botanist application, this high level of accuracy means that our model may be trustworthy enough to use. In later chapters we will discuss how we can improve performance, and what caveats there are in tuning a model.

1.8 Summary and Outlook

Let's summarize what we learned in this chapter. We started with a brief introduction to machine learning and its applications, then discussed the distinction between supervised and unsupervised learning and gave an overview of the tools we'll be using in this book. Then, we formulated the task of predicting which species of iris a particular flower belongs to by using physical measurements of the flower. We used a dataset of measurements that was annotated by an expert with the correct species to build our model, making this a supervised learning task. There were three possible species, *setosa*, *versicolor*, or *virginica*, which made the task a three-class classification problem. The possible species are called *classes* in the classification problem, and the species of a single iris is called its *label*.

The Iris dataset consists of two NumPy arrays: one containing the data, which is referred to as `X` in `scikit-learn`, and one containing the correct or desired outputs, which is called `y`. The array `X` is a two-dimensional array of features, with one row per data point and one column per feature. The array `y` is a one-dimensional array, which here contains one class label, an integer ranging from 0 to 2, for each of the samples.

We split our dataset into a *training set*, to build our model, and a *test set*, to evaluate how well our model will generalize to new, previously unseen data.

We chose the *k*-nearest neighbors classification algorithm, which makes predictions for a new data point by considering its closest neighbor(s) in the training set. This is implemented in the `KNeighborsClassifier` class, which contains the algorithm that builds the model as well as the algorithm that makes a prediction using the model. We instantiated the class, setting parameters. Then we built the model by calling the `fit` method, passing the training data (`X_train`) and training outputs (`y_train`) as parameters. We evaluated the model using the `score` method, which computes the accuracy of the model. We applied the `score` method to the test set data and the test set labels and found that our model is about 97% accurate, meaning it is correct 97% of the time on the test set.

This gave us the confidence to apply the model to new data (in our example, new flower measurements) and trust that the model will be correct about 97% of the time.

Here is a summary of the code needed for the whole training and evaluation procedure:

In[31]:

```
X_train, X_test, y_train, y_test = train_test_split(
    iris_dataset['data'], iris_dataset['target'], random_state=0)

knn = KNeighborsClassifier(n_neighbors=1)
knn.fit(X_train, y_train)

print("Test set score: {:.2f}".format(knn.score(X_test, y_test)))
```

Out[31]:

```
Test set score: 0.97
```

This snippet contains the core code for applying any machine learning algorithm using `scikit-learn`. The `fit`, `predict`, and `score` methods are the common interface to supervised models in `scikit-learn`, and with the concepts introduced in this chapter, you can apply these models to many machine learning tasks. In the next chapter, we will go into more depth about the different kinds of supervised models in `scikit-learn` and how to apply them successfully.

CHAPTER 2

Supervised Learning

As we mentioned earlier, supervised machine learning is one of the most commonly used and successful types of machine learning. In this chapter, we will describe supervised learning in more detail and explain several popular supervised learning algorithms. We already saw an application of supervised machine learning in Chapter 1: classifying iris flowers into several species using physical measurements of the flowers.

Remember that supervised learning is used whenever we want to predict a certain outcome from a given input, and we have examples of input/output pairs. We build a machine learning model from these input/output pairs, which comprise our training set. Our goal is to make accurate predictions for new, never-before-seen data. Supervised learning often requires human effort to build the training set, but afterward automates and often speeds up an otherwise laborious or infeasible task.

2.1 Classification and Regression

There are two major types of supervised machine learning problems, called *classification* and *regression.*

In classification, the goal is to predict a *class label*, which is a choice from a predefined list of possibilities. In Chapter 1 we used the example of classifying irises into one of three possible species. Classification is sometimes separated into *binary classification*, which is the special case of distinguishing between exactly two classes, and *multiclass classification*, which is classification between more than two classes. You can think of binary classification as trying to answer a yes/no question. Classifying emails as either spam or not spam is an example of a binary classification problem. In this binary classification task, the yes/no question being asked would be "Is this email spam?"

In binary classification we often speak of one class being the *positive* class and the other class being the *negative* class. Here, positive doesn't represent having benefit or value, but rather what the object of the study is. So, when looking for spam, "positive" could mean the spam class. Which of the two classes is called positive is often a subjective matter, and specific to the domain.

The iris example, on the other hand, is an example of a multiclass classification problem. Another example is predicting what language a website is in from the text on the website. The classes here would be a pre-defined list of possible languages.

For regression tasks, the goal is to predict a continuous number, or a *floating-point number* in programming terms (or *real number* in mathematical terms). Predicting a person's annual income from their education, their age, and where they live is an example of a regression task. When predicting income, the predicted value is an *amount*, and can be any number in a given range. Another example of a regression task is predicting the yield of a corn farm given attributes such as previous yields, weather, and number of employees working on the farm. The yield again can be an arbitrary number.

An easy way to distinguish between classification and regression tasks is to ask whether there is some kind of continuity in the output. If there is continuity between possible outcomes, then the problem is a regression problem. Think about predicting annual income. There is a clear continuity in the output. Whether a person makes $40,000 or $40,001 a year does not make a tangible difference, even though these are different amounts of money; if our algorithm predicts $39,999 or $40,001 when it should have predicted $40,000, we don't mind that much.

By contrast, for the task of recognizing the language of a website (which is a classification problem), there is no matter of degree. A website is in one language, or it is in another. There is no continuity between languages, and there is no language that is *between* English and French.[1]

2.2 Generalization, Overfitting, and Underfitting

In supervised learning, we want to build a model on the training data and then be able to make accurate predictions on new, unseen data that has the same characteristics as the training set that we used. If a model is able to make accurate predictions on unseen data, we say it is able to *generalize* from the training set to the test set. We want to build a model that is able to generalize as accurately as possible.

1 We ask linguists to excuse the simplified presentation of languages as distinct and fixed entities.

Usually we build a model in such a way that it can make accurate predictions on the training set. If the training and test sets have enough in common, we expect the model to also be accurate on the test set. However, there are some cases where this can go wrong. For example, if we allow ourselves to build very complex models, we can always be as accurate as we like on the training set.

Let's take a look at a made-up example to illustrate this point. Say a novice data scientist wants to predict whether a customer will buy a boat, given records of previous boat buyers and customers who we know are not interested in buying a boat.[2] The goal is to send out promotional emails to people who are likely to actually make a purchase, but not bother those customers who won't be interested.

Suppose we have the customer records shown in Table 2-1.

Table 2-1. Example data about customers

Age	Number of cars owned	Owns house	Number of children	Marital status	Owns a dog	Bought a boat
66	1	yes	2	widowed	no	yes
52	2	yes	3	married	no	yes
22	0	no	0	married	yes	no
25	1	no	1	single	no	no
44	0	no	2	divorced	yes	no
39	1	yes	2	married	yes	no
26	1	no	2	single	no	no
40	3	yes	1	married	yes	no
53	2	yes	2	divorced	no	yes
64	2	yes	3	divorced	no	no
58	2	yes	2	married	yes	yes
33	1	no	1	single	no	no

After looking at the data for a while, our novice data scientist comes up with the following rule: "If the customer is older than 45, and has less than 3 children or is not divorced, then they want to buy a boat." When asked how well this rule of his does, our data scientist answers, "It's 100 percent accurate!" And indeed, on the data that is in the table, the rule is perfectly accurate. There are many possible rules we could come up with that would explain perfectly if someone in this dataset wants to buy a boat. No age appears twice in the data, so we could say people who are 66, 52, 53, or

2 In the real world, this is actually a tricky problem. While we know that the other customers haven't bought a boat from us yet, they might have bought one from someone else, or they may still be saving and plan to buy one in the future.

58 years old want to buy a boat, while all others don't. While we can make up many rules that work well on this data, remember that we are not interested in making predictions for this dataset; we already know the answers for these customers. We want to know if *new customers* are likely to buy a boat. We therefore want to find a rule that will work well for new customers, and achieving 100 percent accuracy on the training set does not help us there. We might not expect that the rule our data scientist came up with will work very well on new customers. It seems too complex, and it is supported by very little data. For example, the "or is not divorced" part of the rule hinges on a single customer.

The only measure of whether an algorithm will perform well on new data is the evaluation on the test set. However, intuitively[3] we expect simple models to generalize better to new data. If the rule was "People older than 50 want to buy a boat," and this would explain the behavior of all the customers, we would trust it more than the rule involving children and marital status in addition to age. Therefore, we always want to find the simplest model. Building a model that is too complex for the amount of information we have, as our novice data scientist did, is called *overfitting*. Overfitting occurs when you fit a model too closely to the particularities of the training set and obtain a model that works well on the training set but is not able to generalize to new data. On the other hand, if your model is too simple—say, "Everybody who owns a house buys a boat"—then you might not be able to capture all the aspects of and variability in the data, and your model will do badly even on the training set. Choosing too simple a model is called *underfitting*.

The more complex we allow our model to be, the better we will be able to predict on the training data. However, if our model becomes too complex, we start focusing too much on each individual data point in our training set, and the model will not generalize well to new data.

There is a sweet spot in between that will yield the best generalization performance. This is the model we want to find.

The trade-off between overfitting and underfitting is illustrated in Figure 2-1.

3 And also provably, with the right math.

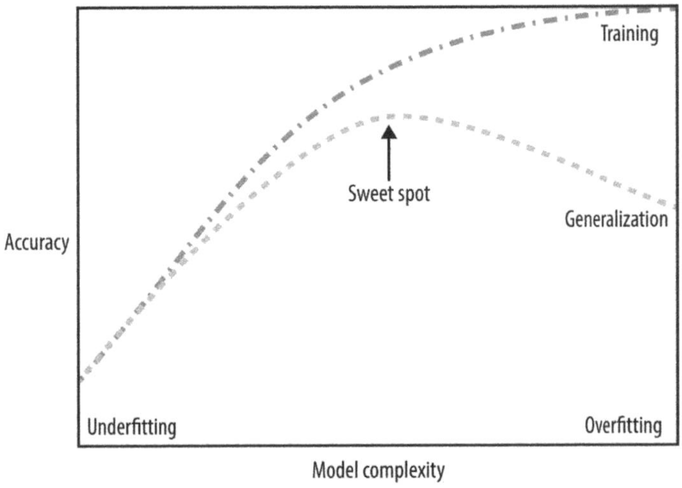

Figure 2-1. Trade-off of model complexity against training and test accuracy

2.2.1 Relation of Model Complexity to Dataset Size

It's important to note that model complexity is intimately tied to the variation of inputs contained in your training dataset: the larger variety of data points your dataset contains, the more complex a model you can use without overfitting. Usually, collecting more data points will yield more variety, so larger datasets allow building more complex models. However, simply duplicating the same data points or collecting very similar data will not help.

Going back to the boat selling example, if we saw 10,000 more rows of customer data, and all of them complied with the rule "If the customer is older than 45, and has less than 3 children or is not divorced, then they want to buy a boat," we would be much more likely to believe this to be a good rule than when it was developed using only the 12 rows in Table 2-1.

Having more data and building appropriately more complex models can often work wonders for supervised learning tasks. In this book, we will focus on working with datasets of fixed sizes. In the real world, you often have the ability to decide how much data to collect, which might be more beneficial than tweaking and tuning your model. Never underestimate the power of more data.

2.3 Supervised Machine Learning Algorithms

We will now review the most popular machine learning algorithms and explain how they learn from data and how they make predictions. We will also discuss how the concept of model complexity plays out for each of these models, and provide an overview of how each algorithm builds a model. We will examine the strengths and weaknesses of each algorithm, and what kind of data they can best be applied to. We will also explain the meaning of the most important parameters and options.[4] Many algorithms have a classification and a regression variant, and we will describe both.

It is not necessary to read through the descriptions of each algorithm in detail, but understanding the models will give you a better feeling for the different ways machine learning algorithms can work. This chapter can also be used as a reference guide, and you can come back to it when you are unsure about the workings of any of the algorithms.

2.3.1 Some Sample Datasets

We will use several datasets to illustrate the different algorithms. Some of the datasets will be small and synthetic (meaning made-up), designed to highlight particular aspects of the algorithms. Other datasets will be large, real-world examples.

An example of a synthetic two-class classification dataset is the `forge` dataset, which has two features. The following code creates a scatter plot (Figure 2-2) visualizing all of the data points in this dataset. The plot has the first feature on the x-axis and the second feature on the y-axis. As is always the case in scatter plots, each data point is represented as one dot. The color and shape of the dot indicates its class:

In[1]:

```
# generate dataset
X, y = mglearn.datasets.make_forge()
# plot dataset
mglearn.discrete_scatter(X[:, 0], X[:, 1], y)
plt.legend(["Class 0", "Class 1"], loc=4)
plt.xlabel("First feature")
plt.ylabel("Second feature")
print("X.shape:", X.shape)
```

Out[1]:

```
X.shape: (26, 2)
```

4 Discussing all of them is beyond the scope of the book, and we refer you to the `scikit-learn` documentation (*http://scikit-learn.org/stable/documentation*) for more details.

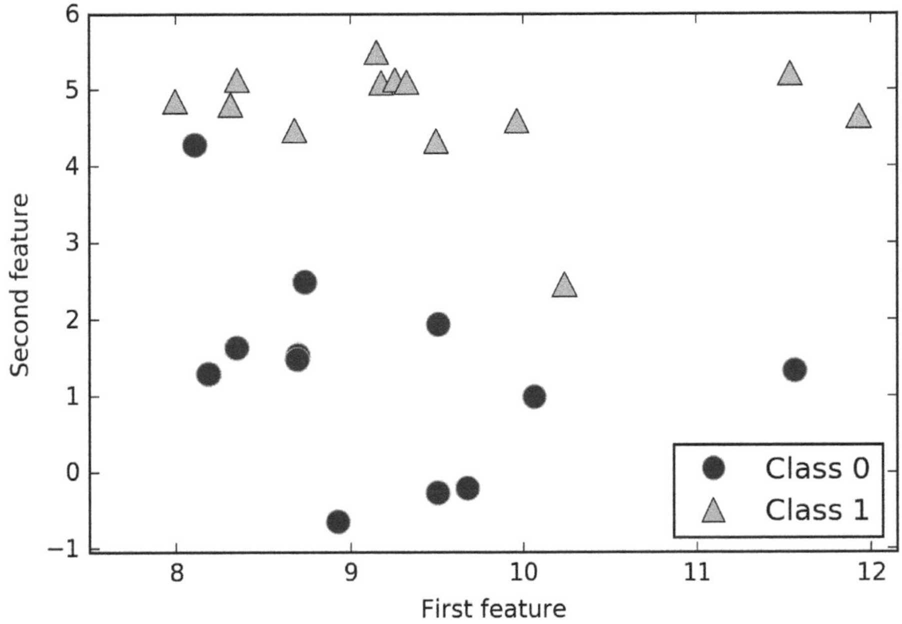

Figure 2-2. Scatter plot of the forge dataset

As you can see from `X.shape`, this dataset consists of 26 data points, with 2 features.

To illustrate regression algorithms, we will use the synthetic `wave` dataset. The `wave` dataset has a single input feature and a continuous target variable (or *response*) that we want to model. The plot created here (Figure 2-3) shows the single feature on the x-axis and the regression target (the output) on the y-axis:

In[2]:

```
X, y = mglearn.datasets.make_wave(n_samples=40)
plt.plot(X, y, 'o')
plt.ylim(-3, 3)
plt.xlabel("Feature")
plt.ylabel("Target")
```

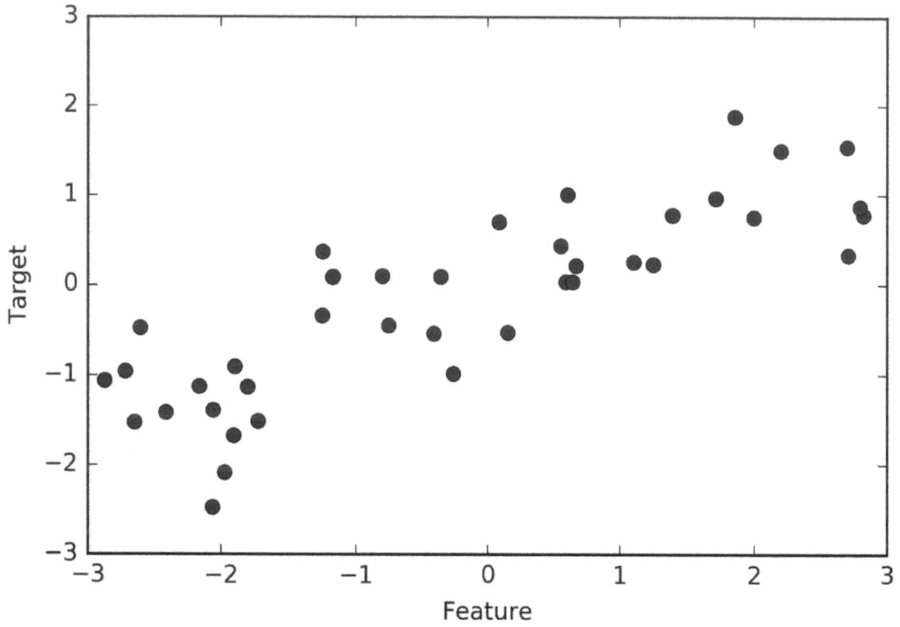

Figure 2-3. Plot of the wave dataset, with the x-axis showing the feature and the y-axis showing the regression target

We are using these very simple, low-dimensional datasets because we can easily visualize them—a printed page has two dimensions, so data with more than two features is hard to show. Any intuition derived from datasets with few features (also called *low-dimensional* datasets) might not hold in datasets with many features (*high-dimensional* datasets). As long as you keep that in mind, inspecting algorithms on low-dimensional datasets can be very instructive.

We will complement these small synthetic datasets with two real-world datasets that are included in `scikit-learn`. One is the Wisconsin Breast Cancer dataset (`cancer`, for short), which records clinical measurements of breast cancer tumors. Each tumor is labeled as "benign" (for harmless tumors) or "malignant" (for cancerous tumors), and the task is to learn to predict whether a tumor is malignant based on the measurements of the tissue.

The data can be loaded using the `load_breast_cancer` function from `scikit-learn`:

In[3]:

```
from sklearn.datasets import load_breast_cancer
cancer = load_breast_cancer()
print("cancer.keys():\n", cancer.keys())
```

Out[3]:

```
cancer.keys():
 dict_keys(['data', 'target', 'target_names', 'DESCR', 'feature_names', 'filename'])
```

> Datasets that are included in `scikit-learn` are usually stored as `Bunch` objects, which contain some information about the dataset as well as the actual data. All you need to know about `Bunch` objects is that they behave like dictionaries, with the added benefit that you can access values using a dot (as in `bunch.key` instead of `bunch['key']`).

The dataset consists of 569 data points, with 30 features each:

In[4]:

```
print("Shape of cancer data:", cancer.data.shape)
```

Out[4]:

```
Shape of cancer data: (569, 30)
```

Of these 569 data points, 212 are labeled as malignant and 357 as benign:

In[5]:

```
print("Sample counts per class:\n",
      {n: v for n, v in zip(cancer.target_names, np.bincount(cancer.target))})
```

Out[5]:

```
Sample counts per class:
 {'malignant': 212, 'benign': 357}
```

To get a description of the semantic meaning of each feature, we can have a look at the `feature_names` attribute:

In[6]:

```
print("Feature names:\n", cancer.feature_names)
```

Out[6]:

```
Feature names:
['mean radius' 'mean texture' 'mean perimeter' 'mean area'
 'mean smoothness' 'mean compactness' 'mean concavity'
 'mean concave points' 'mean symmetry' 'mean fractal dimension'
 'radius error' 'texture error' 'perimeter error' 'area error'
 'smoothness error' 'compactness error' 'concavity error'
 'concave points error' 'symmetry error' 'fractal dimension error'
 'worst radius' 'worst texture' 'worst perimeter' 'worst area'
 'worst smoothness' 'worst compactness' 'worst concavity'
 'worst concave points' 'worst symmetry' 'worst fractal dimension']
```

You can find out more about the data by reading `cancer.DESCR` if you are interested.

We will also be using a real-world regression dataset, the Boston Housing dataset. The task associated with this dataset is to predict the median value of homes in several Boston neighborhoods in the 1970s, using information such as crime rate, proximity to the Charles River, highway accessibility, and so on. The dataset contains 506 data points, described by 13 features:

In[7]:

```
from sklearn.datasets import load_boston
boston = load_boston()
print("Data shape:", boston.data.shape)
```

Out[7]:

```
Data shape: (506, 13)
```

Again, you can get more information about the dataset by reading the `DESCR` attribute of `boston`. For our purposes here, we will actually expand this dataset by not only considering these 13 measurements as input features, but also looking at all products (also called *interactions*) between features. In other words, we will not only consider crime rate and highway accessibility as features, but also the product of crime rate and highway accessibility. Including derived feature like these is called *feature engineering*, which we will discuss in more detail in Chapter 4. This derived dataset can be loaded using the `load_extended_boston` function:

In[8]:

```
X, y = mglearn.datasets.load_extended_boston()
print("X.shape:", X.shape)
```

Out[8]:

```
X.shape: (506, 104)
```

The resulting 104 features are the 13 original features together with the 91 possible combinations of two features within those 13 (with replacement).[5]

We will use these datasets to explain and illustrate the properties of the different machine learning algorithms. But for now, let's get to the algorithms themselves. First, we will revisit the *k*-nearest neighbors (*k*-NN) algorithm that we saw in the previous chapter.

5 This is 13 interactions for the first feature, plus 12 for the second not involving the first, plus 11 for the third and so on (13 + 12 + 11 + … + 1 = 91).

2.3.2 k-Nearest Neighbors

The *k*-NN algorithm is arguably the simplest machine learning algorithm. Building the model consists only of storing the training dataset. To make a prediction for a new data point, the algorithm finds the closest data points in the training dataset—its "nearest neighbors."

k-Neighbors classification

In its simplest version, the *k*-NN algorithm only considers exactly one nearest neighbor, which is the closest training data point to the point we want to make a prediction for. The prediction is then simply the known output for this training point. Figure 2-4 illustrates this for the case of classification on the `forge` dataset:

In[9]:

```
mglearn.plots.plot_knn_classification(n_neighbors=1)
```

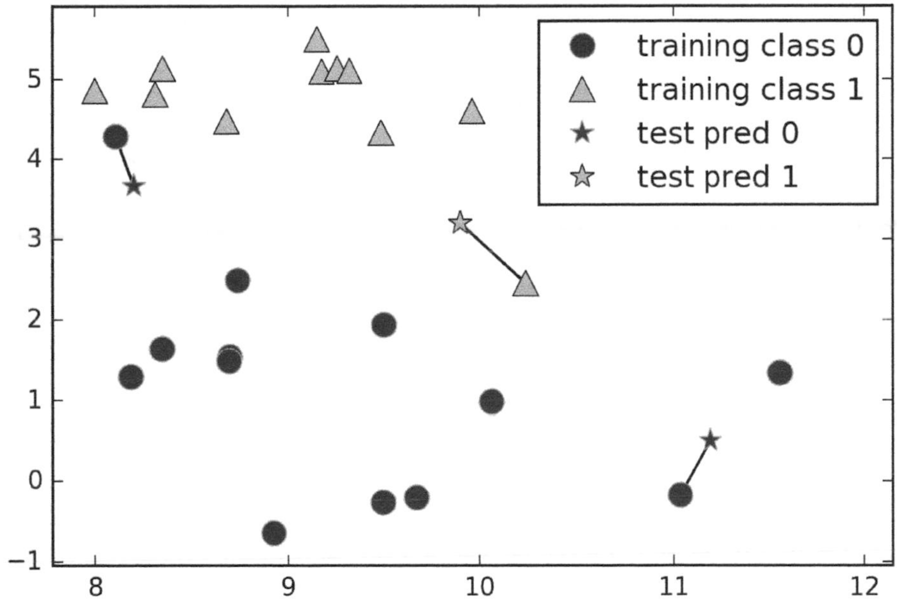

Figure 2-4. Predictions made by the one-nearest-neighbor model on the forge dataset

Here, we added three new data points, shown as stars. For each of them, we marked the closest point in the training set. The prediction of the one-nearest-neighbor algorithm is the label of that point (shown by the color of the cross).

Instead of considering only the closest neighbor, we can also consider an arbitrary number, *k*, of neighbors. This is where the name of the *k*-nearest neighbors algorithm comes from. When considering more than one neighbor, we use *voting* to assign a label. This means that for each test point, we count how many neighbors belong to class 0 and how many neighbors belong to class 1. We then assign the class that is more frequent: in other words, the majority class among the *k*-nearest neighbors. The following example (Figure 2-5) uses the three closest neighbors:

In[10]:

```
mglearn.plots.plot_knn_classification(n_neighbors=3)
```

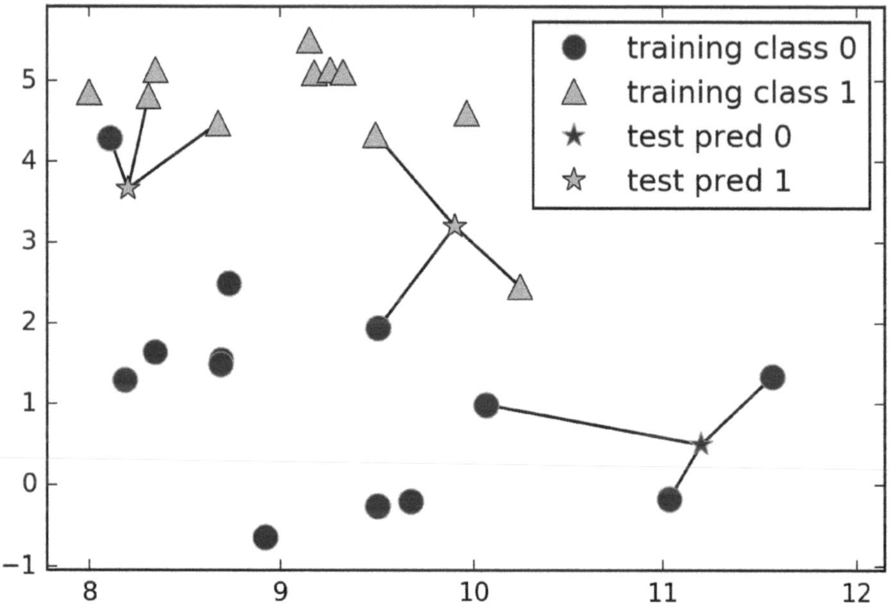

Figure 2-5. Predictions made by the three-nearest-neighbors model on the forge dataset

Again, the prediction is shown as the color of the cross. You can see that the prediction for the new data point at the top left is not the same as the prediction when we used only one neighbor.

While this illustration is for a binary classification problem, this method can be applied to datasets with any number of classes. For more classes, we count how many neighbors belong to each class and again predict the most common class.

Now let's look at how we can apply the *k*-nearest neighbors algorithm using `scikit-learn`. First, we split our data into a training and a test set so we can evaluate generalization performance, as discussed in Chapter 1:

In[11]:

```
from sklearn.model_selection import train_test_split
X, y = mglearn.datasets.make_forge()

X_train, X_test, y_train, y_test = train_test_split(X, y, random_state=0)
```

Next, we import and instantiate the class. This is when we can set parameters, like the number of neighbors to use. Here, we set it to 3:

In[12]:

```
from sklearn.neighbors import KNeighborsClassifier
clf = KNeighborsClassifier(n_neighbors=3)
```

Now, we fit the classifier using the training set. For `KNeighborsClassifier` this means storing the dataset, so we can compute neighbors during prediction:

In[13]:

```
clf.fit(X_train, y_train)
```

To make predictions on the test data, we call the `predict` method. For each data point in the test set, this computes its nearest neighbors in the training set and finds the most common class among these:

In[14]:

```
print("Test set predictions:", clf.predict(X_test))
```

Out[14]:

```
Test set predictions: [1 0 1 0 1 0 0]
```

To evaluate how well our model generalizes, we can call the `score` method with the test data together with the test labels:

In[15]:

```
print("Test set accuracy: {:.2f}".format(clf.score(X_test, y_test)))
```

Out[15]:

```
Test set accuracy: 0.86
```

We see that our model is about 86% accurate, meaning the model predicted the class correctly for 86% of the samples in the test dataset.

Analyzing KNeighborsClassifier

For two-dimensional datasets, we can also illustrate the prediction for all possible test points in the xy-plane. We color the plane according to the class that would be assigned to a point in this region. This lets us view the *decision boundary*, which is the divide between where the algorithm assigns class 0 versus where it assigns class 1.

The following code produces the visualizations of the decision boundaries for one, three, and nine neighbors shown in Figure 2-6:

In[16]:

```
fig, axes = plt.subplots(1, 3, figsize=(10, 3))

for n_neighbors, ax in zip([1, 3, 9], axes):
    # the fit method returns the object self, so we can instantiate
    # and fit in one line
    clf = KNeighborsClassifier(n_neighbors=n_neighbors).fit(X, y)
    mglearn.plots.plot_2d_separator(clf, X, fill=True, eps=0.5, ax=ax, alpha=.4)
    mglearn.discrete_scatter(X[:, 0], X[:, 1], y, ax=ax)
    ax.set_title("{} neighbor(s)".format(n_neighbors))
    ax.set_xlabel("feature 0")
    ax.set_ylabel("feature 1")
axes[0].legend(loc=3)
```

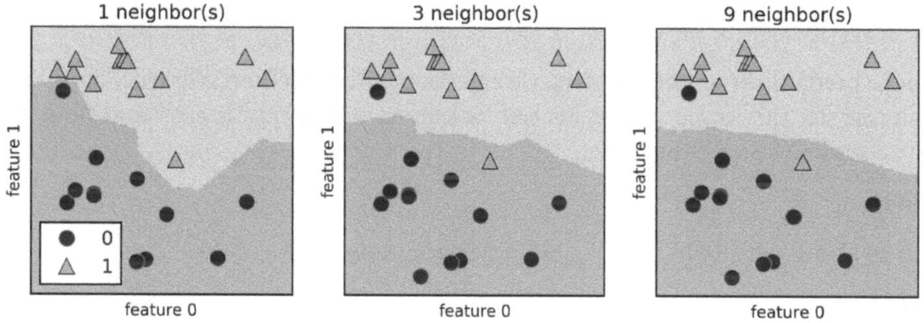

Figure 2-6. Decision boundaries created by the nearest neighbors model for different values of n_neighbors

As you can see on the left in the figure, using a single neighbor results in a decision boundary that follows the training data closely. Considering more and more neighbors leads to a smoother decision boundary. A smoother boundary corresponds to a simpler model. In other words, using few neighbors corresponds to high model complexity (as shown on the right side of Figure 2-1), and using many neighbors corresponds to low model complexity (as shown on the left side of Figure 2-1). If you consider the extreme case where the number of neighbors is the number of all data points in the training set, each test point would have exactly the same neighbors (all training points) and all predictions would be the same: the class that is most frequent in the training set.

Let's investigate whether we can confirm the connection between model complexity and generalization that we discussed earlier. We will do this on the real-world Breast Cancer dataset. We begin by splitting the dataset into a training and a test set. Then we evaluate training and test set performance with different numbers of neighbors. The results are shown in Figure 2-7:

In[17]:

```
from sklearn.datasets import load_breast_cancer

cancer = load_breast_cancer()
X_train, X_test, y_train, y_test = train_test_split(
    cancer.data, cancer.target, stratify=cancer.target, random_state=66)

training_accuracy = []
test_accuracy = []
# try n_neighbors from 1 to 10
neighbors_settings = range(1, 11)

for n_neighbors in neighbors_settings:
    # build the model
    clf = KNeighborsClassifier(n_neighbors=n_neighbors)
    clf.fit(X_train, y_train)
    # record training set accuracy
    training_accuracy.append(clf.score(X_train, y_train))
    # record generalization accuracy
    test_accuracy.append(clf.score(X_test, y_test))

plt.plot(neighbors_settings, training_accuracy, label="training accuracy")
plt.plot(neighbors_settings, test_accuracy, label="test accuracy")
plt.ylabel("Accuracy")
plt.xlabel("n_neighbors")
plt.legend()
```

The plot shows the training and test set accuracy on the y-axis against the setting of `n_neighbors` on the x-axis. While real-world plots are rarely very smooth, we can still recognize some of the characteristics of overfitting and underfitting (note that because considering fewer neighbors corresponds to a more complex model, the plot is horizontally flipped relative to the illustration in Figure 2-1). Considering a single nearest neighbor, the prediction on the training set is perfect. But when more neighbors are considered, the model becomes simpler and the training accuracy drops. The test set accuracy for using a single neighbor is lower than when using more neighbors, indicating that using the single nearest neighbor leads to a model that is too complex. On the other hand, when considering 10 neighbors, the model is too simple and performance is even worse. The best performance is somewhere in the middle, using around six neighbors. Still, it is good to keep the scale of the plot in mind. The worst performance is around 88% accuracy, which might still be acceptable.

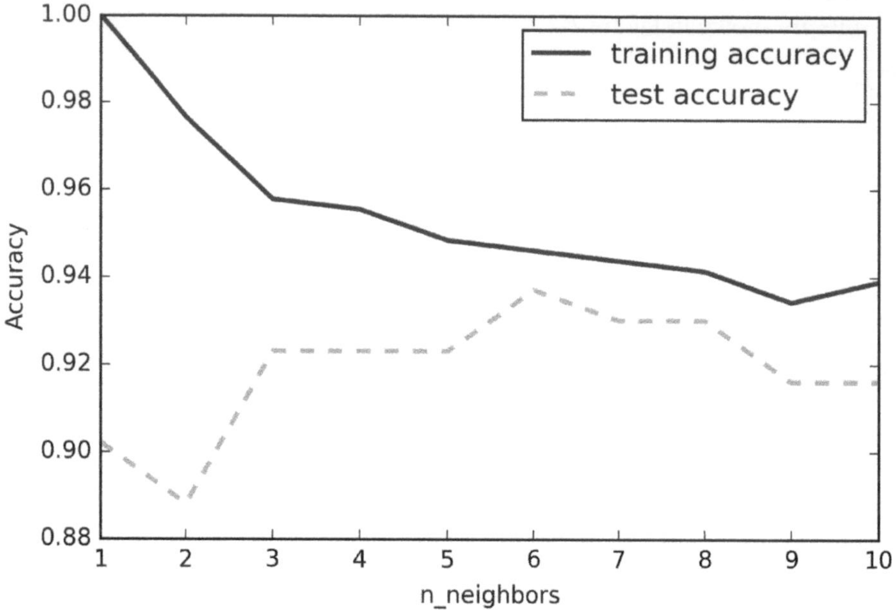

Figure 2-7. Comparison of training and test accuracy as a function of n_neighbors

k-neighbors regression

There is also a regression variant of the *k*-nearest neighbors algorithm. Again, let's start by using the single nearest neighbor, this time using the `wave` dataset. We've added three test data points as green stars on the x-axis. The prediction using a single neighbor is just the target value of the nearest neighbor. These are shown as blue stars in Figure 2-8:

In[18]:

```
mglearn.plots.plot_knn_regression(n_neighbors=1)
```

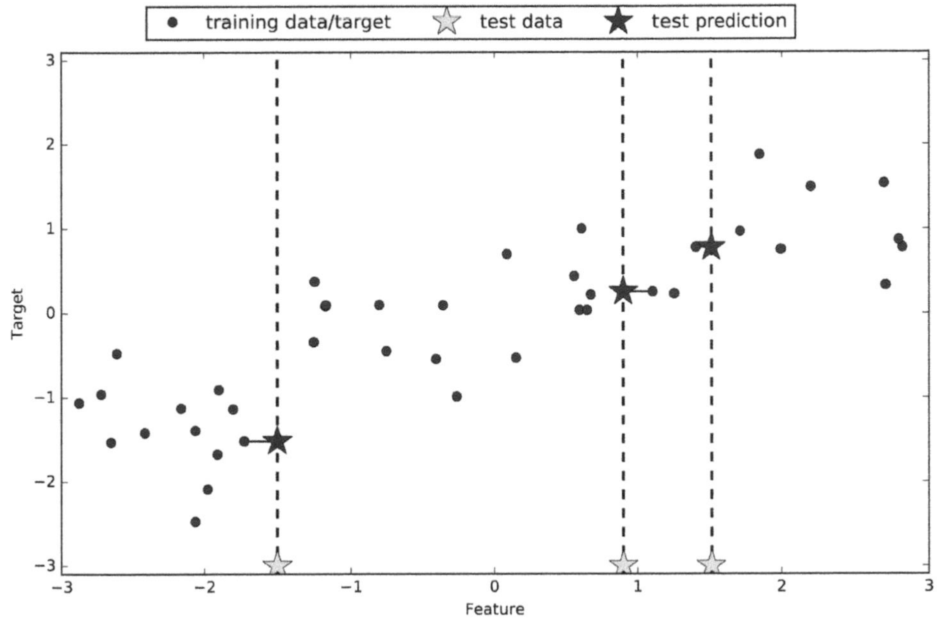

Figure 2-8. Predictions made by one-nearest-neighbor regression on the wave dataset

Again, we can use more than the single closest neighbor for regression. When using multiple nearest neighbors, the prediction is the average, or mean, of the relevant neighbors (Figure 2-9):

In[19]:

```
mglearn.plots.plot_knn_regression(n_neighbors=3)
```

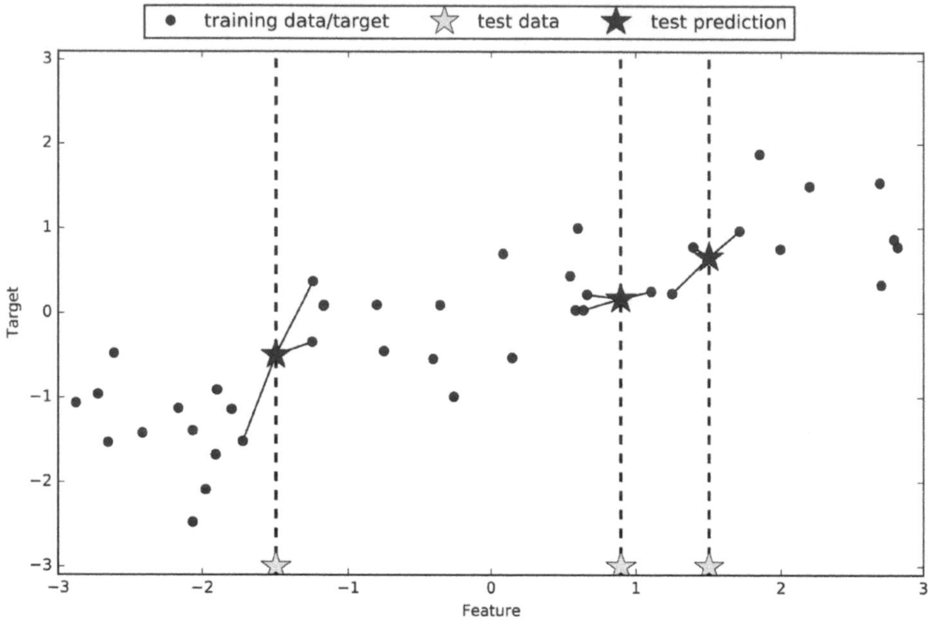

Figure 2-9. Predictions made by three-nearest-neighbors regression on the wave dataset

The *k*-nearest neighbors algorithm for regression is implemented in the `KNeighbors Regressor` class in `scikit-learn`. It's used similarly to `KNeighborsClassifier`:

In[20]:

```
from sklearn.neighbors import KNeighborsRegressor

X, y = mglearn.datasets.make_wave(n_samples=40)

# split the wave dataset into a training and a test set
X_train, X_test, y_train, y_test = train_test_split(X, y, random_state=0)

# instantiate the model and set the number of neighbors to consider to 3
reg = KNeighborsRegressor(n_neighbors=3)
# fit the model using the training data and training targets
reg.fit(X_train, y_train)
```

Now we can make predictions on the test set:

In[21]:

```
print("Test set predictions:\n", reg.predict(X_test))
```

Out[21]:

```
Test set predictions:
[-0.054  0.357  1.137 -1.894 -1.139 -1.631  0.357  0.912 -0.447 -1.139]
```

We can also evaluate the model using the `score` method, which for regressors returns the R^2 score. The R^2 score, also known as the coefficient of determination, is a measure of goodness of a prediction for a regression model, and yields a score that's usually between 0 and 1. A value of 1 corresponds to a perfect prediction, and a value of 0 corresponds to a constant model that just predicts the mean of the training set responses, `y_train`. The formulation of R^2 used here can even be negative, which can indicate anticorrelated predictions.

In[22]:

```
print("Test set R^2: {:.2f}".format(reg.score(X_test, y_test)))
```

Out[22]:

```
Test set R^2: 0.83
```

Here, the score is 0.83, which indicates a relatively good model fit.

Analyzing KNeighborsRegressor

For our one-dimensional dataset, we can see what the predictions look like for all possible feature values (Figure 2-10). To do this, we create a test dataset consisting of many points on the x-axis, which corresponds to the single feature:

In[23]:

```
fig, axes = plt.subplots(1, 3, figsize=(15, 4))
# create 1,000 data points, evenly spaced between -3 and 3
line = np.linspace(-3, 3, 1000).reshape(-1, 1)
for n_neighbors, ax in zip([1, 3, 9], axes):
    # make predictions using 1, 3, or 9 neighbors
    reg = KNeighborsRegressor(n_neighbors=n_neighbors)
    reg.fit(X_train, y_train)
    ax.plot(line, reg.predict(line))
    ax.plot(X_train, y_train, '^', c=mglearn.cm2(0), markersize=8)
    ax.plot(X_test, y_test, 'v', c=mglearn.cm2(1), markersize=8)

    ax.set_title(
        "{} neighbor(s)\n train score: {:.2f} test score: {:.2f}".format(
            n_neighbors, reg.score(X_train, y_train),
            reg.score(X_test, y_test)))
    ax.set_xlabel("Feature")
    ax.set_ylabel("Target")
axes[0].legend(["Model predictions", "Training data/target",
                "Test data/target"], loc="best")
```

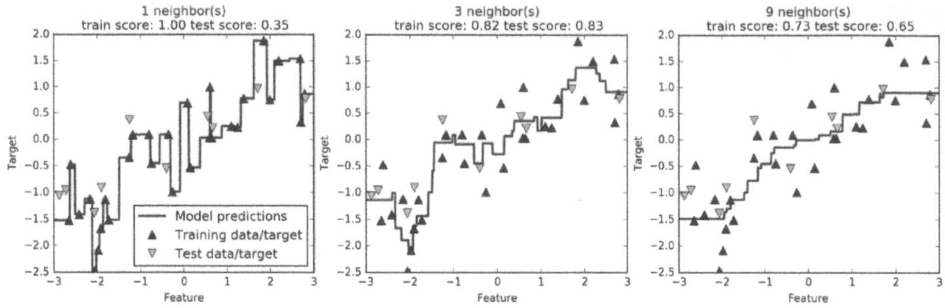

Figure 2-10. Comparing predictions made by nearest neighbors regression for different values of `n_neighbors`

As we can see from the plot, using only a single neighbor, each point in the training set has an obvious influence on the predictions, and the predicted values go through all of the data points. This leads to a very unsteady prediction. Considering more neighbors leads to smoother predictions, but these do not fit the training data as well.

Strengths, weaknesses, and parameters

In principle, there are two important parameters to the `KNeighbors` classifier: the number of neighbors and how you measure distance between data points. In practice, using a small number of neighbors like three or five often works well, but you should certainly adjust this parameter. Choosing the right distance measure is somewhat beyond the scope of this book. By default, Euclidean distance is used, which works well in many settings.

One of the strengths of *k*-NN is that the model is very easy to understand, and often gives reasonable performance without a lot of adjustments. Using this algorithm is a good baseline method to try before considering more advanced techniques. Building the nearest neighbors model is usually very fast, but when your training set is very large (either in number of features or in number of samples) prediction can be slow. When using the *k*-NN algorithm, it's important to preprocess your data (see Chapter 3). This approach often does not perform well on datasets with many features (hundreds or more), and it does particularly badly with datasets where most features are 0 most of the time (so-called *sparse datasets*).

So, while the *k*-nearest neighbors algorithm is easy to understand, it is not often used in practice, due to prediction being slow and its inability to handle many features. The method we discuss next has neither of these drawbacks.

2.3.3 Linear Models

Linear models are a class of models that are widely used in practice and have been studied extensively in the last few decades, with roots going back over a hundred years. Linear models make a prediction using a *linear function* of the input features, which we will explain shortly.

Linear models for regression

For regression, the general prediction formula for a linear model looks as follows:

$$\hat{y} = w[0] * x[0] + w[1] * x[1] + ... + w[p] * x[p] + b$$

Here, $x[0]$ to $x[p]$ denotes the features (in this example, the number of features is $p+1$) of a single data point, w and b are parameters of the model that are learned, and $\hat{y}$ is the prediction the model makes. For a dataset with a single feature, this is:

$$\hat{y} = w[0] * x[0] + b$$

which you might remember from high school mathematics as the equation for a line. Here, $w[0]$ is the slope and b is the y-axis offset. For more features, w contains the slopes along each feature axis. Alternatively, you can think of the predicted response as being a weighted sum of the input features, with weights (which can be negative) given by the entries of w.

Trying to learn the parameters $w[0]$ and b on our one-dimensional `wave` dataset might lead to the following line (see Figure 2-11):

In[24]:

```
mglearn.plots.plot_linear_regression_wave()
```

Out[24]:

```
w[0]: 0.393906  b: -0.031804
```

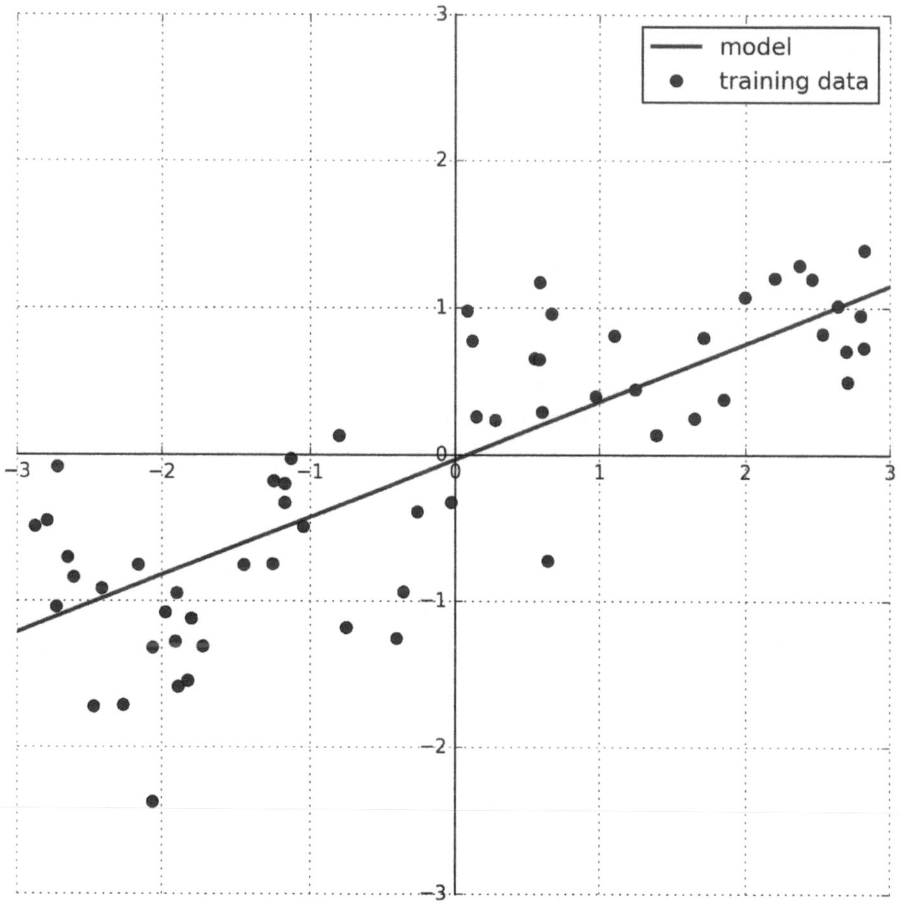

Figure 2-11. Predictions of a linear model on the wave dataset

We added a coordinate cross into the plot to make it easier to understand the line. Looking at `w[0]` we see that the slope should be around 0.4, which we can confirm visually in the plot. The intercept is where the prediction line should cross the y-axis: this is slightly below zero, which you can also confirm in the image.

Linear models for regression can be characterized as regression models for which the prediction is a line for a single feature, a plane when using two features, or a hyperplane in higher dimensions (that is, when using more features).

If you compare the predictions made by the straight line with those made by the `KNeighborsRegressor` in Figure 2-10, using a straight line to make predictions seems very restrictive. It looks like all the fine details of the data are lost. In a sense, this is true. It is a strong (and somewhat unrealistic) assumption that our target *y* is a linear combination of the features. But looking at one-dimensional data gives a somewhat skewed perspective. For datasets with many features, linear models can be very powerful. In particular, if you have more features than training data points, any target *y* can be perfectly modeled (on the training set) as a linear function.[6]

There are many different linear models for regression. The difference between these models lies in how the model parameters *w* and *b* are learned from the training data, and how model complexity can be controlled. We will now take a look at the most popular linear models for regression.

Linear regression (aka ordinary least squares)

Linear regression, or *ordinary least squares* (OLS), is the simplest and most classic linear method for regression. Linear regression finds the parameters *w* and *b* that minimize the *mean squared error* between predictions and the true regression targets, *y*, on the training set. The mean squared error is the sum of the squared differences between the predictions and the true values, divided by the number of samples. Linear regression has no parameters, which is a benefit, but it also has no way to control model complexity.

Here is the code that produces the model you can see in Figure 2-11:

In[25]:

```
from sklearn.linear_model import LinearRegression
X, y = mglearn.datasets.make_wave(n_samples=60)
X_train, X_test, y_train, y_test = train_test_split(X, y, random_state=42)

lr = LinearRegression().fit(X_train, y_train)
```

The "slope" parameters (*w*), also called weights or *coefficients*, are stored in the `coef_` attribute, while the offset or *intercept* (*b*) is stored in the `intercept_` attribute:

In[26]:

```
print("lr.coef_:", lr.coef_)
print("lr.intercept_:", lr.intercept_)
```

Out[26]:

```
lr.coef_: [0.394]
lr.intercept_: -0.031804343026759746
```

6 This is easy to see if you know some linear algebra.

You might notice the strange-looking trailing underscore at the end of `coef_` and `intercept_`. `scikit-learn` always stores anything that is derived from the training data in attributes that end with a trailing underscore. That is to separate them from parameters that are set by the user.

The `intercept_` attribute is always a single float number, while the `coef_` attribute is a NumPy array with one entry per input feature. As we only have a single input feature in the `wave` dataset, `lr.coef_` only has a single entry.

Let's look at the training set and test set performance:

In[27]:

```
print("Training set score: {:.2f}".format(lr.score(X_train, y_train)))
print("Test set score: {:.2f}".format(lr.score(X_test, y_test)))
```

Out[27]:

```
Training set score: 0.67
Test set score: 0.66
```

An R^2 of around 0.66 is not very good, but we can see that the scores on the training and test sets are very close together. This means we are likely underfitting, not overfitting. For this one-dimensional dataset, there is little danger of overfitting, as the model is very simple (or restricted). However, with higher-dimensional datasets (meaning datasets with a large number of features), linear models become more powerful, and there is a higher chance of overfitting. Let's take a look at how `LinearRegression` performs on a more complex dataset, like the Boston Housing dataset. Remember that this dataset has 506 samples and 104 derived features. First, we load the dataset and split it into a training and a test set. Then we build the linear regression model as before:

In[28]:

```
X, y = mglearn.datasets.load_extended_boston()

X_train, X_test, y_train, y_test = train_test_split(X, y, random_state=0)
lr = LinearRegression().fit(X_train, y_train)
```

When comparing training set and test set scores, we find that we predict very accurately on the training set, but the R^2 on the test set is much worse:

In[29]:

```
print("Training set score: {:.2f}".format(lr.score(X_train, y_train)))
print("Test set score: {:.2f}".format(lr.score(X_test, y_test)))
```

Out[29]:

```
Training set score: 0.95
Test set score: 0.61
```

This discrepancy between performance on the training set and the test set is a clear sign of overfitting, and therefore we should try to find a model that allows us to control complexity. One of the most commonly used alternatives to standard linear regression is *ridge regression*, which we will look into next.

Ridge regression

Ridge regression is also a linear model for regression, so the formula it uses to make predictions is the same one used for ordinary least squares. In ridge regression, though, the coefficients (*w*) are chosen not only so that they predict well on the training data, but also to fit an additional constraint. We also want the magnitude of coefficients to be as small as possible; in other words, all entries of *w* should be close to zero. Intuitively, this means each feature should have as little effect on the outcome as possible (which translates to having a small slope), while still predicting well. This constraint is an example of what is called *regularization*. Regularization means explicitly restricting a model to avoid overfitting. The particular kind used by ridge regression is known as L2 regularization.[7]

Ridge regression is implemented in `linear_model.Ridge`. Let's see how well it does on the extended Boston Housing dataset:

In[30]:

```
from sklearn.linear_model import Ridge

ridge = Ridge().fit(X_train, y_train)
print("Training set score: {:.2f}".format(ridge.score(X_train, y_train)))
print("Test set score: {:.2f}".format(ridge.score(X_test, y_test)))
```

Out[30]:

```
Training set score: 0.89
Test set score: 0.75
```

As you can see, the training set score of `Ridge` is *lower* than for `LinearRegression`, while the test set score is *higher*. This is consistent with our expectation. With linear regression, we were overfitting our data. `Ridge` is a more restricted model, so we are less likely to overfit. A less complex model means worse performance on the training set, but better generalization. As we are only interested in generalization performance, we should choose the `Ridge` model over the `LinearRegression` model.

7 Mathematically, `Ridge` penalizes the squared L2 norm of the coefficients, or the Euclidean length of *w*.

The Ridge model makes a trade-off between the simplicity of the model (near-zero coefficients) and its performance on the training set. How much importance the model places on simplicity versus training set performance can be specified by the user, using the alpha parameter. In the previous example, we used the default parameter alpha=1.0. There is no reason why this will give us the best trade-off, though. The optimum setting of alpha depends on the particular dataset we are using. Increasing alpha forces coefficients to move more toward zero, which decreases training set performance but might help generalization. For example:

In[31]:

```
ridge10 = Ridge(alpha=10).fit(X_train, y_train)
print("Training set score: {:.2f}".format(ridge10.score(X_train, y_train)))
print("Test set score: {:.2f}".format(ridge10.score(X_test, y_test)))
```

Out[31]:

```
Training set score: 0.79
Test set score: 0.64
```

Decreasing alpha allows the coefficients to be less restricted, meaning we move right in Figure 2-1. For very small values of alpha, coefficients are barely restricted at all, and we end up with a model that resembles LinearRegression:

In[32]:

```
ridge01 = Ridge(alpha=0.1).fit(X_train, y_train)
print("Training set score: {:.2f}".format(ridge01.score(X_train, y_train)))
print("Test set score: {:.2f}".format(ridge01.score(X_test, y_test)))
```

Out[32]:

```
Training set score: 0.93
Test set score: 0.77
```

Here, alpha=0.1 seems to be working well. We could try decreasing alpha even more to improve generalization. For now, notice how the parameter alpha corresponds to the model complexity as shown in Figure 2-1. We will discuss methods to properly select parameters in Chapter 5.

We can also get a more qualitative insight into how the alpha parameter changes the model by inspecting the coef_ attribute of models with different values of alpha. A higher alpha means a more restricted model, so we expect the entries of coef_ to have smaller magnitude for a high value of alpha than for a low value of alpha. This is confirmed in the plot in Figure 2-12:

In[33]:

```
plt.plot(ridge.coef_, 's', label="Ridge alpha=1")
plt.plot(ridge10.coef_, '^', label="Ridge alpha=10")
plt.plot(ridge01.coef_, 'v', label="Ridge alpha=0.1")

plt.plot(lr.coef_, 'o', label="LinearRegression")
plt.xlabel("Coefficient index")
plt.ylabel("Coefficient magnitude")
plt.hlines(0, 0, len(lr.coef_))
plt.ylim(-25, 25)
plt.legend()
```

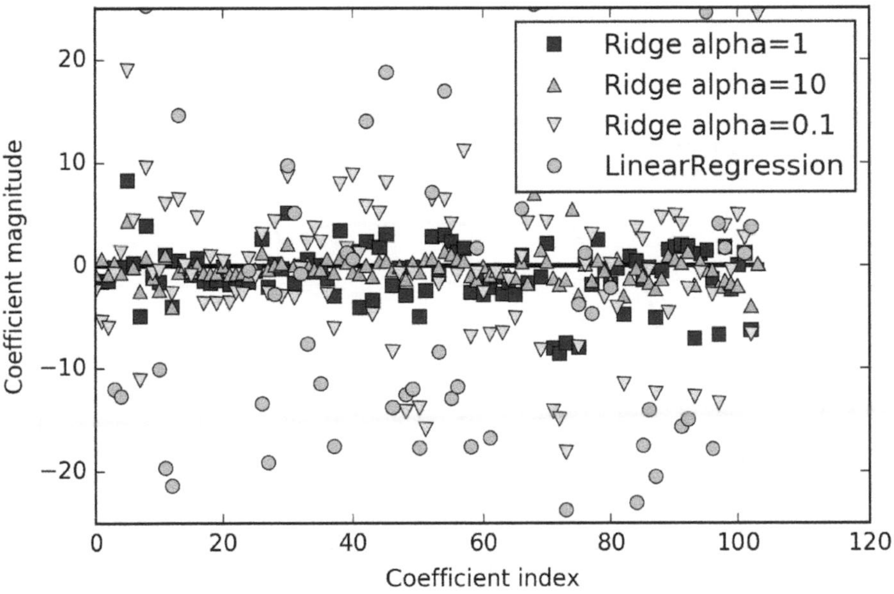

Figure 2-12. Comparing coefficient magnitudes for ridge regression with different values of alpha and linear regression

Here, the x-axis enumerates the entries of `coef_`: `x=0` shows the coefficient associated with the first feature, `x=1` the coefficient associated with the second feature, and so on up to `x=100`. The y-axis shows the numeric values of the corresponding values of the coefficients. The main takeaway here is that for `alpha=10`, the coefficients are mostly between around –3 and 3. The coefficients for the `Ridge` model with `alpha=1`, are somewhat larger. The dots corresponding to `alpha=0.1` have larger magnitude still, and many of the dots corresponding to linear regression without any regularization (which would be `alpha=0`) are so large they are outside of the chart.

Another way to understand the influence of regularization is to fix a value of `alpha` but vary the amount of training data available. For Figure 2-13, we subsampled the Boston Housing dataset and evaluated `LinearRegression` and `Ridge(alpha=1)` on subsets of increasing size (plots that show model performance as a function of dataset size are called *learning curves*):

In[34]:

```
mglearn.plots.plot_ridge_n_samples()
```

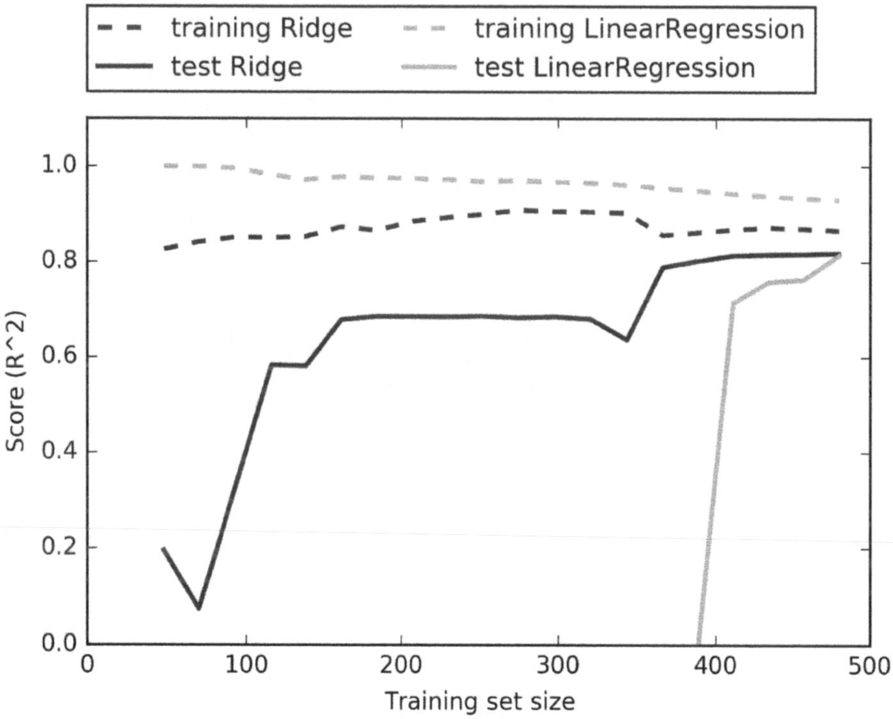

Figure 2-13. Learning curves for ridge regression and linear regression on the Boston Housing dataset

As one would expect, the training score is higher than the test score for all dataset sizes, for both ridge and linear regression. Because ridge is regularized, the training score of ridge is lower than the training score for linear regression across the board. However, the test score for ridge is better, particularly for small subsets of the data. For less than 400 data points, linear regression is not able to learn anything. As more and more data becomes available to the model, both models improve, and linear regression catches up with ridge in the end. The lesson here is that with enough training data, regularization becomes less important, and given enough data, ridge and linear regression will have the same performance (the fact that this happens here when using the full dataset is just by chance). Another interesting aspect of Figure 2-13 is the decrease in training performance for linear regression. If more data is added, it becomes harder for a model to overfit, or memorize the data.

Lasso

An alternative to `Ridge` for regularizing linear regression is `Lasso`. As with ridge regression, the lasso also restricts coefficients to be close to zero, but in a slightly different way, called L1 regularization.[8] The consequence of L1 regularization is that when using the lasso, some coefficients are *exactly zero*. This means some features are entirely ignored by the model. This can be seen as a form of automatic feature selection. Having some coefficients be exactly zero often makes a model easier to interpret, and can reveal the most important features of your model.

Let's apply the lasso to the extended Boston Housing dataset:

In[35]:

```
from sklearn.linear_model import Lasso

lasso = Lasso().fit(X_train, y_train)
print("Training set score: {:.2f}".format(lasso.score(X_train, y_train)))
print("Test set score: {:.2f}".format(lasso.score(X_test, y_test)))
print("Number of features used:", np.sum(lasso.coef_ != 0))
```

Out[35]:

```
Training set score: 0.29
Test set score: 0.21
Number of features used: 4
```

As you can see, `Lasso` does quite badly, both on the training and the test set. This indicates that we are underfitting, and we find that it used only 4 of the 104 features. Similarly to `Ridge`, the Lasso also has a regularization parameter, `alpha`, that controls how strongly coefficients are pushed toward zero. In the previous example, we used the default of `alpha=1.0`. To reduce underfitting, let's try decreasing `alpha`. When we do this, we also need to increase the default setting of `max_iter` (the maximum number of iterations to run):

8 The lasso penalizes the L1 norm of the coefficient vector—or in other words, the sum of the absolute values of the coefficients.

In[36]:

```
# we increase the default setting of "max_iter",
# otherwise the model would warn us that we should increase max_iter.
lasso001 = Lasso(alpha=0.01, max_iter=100000).fit(X_train, y_train)
print("Training set score: {:.2f}".format(lasso001.score(X_train, y_train)))
print("Test set score: {:.2f}".format(lasso001.score(X_test, y_test)))
print("Number of features used:", np.sum(lasso001.coef_ != 0))
```

Out[36]:

```
Training set score: 0.90
Test set score: 0.77
Number of features used: 33
```

A lower `alpha` allowed us to fit a more complex model, which worked better on the training and test data. The performance is slightly better than using `Ridge`, and we are using only 33 of the 104 features. This makes this model potentially easier to understand.

If we set `alpha` too low, however, we again remove the effect of regularization and end up overfitting, with a result similar to `LinearRegression`:

In[37]:

```
lasso00001 = Lasso(alpha=0.0001, max_iter=100000).fit(X_train, y_train)
print("Training set score: {:.2f}".format(lasso00001.score(X_train, y_train)))
print("Test set score: {:.2f}".format(lasso00001.score(X_test, y_test)))
print("Number of features used:", np.sum(lasso00001.coef_ != 0))
```

Out[37]:

```
Training set score: 0.95
Test set score: 0.64
Number of features used: 94
```

Again, we can plot the coefficients of the different models, similarly to Figure 2-12. The result is shown in Figure 2-14:

In[38]:

```
plt.plot(lasso.coef_, 's', label="Lasso alpha=1")
plt.plot(lasso001.coef_, '^', label="Lasso alpha=0.01")
plt.plot(lasso00001.coef_, 'v', label="Lasso alpha=0.0001")

plt.plot(ridge01.coef_, 'o', label="Ridge alpha=0.1")
plt.legend(ncol=2, loc=(0, 1.05))
plt.ylim(-25, 25)
plt.xlabel("Coefficient index")
plt.ylabel("Coefficient magnitude")
```

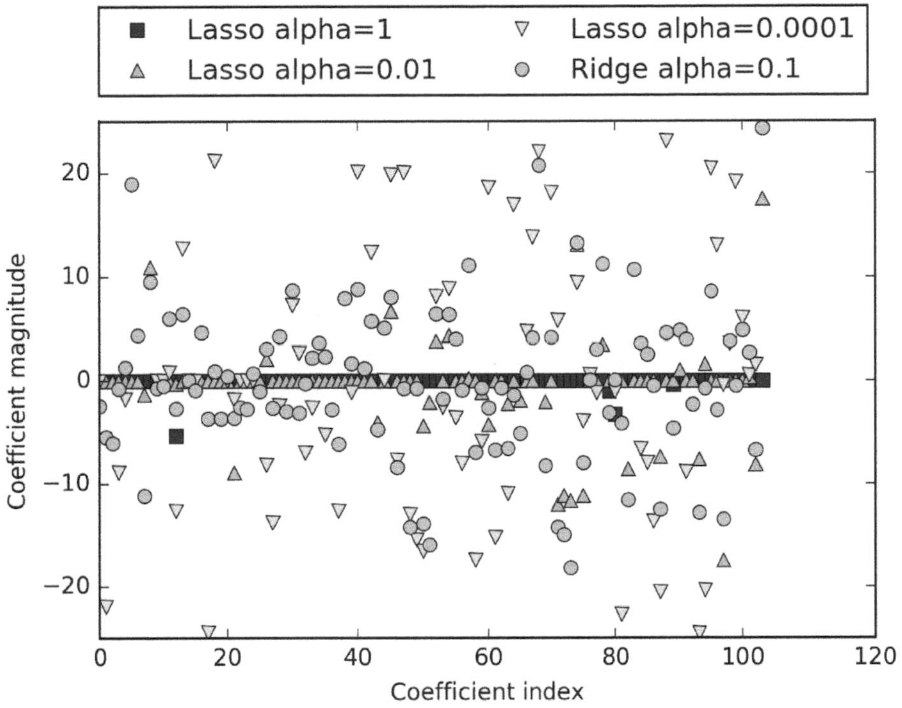

Figure 2-14. Comparing coefficient magnitudes for lasso regression with different values of alpha and ridge regression

For `alpha=1`, we not only see that most of the coefficients are zero (which we already knew), but that the remaining coefficients are also small in magnitude. Decreasing `alpha` to `0.01`, we obtain the solution shown as an upward pointing triangle, which causes most features to be exactly zero. Using `alpha=0.0001`, we get a model that is quite unregularized, with most coefficients nonzero and of large magnitude. For comparison, the best `Ridge` solution is shown as circles. The `Ridge` model with `alpha=0.1` has similar predictive performance as the lasso model with `alpha=0.01`, but using `Ridge`, all coefficients are nonzero.

In practice, ridge regression is usually the first choice between these two models. However, if you have a large amount of features and expect only a few of them to be important, `Lasso` might be a better choice. Similarly, if you would like to have a model that is easy to interpret, `Lasso` will provide a model that is easier to understand, as it will select only a subset of the input features. `scikit-learn` also provides the `ElasticNet` class, which combines the penalties of `Lasso` and `Ridge`. In practice, this combination works best, though at the price of having two parameters to adjust: one for the L1 regularization, and one for the L2 regularization.

Linear models for classification

Linear models are also extensively used for classification. Let's look at binary classification first. In this case, a prediction is made using the following formula:

$$\hat{y} = w[0] * x[0] + w[1] * x[1] + ... + w[p] * x[p] + b > 0$$

The formula looks very similar to the one for linear regression, but instead of just returning the weighted sum of the features, we threshold the predicted value at zero. If the function is smaller than zero, we predict the class –1; if it is larger than zero, we predict the class +1. This prediction rule is common to all linear models for classification. Again, there are many different ways to find the coefficients (w) and the intercept (b).

For linear models for regression, the output, $\hat{y}$, is a linear function of the features: a line, plane, or hyperplane (in higher dimensions). For linear models for classification, the *decision boundary* is a linear function of the input. In other words, a (binary) linear classifier is a classifier that separates two classes using a line, a plane, or a hyperplane. We will see examples of that in this section.

There are many algorithms for learning linear models. These algorithms all differ in the following two ways:

- The way in which they measure how well a particular combination of coefficients and intercept fits the training data
- If and what kind of regularization they use

Different algorithms choose different ways to measure what "fitting the training set well" means. For technical mathematical reasons, it is not possible to adjust w and b to minimize the number of misclassifications the algorithms produce, as one might hope. For our purposes, and many applications, the different choices for item 1 in the preceding list (called *loss functions*) are of little significance.

The two most common linear classification algorithms are *logistic regression*, implemented in `linear_model.LogisticRegression`, and *linear support vector machines* (linear SVMs), implemented in `svm.LinearSVC` (SVC stands for support vector classifier). Despite its name, `LogisticRegression` is a classification algorithm and not a regression algorithm, and it should not be confused with `LinearRegression`.

We can apply the `LogisticRegression` and `LinearSVC` models to the `forge` dataset, and visualize the decision boundary as found by the linear models (Figure 2-15):

In[39]:

```
from sklearn.linear_model import LogisticRegression
from sklearn.svm import LinearSVC

X, y = mglearn.datasets.make_forge()

fig, axes = plt.subplots(1, 2, figsize=(10, 3))

for model, ax in zip([LinearSVC(), LogisticRegression()], axes):
    clf = model.fit(X, y)
    mglearn.plots.plot_2d_separator(clf, X, fill=False, eps=0.5,
                                    ax=ax, alpha=.7)
    mglearn.discrete_scatter(X[:, 0], X[:, 1], y, ax=ax)
    ax.set_title(clf.__class__.__name__)
    ax.set_xlabel("Feature 0")
    ax.set_ylabel("Feature 1")
axes[0].legend()
```

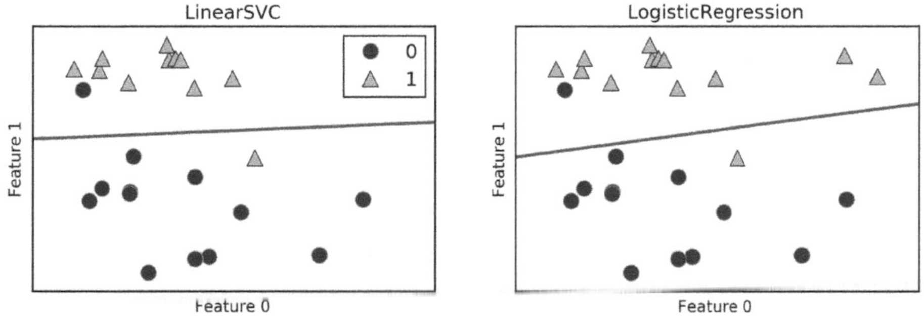

Figure 2-15. Decision boundaries of a linear SVM and logistic regression on the forge dataset with the default parameters

In this figure, we have the first feature of the `forge` dataset on the x-axis and the second feature on the y-axis, as before. We display the decision boundaries found by `LinearSVC` and `LogisticRegression` respectively as straight lines, separating the area classified as class 1 on the top from the area classified as class 0 on the bottom. In other words, any new data point that lies above the black line will be classified as class 1 by the respective classifier, while any point that lies below the black line will be classified as class 0.

The two models come up with similar decision boundaries. Note that both misclassify two of the points. By default, both models apply an L2 regularization, in the same way that `Ridge` does for regression.

For `LogisticRegression` and `LinearSVC` the trade-off parameter that determines the strength of the regularization is called `C`, and higher values of `C` correspond to *less* regularization. In other words, when you use a high value for the parameter `C`, `LogisticRegression` and `LinearSVC` try to fit the training set as best as possible, while with low values of the parameter `C`, the models put more emphasis on finding a coefficient vector (*w*) that is close to zero.

There is another interesting aspect of how the parameter `C` acts. Using low values of `C` will cause the algorithms to try to adjust to the "majority" of data points, while using a higher value of `C` stresses the importance that each individual data point be classified correctly. Here is an illustration using `LinearSVC` (Figure 2-16):

In[40]:

```
mglearn.plots.plot_linear_svc_regularization()
```

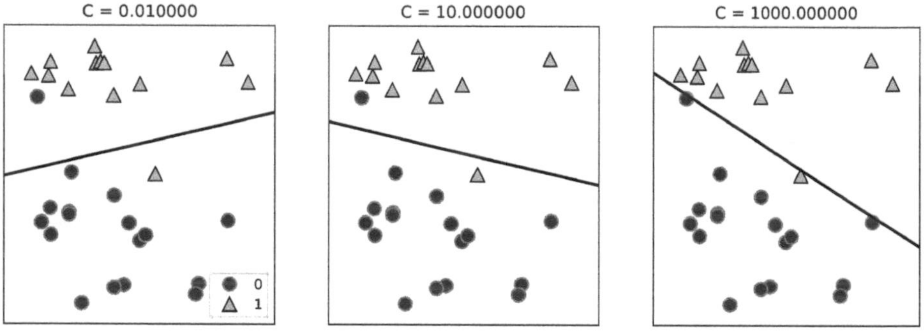

Figure 2-16. Decision boundaries of a linear SVM on the forge dataset for different values of C

On the lefthand side, we have a very small `C` corresponding to a lot of regularization. Most of the points in class 0 are at the bottom, and most of the points in class 1 are at the top. The strongly regularized model chooses a relatively horizontal line, misclassifying two points. In the center plot, `C` is slightly higher, and the model focuses more on the two misclassified samples, tilting the decision boundary. Finally, on the righthand side, the very high value of `C` in the model tilts the decision boundary a lot, now correctly classifying all points in class 0. One of the points in class 1 is still misclassified, as it is not possible to correctly classify all points in this dataset using a straight line. The model illustrated on the righthand side tries hard to correctly classify all points, but might not capture the overall layout of the classes well. In other words, this model is likely overfitting.

Similarly to the case of regression, linear models for classification might seem very restrictive in low-dimensional spaces, only allowing for decision boundaries that are straight lines or planes. Again, in high dimensions, linear models for classification become very powerful, and guarding against overfitting becomes increasingly important when considering more features.

Let's analyze `LogisticRegression` in more detail on the Breast Cancer dataset:

In[41]:

```
from sklearn.datasets import load_breast_cancer
cancer = load_breast_cancer()
X_train, X_test, y_train, y_test = train_test_split(
    cancer.data, cancer.target, stratify=cancer.target, random_state=42)
logreg = LogisticRegression().fit(X_train, y_train)
print("Training set score: {:.3f}".format(logreg.score(X_train, y_train)))
print("Test set score: {:.3f}".format(logreg.score(X_test, y_test)))
```

Out[41]:

```
Training set score: 0.953
Test set score: 0.958
```

The default value of `C=1` provides quite good performance, with 95% accuracy on both the training and the test set. But as training and test set performance are very close, it is likely that we are underfitting. Let's try to increase `C` to fit a more flexible model:

In[42]:

```
logreg100 = LogisticRegression(C=100).fit(X_train, y_train)
print("Training set score: {:.3f}".format(logreg100.score(X_train, y_train)))
print("Test set score: {:.3f}".format(logreg100.score(X_test, y_test)))
```

Out[42]:

```
Training set score: 0.972
Test set score: 0.965
```

Using `C=100` results in higher training set accuracy, and also a slightly increased test set accuracy, confirming our intuition that a more complex model should perform better.

We can also investigate what happens if we use an even more regularized model than the default of `C=1`, by setting `C=0.01`:

In[43]:

```
logreg001 = LogisticRegression(C=0.01).fit(X_train, y_train)
print("Training set score: {:.3f}".format(logreg001.score(X_train, y_train)))
print("Test set score: {:.3f}".format(logreg001.score(X_test, y_test)))
```

Out[43]:

```
Training set score: 0.934
Test set score: 0.930
```

As expected, when moving more to the left along the scale shown in Figure 2-1 from an already underfit model, both training and test set accuracy decrease relative to the default parameters.

Finally, let's look at the coefficients learned by the models with the three different settings of the regularization parameter C (Figure 2-17):

In[44]:

```
plt.plot(logreg.coef_.T, 'o', label="C=1")
plt.plot(logreg100.coef_.T, '^', label="C=100")
plt.plot(logreg001.coef_.T, 'v', label="C=0.001")
plt.xticks(range(cancer.data.shape[1]), cancer.feature_names, rotation=90)
plt.hlines(0, 0, cancer.data.shape[1])
plt.ylim(-5, 5)
plt.xlabel("Feature")
plt.ylabel("Coefficient magnitude")
plt.legend()
```

As `LogisticRegression` applies an L2 regularization by default, the result looks similar to that produced by `Ridge` in Figure 2-12. Stronger regularization pushes coefficients more and more toward zero, though coefficients never become exactly zero. Inspecting the plot more closely, we can also see an interesting effect in the third coefficient, for "mean perimeter." For `C=100` and `C=1`, the coefficient is negative, while for `C=0.001`, the coefficient is positive, with a magnitude that is even larger than for `C=1`. Interpreting a model like this, one might think the coefficient tells us which class a feature is associated with. For example, one might think that a high "texture error" feature is related to a sample being "malignant." However, the change of sign in the coefficient for "mean perimeter" means that depending on which model we look at, a high "mean perimeter" could be taken as being either indicative of "benign" or indicative of "malignant." This illustrates that interpretations of coefficients of linear models should always be taken with a grain of salt.

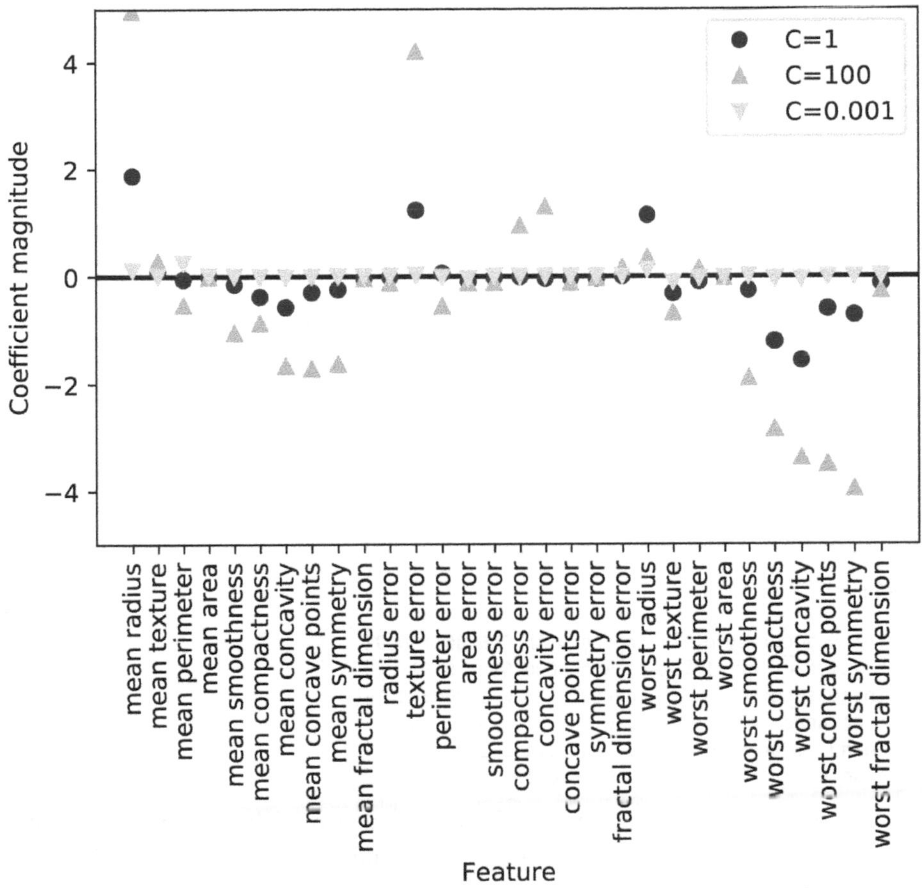

Figure 2-17. Coefficients learned by logistic regression on the Breast Cancer dataset for different values of C

If we desire a more interpretable model, using L1 regularization might help, as it limits the model to using only a few features. Here is the coefficient plot and classification accuracies for L1 regularization (Figure 2-18):

In[45]:

```
for C, marker in zip([0.001, 1, 100], ['o', '^', 'v']):
    lr_l1 = LogisticRegression(C=C, penalty="l1").fit(X_train, y_train)
    print("Training accuracy of l1 logreg with C={:.3f}: {:.2f}".format(
          C, lr_l1.score(X_train, y_train)))
    print("Test accuracy of l1 logreg with C={:.3f}: {:.2f}".format(
          C, lr_l1.score(X_test, y_test)))
    plt.plot(lr_l1.coef_.T, marker, label="C={:.3f}".format(C))

plt.xticks(range(cancer.data.shape[1]), cancer.feature_names, rotation=90)
plt.hlines(0, 0, cancer.data.shape[1])
plt.xlabel("Feature")
plt.ylabel("Coefficient magnitude")

plt.ylim(-5, 5)
plt.legend(loc=3)
```

Out[45]:

```
Training accuracy of l1 logreg with C=0.001: 0.91
Test accuracy of l1 logreg with C=0.001: 0.92
Training accuracy of l1 logreg with C=1.000: 0.96
Test accuracy of l1 logreg with C=1.000: 0.96
Training accuracy of l1 logreg with C=100.000: 0.99
Test accuracy of l1 logreg with C=100.000: 0.98
```

As you can see, there are many parallels between linear models for binary classification and linear models for regression. As in regression, the main difference between the models is the `penalty` parameter, which influences the regularization and whether the model will use all available features or select only a subset.

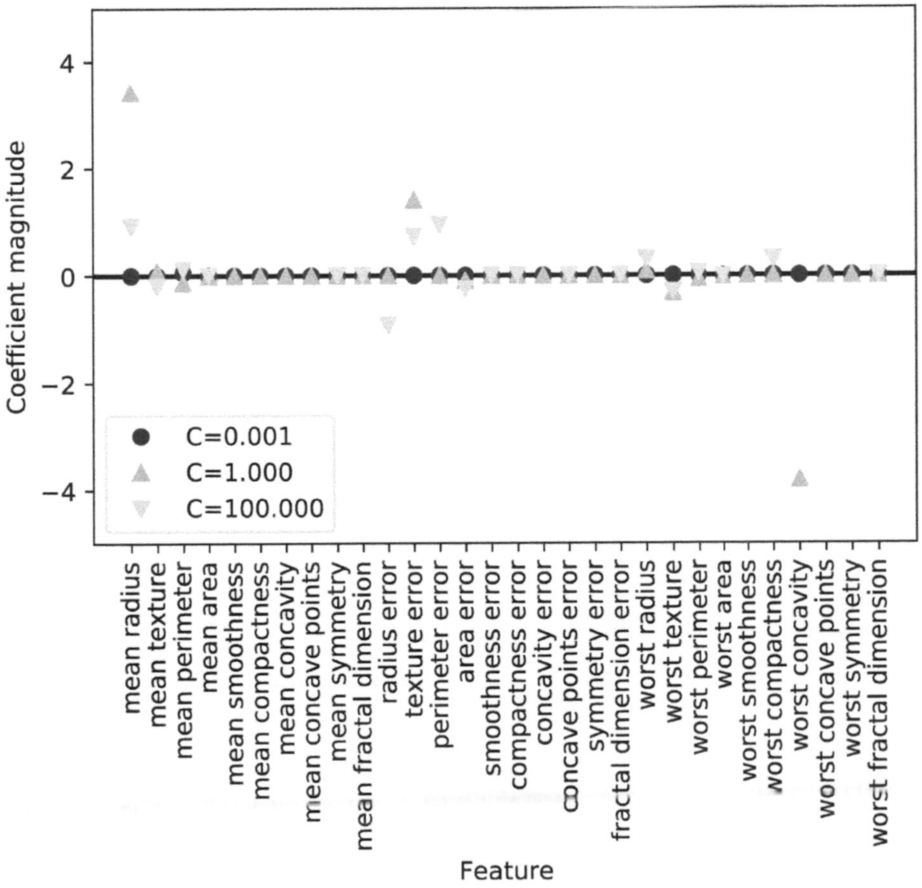

Figure 2-18. Coefficients learned by logistic regression with L1 penalty on the Breast Cancer dataset for different values of C

Linear models for multiclass classification

Many linear classification models are for binary classification only, and don't extend naturally to the multiclass case (with the exception of logistic regression). A common technique to extend a binary classification algorithm to a multiclass classification algorithm is the *one-vs.-rest* approach. In the one-vs.-rest approach, a binary model is learned for each class that tries to separate that class from all of the other classes, resulting in as many binary models as there are classes. To make a prediction, all binary classifiers are run on a test point. The classifier that has the highest score on its single class "wins," and this class label is returned as the prediction.

Having one binary classifier per class results in having one vector of coefficients (w) and one intercept (b) for each class. The class for which the result of the classification confidence formula given here is highest is the assigned class label:

$$w[0] * x[0] + w[1] * x[1] + ... + w[p] * x[p] + b$$

The mathematics behind multiclass logistic regression differ somewhat from the one-vs.-rest approach, but they also result in one coefficient vector and intercept per class, and the same method of making a prediction is applied.

Let's apply the one-vs.-rest method to a simple three-class classification dataset. We use a two-dimensional dataset, where each class is given by data sampled from a Gaussian distribution (see Figure 2-19):

In[46]:

```
from sklearn.datasets import make_blobs

X, y = make_blobs(random_state=42)
mglearn.discrete_scatter(X[:, 0], X[:, 1], y)
plt.xlabel("Feature 0")
plt.ylabel("Feature 1")
plt.legend(["Class 0", "Class 1", "Class 2"])
```

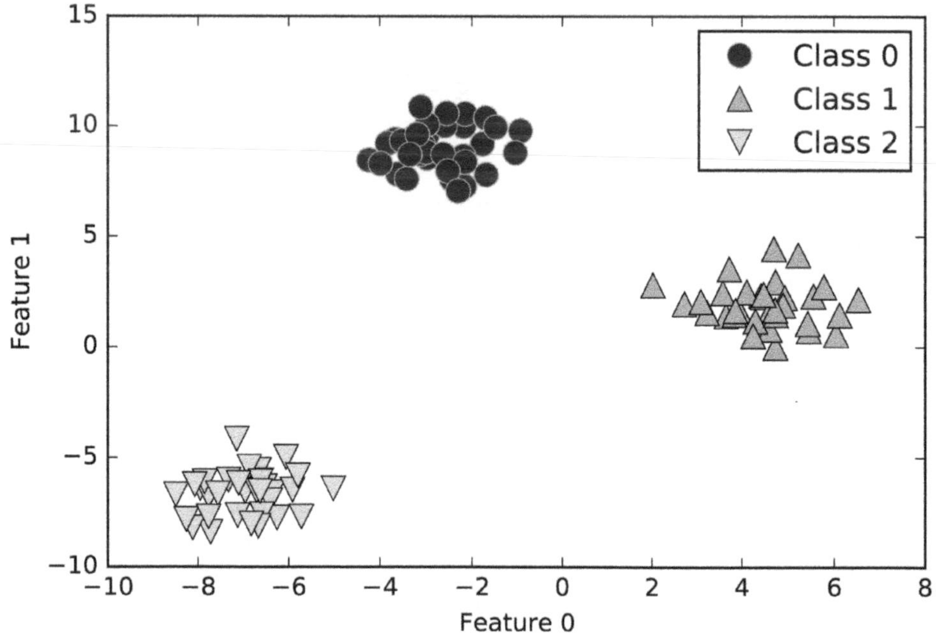

Figure 2-19. Two-dimensional toy dataset containing three classes

Now, we train a LinearSVC classifier on the dataset:

In[47]:

```
linear_svm = LinearSVC().fit(X, y)
print("Coefficient shape: ", linear_svm.coef_.shape)
print("Intercept shape: ", linear_svm.intercept_.shape)
```

Out[47]:

```
Coefficient shape:  (3, 2)
Intercept shape:  (3,)
```

We see that the shape of the `coef_` is `(3, 2)`, meaning that each row of `coef_` contains the coefficient vector for one of the three classes and each column holds the coefficient value for a specific feature (there are two in this dataset). The `intercept_` is now a one-dimensional array, storing the intercepts for each class.

Let's visualize the lines given by the three binary classifiers (Figure 2-20):

In[48]:

```
mglearn.discrete_scatter(X[:, 0], X[:, 1], y)
line = np.linspace(-15, 15)
for coef, intercept, color in zip(linear_svm.coef_, linear_svm.intercept_,
                                  mglearn.cm3.colors):
    plt.plot(line, -(line * coef[0] + intercept) / coef[1], c=color)
plt.ylim(-10, 15)
plt.xlim(-10, 8)
plt.xlabel("Feature 0")
plt.ylabel("Feature 1")
plt.legend(['Class 0', 'Class 1', 'Class 2', 'Line class 0', 'Line class 1',
            'Line class 2'], loc=(1.01, 0.3))
```

You can see that all the points belonging to class 0 in the training data are above the line corresponding to class 0, which means they are on the "class 0" side of this binary classifier. The points in class 0 are above the line corresponding to class 2, which means they are classified as "rest" by the binary classifier for class 2. The points belonging to class 0 are to the left of the line corresponding to class 1, which means the binary classifier for class 1 also classifies them as "rest." Therefore, any point in this area will be classified as class 0 by the final classifier (the result of the classification confidence formula for classifier 0 is greater than zero, while it is smaller than zero for the other two classes).

But what about the triangle in the middle of the plot? All three binary classifiers classify points there as "rest." Which class would a point there be assigned to? The answer is the one with the highest value for the classification formula: the class of the closest line.

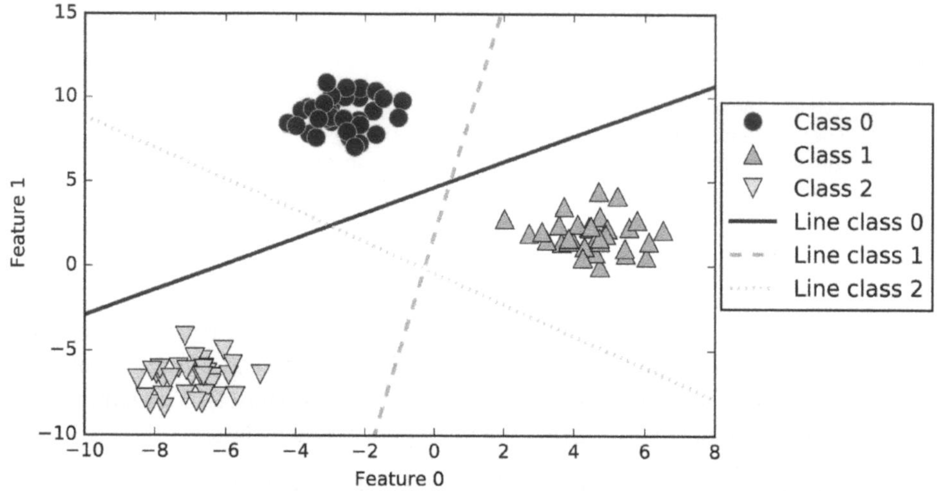

Figure 2-20. Decision boundaries learned by the three one-vs.-rest classifiers

The following example (Figure 2-21) shows the predictions for all regions of the 2D space:

In[49]:

```
mglearn.plots.plot_2d_classification(linear_svm, X, fill=True, alpha=.7)
mglearn.discrete_scatter(X[:, 0], X[:, 1], y)
line = np.linspace(-15, 15)
for coef, intercept, color in zip(linear_svm.coef_, linear_svm.intercept_,
                                  mglearn.cm3.colors):
    plt.plot(line, -(line * coef[0] + intercept) / coef[1], c=color)
plt.legend(['Class 0', 'Class 1', 'Class 2', 'Line class 0', 'Line class 1',
            'Line class 2'], loc=(1.01, 0.3))
plt.xlabel("Feature 0")
plt.ylabel("Feature 1")
```

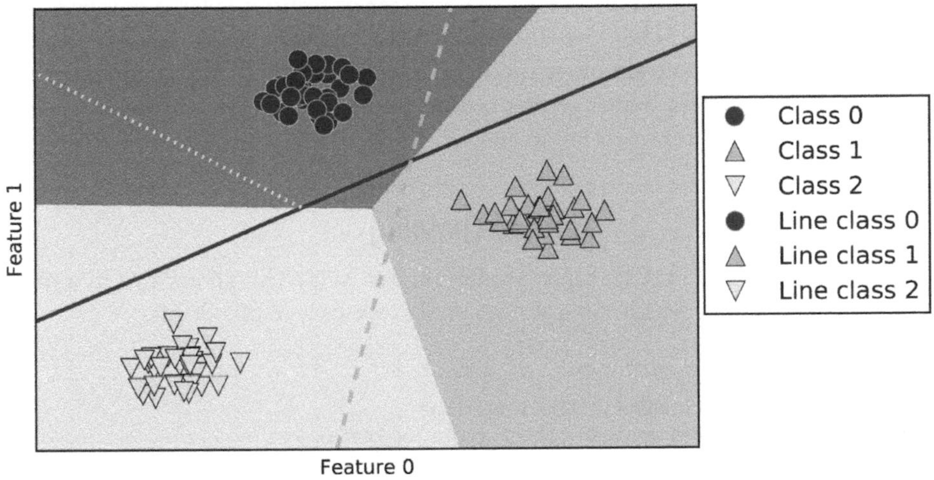

Figure 2-21. Multiclass decision boundaries derived from the three one-vs.-rest classifiers

Strengths, weaknesses, and parameters

The main parameter of linear models is the regularization parameter, called `alpha` in the regression models and `C` in `LinearSVC` and `LogisticRegression`. Large values for `alpha` or small values for `C` mean simple models. In particular for the regression models, tuning these parameters is quite important. Usually `C` and `alpha` are searched for on a logarithmic scale. The other decision you have to make is whether you want to use L1 regularization or L2 regularization. If you assume that only a few of your features are actually important, you should use L1. Otherwise, you should default to L2. L1 can also be useful if interpretability of the model is important. As L1 will use only a few features, it is easier to explain which features are important to the model, and what the effects of these features are.

Linear models are very fast to train, and also fast to predict. They scale to very large datasets and work well with sparse data. If your data consists of hundreds of thousands or millions of samples, you might want to investigate using the `solver='sag'` option in `LogisticRegression` and `Ridge`, which can be faster than the default on large datasets. Other options are the `SGDClassifier` class and the `SGDRegressor` class, which implement even more scalable versions of the linear models described here.

Another strength of linear models is that they make it relatively easy to understand how a prediction is made, using the formulas we saw earlier for regression and classification. Unfortunately, it is often not entirely clear why coefficients are the way they are. This is particularly true if your dataset has highly correlated features; in these cases, the coefficients might be hard to interpret.

Linear models often perform well when the number of features is large compared to the number of samples. They are also often used on very large datasets, simply because it's not feasible to train other models. However, in lower-dimensional spaces, other models might yield better generalization performance. We will look at some examples in which linear models fail in Section 2.3.7.

Method Chaining

The `fit` method of all `scikit-learn` models returns `self`. This allows you to write code like the following, which we've already used extensively in this chapter:

In[50]:

```
# instantiate model and fit it in one line
logreg = LogisticRegression().fit(X_train, y_train)
```

Here, we used the return value of `fit` (which is `self`) to assign the trained model to the variable `logreg`. This concatenation of method calls (here `__init__` and then `fit`) is known as *method chaining*. Another common application of method chaining in `scikit-learn` is to `fit` and `predict` in one line:

In[51]:

```
logreg = LogisticRegression()
y_pred = logreg.fit(X_train, y_train).predict(X_test)
```

Finally, you can even do model instantiation, fitting, and predicting in one line:

In[52]:

```
y_pred = LogisticRegression().fit(X_train, y_train).predict(X_test)
```

This very short variant is not ideal, though. A lot is happening in a single line, which might make the code hard to read. Additionally, the fitted logistic regression model isn't stored in any variable, so we can't inspect it or use it to predict on any other data.

2.3.4 Naive Bayes Classifiers

Naive Bayes classifiers are a family of classifiers that are quite similar to the linear models discussed in the previous section. However, they tend to be even faster in training. The price paid for this efficiency is that naive Bayes models often provide generalization performance that is slightly worse than that of linear classifiers like `LogisticRegression` and `LinearSVC`.

The reason that naive Bayes models are so efficient is that they learn parameters by looking at each feature individually and collect simple per-class statistics from each feature. There are three kinds of naive Bayes classifiers implemented in `scikit-learn`: `GaussianNB`, `BernoulliNB`, and `MultinomialNB`. `GaussianNB` can be applied to any continuous data, while `BernoulliNB` assumes binary data and `MultinomialNB` assumes count data (that is, that each feature represents an integer count of something, like how often a word appears in a sentence). `BernoulliNB` and `MultinomialNB` are mostly used in text data classification.

The `BernoulliNB` classifier counts how often every feature of each class is not zero. This is most easily understood with an example:

In[53]:

```
X = np.array([[0, 1, 0, 1],
              [1, 0, 1, 1],
              [0, 0, 0, 1],
              [1, 0, 1, 0]])
y = np.array([0, 1, 0, 1])
```

Here, we have four data points, with four binary features each. There are two classes, 0 and 1. For class 0 (the first and third data points), the first feature is zero two times and nonzero zero times, the second feature is zero one time and nonzero one time, and so on. These same counts are then calculated for the data points in the second class. Counting the nonzero entries per class in essence looks like this:

In[54]:

```
counts = {}
for label in np.unique(y):
    # iterate over each class
    # count (sum) entries of 1 per feature
    counts[label] = X[y == label].sum(axis=0)
print("Feature counts:\n", counts)
```

Out[54]:

```
Feature counts:
{0: array([0, 1, 0, 2]), 1: array([2, 0, 2, 1])}
```

The other two naive Bayes models, `MultinomialNB` and `GaussianNB`, are slightly different in what kinds of statistics they compute. `MultinomialNB` takes into account the average value of each feature for each class, while `GaussianNB` stores the average value as well as the standard deviation of each feature for each class.

To make a prediction, a data point is compared to the statistics for each of the classes, and the best matching class is predicted. Interestingly, for both `MultinomialNB` and `BernoulliNB`, this leads to a prediction formula that is of the same form as in the linear models (see "Linear models for classification" on page 58). Unfortunately, `coef_` for the naive Bayes models has a somewhat different meaning than in the linear models, in that `coef_` is not the same as *w*.

Strengths, weaknesses, and parameters

`MultinomialNB` and `BernoulliNB` have a single parameter, `alpha`, which controls model complexity. The way `alpha` works is that the algorithm adds to the data `alpha` many virtual data points that have positive values for all the features. This results in a "smoothing" of the statistics. A large `alpha` means more smoothing, resulting in less complex models. The algorithm's performance is relatively robust to the setting of `alpha`, meaning that setting `alpha` is not critical for good performance. However, tuning it usually improves accuracy somewhat.

`GaussianNB` is mostly used on very high-dimensional data, while the other two variants of naive Bayes are widely used for sparse count data such as text. `MultinomialNB` usually performs better than `BernoulliNB`, particularly on datasets with a relatively large number of nonzero features (i.e., large documents).

The naive Bayes models share many of the strengths and weaknesses of the linear models. They are very fast to train and to predict, and the training procedure is easy to understand. The models work very well with high-dimensional sparse data and are relatively robust to the parameters. Naive Bayes models are great baseline models and are often used on very large datasets, where training even a linear model might take too long.

2.3.5 Decision Trees

Decision trees are widely used models for classification and regression tasks. Essentially, they learn a hierarchy of if/else questions, leading to a decision.

These questions are similar to the questions you might ask in a game of 20 Questions. Imagine you want to distinguish between the following four animals: bears, hawks, penguins, and dolphins. Your goal is to get to the right answer by asking as few if/else questions as possible. You might start off by asking whether the animal has feathers, a question that narrows down your possible animals to just two. If the answer is "yes," you can ask another question that could help you distinguish between hawks and penguins. For example, you could ask whether the animal can fly. If the animal doesn't have feathers, your possible animal choices are dolphins and bears, and you will need to ask a question to distinguish between these two animals—for example, asking whether the animal has fins.

This series of questions can be expressed as a decision tree, as shown in Figure 2-22.

In[55]:

```
mglearn.plots.plot_animal_tree()
```

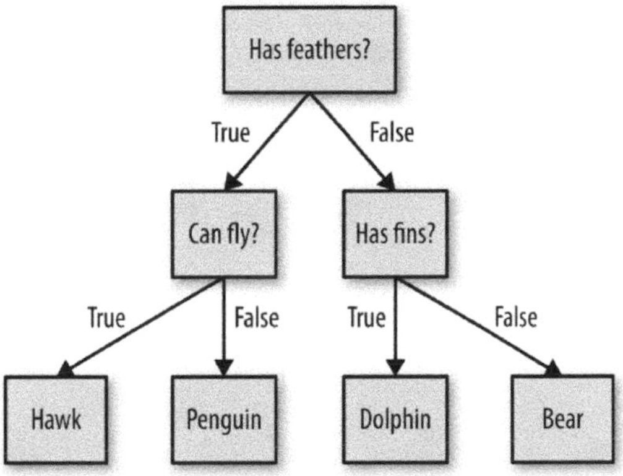

Figure 2-22. A decision tree to distinguish among several animals

In this illustration, each node in the tree either represents a question or a terminal node (also called a *leaf*) that contains the answer. The edges connect the answers to a question with the next question you would ask.

In machine learning parlance, we built a model to distinguish between four classes of animals (hawks, penguins, dolphins, and bears) using the three features "has feathers," "can fly," and "has fins." Instead of building these models by hand, we can learn them from data using supervised learning.

Building decision trees

Let's go through the process of building a decision tree for the 2D classification dataset shown in Figure 2-23. The dataset consists of two half-moon shapes, with each class consisting of 75 data points. We will refer to this dataset as `two_moons`.

Learning a decision tree means learning the sequence of if/else questions that gets us to the true answer most quickly. In the machine learning setting, these questions are called *tests* (not to be confused with the test set, which is the data we use to test to see how generalizable our model is). Usually data does not come in the form of binary yes/no features as in the animal example, but is instead represented as continuous features such as in the 2D dataset shown in Figure 2-23. The tests that are used on continuous data are of the form "Is feature *i* larger than value *a*?"

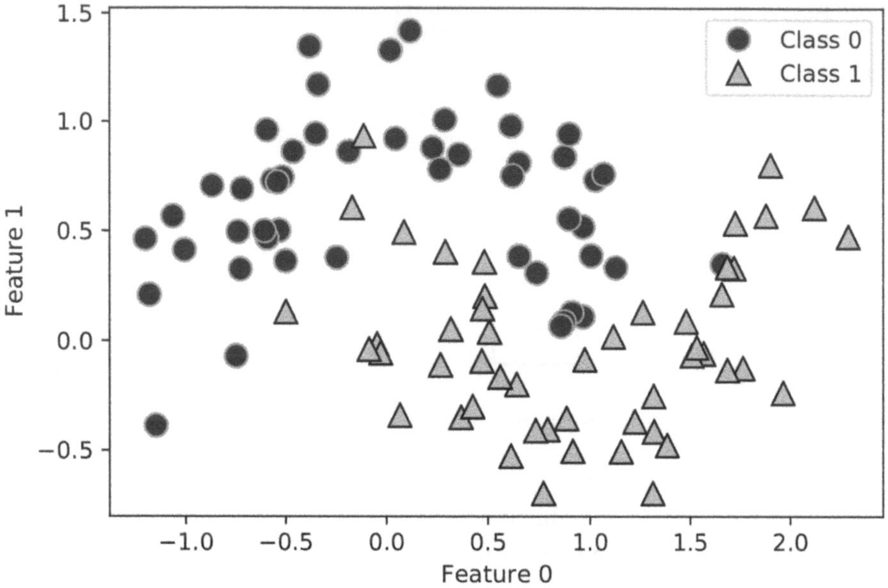

Figure 2-23. Two-moons dataset on which the decision tree will be built

To build a tree, the algorithm searches over all possible tests and finds the one that is most informative about the target variable. Figure 2-24 shows the first test that is picked. Splitting the dataset horizontally at `x[1]=0.0596` yields the most information; it best separates the points in class 0 from the points in class 1. The top node, also called the *root*, represents the whole dataset, consisting of 50 points belonging to class 0 and 50 points belonging to class 1. The split is done by testing whether `x[1] <= 0.0596`, indicated by a black line. If the test is true, a point is assigned to the left node, which contains 2 points belonging to class 0 and 32 points belonging to class 1. Otherwise the point is assigned to the right node, which contains 48 points belonging to class 0 and 18 points belonging to class 1. These two nodes correspond to the top and bottom regions shown in Figure 2-24. Even though the first split did a good job of separating the two classes, the bottom region still contains points belonging to class 0, and the top region still contains points belonging to class 1. We can build a more accurate model by repeating the process of looking for the best test in both regions. Figure 2-25 shows that the most informative next split for the left and the right region is based on `x[0]`.

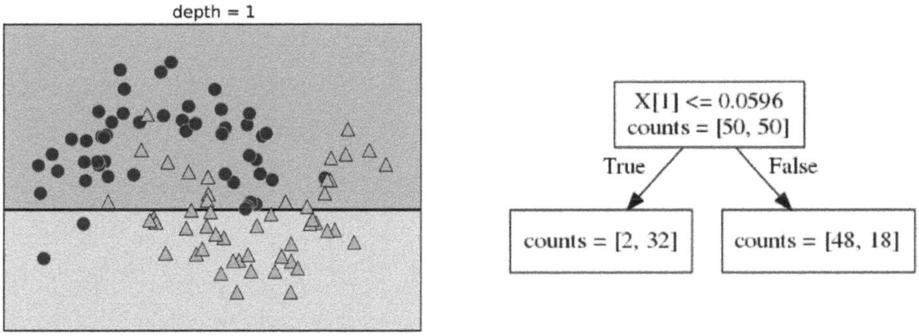

Figure 2-24. Decision boundary of tree with depth 1 (left) and corresponding tree (right)

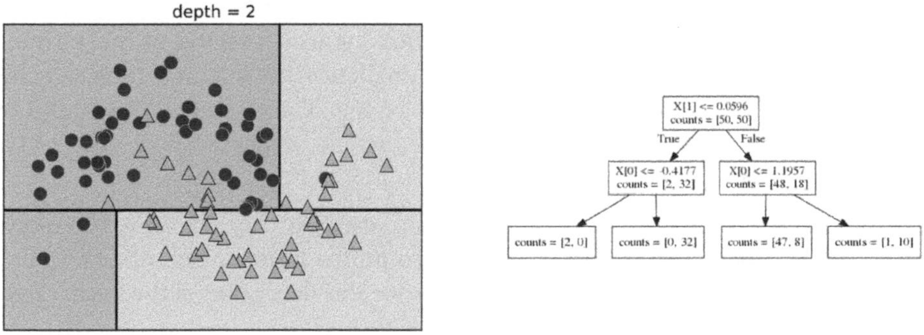

Figure 2-25. Decision boundary of tree with depth 2 (left) and corresponding decision tree (right)

This recursive process yields a binary tree of decisions, with each node containing a test. Alternatively, you can think of each test as splitting the part of the data that is currently being considered along one axis. This yields a view of the algorithm as building a hierarchical partition. As each test concerns only a single feature, the regions in the resulting partition always have axis-parallel boundaries.

The recursive partitioning of the data is repeated until each region in the partition (each leaf in the decision tree) only contains a single target value (a single class or a single regression value). A leaf of the tree that contains data points that all share the same target value is called *pure*. The final partitioning for this dataset is shown in Figure 2-26.

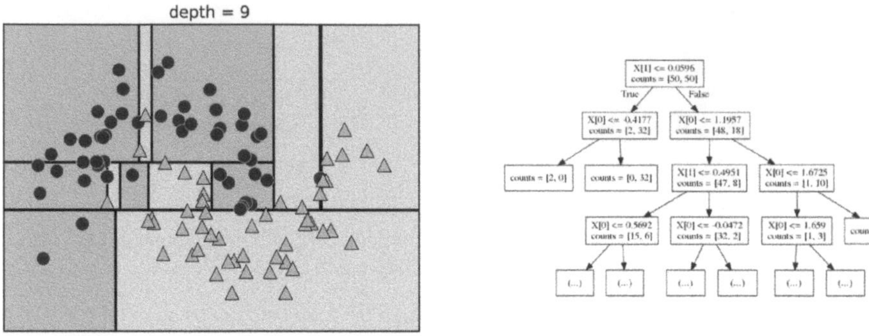

Figure 2-26. Decision boundary of tree with depth 9 (left) and part of the corresponding tree (right); the full tree is quite large and hard to visualize

A prediction on a new data point is made by checking which region of the partition of the feature space the point lies in, and then predicting the majority target (or the single target in the case of pure leaves) in that region. The region can be found by traversing the tree from the root and going left or right, depending on whether the test is fulfilled or not.

It is also possible to use trees for regression tasks, using exactly the same technique. To make a prediction, we traverse the tree based on the tests in each node and find the leaf the new data point falls into. The output for this data point is the mean target of the training points in this leaf.

Controlling complexity of decision trees

Typically, building a tree as described here and continuing until all leaves are pure leads to models that are very complex and highly overfit to the training data. The presence of pure leaves mean that a tree is 100% accurate on the training set; each data point in the training set is in a leaf that has the correct majority class. The overfitting can be seen on the left of Figure 2-26. You can see the regions determined to belong to class 1 in the middle of all the points belonging to class 0. On the other hand, there is a small strip predicted as class 0 around the point belonging to class 0 to the very right. This is not how one would imagine the decision boundary to look, and the decision boundary focuses a lot on single outlier points that are far away from the other points in that class.

There are two common strategies to prevent overfitting: stopping the creation of the tree early (also called *pre-pruning*), or building the tree but then removing or collapsing nodes that contain little information (also called *post-pruning* or just *pruning*). Possible criteria for pre-pruning include limiting the maximum depth of the tree, limiting the maximum number of leaves, or requiring a minimum number of points in a node to keep splitting it.

Decision trees in scikit-learn are implemented in the DecisionTreeRegressor and DecisionTreeClassifier classes. scikit-learn only implements pre-pruning, not post-pruning.

Let's look at the effect of pre-pruning in more detail on the Breast Cancer dataset. As always, we import the dataset and split it into a training and a test part. Then we build a model using the default setting of fully developing the tree (growing the tree until all leaves are pure). We fix the random_state in the tree, which is used for tie-breaking internally:

In[56]:

```
from sklearn.tree import DecisionTreeClassifier

cancer = load_breast_cancer()
X_train, X_test, y_train, y_test = train_test_split(
    cancer.data, cancer.target, stratify=cancer.target, random_state=42)
tree = DecisionTreeClassifier(random_state=0)
tree.fit(X_train, y_train)
print("Accuracy on training set: {:.3f}".format(tree.score(X_train, y_train)))
print("Accuracy on test set: {:.3f}".format(tree.score(X_test, y_test)))
```

Out[56]:

```
Accuracy on training set: 1.000
Accuracy on test set: 0.937
```

As expected, the accuracy on the training set is 100%—because the leaves are pure, the tree was grown deep enough that it could perfectly memorize all the labels on the training data. The test set accuracy is slightly worse than for the linear models we looked at previously, which had around 95% accuracy.

If we don't restrict the depth of a decision tree, the tree can become arbitrarily deep and complex. Unpruned trees are therefore prone to overfitting and not generalizing well to new data. Now let's apply pre-pruning to the tree, which will stop developing the tree before we perfectly fit to the training data. One option is to stop building the tree after a certain depth has been reached. Here we set max_depth=4, meaning only four consecutive questions can be asked (cf. Figures 2-24 and 2-26). Limiting the depth of the tree decreases overfitting. This leads to a lower accuracy on the training set, but an improvement on the test set:

In[57]:

```
tree = DecisionTreeClassifier(max_depth=4, random_state=0)
tree.fit(X_train, y_train)

print("Accuracy on training set: {:.3f}".format(tree.score(X_train, y_train)))
print("Accuracy on test set: {:.3f}".format(tree.score(X_test, y_test)))
```

Out[57]:

```
Accuracy on training set: 0.988
Accuracy on test set: 0.951
```

Analyzing decision trees

We can visualize the tree using the `export_graphviz` function from the `tree` module. This writes a file in the *.dot* file format, which is a text file format for storing graphs. We set an option to color the nodes to reflect the majority class in each node and pass the class and features names so the tree can be properly labeled:

In[58]:

```
from sklearn.tree import export_graphviz
export_graphviz(tree, out_file="tree.dot", class_names=["malignant", "benign"],
                feature_names=cancer.feature_names, impurity=False, filled=True)
```

We can read this file and visualize it, as seen in Figure 2-27, using the `graphviz` module (or you can use any program that can read *.dot* files):

In[59]:

```
import graphviz

with open("tree.dot") as f:
    dot_graph = f.read()
display(graphviz.Source(dot_graph))
```

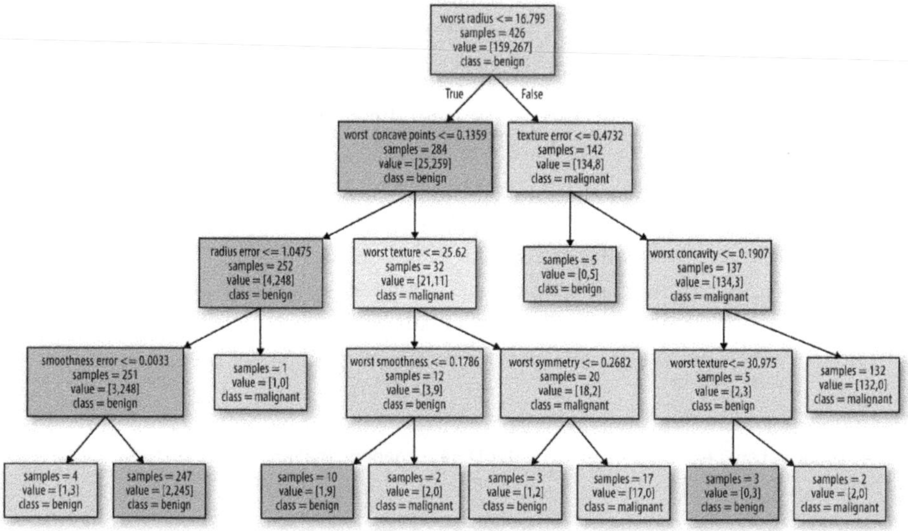

Figure 2-27. Visualization of the decision tree built on the Breast Cancer dataset

The visualization of the tree provides a great in-depth view of how the algorithm makes predictions, and is a good example of a machine learning algorithm that is easily explained to nonexperts. However, even with a tree of depth four, as seen here, the tree can become a bit overwhelming. Deeper trees (a depth of 10 is not uncommon) are even harder to grasp. One method of inspecting the tree that may be helpful is to find out which path most of the data actually takes. The `samples` shown in each node in Figure 2-27 gives the number of samples in that node, while `value` provides the number of samples per class. Following the branches to the right, we see that `worst radius > 16.795` creates a node that contains only 8 benign but 134 malignant samples. The rest of this side of the tree then uses some finer distinctions to split off these 8 remaining benign samples. Of the 142 samples that went to the right in the initial split, nearly all of them (132) end up in the leaf to the very right.

Taking a left at the root, for `worst radius <= 16.795` we end up with 25 malignant and 259 benign samples. Nearly all of the benign samples end up in the second leaf from the left, with most of the other leaves containing very few samples.

Feature importance in trees

Instead of looking at the whole tree, which can be taxing, there are some useful properties that we can derive to summarize the workings of the tree. The most commonly used summary is *feature importance*, which rates how important each feature is for the decision a tree makes. It is a number between 0 and 1 for each feature, where 0 means "not used at all" and 1 means "perfectly predicts the target." The feature importances always sum to 1:

In[60]:

```
print("Feature importances:")
print(tree.feature_importances_)
```

Out[60]:

```
Feature importances:
[0.    0.    0.    0.    0.    0.    0.    0.    0.    0.    0.01  0.048
 0.    0.    0.002 0.    0.    0.    0.    0.    0.727 0.046 0.    0.
 0.014 0.    0.018 0.122 0.012 0.   ]
```

We can visualize the feature importances in a way that is similar to the way we visualize the coefficients in the linear model (Figure 2-28):

In[61]:

```
def plot_feature_importances_cancer(model):
    n_features = cancer.data.shape[1]
    plt.barh(np.arange(n_features), model.feature_importances_, align='center')
    plt.yticks(np.arange(n_features), cancer.feature_names)
    plt.xlabel("Feature importance")
    plt.ylabel("Feature")
    plt.ylim(-1, n_features)
```

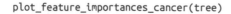

```
plot_feature_importances_cancer(tree)
```

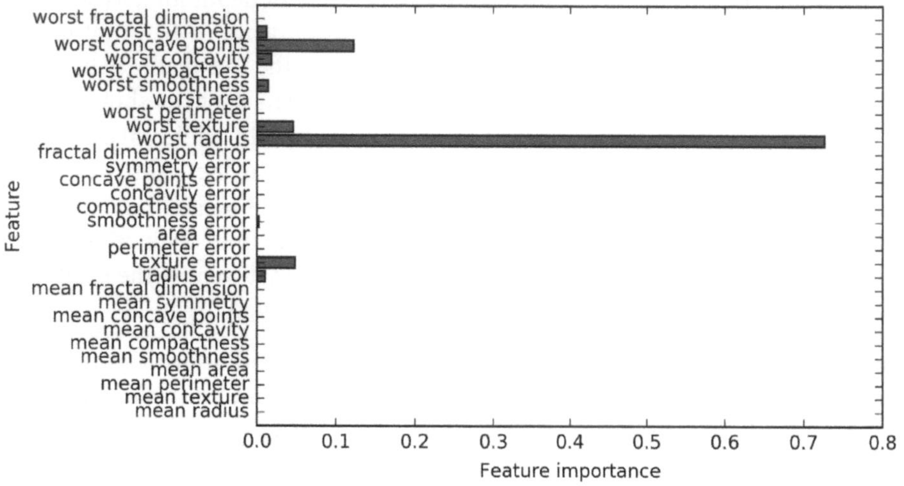

Figure 2-28. Feature importances computed from a decision tree learned on the Breast Cancer dataset

Here we see that the feature used in the top split ("worst radius") is by far the most important feature. This confirms our observation in analyzing the tree that the first level already separates the two classes fairly well.

However, if a feature has a low value in `feature_importance_`, it doesn't mean that this feature is uninformative. It only means that the feature was not picked by the tree, likely because another feature encodes the same information.

In contrast to the coefficients in linear models, feature importances are always positive, and don't encode which class a feature is indicative of. The feature importances tell us that "worst radius" is important, but not whether a high radius is indicative of a sample being benign or malignant. In fact, there might not be such a simple relationship between features and class, as you can see in the following example (Figures 2-29 and 2-30):

In[62]:

```
tree = mglearn.plots.plot_tree_not_monotone()
display(tree)
```

Out[62]:

```
Feature importances: [ 0.  1.]
```

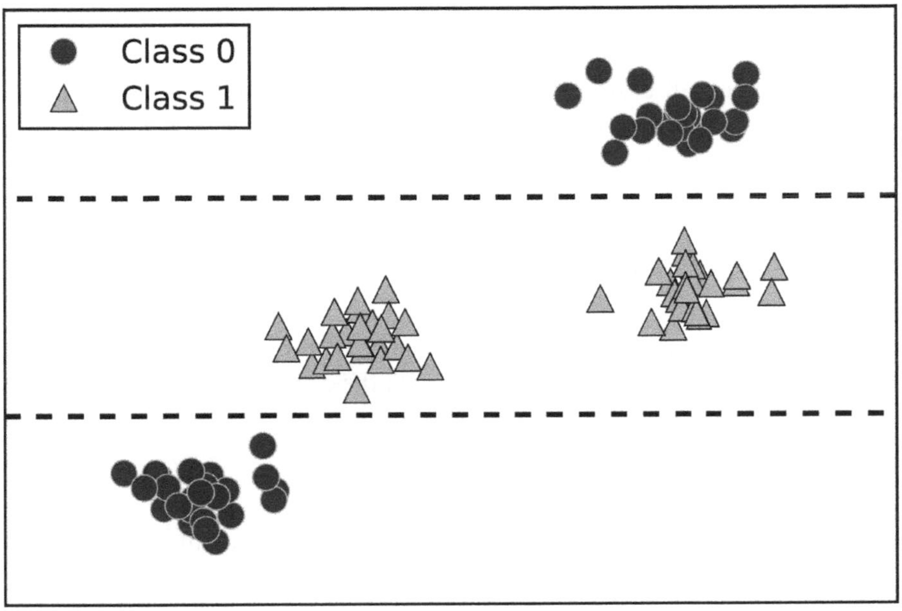

Figure 2-29. A two-dimensional dataset in which the feature on the y-axis has a nonmonotonous relationship with the class label, and the decision boundaries found by a decision tree

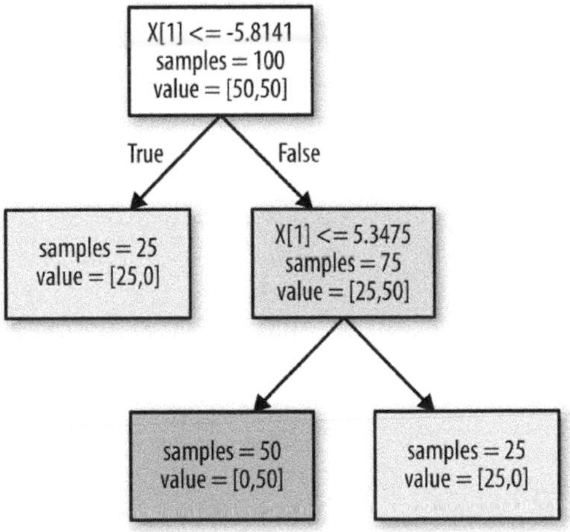

Figure 2-30. Decision tree learned on the data shown in Figure 2-29

The plot shows a dataset with two features and two classes. Here, all the information is contained in `X[1]`, and `X[0]` is not used at all. But the relation between `X[1]` and the output class is not monotonous, meaning we cannot say "a high value of X[1] means class 0, and a low value means class 1" (or vice versa).

While we focused our discussion here on decision trees for classification, all that was said is similarly true for decision trees for regression, as implemented in DecisionTreeRegressor. The usage and analysis of regression trees is very similar to that of classification trees. There is one particular property of using tree-based models for regression that we want to point out, though. The DecisionTreeRegressor (and all other tree-based regression models) is not able to *extrapolate*, or make predictions outside of the range of the training data.

Let's look into this in more detail, using a dataset of historical computer memory (RAM) prices. Figure 2-31 shows the dataset, with the date on the x-axis and the price of one megabyte of RAM in that year on the y-axis:

In[63]:

```
import os
ram_prices = pd.read_csv(os.path.join(mglearn.datasets.DATA_PATH,
                                      "ram_price.csv"))

plt.semilogy(ram_prices.date, ram_prices.price)
plt.xlabel("Year")
plt.ylabel("Price in $/Mbyte")
```

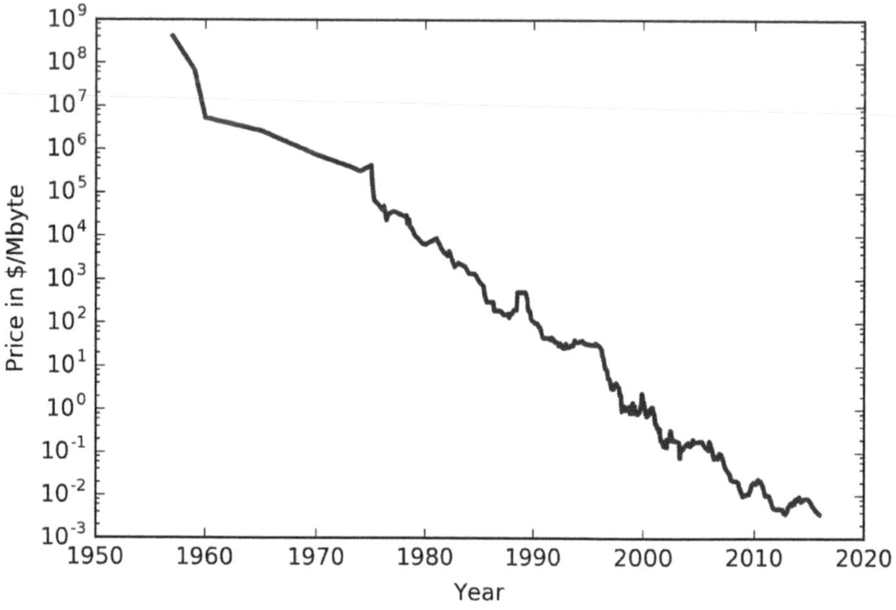

Figure 2-31. Historical development of the price of RAM, plotted on a log scale

Note the logarithmic scale of the y-axis. When plotting logarithmically, the relation seems to be quite linear and so should be relatively easy to predict, apart from some bumps.

We will make a forecast for the years after 2000 using the historical data up to that point, with the date as our only feature. We will compare two simple models: a `DecisionTreeRegressor` and `LinearRegression`. We rescale the prices using a logarithm, so that the relationship is relatively linear. This doesn't make a difference for the `DecisionTreeRegressor`, but it makes a big difference for `LinearRegression` (we will discuss this in more depth in Chapter 4). After training the models and making predictions, we apply the exponential map to undo the logarithm transform. We make predictions on the whole dataset for visualization purposes here, but for a quantitative evaluation we would only consider the test dataset:

In[64]:

```
from sklearn.tree import DecisionTreeRegressor
# use historical data to forecast prices after the year 2000
data_train = ram_prices[ram_prices.date < 2000]
data_test = ram_prices[ram_prices.date >= 2000]

# predict prices based on date
X_train = data_train.date[:, np.newaxis]
# we use a log-transform to get a simpler relationship of data to target
y_train = np.log(data_train.price)

tree = DecisionTreeRegressor(max_depth=3).fit(X_train, y_train)
linear_reg = LinearRegression().fit(X_train, y_train)

# predict on all data
X_all = ram_prices.date[:, np.newaxis]

pred_tree = tree.predict(X_all)
pred_lr = linear_reg.predict(X_all)

# undo log-transform
price_tree = np.exp(pred_tree)
price_lr = np.exp(pred_lr)
```

Figure 2-32, created here, compares the predictions of the decision tree and the linear regression model with the ground truth:

In[65]:

```
plt.semilogy(data_train.date, data_train.price, label="Training data")
plt.semilogy(data_test.date, data_test.price, label="Test data")
plt.semilogy(ram_prices.date, price_tree, label="Tree prediction")
plt.semilogy(ram_prices.date, price_lr, label="Linear prediction")
plt.legend()
```

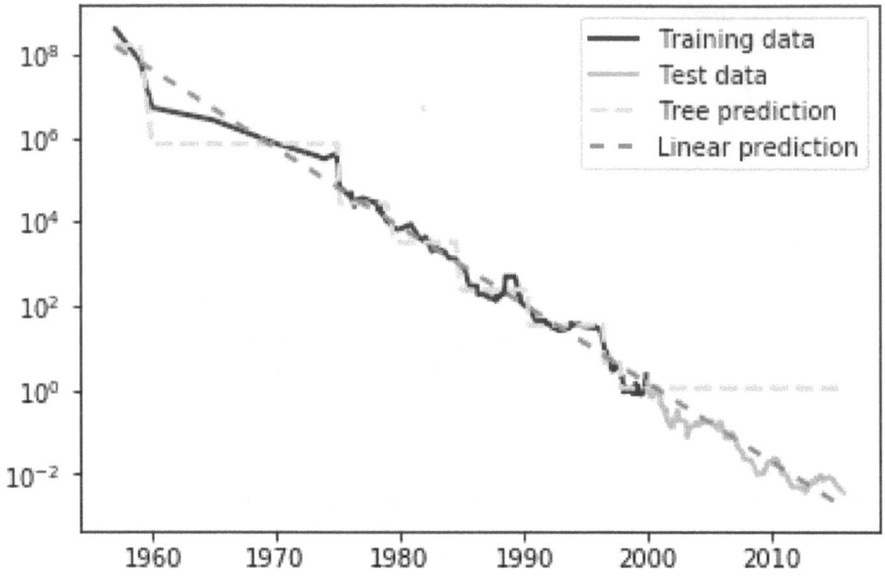

Figure 2-32. Comparison of predictions made by a linear model and predictions made by a regression tree on the RAM price data

The difference between the models is quite striking. The linear model approximates the data with a line, as we knew it would. This line provides quite a good forecast for the test data (the years after 2000), while glossing over some of the finer variations in both the training and the test data. The tree model, on the other hand, makes perfect predictions on the training data; we did not restrict the complexity of the tree, so it learned the whole dataset by heart. However, once we leave the data range for which the model has data, the model simply keeps predicting the last known point. The tree has no ability to generate "new" responses, outside of what was seen in the training data. This shortcoming applies to all models based on trees.[9]

Strengths, weaknesses, and parameters

As discussed earlier, the parameters that control model complexity in decision trees are the pre-pruning parameters that stop the building of the tree before it is fully developed. Usually, picking one of the pre-pruning strategies—setting either

9 It is actually possible to make very good forecasts with tree-based models (for example, when trying to predict whether a price will go up or down). The point of this example was not to show that trees are a bad model for time series, but to illustrate a particular property of how trees make predictions.

`max_depth`, `max_leaf_nodes`, or `min_samples_leaf`—is sufficient to prevent overfitting.

Decision trees have two advantages over many of the algorithms we've discussed so far: the resulting model can easily be visualized and understood by nonexperts (at least for smaller trees), and the algorithms are completely invariant to scaling of the data. As each feature is processed separately, and the possible splits of the data don't depend on scaling, no preprocessing like normalization or standardization of features is needed for decision tree algorithms. In particular, decision trees work well when you have features that are on completely different scales, or a mix of binary and continuous features.

The main downside of decision trees is that even with the use of pre-pruning, they tend to overfit and provide poor generalization performance. Therefore, in most applications, the ensemble methods we discuss next are usually used in place of a single decision tree.

2.3.6 Ensembles of Decision Trees

Ensembles are methods that combine multiple machine learning models to create more powerful models. There are many models in the machine learning literature that belong to this category, but there are two ensemble models that have proven to be effective on a wide range of datasets for classification and regression, both of which use decision trees as their building blocks: random forests and gradient boosted decision trees.

Random forests

As we just observed, a main drawback of decision trees is that they tend to overfit the training data. Random forests are one way to address this problem. A random forest is essentially a collection of decision trees, where each tree is slightly different from the others. The idea behind random forests is that each tree might do a relatively good job of predicting, but will likely overfit on part of the data. If we build many trees, all of which work well and overfit in different ways, we can reduce the amount of overfitting by averaging their results. This reduction in overfitting, while retaining the predictive power of the trees, can be shown using rigorous mathematics.

To implement this strategy, we need to build many decision trees. Each tree should do an acceptable job of predicting the target, and should also be different from the other trees. Random forests get their name from injecting randomness into the tree building to ensure each tree is different. There are two ways in which the trees in a random forest are randomized: by selecting the data points used to build a tree and by selecting the features in each split test. Let's go into this process in more detail.

Building random forests. To build a random forest model, you need to decide on the number of trees to build (the `n_estimators` parameter of `RandomForestRegressor` or `RandomForestClassifier`). Let's say we want to build 10 trees. These trees will be built completely independently from each other, and the algorithm will make different random choices for each tree to make sure the trees are distinct. To build a tree, we first take what is called a *bootstrap sample* of our data. That is, from our `n_samples` data points, we repeatedly draw an example randomly with replacement (meaning the same sample can be picked multiple times), `n_samples` times. This will create a dataset that is as big as the original dataset, but some data points will be missing from it (approximately one third), and some will be repeated.

To illustrate, let's say we want to create a bootstrap sample of the list `['a', 'b', 'c', 'd']`. A possible bootstrap sample would be `['b', 'd', 'd', 'c']`. Another possible sample would be `['d', 'a', 'd', 'a']`.

Next, a decision tree is built based on this newly created dataset. However, the algorithm we described for the decision tree is slightly modified. Instead of looking for the best test for each node, in each node the algorithm randomly selects a subset of the features, and it looks for the best possible test involving one of these features. The number of features that are selected is controlled by the `max_features` parameter. This selection of a subset of features is repeated separately in each node, so that each node in a tree can make a decision using a different subset of the features.

The bootstrap sampling leads to each decision tree in the random forest being built on a slightly different dataset. Because of the selection of features in each node, each split in each tree operates on a different subset of features. Together, these two mechanisms ensure that all the trees in the random forest are different.

A critical parameter in this process is `max_features`. If we set `max_features` to `n_features`, that means that each split can look at all features in the dataset, and no randomness will be injected in the feature selection (the randomness due to the bootstrapping remains, though). If we set `max_features` to `1`, that means that the splits have no choice at all on which feature to test, and can only search over different thresholds for the feature that was selected randomly. Therefore, a high `max_features` means that the trees in the random forest will be quite similar, and they will be able to fit the data easily, using the most distinctive features. A low `max_features` means that the trees in the random forest will be quite different, and that each tree might need to be very deep in order to fit the data well.

To make a prediction using the random forest, the algorithm first makes a prediction for every tree in the forest. For regression, we can average these results to get our final prediction. For classification, a "soft voting" strategy is used. This means each algorithm makes a "soft" prediction, providing a probability for each possible output label. The probabilities predicted by all the trees are averaged, and the class with the highest probability is predicted.

Analyzing random forests. Let's apply a random forest consisting of five trees to the two_moons dataset we studied earlier:

In[66]:

```
from sklearn.ensemble import RandomForestClassifier
from sklearn.datasets import make_moons

X, y = make_moons(n_samples=100, noise=0.25, random_state=3)
X_train, X_test, y_train, y_test = train_test_split(X, y, stratify=y,
                                                    random_state=42)

forest = RandomForestClassifier(n_estimators=5, random_state=2)
forest.fit(X_train, y_train)
```

The trees that are built as part of the random forest are stored in the estimator_ attribute. Let's visualize the decision boundaries learned by each tree, together with their aggregate prediction as made by the forest (Figure 2-33):

In[67]:

```
fig, axes = plt.subplots(2, 3, figsize=(20, 10))
for i, (ax, tree) in enumerate(zip(axes.ravel(), forest.estimators_)):
    ax.set_title("Tree {}".format(i))
    mglearn.plots.plot_tree_partition(X_train, y_train, tree, ax=ax)

mglearn.plots.plot_2d_separator(forest, X_train, fill=True, ax=axes[-1, -1],
                                alpha=.4)
axes[-1, -1].set_title("Random Forest")
mglearn.discrete_scatter(X_train[:, 0], X_train[:, 1], y_train)
```

You can clearly see that the decision boundaries learned by the five trees are quite different. Each of them makes some mistakes, as some of the training points that are plotted here were not actually included in the training sets of the trees, due to the bootstrap sampling.

The random forest overfits less than any of the trees individually, and provides a much more intuitive decision boundary. In any real application, we would use many more trees (often hundreds or thousands), leading to even smoother boundaries.

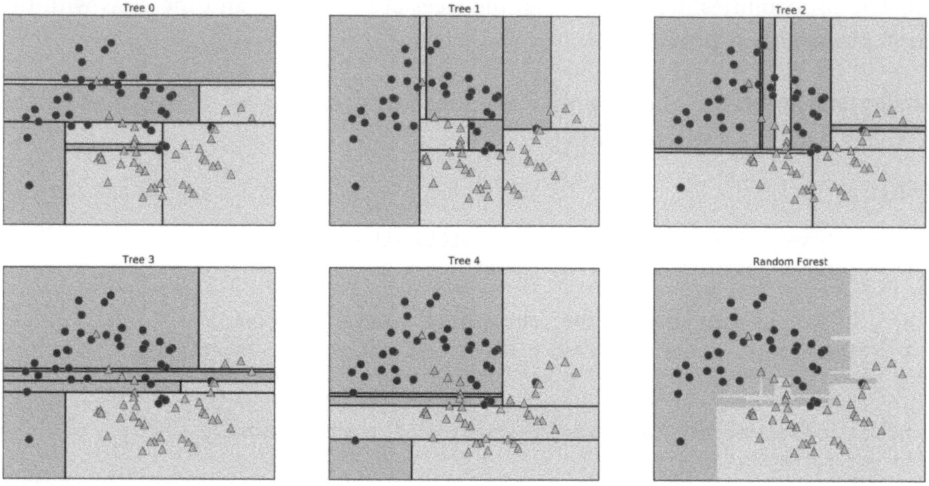

Figure 2-33. Decision boundaries found by five randomized decision trees and the decision boundary obtained by averaging their predicted probabilities

As another example, let's apply a random forest consisting of 100 trees on the Breast Cancer dataset:

In[68]:

```
X_train, X_test, y_train, y_test = train_test_split(
    cancer.data, cancer.target, random_state=0)
forest = RandomForestClassifier(n_estimators=100, random_state=0)
forest.fit(X_train, y_train)

print("Accuracy on training set: {:.3f}".format(forest.score(X_train, y_train)))
print("Accuracy on test set: {:.3f}".format(forest.score(X_test, y_test)))
```

Out[68]:

```
Accuracy on training set: 1.000
Accuracy on test set: 0.972
```

The random forest gives us an accuracy of 97%, better than the linear models or a single decision tree, without tuning any parameters. We could adjust the `max_features` setting, or apply pre-pruning as we did for the single decision tree. However, often the default parameters of the random forest already work quite well.

Similarly to the decision tree, the random forest provides feature importances, which are computed by aggregating the feature importances over the trees in the forest. Typically, the feature importances provided by the random forest are more reliable than the ones provided by a single tree. Take a look at Figure 2-34.

In[69]:

```
plot_feature_importances_cancer(forest)
```

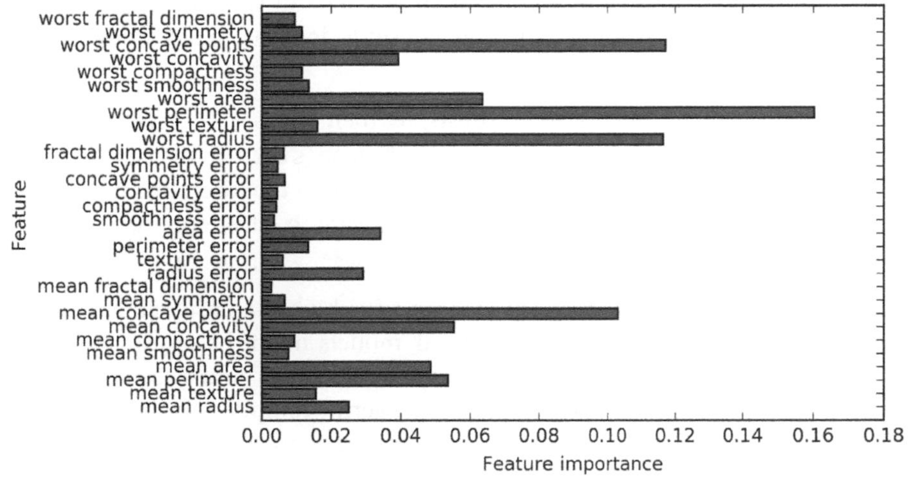

Figure 2-34. Feature importances computed from a random forest that was fit to the Breast Cancer dataset

As you can see, the random forest gives nonzero importance to many more features than the single tree. Similarly to the single decision tree, the random forest also gives a lot of importance to the "worst radius" feature, but it actually chooses "worst perimeter" to be the most informative feature overall. The randomness in building the random forest forces the algorithm to consider many possible explanations, the result being that the random forest captures a much broader picture of the data than a single tree.

Strengths, weaknesses, and parameters. Random forests for regression and classification are currently among the most widely used machine learning methods. They are very powerful, often work well without heavy tuning of the parameters, and don't require scaling of the data.

Essentially, random forests share all of the benefits of decision trees, while making up for some of their deficiencies. One reason to still use decision trees is if you need a compact representation of the decision-making process. It is basically impossible to interpret tens or hundreds of trees in detail, and trees in random forests tend to be deeper than decision trees (because of the use of feature subsets). Therefore, if you need to summarize the prediction making in a visual way to nonexperts, a single decision tree might be a better choice. While building random forests on large datasets might be somewhat time consuming, it can be parallelized across multiple CPU cores within a computer easily. If you are using a multi-core processor (as nearly all modern computers do), you can use the n_jobs parameter to adjust the number of cores to use. Using more CPU cores will result in linear speed-ups (using two cores, the training of the random forest will be twice as fast), but specifying n_jobs larger than the number of cores will not help. You can set n_jobs=-1 to use all the cores in your computer.

You should keep in mind that random forests, by their nature, are random, and setting different random states (or not setting the random_state at all) can drastically change the model that is built. The more trees there are in the forest, the more robust it will be against the choice of random state. If you want to have reproducible results, it is important to fix the random_state.

Random forests don't tend to perform well on very high dimensional, sparse data, such as text data. For this kind of data, linear models might be more appropriate. Random forests usually work well even on very large datasets, and training can easily be parallelized over many CPU cores within a powerful computer. However, random forests require more memory and are slower to train and to predict than linear models. If time and memory are important in an application, it might make sense to use a linear model instead.

The important parameters to adjust are n_estimators, max_features, and possibly pre-pruning options like max_depth. For n_estimators, larger is always better. Averaging more trees will yield a more robust ensemble by reducing overfitting. However, there are diminishing returns, and more trees need more memory and more time to train. A common rule of thumb is to build "as many as you have time/memory for."

As described earlier, max_features determines how random each tree is, and a smaller max_features reduces overfitting. In general, it's a good rule of thumb to use the default values: max_features=sqrt(n_features) for classification and max_features=n_features for regression. Adding max_features or max_leaf_nodes might sometimes improve performance. It can also drastically reduce space and time requirements for training and prediction.

Gradient boosted regression trees (gradient boosting machines)

The gradient boosted regression tree is another ensemble method that combines multiple decision trees to create a more powerful model. Despite the "regression" in the name, these models can be used for regression and classification. In contrast to the random forest approach, gradient boosting works by building trees in a serial manner, where each tree tries to correct the mistakes of the previous one. By default, there is no randomization in gradient boosted regression trees; instead, strong pre-pruning is used. Gradient boosted trees often use very shallow trees, of depth one to five, which makes the model smaller in terms of memory and makes predictions faster.

The main idea behind gradient boosting is to combine many simple models (in this context known as *weak learners*), like shallow trees. Each tree can only provide good predictions on part of the data, and so more and more trees are added to iteratively improve performance.

Gradient boosted trees are frequently the winning entries in machine learning competitions, and are widely used in industry. They are generally a bit more sensitive to parameter settings than random forests, but can provide better accuracy if the parameters are set correctly.

Apart from the pre-pruning and the number of trees in the ensemble, another important parameter of gradient boosting is the `learning_rate`, which controls how strongly each tree tries to correct the mistakes of the previous trees. A higher learning rate means each tree can make stronger corrections, allowing for more complex models. Adding more trees to the ensemble, which can be accomplished by increasing `n_estimators`, also increases the model complexity, as the model has more chances to correct mistakes on the training set.

Here is an example of using `GradientBoostingClassifier` on the Breast Cancer dataset. By default, 100 trees of maximum depth 3 and a learning rate of 0.1 are used:

In[70]:

```
from sklearn.ensemble import GradientBoostingClassifier

X_train, X_test, y_train, y_test = train_test_split(
    cancer.data, cancer.target, random_state=0)

gbrt = GradientBoostingClassifier(random_state=0)
gbrt.fit(X_train, y_train)

print("Accuracy on training set: {:.3f}".format(gbrt.score(X_train, y_train)))
print("Accuracy on test set: {:.3f}".format(gbrt.score(X_test, y_test)))
```

Out[70]:

```
Accuracy on training set: 1.000
Accuracy on test set: 0.958
```

As the training set accuracy is 100%, we are likely to be overfitting. To reduce overfitting, we could either apply stronger pre-pruning by limiting the maximum depth or lower the learning rate:

In[71]:

```
gbrt = GradientBoostingClassifier(random_state=0, max_depth=1)
gbrt.fit(X_train, y_train)

print("Accuracy on training set: {:.3f}".format(gbrt.score(X_train, y_train)))
print("Accuracy on test set: {:.3f}".format(gbrt.score(X_test, y_test)))
```

Out[71]:

```
Accuracy on training set: 0.991
Accuracy on test set: 0.972
```

In[72]:

```
gbrt = GradientBoostingClassifier(random_state=0, learning_rate=0.01)
gbrt.fit(X_train, y_train)

print("Accuracy on training set: {:.3f}".format(gbrt.score(X_train, y_train)))
print("Accuracy on test set: {:.3f}".format(gbrt.score(X_test, y_test)))
```

Out[72]:

```
Accuracy on training set: 0.988
Accuracy on test set: 0.965
```

Both methods of decreasing the model complexity reduced the training set accuracy, as expected. In this case, lowering the maximum depth of the trees provided a significant improvement of the model, while lowering the learning rate only increased the generalization performance slightly.

As for the other decision tree–based models, we can again visualize the feature importances to get more insight into our model (Figure 2-35). As we used 100 trees, it is impractical to inspect them all, even if they are all of depth 1:

In[73]:

```
gbrt = GradientBoostingClassifier(random_state=0, max_depth=1)
gbrt.fit(X_train, y_train)

plot_feature_importances_cancer(gbrt)
```

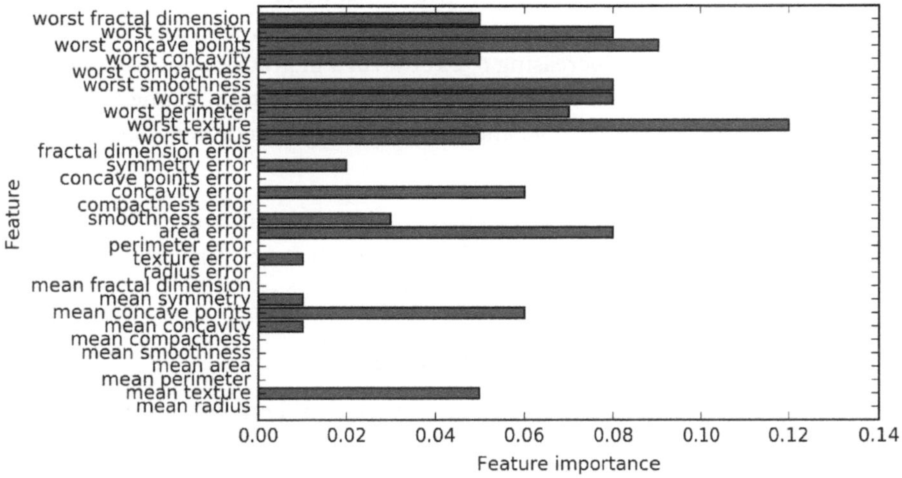

Figure 2-35. Feature importances computed from a gradient boosting classifier that was fit to the Breast Cancer dataset

We can see that the feature importances of the gradient boosted trees are somewhat similar to the feature importances of the random forests, though the gradient boosting completely ignored some of the features.

As both gradient boosting and random forests perform well on similar kinds of data, a common approach is to first try random forests, which work quite robustly. If random forests work well but prediction time is at a premium, or it is important to squeeze out the last percentage of accuracy from the machine learning model, moving to gradient boosting often helps.

If you want to apply gradient boosting to a large-scale problem, it might be worth looking into the `xgboost` package and its Python interface, which at the time of writing is faster (and sometimes easier to tune) than the `scikit-learn` implementation of gradient boosting on many datasets.

Strengths, weaknesses, and parameters. Gradient boosted decision trees are among the most powerful and widely used models for supervised learning. Their main drawback is that they require careful tuning of the parameters and may take a long time to train. Similarly to other tree-based models, the algorithm works well without scaling and on a mixture of binary and continuous features. As with other tree-based models, it also often does not work well on high-dimensional sparse data.

The main parameters of gradient boosted tree models are the number of trees, `n_estimators`, and the `learning_rate`, which controls the degree to which each tree is allowed to correct the mistakes of the previous trees. These two parameters are highly interconnected, as a lower `learning_rate` means that more trees are needed to build a model of similar complexity. In contrast to random forests, where a higher `n_estimators` value is always better, increasing `n_estimators` in gradient boosting leads to a more complex model, which may lead to overfitting. A common practice is to fit `n_estimators` depending on the time and memory budget, and then search over different `learning_rate`s.

Another important parameter is `max_depth` (or alternatively `max_leaf_nodes`), to reduce the complexity of each tree. Usually `max_depth` is set very low for gradient boosted models, often not deeper than five splits.

2.3.7 Kernelized Support Vector Machines

The next type of supervised model we will discuss is kernelized support vector machines. We explored the use of linear support vector machines for classification in "Linear models for classification" on page 58. Kernelized support vector machines (often just referred to as SVMs) are an extension that allows for more complex models that are not defined simply by hyperplanes in the input space. While there are support vector machines for classification and regression, we will restrict ourselves to the classification case, as implemented in `SVC`. Similar concepts apply to support vector regression, as implemented in `SVR`.

The math behind kernelized support vector machines is a bit involved, and is beyond the scope of this book. You can find the details in Chapter 12 of Hastie, Tibshirani, and Friedman's *The Elements of Statistical Learning* (*http://statweb.stanford.edu/~tibs/ElemStatLearn/*). However, we will try to give you some sense of the idea behind the method.

Linear models and nonlinear features

As you saw in Figure 2-15, linear models can be quite limiting in low-dimensional spaces, as lines and hyperplanes have limited flexibility. One way to make a linear model more flexible is by adding more features—for example, by adding interactions or polynomials of the input features.

Let's look at the synthetic dataset we used in "Feature importance in trees" on page 79 (see Figure 2-29):

In[74]:

```
X, y = make_blobs(centers=4, random_state=8)
y = y % 2

mglearn.discrete_scatter(X[:, 0], X[:, 1], y)
plt.xlabel("Feature 0")
plt.ylabel("Feature 1")
```

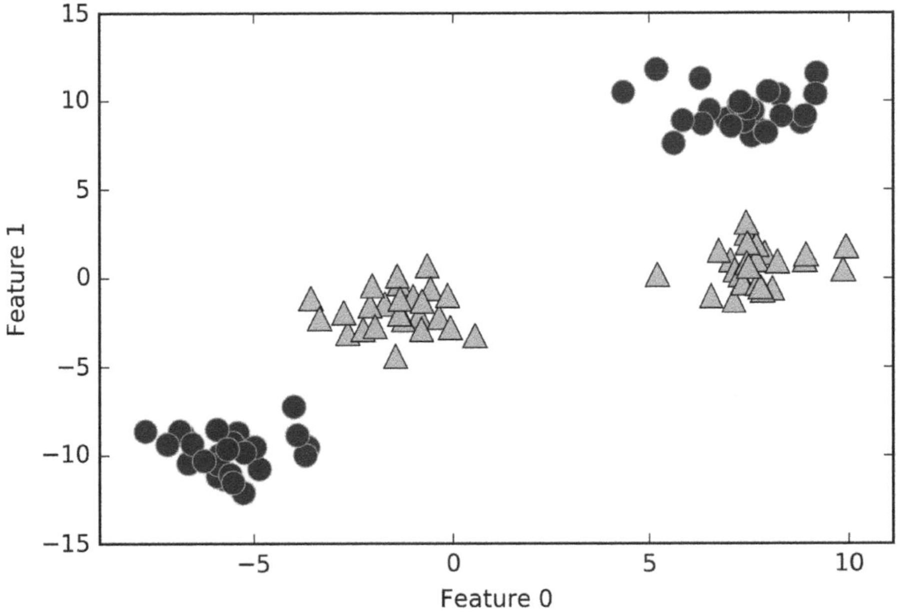

Figure 2-36. Two-class classification dataset in which classes are not linearly separable

A linear model for classification can only separate points using a line, and will not be able to do a very good job on this dataset (see Figure 2-37):

In[75]:

```
from sklearn.svm import LinearSVC
linear_svm = LinearSVC().fit(X, y)

mglearn.plots.plot_2d_separator(linear_svm, X)
mglearn.discrete_scatter(X[:, 0], X[:, 1], y)
plt.xlabel("Feature 0")
plt.ylabel("Feature 1")
```

Now let's expand the set of input features, say by also adding `feature1 ** 2`, the square of the second feature, as a new feature. Instead of representing each data point as a two-dimensional point, `(feature0, feature1)`, we now represent it as a three-dimensional point, `(feature0, feature1, feature1 ** 2)`.[10] This new representation is illustrated in Figure 2-38 in a three-dimensional scatter plot:

10 We picked this particular feature to add for illustration purposes. The choice is not particularly important.

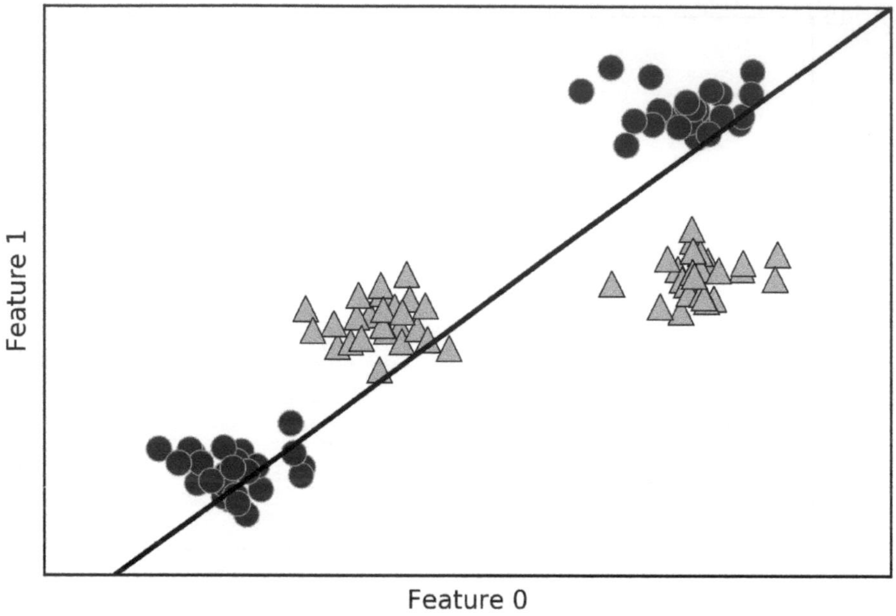

Figure 2-37. Decision boundary found by a linear SVM

In[76]:

```
# add the squared second feature
X_new = np.hstack([X, X[:, 1:] ** 2])

from mpl_toolkits.mplot3d import Axes3D, axes3d
figure = plt.figure()
# visualize in 3D
ax = Axes3D(figure, elev=-152, azim=-26)
# plot first all the points with y == 0, then all with y == 1
mask = y == 0
ax.scatter(X_new[mask, 0], X_new[mask, 1], X_new[mask, 2], c='b',
           cmap=mglearn.cm2, s=60, edgecolor='k')
ax.scatter(X_new[~mask, 0], X_new[~mask, 1], X_new[~mask, 2], c='r', marker='^',
           cmap=mglearn.cm2, s=60, edgecolor='k')
ax.set_xlabel("feature0")
ax.set_ylabel("feature1")
ax.set_zlabel("feature1 ** 2")
```

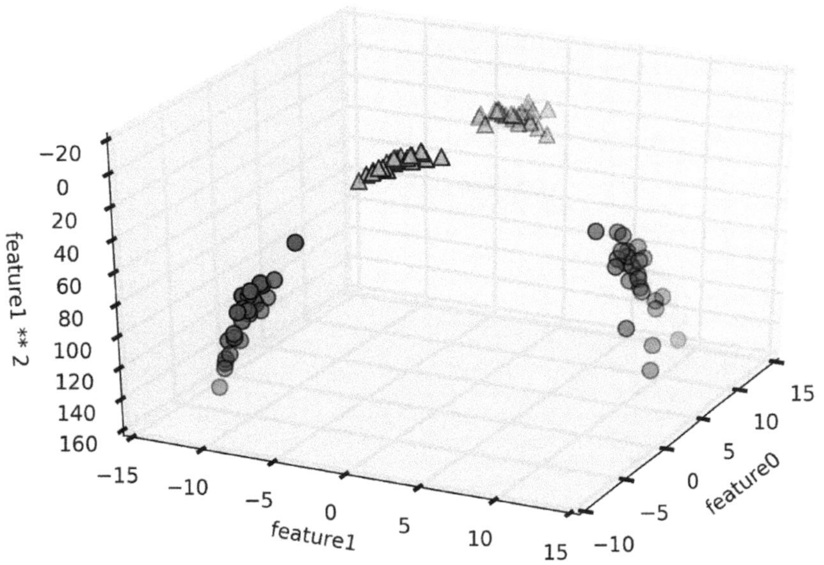

Figure 2-38. Expansion of the dataset shown in Figure 2-37, created by adding a third feature derived from feature1

In the new representation of the data, it is now indeed possible to separate the two classes using a linear model, a plane in three dimensions. We can confirm this by fitting a linear model to the augmented data (see Figure 2-39):

In[77]:

```
linear_svm_3d = LinearSVC().fit(X_new, y)
coef, intercept = linear_svm_3d.coef_.ravel(), linear_svm_3d.intercept_

# show linear decision boundary
figure = plt.figure()
ax = Axes3D(figure, elev=-152, azim=-26)
xx = np.linspace(X_new[:, 0].min() - 2, X_new[:, 0].max() + 2, 50)
yy = np.linspace(X_new[:, 1].min() - 2, X_new[:, 1].max() + 2, 50)

XX, YY = np.meshgrid(xx, yy)
ZZ = (coef[0] * XX + coef[1] * YY + intercept) / -coef[2]
ax.plot_surface(XX, YY, ZZ, rstride=8, cstride=8, alpha=0.3)
ax.scatter(X_new[mask, 0], X_new[mask, 1], X_new[mask, 2], c='b',
           cmap=mglearn.cm2, s=60, edgecolor='k')
ax.scatter(X_new[~mask, 0], X_new[~mask, 1], X_new[~mask, 2], c='r', marker='^',
           cmap=mglearn.cm2, s=60, edgecolor='k')

ax.set_xlabel("feature0")
ax.set_ylabel("feature1")
ax.set_zlabel("feature1 ** 2")
```

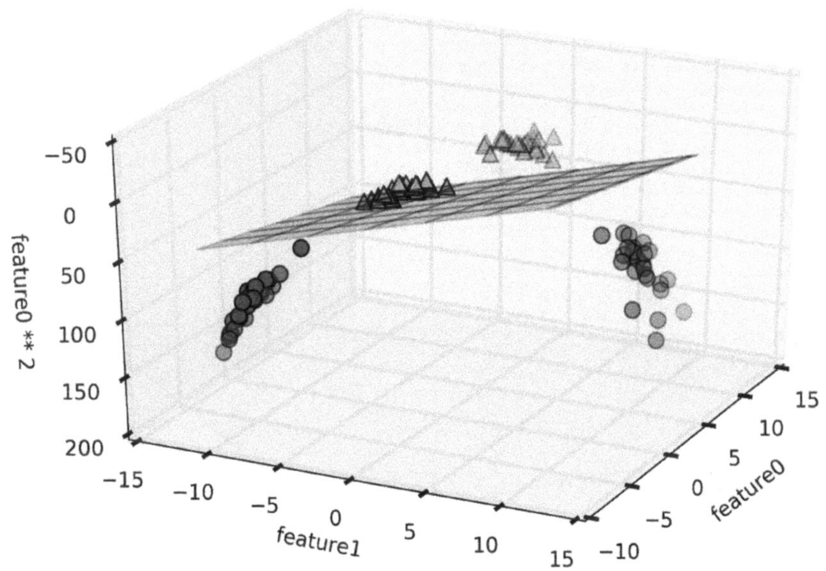

Figure 2-39. Decision boundary found by a linear SVM on the expanded three-dimensional dataset

As a function of the original features, the linear SVM model is not actually linear anymore. It is not a line, but more of an ellipse, as you can see from the plot created here (Figure 2-40):

In[78]:

```
ZZ = YY ** 2
dec = linear_svm_3d.decision_function(np.c_[XX.ravel(), YY.ravel(), ZZ.ravel()])
plt.contourf(XX, YY, dec.reshape(XX.shape), levels=[dec.min(), 0, dec.max()],
             cmap=mglearn.cm2, alpha=0.5)
mglearn.discrete_scatter(X[:, 0], X[:, 1], y)
plt.xlabel("Feature 0")
plt.ylabel("Feature 1")
```

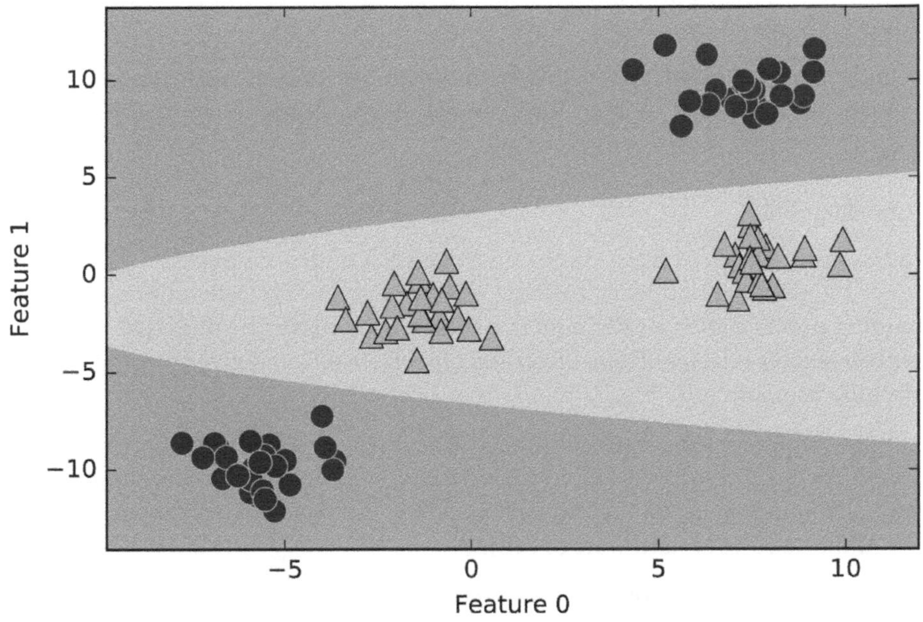

Figure 2-40. The decision boundary from Figure 2-39 as a function of the original two features

The kernel trick

The lesson here is that adding nonlinear features to the representation of our data can make linear models much more powerful. However, often we don't know which features to add, and adding many features (like all possible interactions in a 100-dimensional feature space) might make computation very expensive. Luckily, there is a clever mathematical trick that allows us to learn a classifier in a higher-dimensional space without actually computing the new, possibly very large representation. This is known as the *kernel trick*, and it works by directly computing the distance (more precisely, the scalar products) of the data points for the expanded feature representation, without ever actually computing the expansion.

There are two ways to map your data into a higher-dimensional space that are commonly used with support vector machines: the polynomial kernel, which computes all possible polynomials up to a certain degree of the original features (like `feature1 ** 2 * feature2 ** 5`); and the radial basis function (RBF) kernel, also known as the Gaussian kernel. The Gaussian kernel is a bit harder to explain, as it corresponds to an infinite-dimensional feature space. One way to explain the Gaussian kernel is that it considers all possible polynomials of all degrees, but the importance of the features decreases for higher degrees.[11]

In practice, the mathematical details behind the kernel SVM are not that important, though, and how an SVM with an RBF kernel makes a decision can be summarized quite easily—we'll do so in the next section.

Understanding SVMs

During training, the SVM learns how important each of the training data points is to represent the decision boundary between the two classes. Typically only a subset of the training points matter for defining the decision boundary: the ones that lie on the border between the classes. These are called *support vectors* and give the support vector machine its name.

To make a prediction for a new point, the distance to each of the support vectors is measured. A classification decision is made based on the distances to the support vector, and the importance of the support vectors that was learned during training (stored in the `dual_coef_` attribute of `SVC`).

The distance between data points is measured by the Gaussian kernel:

$$k_{rbf}(x_1, x_2) = \exp(-\gamma \|x_1 - x_2\|^2)$$

Here, x_1 and x_2 are data points, $\| x_1 - x_2 \|$ denotes Euclidean distance, and γ (gamma) is a parameter that controls the width of the Gaussian kernel.

Figure 2-41 shows the result of training a support vector machine on a two-dimensional two-class dataset. The decision boundary is shown in black, and the support vectors are larger points with the wide outline. The following code creates this plot by training an SVM on the `forge` dataset:

In[79]:

```
from sklearn.svm import SVC
X, y = mglearn.tools.make_handcrafted_dataset()
svm = SVC(kernel='rbf', C=10, gamma=0.1).fit(X, y)
mglearn.plots.plot_2d_separator(svm, X, eps=.5)
mglearn.discrete_scatter(X[:, 0], X[:, 1], y)
# plot support vectors
sv = svm.support_vectors_
# class labels of support vectors are given by the sign of the dual coefficients
sv_labels = svm.dual_coef_.ravel() > 0
mglearn.discrete_scatter(sv[:, 0], sv[:, 1], sv_labels, s=15, markeredgewidth=3)
plt.xlabel("Feature 0")
plt.ylabel("Feature 1")
```

11 This follows from the Taylor expansion of the exponential map.

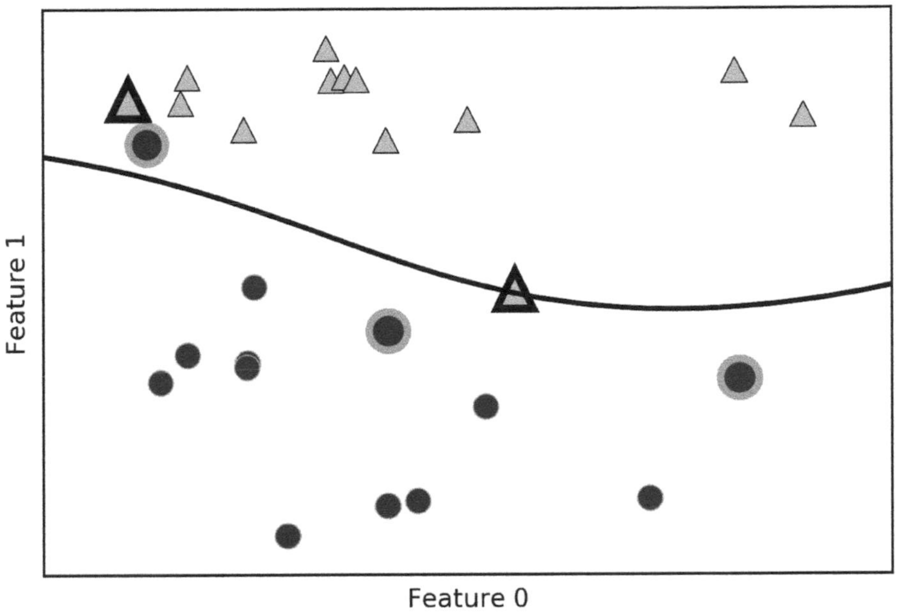

Figure 2-41. Decision boundary and support vectors found by an SVM with RBF kernel

In this case, the SVM yields a very smooth and nonlinear (not a straight line) boundary. We adjusted two parameters here: the `C` parameter and the `gamma` parameter, which we will now discuss in detail.

Tuning SVM parameters

The `gamma` parameter is the one shown in the formula given in the previous section, which corresponds to the inverse of the width of the Gaussian kernel. Intuitively, the gamma parameter determines how far the influence of a single training example reaches, with low values meaning corresponding to a far reach, and high values to a limited reach. In other words, the wider the radius of the Gaussian kernel, the further the influence of each training example. The `C` parameter is a regularization parameter, similar to that used in the linear models. It limits the importance of each point (or more precisely, their `dual_coef_`).

Let's have a look at what happens when we vary these parameters (Figure 2-42):

In[80]:

```
fig, axes = plt.subplots(3, 3, figsize=(15, 10))

for ax, C in zip(axes, [-1, 0, 3]):
    for a, gamma in zip(ax, range(-1, 2)):
```

```
        mglearn.plots.plot_svm(log_C=C, log_gamma=gamma, ax=a)

axes[0, 0].legend(["class 0", "class 1", "sv class 0", "sv class 1"],
                  ncol=4, loc=(.9, 1.2))
```

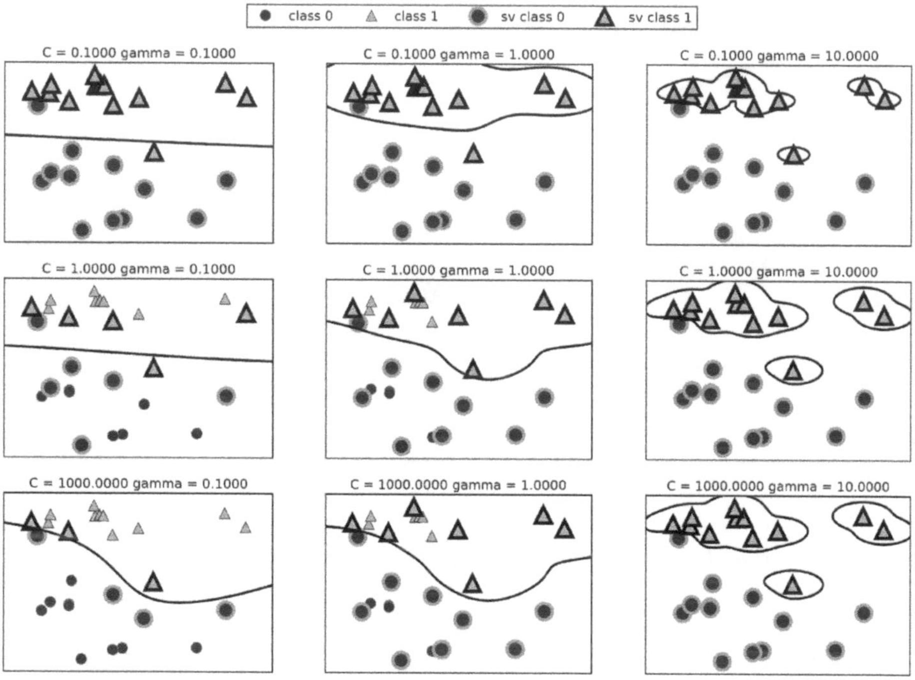

Figure 2-42. Decision boundaries and support vectors for different settings of the parameters C and gamma

Going from left to right, we increase the value of the parameter `gamma` from `0.1` to `10`. A small `gamma` means a large radius for the Gaussian kernel, which means that many points are considered close by. This is reflected in very smooth decision boundaries on the left, and boundaries that focus more on single points further to the right. A low value of `gamma` means that the decision boundary will vary slowly, which yields a model of low complexity, while a high value of `gamma` yields a more complex model.

Going from top to bottom, we increase the `C` parameter from `0.1` to `1000`. As with the linear models, a small `C` means a very restricted model, where each data point can only have very limited influence. You can see that at the top left the decision boundary looks nearly linear, with the misclassified points barely having any influence on the line. Increasing `C`, as shown on the bottom left, allows these points to have a stronger influence on the model and makes the decision boundary bend to correctly classify them.

Let's apply the RBF kernel SVM to the Breast Cancer dataset. By default, C=1 and gamma=1/n_features:

In[81]:

```
X_train, X_test, y_train, y_test = train_test_split(
    cancer.data, cancer.target, random_state=0)

svc = SVC()
svc.fit(X_train, y_train)

print("Accuracy on training set: {:.2f}".format(svc.score(X_train, y_train)))
print("Accuracy on test set: {:.2f}".format(svc.score(X_test, y_test)))
```

Out[81]:

```
Accuracy on training set: 1.00
Accuracy on test set: 0.63
```

The model overfits quite substantially, with a perfect score on the training set and only 63% accuracy on the test set. While SVMs often perform quite well, they are very sensitive to the settings of the parameters and to the scaling of the data. In particular, they require all the features to vary on a similar scale. Let's look at the minimum and maximum values for each feature, plotted in log-space (Figure 2-43):

In[82]:

```
plt.boxplot(X_train, manage_xticks=False)
plt.yscale("symlog")
plt.xlabel("Feature index")
plt.ylabel("Feature magnitude")
```

From this plot we can determine that features in the Breast Cancer dataset are of completely different orders of magnitude. This can be somewhat of a problem for other models (like linear models), but it has devastating effects for the kernel SVM. Let's examine some ways to deal with this issue.

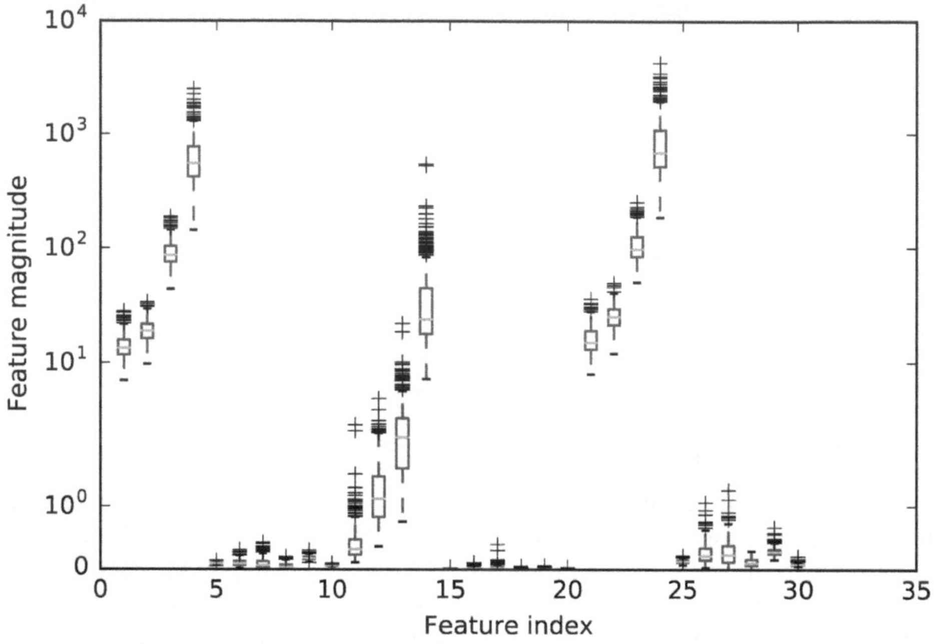

Figure 2-43. Feature ranges for the Breast Cancer dataset (note that the y axis has a logarithmic scale)

Preprocessing data for SVMs

One way to resolve this problem is by rescaling each feature so that they are all approximately on the same scale. A common rescaling method for kernel SVMs is to scale the data such that all features have 0 mean and unit variance, or that all features are between 0 and 1. We will see how to do this using the `StandardScaler` or `MinMaxScaler` preprocessing method in Chapter 3, where we'll give more details. The best choice of preprocessing method depends on the properties of the dataset. For now, let's do this "by hand":

In[83]:

```
# compute the minimum value per feature on the training set
min_on_training = X_train.min(axis=0)
# compute the range of each feature (max - min) on the training set
range_on_training = (X_train - min_on_training).max(axis=0)

# subtract the min, and divide by range
# afterward, min=0 and max=1 for each feature
X_train_scaled = (X_train - min_on_training) / range_on_training
print("Minimum for each feature\n", X_train_scaled.min(axis=0))
print("Maximum for each feature\n", X_train_scaled.max(axis=0))
```

Out[83]:

```
Minimum for each feature
[0. 0. 0. 0. 0. 0. 0. 0. 0. 0. 0. 0. 0. 0. 0. 0. 0. 0. 0. 0. 0. 0. 0. 0.
 0. 0. 0. 0. 0. 0.]
Maximum for each feature
 [1. 1. 1. 1. 1. 1. 1. 1. 1. 1. 1. 1. 1. 1. 1. 1. 1. 1. 1. 1. 1. 1. 1. 1.
 1. 1. 1. 1. 1. 1.]
```

In[84]:

```
# use THE SAME transformation on the test set,
# using min and range of the training set (see Chapter 3 for details)
X_test_scaled = (X_test - min_on_training) / range_on_training
```

In[85]:

```
svc = SVC()
svc.fit(X_train_scaled, y_train)

print("Accuracy on training set: {:.3f}".format(
        svc.score(X_train_scaled, y_train)))
print("Accuracy on test set: {:.3f}".format(svc.score(X_test_scaled, y_test)))
```

Out[85]:

```
Accuracy on training set: 0.948
Accuracy on test set: 0.951
```

Scaling the data made a huge difference! Now we are actually in an underfitting regime, where training and test set performance are quite similar but less close to 100% accuracy. From here, we can try increasing either `C` or `gamma` to fit a more complex model. For example:

In[86]:

```
svc = SVC(C=1000)
svc.fit(X_train_scaled, y_train)

print("Accuracy on training set: {:.3f}".format(
    svc.score(X_train_scaled, y_train)))
print("Accuracy on test set: {:.3f}".format(svc.score(X_test_scaled, y_test)))
```

Out[86]:

```
Accuracy on training set: 0.988
Accuracy on test set: 0.972
```

Here, increasing `C` allows us to improve the model significantly, resulting in 97.2% accuracy.

Strengths, weaknesses, and parameters

Kernelized support vector machines are powerful models and perform well on a variety of datasets. SVMs allow for complex decision boundaries, even if the data has only a few features. They work well on low-dimensional and high-dimensional data (i.e., few and many features), but don't scale very well with the number of samples. Running an SVM on data with up to 10,000 samples might work well, but working with datasets of size 100,000 or more can become challenging in terms of runtime and memory usage.

Another downside of SVMs is that they require careful preprocessing of the data and tuning of the parameters. This is why, these days, most people instead use tree-based models such as random forests or gradient boosting (which require little or no preprocessing) in many applications. Furthermore, SVM models are hard to inspect; it can be difficult to understand why a particular prediction was made, and it might be tricky to explain the model to a nonexpert.

Still, it might be worth trying SVMs, particularly if all of your features represent measurements in similar units (e.g., all are pixel intensities) and they are on similar scales.

The important parameters in kernel SVMs are the regularization parameter `C`, the choice of the kernel, and the kernel-specific parameters. Although we primarily focused on the RBF kernel, other choices are available in `scikit-learn`. The RBF kernel has only one parameter, `gamma`, which is the inverse of the width of the Gaussian kernel. `gamma` and `C` both control the complexity of the model, with large values in either resulting in a more complex model. Therefore, good settings for the two parameters are usually strongly correlated, and `C` and `gamma` should be adjusted together.

2.3.8 Neural Networks (Deep Learning)

A family of algorithms known as neural networks has recently seen a revival under the name "deep learning." While deep learning shows great promise in many machine learning applications, deep learning algorithms are often tailored very carefully to a specific use case. Here, we will only discuss some relatively simple methods, namely *multilayer perceptrons* for classification and regression, that can serve as a starting point for more involved deep learning methods. Multilayer perceptrons (MLPs) are also known as (vanilla) feed-forward neural networks, or sometimes just neural networks.

The neural network model

MLPs can be viewed as generalizations of linear models that perform multiple stages of processing to come to a decision.

Remember that the prediction by a linear regressor is given as:

$$\hat{y} = w[0] * x[0] + w[1] * x[1] + ... + w[p] * x[p] + b$$

In plain English, $\hat{y}$ is a weighted sum of the input features $x[0]$ to $x[p]$, weighted by the learned coefficients $w[0]$ to $w[p]$. We could visualize this graphically as shown in Figure 2-44:

In[87]:

```
display(mglearn.plots.plot_logistic_regression_graph())
```

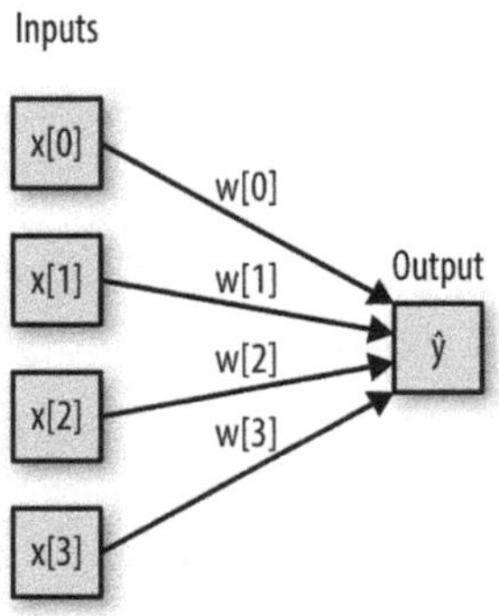

Figure 2-44. Visualization of logistic regression, where input features and predictions are shown as nodes, and the coefficients are connections between the nodes

Here, each node on the left represents an input feature, the connecting lines represent the learned coefficients, and the node on the right represents the output, which is a weighted sum of the inputs.

In an MLP this process of computing weighted sums is repeated multiple times, first computing *hidden units* that represent an intermediate processing step, which are again combined using weighted sums to yield the final result (Figure 2-45):

In[88]:

```
display(mglearn.plots.plot_single_hidden_layer_graph())
```

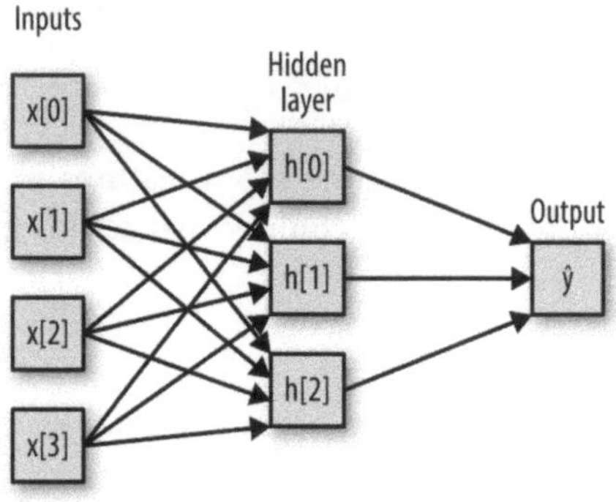

Figure 2-45. Illustration of a multilayer perceptron with a single hidden layer

This model has a lot more coefficients (also called weights) to learn: there is one between every input and every hidden unit (which make up the *hidden layer*), and one between every unit in the hidden layer and the output.

Computing a series of weighted sums is mathematically the same as computing just one weighted sum, so to make this model truly more powerful than a linear model, we need one extra trick. After computing a weighted sum for each hidden unit, a nonlinear function is applied to the result—usually the *rectifying nonlinearity* (also known as rectified linear unit or relu) or the *tangens hyperbolicus* (tanh). The result of this function is then used in the weighted sum that computes the output, $\hat{y}$. The two functions are visualized in Figure 2-46. The relu cuts off values below zero, while tanh saturates to –1 for low input values and +1 for high input values. Either nonlinear function allows the neural network to learn much more complicated functions than a linear model could:

In[89]:

```
line = np.linspace(-3, 3, 100)
plt.plot(line, np.tanh(line), label="tanh")
plt.plot(line, np.maximum(line, 0), label="relu")
plt.legend(loc="best")
plt.xlabel("x")
plt.ylabel("relu(x), tanh(x)")
```

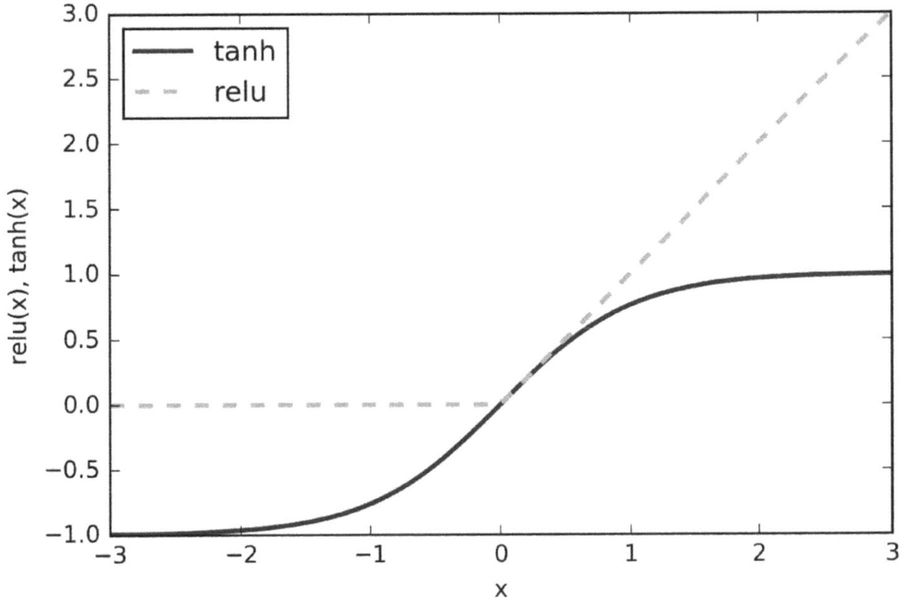

Figure 2-46. The hyperbolic tangent activation function and the rectified linear activation function

For the small neural network pictured in Figure 2-45, the full formula for computing $\hat{y}$ in the case of regression would be (when using a tanh nonlinearity):

$$h[0] = \tanh(w[0, 0] * x[0] + w[1, 0] * x[1] + w[2, 0] * x[2] + w[3, 0] * x[3] + b[0])$$
$$h[1] = \tanh(w[0, 1] * x[0] + w[1, 1] * x[1] + w[2, 1] * x[2] + w[3, 1] * x[3] + b[1])$$
$$h[2] = \tanh(w[0, 2] * x[0] + w[1, 2] * x[1] + w[2, 2] * x[2] + w[3, 2] * x[3] + b[2])$$
$$\hat{y} = v[0] * h[0] + v[1] * h[1] + v[2] * h[2] + b$$

Here, w are the weights between the input x and the hidden layer h, and v are the weights between the hidden layer h and the output $\hat{y}$. The weights v and w are learned from data, x are the input features, $\hat{y}$ is the computed output, and h are intermediate computations. An important parameter that needs to be set by the user is the number of nodes in the hidden layer. This can be as small as 10 for very small or simple datasets and as big as 10,000 for very complex data. It is also possible to add additional hidden layers, as shown in Figure 2-47:

In[90]:

```
mglearn.plots.plot_two_hidden_layer_graph()
```

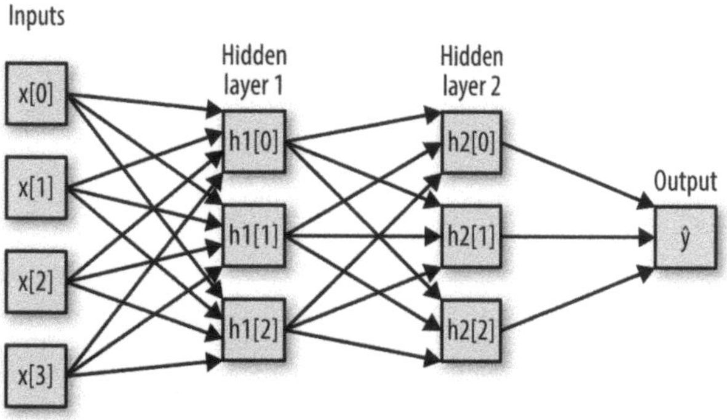

Figure 2-47. A multilayer perceptron with two hidden layers

Having large neural networks made up of many of these layers of computation is what inspired the term "deep learning."

Tuning neural networks

Let's look into the workings of the MLP by applying the `MLPClassifier` to the `two_moons` dataset we used earlier in this chapter. The results are shown in Figure 2-48:

In[91]:

```
from sklearn.neural_network import MLPClassifier
from sklearn.datasets import make_moons

X, y = make_moons(n_samples=100, noise=0.25, random_state=3)

X_train, X_test, y_train, y_test = train_test_split(X, y, stratify=y,
                                                    random_state=42)

mlp = MLPClassifier(solver='lbfgs', random_state=0).fit(X_train, y_train)
mglearn.plots.plot_2d_separator(mlp, X_train, fill=True, alpha=.3)
mglearn.discrete_scatter(X_train[:, 0], X_train[:, 1], y_train)
plt.xlabel("Feature 0")
plt.ylabel("Feature 1")
```

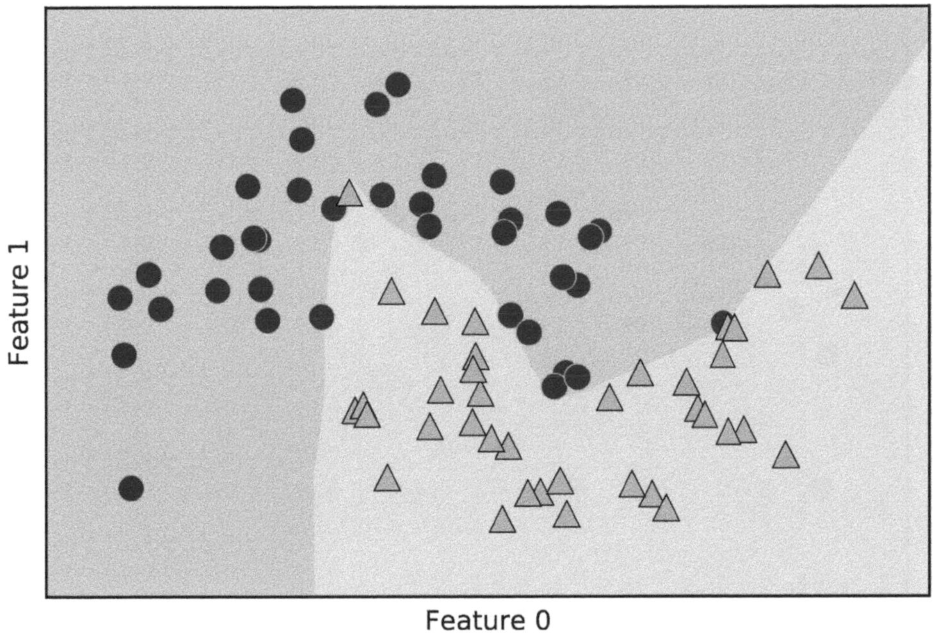

Figure 2-48. Decision boundary learned by a neural network with 100 hidden units on the two_moons dataset

As you can see, the neural network learned a very nonlinear but relatively smooth decision boundary. We used `solver='lbfgs'`, which we will discuss later.

By default, the MLP uses 100 hidden nodes, which is quite a lot for this small dataset. We can reduce the number (which reduces the complexity of the model) and still get a good result (Figure 2-49):

In[92]:

```
mlp = MLPClassifier(solver='lbfgs', random_state=0, hidden_layer_sizes=[10])
mlp.fit(X_train, y_train)
mglearn.plots.plot_2d_separator(mlp, X_train, fill=True, alpha=.3)
mglearn.discrete_scatter(X_train[:, 0], X_train[:, 1], y_train)
plt.xlabel("Feature 0")
plt.ylabel("Feature 1")
```

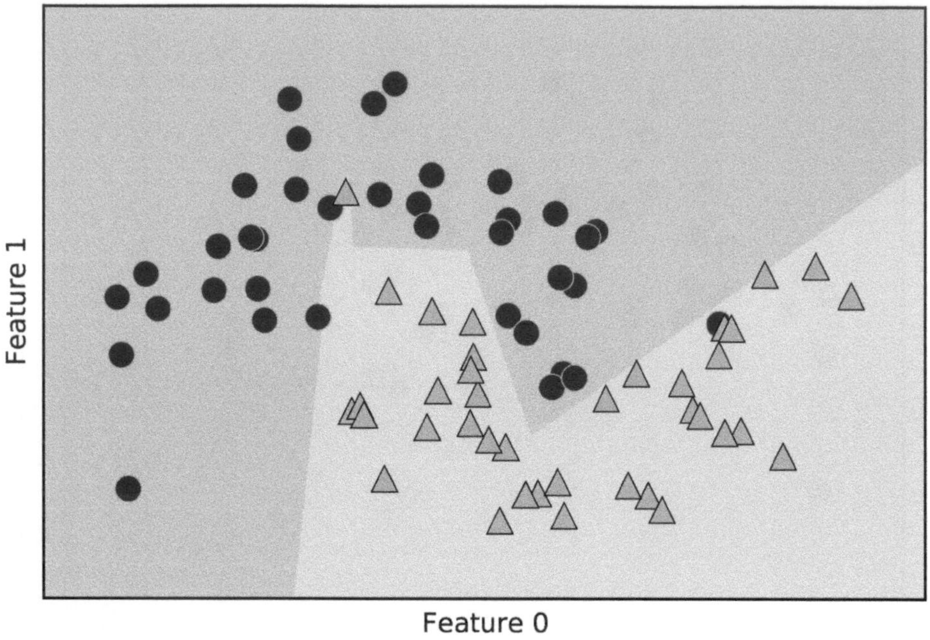

Figure 2-49. Decision boundary learned by a neural network with 10 hidden units on the two_moons dataset

With only 10 hidden units, the decision boundary looks somewhat more ragged. The default nonlinearity is relu, shown in Figure 2-46. With a single hidden layer, this means the decision function will be made up of 10 straight line segments. If we want a smoother decision boundary, we could add more hidden units (as in Figure 2-48), add a second hidden layer (Figure 2-50), or use the tanh nonlinearity (Figure 2-51):

In[93]:

```
# using two hidden layers, with 10 units each
mlp = MLPClassifier(solver='lbfgs', random_state=0,
                    hidden_layer_sizes=[10, 10])
mlp.fit(X_train, y_train)
mglearn.plots.plot_2d_separator(mlp, X_train, fill=True, alpha=.3)
mglearn.discrete_scatter(X_train[:, 0], X_train[:, 1], y_train)
plt.xlabel("Feature 0")
plt.ylabel("Feature 1")
```

In[94]:

```
# using two hidden layers, with 10 units each, now with tanh nonlinearity
mlp = MLPClassifier(solver='lbfgs', activation='tanh',
                    random_state=0, hidden_layer_sizes=[10, 10])
mlp.fit(X_train, y_train)
mglearn.plots.plot_2d_separator(mlp, X_train, fill=True, alpha=.3)
mglearn.discrete_scatter(X_train[:, 0], X_train[:, 1], y_train)
plt.xlabel("Feature 0")
plt.ylabel("Feature 1")
```

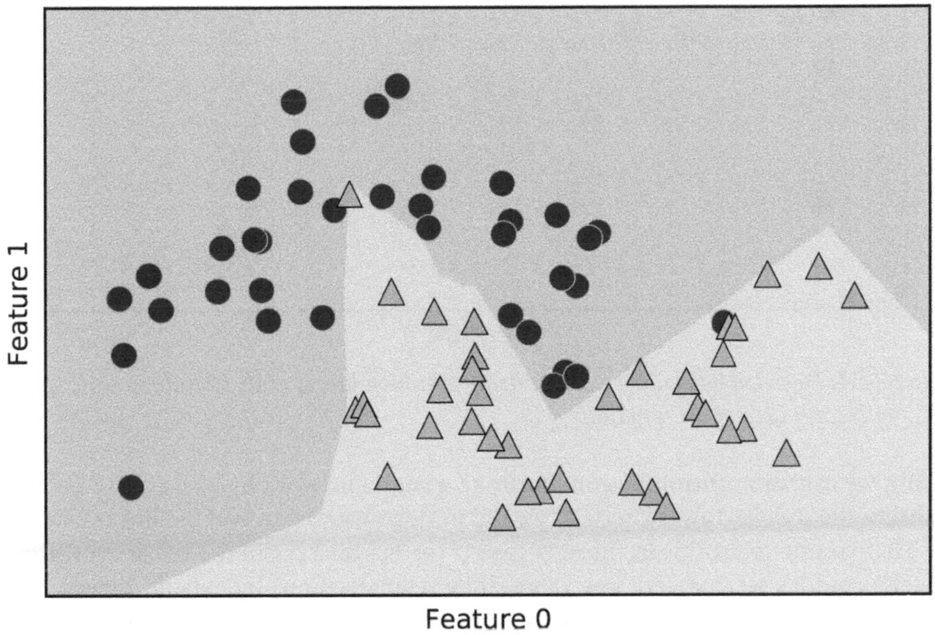

Figure 2-50. Decision boundary learned using 2 hidden layers with 10 hidden units each, with rect activation function

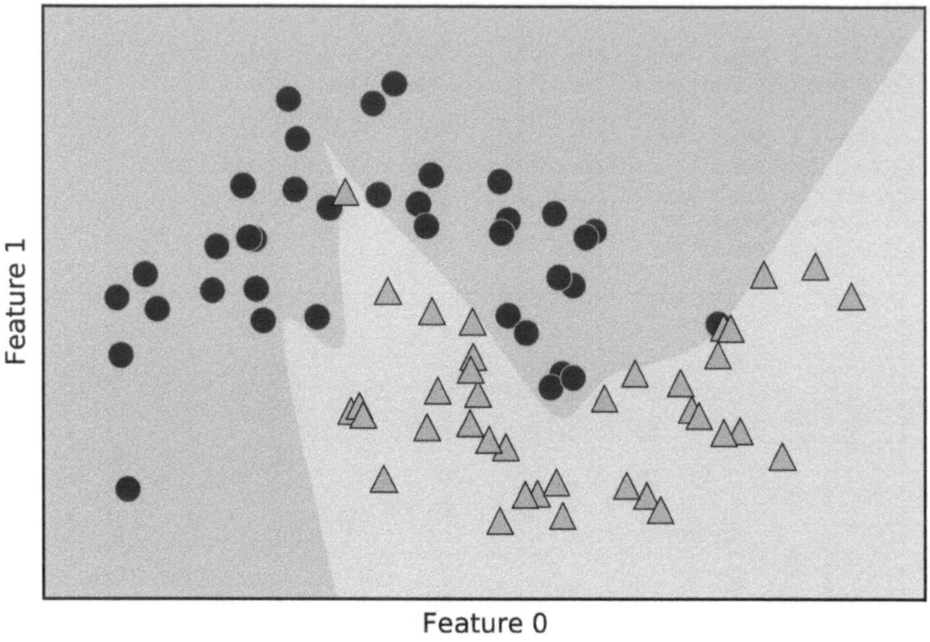

Figure 2-51. Decision boundary learned using 2 hidden layers with 10 hidden units each, with tanh activation function

Finally, we can also control the complexity of a neural network by using an `l2` penalty to shrink the weights toward zero, as we did in ridge regression and the linear classifiers. The parameter for this in the `MLPClassifier` is `alpha` (as in the linear regression models), and it's set to a very low value (little regularization) by default. Figure 2-52 shows the effect of different values of `alpha` on the `two_moons` dataset, using two hidden layers of 10 or 100 units each:

In[95]:

```
fig, axes = plt.subplots(2, 4, figsize=(20, 8))
for axx, n_hidden_nodes in zip(axes, [10, 100]):
    for ax, alpha in zip(axx, [0.0001, 0.01, 0.1, 1]):
        mlp = MLPClassifier(solver='lbfgs', random_state=0,
                            hidden_layer_sizes=[n_hidden_nodes, n_hidden_nodes],
                            alpha=alpha)
        mlp.fit(X_train, y_train)
        mglearn.plots.plot_2d_separator(mlp, X_train, fill=True, alpha=.3, ax=ax)
        mglearn.discrete_scatter(X_train[:, 0], X_train[:, 1], y_train, ax=ax)
        ax.set_title("n_hidden=[{}, {}]\nalpha={:.4f}".format(
                     n_hidden_nodes, n_hidden_nodes, alpha))
```

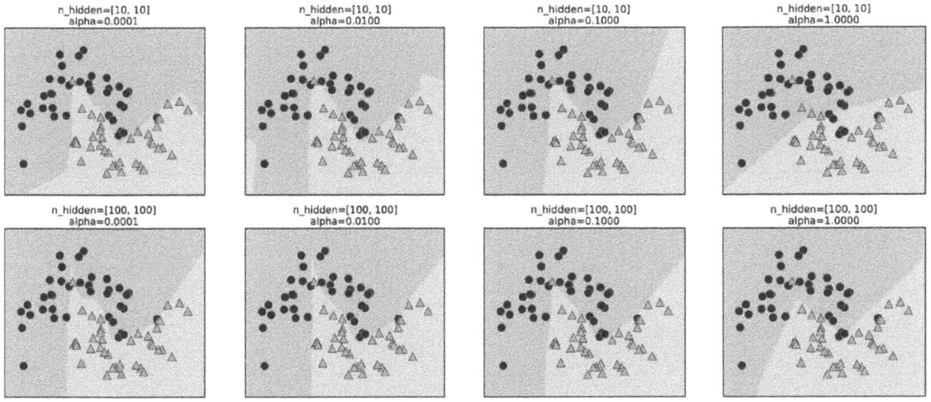

Figure 2-52. Decision functions for different numbers of hidden units and different settings of the alpha parameter

As you probably have realized by now, there are many ways to control the complexity of a neural network: the number of hidden layers, the number of units in each hidden layer, and the regularization (`alpha`). There are actually even more, which we won't go into here.

An important property of neural networks is that their weights are set randomly before learning is started, and this random initialization affects the model that is learned. That means that even when using exactly the same parameters, we can obtain very different models when using different random seeds. If the networks are large, and their complexity is chosen properly, this should not affect accuracy too much, but it is worth keeping in mind (particularly for smaller networks). Figure 2-53 shows plots of several models, all learned with the same settings of the parameters:

In[96]:

```
fig, axes = plt.subplots(2, 4, figsize=(20, 8))
for i, ax in enumerate(axes.ravel()):
    mlp = MLPClassifier(solver='lbfgs', random_state=i,
                        hidden_layer_sizes=[100, 100])
    mlp.fit(X_train, y_train)
    mglearn.plots.plot_2d_separator(mlp, X_train, fill=True, alpha=.3, ax=ax)
    mglearn.discrete_scatter(X_train[:, 0], X_train[:, 1], y_train, ax=ax)
```

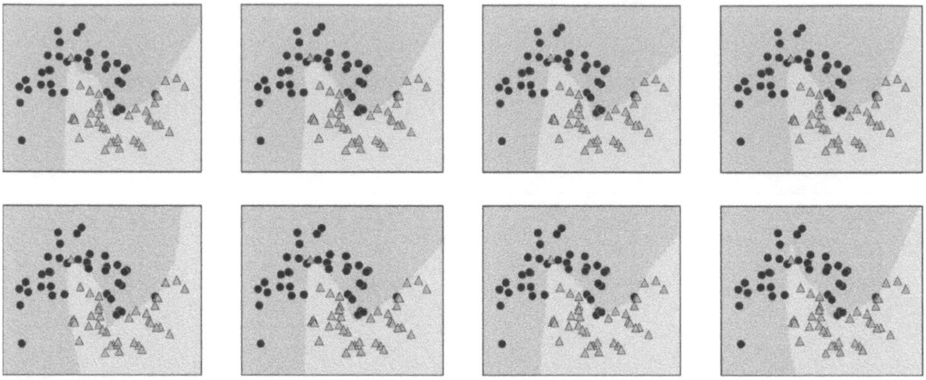

Figure 2-53. Decision functions learned with the same parameters but different random initializations

To get a better understanding of neural networks on real-world data, let's apply the `MLPClassifier` to the Breast Cancer dataset. We start with the default parameters:

In[97]:

```
print("Cancer data per-feature maxima:\n{}".format(cancer.data.max(axis=0)))
```

Out[97]:

```
Cancer data per-feature maxima:
[  28.11     39.28    188.5    2501.        0.163     0.345     0.427     0.201
    0.304     0.097     2.873     4.885    21.98    542.2       0.031     0.135
    0.396     0.053     0.079     0.03     36.04     49.54    251.2    4254.
    0.223     1.058     1.252     0.291     0.664     0.207]
```

In[98]:

```
X_train, X_test, y_train, y_test = train_test_split(
    cancer.data, cancer.target, random_state=0)

mlp = MLPClassifier(random_state=42)
mlp.fit(X_train, y_train)

print("Accuracy on training set: {:.2f}".format(mlp.score(X_train, y_train)))
print("Accuracy on test set: {:.2f}".format(mlp.score(X_test, y_test)))
```

Out[98]:

```
Accuracy on training set: 0.92
Accuracy on test set: 0.90
```

The accuracy of the MLP is quite good, but not as good as the other models. As in the earlier SVC example, this is likely due to scaling of the data. Neural networks also expect all input features to vary in a similar way, and ideally to have a mean of 0, and a variance of 1. We must rescale our data so that it fulfills these requirements. Again, we will do this by hand here, but we'll introduce the `StandardScaler` to do this automatically in Chapter 3:

In[99]:

```
# compute the mean value per feature on the training set
mean_on_train = X_train.mean(axis=0)
# compute the standard deviation of each feature on the training set
std_on_train = X_train.std(axis=0)

# subtract the mean, and scale by inverse standard deviation
# afterward, mean=0 and std=1
X_train_scaled = (X_train - mean_on_train) / std_on_train
# use THE SAME transformation (using training mean and std) on the test set
X_test_scaled = (X_test - mean_on_train) / std_on_train

mlp = MLPClassifier(random_state=0)
mlp.fit(X_train_scaled, y_train)

print("Accuracy on training set: {:.3f}".format(
    mlp.score(X_train_scaled, y_train)))
print("Accuracy on test set: {:.3f}".format(mlp.score(X_test_scaled, y_test)))
```

Out[99]:

```
Accuracy on training set: 0.991
Accuracy on test set: 0.965

ConvergenceWarning:
    Stochastic Optimizer: Maximum iterations reached and the optimization
    hasn't converged yet.
```

The results are much better after scaling, and already quite competitive. We got a warning from the model, though, that tells us that the maximum number of iterations has been reached. This is part of the `adam` algorithm for learning the model, and tells us that we should increase the number of iterations:

In[100]:

```
mlp = MLPClassifier(max_iter=1000, random_state=0)
mlp.fit(X_train_scaled, y_train)

print("Accuracy on training set: {:.3f}".format(
    mlp.score(X_train_scaled, y_train)))
print("Accuracy on test set: {:.3f}".format(mlp.score(X_test_scaled, y_test)))
```

Out[100]:

```
Accuracy on training set: 0.995
Accuracy on test set: 0.965
```

Increasing the number of iterations only increased the training set performance, not the generalization performance. Still, the model is performing quite well. As there is some gap between the training and the test performance, we might try to decrease the model's complexity to get better generalization performance. Here, we choose to increase the `alpha` parameter (quite aggressively, from `0.0001` to `1`) to add stronger regularization of the weights:

In[101]:

```
mlp = MLPClassifier(max_iter=1000, alpha=1, random_state=0)
mlp.fit(X_train_scaled, y_train)

print("Accuracy on training set: {:.3f}".format(
    mlp.score(X_train_scaled, y_train)))
print("Accuracy on test set: {:.3f}".format(mlp.score(X_test_scaled, y_test)))
```

Out[101]:

```
Accuracy on training set: 0.988
Accuracy on test set: 0.972
```

This leads to a performance on par with the best models so far.[12]

While it is possible to analyze what a neural network has learned, this is usually much trickier than analyzing a linear model or a tree-based model. One way to inspect what was learned is to look at the weights in the model. You can see an example of this in the `scikit-learn` example gallery (*http://scikit-learn.org/stable/auto_examples/neural_networks/plot_mnist_filters.html*). For the Breast Cancer dataset, this might be a bit hard to understand. The following plot (Figure 2-54) shows the weights that were learned connecting the input to the first hidden layer. The rows in this plot correspond to the 30 input features, while the columns correspond to the 100 hidden units. Light colors represent large positive values, while dark colors represent negative values:

In[102]:

```
plt.figure(figsize=(20, 5))
plt.imshow(mlp.coefs_[0], interpolation='none', cmap='viridis')
plt.yticks(range(30), cancer.feature_names)
plt.xlabel("Columns in weight matrix")
plt.ylabel("Input feature")
plt.colorbar()
```

12 You might have noticed at this point that many of the well-performing models achieved exactly the same accuracy of 0.972. This means that all of the models make exactly the same number of mistakes, which is four. If you compare the actual predictions, you can even see that they make exactly the same mistakes! This might be a consequence of the dataset being very small, or it may be because these points are really different from the rest.

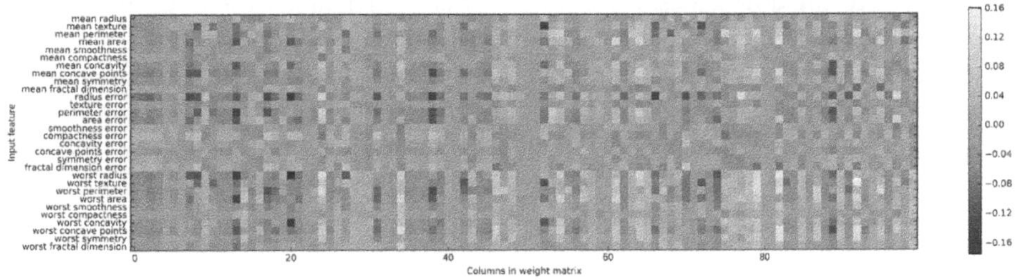

Figure 2-54. Heat map of the first layer weights in a neural network learned on the Breast Cancer dataset

One possible inference we can make is that features that have very small weights for all of the hidden units are "less important" to the model. We can see that "mean smoothness" and "mean compactness," in addition to the features found between "smoothness error" and "fractal dimension error," have relatively low weights compared to other features. This could mean that these are less important features or possibly that we didn't represent them in a way that the neural network could use.

We could also visualize the weights connecting the hidden layer to the output layer, but those are even harder to interpret.

While the `MLPClassifier` and `MLPRegressor` provide easy-to-use interfaces for the most common neural network architectures, they only capture a small subset of what is possible with neural networks. If you are interested in working with more flexible or larger models, we encourage you to look beyond `scikit-learn` into the fantastic deep learning libraries that are out there. For Python users, the most well-established are `keras`, `lasagna`, and `tensor-flow`. `lasagna` builds on the `theano` library, while `keras` can use either `tensor-flow` or `theano`. These libraries provide a much more flexible interface to build neural networks and track the rapid progress in deep learning research. All of the popular deep learning libraries also allow the use of high-performance graphics processing units (GPUs), which `scikit-learn` does not support. Using GPUs allows us to accelerate computations by factors of 10x to 100x, and they are essential for applying deep learning methods to large-scale datasets.

Strengths, weaknesses, and parameters

Neural networks have reemerged as state-of-the-art models in many applications of machine learning. One of their main advantages is that they are able to capture information contained in large amounts of data and build incredibly complex models. Given enough computation time, data, and careful tuning of the parameters, neural networks often beat other machine learning algorithms (for classification and regression tasks).

This brings us to the downsides. Neural networks—particularly the large and powerful ones—often take a long time to train. They also require careful preprocessing of the data, as we saw here. Similarly to SVMs, they work best with "homogeneous" data, where all the features have similar meanings. For data that has very different kinds of features, tree-based models might work better. Tuning neural network parameters is also an art unto itself. In our experiments, we barely scratched the surface of possible ways to adjust neural network models and how to train them.

Estimating complexity in neural networks. The most important parameters are the number of layers and the number of hidden units per layer. You should start with one or two hidden layers, and possibly expand from there. The number of nodes per hidden layer is often similar to the number of input features, but rarely higher than in the low to mid-thousands.

A helpful measure when thinking about the model complexity of a neural network is the number of weights or coefficients that are learned. If you have a binary classification dataset with 100 features, and you have 100 hidden units, then there are 100 * 100 = 10,000 weights between the input and the first hidden layer. There are also 100 * 1 = 100 weights between the hidden layer and the output layer, for a total of around 10,100 weights. If you add a second hidden layer with 100 hidden units, there will be another 100 * 100 = 10,000 weights from the first hidden layer to the second hidden layer, resulting in a total of 20,100 weights. If instead you use one layer with 1,000 hidden units, you are learning 100 * 1,000 = 100,000 weights from the input to the hidden layer and 1,000 * 1 weights from the hidden layer to the output layer, for a total of 101,000. If you add a second hidden layer you add 1,000 * 1,000 = 1,000,000 weights, for a whopping total of 1,101,000—50 times larger than the model with two hidden layers of size 100.

A common way to adjust parameters in a neural network is to first create a network that is large enough to overfit, making sure that the task can actually be learned by the network. Then, once you know the training data can be learned, either shrink the network or increase `alpha` to add regularization, which will improve generalization performance.

In our experiments, we focused mostly on the definition of the model: the number of layers and nodes per layer, the regularization, and the nonlinearity. These define the model we want to learn. There is also the question of *how* to learn the model, or the algorithm that is used for learning the parameters, which is set using the `algorithm` parameter. There are two easy-to-use choices for `algorithm`. The default is `'adam'`, which works well in most situations but is quite sensitive to the scaling of the data (so it is important to always scale your data to 0 mean and unit variance). The other one is `'lbfgs'`, which is quite robust but might take a long time on larger models or larger datasets. There is also the more advanced `'sgd'` option, which is what many deep learning researchers use. The `'sgd'` option comes with many additional parameters that need to be tuned for best results. You can find all of these parameters and their definitions in the user guide. When starting to work with MLPs, we recommend sticking to 'adam' and 'lbfgs'.

> **fit Resets a Model**
>
> An important property of scikit-learn models is that calling fit will always reset everything a model previously learned. So if you build a model on one dataset, and then call fit again on a different dataset, the model will "forget" everything it learned from the first dataset. You can call fit as often as you like on a model, and the outcome will be the same as calling fit on a "new" model.

2.4 Uncertainty Estimates from Classifiers

Another useful part of the scikit-learn interface that we haven't talked about yet is the ability of classifiers to provide uncertainty estimates of predictions. Often, you are not only interested in which class a classifier predicts for a certain test point, but also how certain it is that this is the right class. In practice, different kinds of mistakes lead to very different outcomes in real-world applications. Imagine a medical application testing for cancer. Making a false positive prediction might lead to a patient undergoing additional tests, while a false negative prediction might lead to a serious disease not being treated. We will go into this topic in more detail in Chapter 6.

There are two different functions in scikit-learn that can be used to obtain uncertainty estimates from classifiers: decision_function and predict_proba. Most (but not all) classifiers have at least one of them, and many classifiers have both. Let's look at what these two functions do on a synthetic two-dimensional dataset, when building a GradientBoostingClassifier classifier, which has both a decision_function and a predict_proba method:

In[103]:

```
from sklearn.ensemble import GradientBoostingClassifier
from sklearn.datasets import make_circles
X, y = make_circles(noise=0.25, factor=0.5, random_state=1)

# we rename the classes "blue" and "red" for illustration purposes
y_named = np.array(["blue", "red"])[y]

# we can call train_test_split with arbitrarily many arrays;
# all will be split in a consistent manner
X_train, X_test, y_train_named, y_test_named, y_train, y_test = \
    train_test_split(X, y_named, y, random_state=0)

# build the gradient boosting model
gbrt = GradientBoostingClassifier(random_state=0)
gbrt.fit(X_train, y_train_named)
```

2.4.1 The Decision Function

In the binary classification case, the return value of decision_function is of shape (n_samples,), and it returns one floating-point number for each sample:

In[104]:

```
print("X_test.shape: {}".format(X_test.shape))
print("Decision function shape: {}".format(
      gbrt.decision_function(X_test).shape))
```

Out[104]:

```
X_test.shape: (25, 2)
Decision function shape: (25,)
```

This value encodes how strongly the model believes a data point to belong to the "positive" class, in this case class 1. Positive values indicate a preference for the positive class, and negative values indicate a preference for the "negative" (other) class:

In[105]:

```
# show the first few entries of decision_function
print("Decision function:", gbrt.decision_function(X_test)[:6])
```

Out[105]:

```
Decision function:
[ 4.136 -1.683 -3.951 -3.626  4.29   3.662]
```

We can recover the prediction by looking only at the sign of the decision function:

In[106]:

```
print("Thresholded decision function:\n",
      gbrt.decision_function(X_test) > 0)
print("Predictions:\n", gbrt.predict(X_test))
```

Out[106]:

```
Thresholded decision function:
[ True False False False  True  True False  True  True  True False  True
  True False  True False False False  True  True  True  True  True False
  False]
Predictions:
['red' 'blue' 'blue' 'blue' 'red' 'red' 'blue' 'red' 'red' 'red' 'blue'
 'red' 'red' 'blue' 'red' 'blue' 'blue' 'blue' 'red' 'red' 'red' 'red'
 'red' 'blue' 'blue']
```

For binary classification, the "negative" class is always the first entry of the classes_ attribute, and the "positive" class is the second entry of classes_. So if you want to fully recover the output of predict, you need to make use of the classes_ attribute:

In[107]:

```
# make the boolean True/False into 0 and 1
greater_zero = (gbrt.decision_function(X_test) > 0).astype(int)
# use 0 and 1 as indices into classes_
pred = gbrt.classes_[greater_zero]
# pred is the same as the output of gbrt.predict
print("pred is equal to predictions:",
      np.all(pred == gbrt.predict(X_test)))
```

Out[107]:

```
pred is equal to predictions: True
```

The range of `decision_function` can be arbitrary, and depends on the data and the model parameters:

In[108]:

```
decision_function = gbrt.decision_function(X_test)
print("Decision function minimum: {:.2f} maximum: {:.2f}".format(
      np.min(decision_function), np.max(decision_function)))
```

Out[108]:

```
Decision function minimum: -7.69 maximum: 4.29
```

This arbitrary scaling makes the output of `decision_function` often hard to interpret.

In the following example we plot the `decision_function` for all points in the 2D plane using a color coding, next to a visualization of the decision boundary, as we saw earlier. We show training points as circles and test data as triangles (Figure 2-55):

In[109]:

```
fig, axes = plt.subplots(1, 2, figsize=(13, 5))
mglearn.tools.plot_2d_separator(gbrt, X, ax=axes[0], alpha=.4,
                                fill=True, cm=mglearn.cm2)
scores_image = mglearn.tools.plot_2d_scores(gbrt, X, ax=axes[1],
                                            alpha=.4, cm=mglearn.ReBl)

for ax in axes:
    # plot training and test points
    mglearn.discrete_scatter(X_test[:, 0], X_test[:, 1], y_test,
                             markers='^', ax=ax)
    mglearn.discrete_scatter(X_train[:, 0], X train[:, 1], y_train,
                             markers='o', ax=ax)
    ax.set_xlabel("Feature 0")
    ax.set_ylabel("Feature 1")
cbar = plt.colorbar(scores_image, ax=axes.tolist())
axes[0].legend(["Test class 0", "Test class 1", "Train class 0",
                "Train class 1"], ncol=4, loc=(.1, 1.1))
```

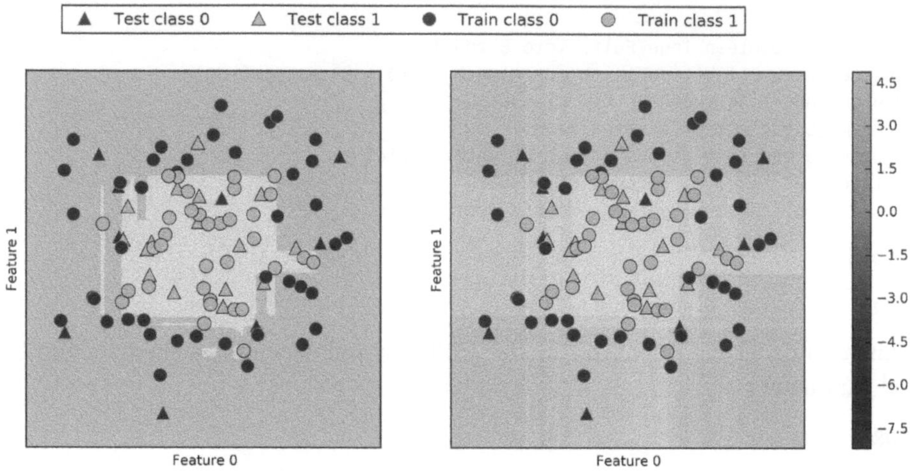

Figure 2-55. Decision boundary (left) and decision function (right) for a gradient boosting model on a two-dimensional toy dataset

Encoding not only the predicted outcome but also how certain the classifier is provides additional information. However, in this visualization, it is hard to make out the boundary between the two classes.

2.4.2 Predicting Probabilities

The output of `predict_proba` is a probability for each class, and is often more easily understood than the output of `decision_function`. It is always of shape `(n_samples, 2)` for binary classification:

In[110]:

```
print("Shape of probabilities:", gbrt.predict_proba(X_test).shape)
```

Out[110]:

```
Shape of probabilities: (25, 2)
```

The first entry in each row is the estimated probability of the first class, and the second entry is the estimated probability of the second class. Because it is a probability, the output of `predict_proba` is always between 0 and 1, and the sum of the entries for both classes is always 1:

In[111]:

```
# show the first few entries of predict_proba
print("Predicted probabilities:")
print(gbrt.predict_proba(X_test[:6]))
```

Out[111]:

```
Predicted probabilities:
[[0.016 0.984]
 [0.846 0.154]
 [0.981 0.019]
 [0.974 0.026]
 [0.014 0.986]
 [0.025 0.975]]
```

Because the probabilities for the two classes sum to 1, exactly one of the classes will be above 50% certainty. That class is the one that is predicted.[13]

You can see in the previous output that the classifier is relatively certain for most points. How well the uncertainty actually reflects uncertainty in the data depends on the model and the parameters. A model that is more overfitted tends to make more certain predictions, even if they might be wrong. A model with less complexity usually has more uncertainty in its predictions. A model is called *calibrated* if the reported uncertainty actually matches how correct it is—in a calibrated model, a prediction made with 70% certainty would be correct 70% of the time.

In the following example (Figure 2-56) we again show the decision boundary on the dataset, next to the class probabilities for the class 1:

In[112]:

```
fig, axes = plt.subplots(1, 2, figsize=(13, 5))

mglearn.tools.plot_2d_separator(
    gbrt, X, ax=axes[0], alpha=.4, fill=True, cm=mglearn.cm2)
scores_image = mglearn.tools.plot_2d_scores(
    gbrt, X, ax=axes[1], alpha=.5, cm=mglearn.ReBl, function='predict_proba')

for ax in axes:
    # plot training and test points
    mglearn.discrete_scatter(X_test[:, 0], X_test[:, 1], y_test,
                             markers='^', ax=ax)
    mglearn.discrete_scatter(X_train[:, 0], X_train[:, 1], y_train,
                             markers='o', ax=ax)
    ax.set_xlabel("Feature 0")
    ax.set_ylabel("Feature 1")
cbar = plt.colorbar(scores_image, ax=axes.tolist())
axes[0].legend(["Test class 0", "Test class 1", "Train class 0",
                "Train class 1"], ncol=4, loc=(.1, 1.1))
```

13 Because the probabilities are floating-point numbers, it is unlikely that they will both be exactly 0.500. However, if that happens, the prediction is made at random.

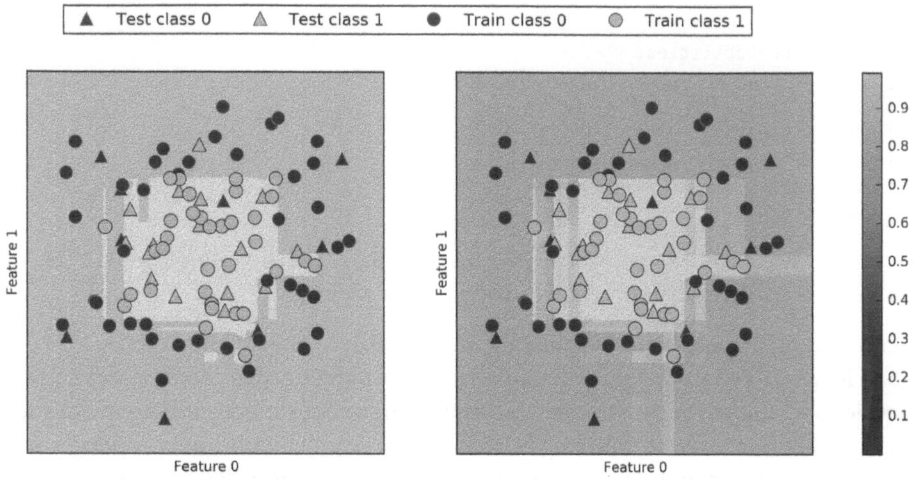

Figure 2-56. Decision boundary (left) and predicted probabilities for the gradient boosting model shown in Figure 2-55

The boundaries in this plot are much more well-defined, and the small areas of uncertainty are clearly visible.

The `scikit-learn` website (*http://bit.ly/2cqCYx6*) has a great comparison of many models and what their uncertainty estimates look like. We've reproduced this in Figure 2-57, and we encourage you to go through the example there.

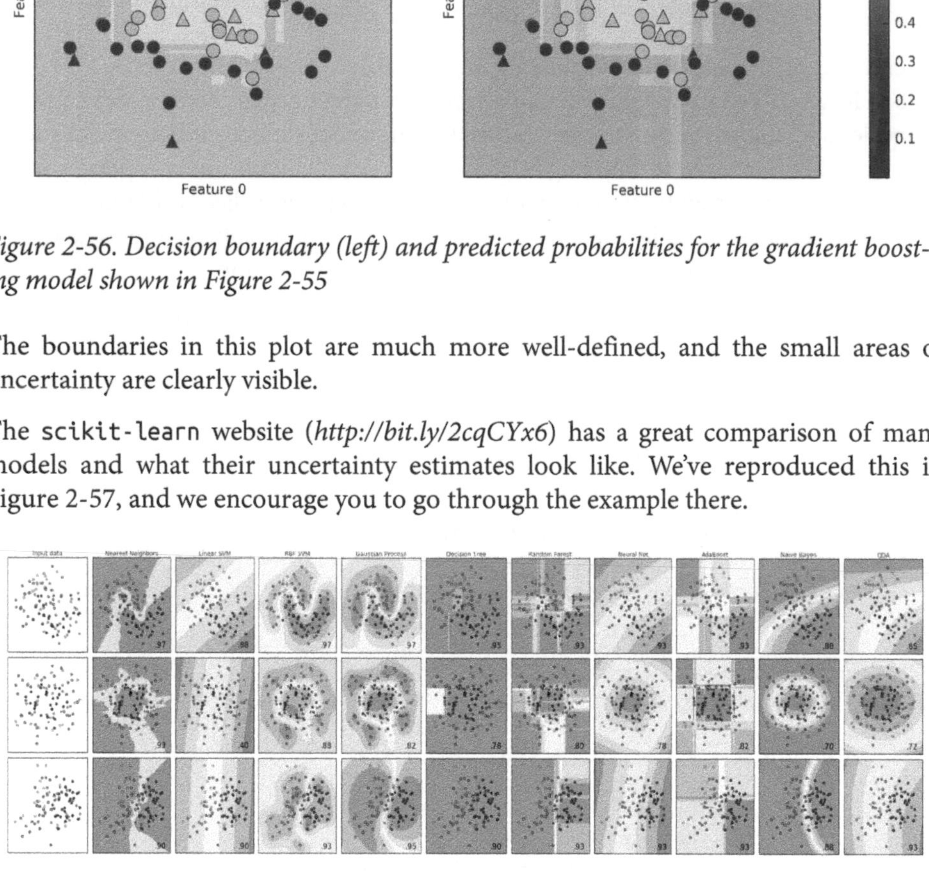

Figure 2-57. Comparison of several classifiers in scikit-learn on synthetic datasets (image courtesy http://scikit-learn.org)

2.4.3 Uncertainty in Multiclass Classification

So far, we've only talked about uncertainty estimates in binary classification. But the `decision_function` and `predict_proba` methods also work in the multiclass setting. Let's apply them on the Iris dataset, which is a three-class classification dataset:

In[113]:

```
from sklearn.datasets import load_iris

iris = load_iris()
X_train, X_test, y_train, y_test = train_test_split(
    iris.data, iris.target, random_state=42)

gbrt = GradientBoostingClassifier(learning_rate=0.01, random_state=0)
gbrt.fit(X_train, y_train)
```

In[114]:

```
print("Decision function shape:", gbrt.decision_function(X_test).shape)
# plot the first few entries of the decision function
print("Decision function:")
print(gbrt.decision_function(X_test)[:6, :])
```

Out[114]:

```
Decision function shape: (38, 3)
Decision function:
[[-0.529  1.466 -0.504]
 [ 1.512 -0.496 -0.503]
 [-0.524 -0.468  1.52 ]
 [-0.529  1.466 -0.504]
 [-0.531  1.282  0.215]
 [ 1.512 -0.496 -0.503]]
```

In the multiclass case, the `decision_function` has the shape `(n_samples, n_classes)` and each column provides a "certainty score" for each class, where a large score means that a class is more likely and a small score means the class is less likely. You can recover the predictions from these scores by finding the maximum entry for each data point:

In[115]:

```
print("Argmax of decision function:")
print(np.argmax(gbrt.decision_function(X_test), axis=1))
print("Predictions:")
print(gbrt.predict(X_test))
```

Out[115]:

```
Argmax of decision function:
[1 0 2 1 1 0 1 2 1 1 2 0 0 0 0 1 2 1 1 2 0 2 0 2 2 2 2 2 0 0 0 0 1 0 0 2 1 0]
Predictions:
[1 0 2 1 1 0 1 2 1 1 2 0 0 0 0 1 2 1 1 2 0 2 0 2 2 2 2 2 0 0 0 0 1 0 0 2 1 0]
```

The output of `predict_proba` has the same shape, `(n_samples, n_classes)`. Again, the probabilities for the possible classes for each data point sum to 1:

In[116]:

```
# show the first few entries of predict_proba
print("Predicted probabilities:")
print(gbrt.predict_proba(X_test)[:6])
# show that sums across rows are one
print("Sums:", gbrt.predict_proba(X_test)[:6].sum(axis=1))
```

Out[116]:

```
Predicted probabilities:
[[0.107 0.784 0.109]
 [0.789 0.106 0.105]
 [0.102 0.108 0.789]
 [0.107 0.784 0.109]
 [0.108 0.663 0.228]
 [0.789 0.106 0.105]]
Sums: [1. 1. 1. 1. 1. 1.]
```

We can again recover the predictions by computing the `argmax` of `predict_proba`:

In[117]:

```
print("Argmax of predicted probabilities:")
print(np.argmax(gbrt.predict_proba(X_test), axis=1))
print("Predictions:")
print(gbrt.predict(X_test))
```

Out[117]:

```
Argmax of predicted probabilities:
[1 0 2 1 1 0 1 2 1 1 2 0 0 0 0 1 2 1 1 2 0 2 0 2 2 2 2 2 0 0 0 0 1 0 0 2 1 0]
Predictions:
[1 0 2 1 1 0 1 2 1 1 2 0 0 0 0 1 2 1 1 2 0 2 0 2 2 2 2 2 0 0 0 0 1 0 0 2 1 0]
```

To summarize, `predict_proba` and `decision_function` always have shape `(n_samples, n_classes)`—apart from `decision_function` in the special binary case. In the binary case, `decision_function` only has one column, corresponding to the "positive" class `classes_[1]`. This is mostly for historical reasons.

You can recover the prediction when there are `n_classes` many columns by computing the `argmax` across columns. Be careful, though, if your classes are strings, or you use integers but they are not consecutive and starting from 0. If you want to compare results obtained with `predict` to results obtained via `decision_function` or `predict_proba`, make sure to use the `classes_` attribute of the classifier to get the actual class names:

In[118]:

```
logreg = LogisticRegression()

# represent each target by its class name in the iris dataset
named_target = iris.target_names[y_train]
logreg.fit(X_train, named_target)
print("unique classes in training data:", logreg.classes_)
print("predictions:", logreg.predict(X_test)[:10])
argmax_dec_func = np.argmax(logreg.decision_function(X_test), axis=1)
print("argmax of decision function:", argmax_dec_func[:10])
print("argmax combined with classes_:",
      logreg.classes_[argmax_dec_func][:10])
```

Out[118]:

```
unique classes in training data: ['setosa' 'versicolor' 'virginica']
predictions: ['versicolor' 'setosa' 'virginica' 'versicolor' 'versicolor'
 'setosa' 'versicolor' 'virginica' 'versicolor' 'versicolor']
argmax of decision function: [1 0 2 1 1 0 1 2 1 1]
argmax combined with classes_: ['versicolor' 'setosa' 'virginica' 'versicolor'
 'versicolor' 'setosa' 'versicolor' 'virginica' 'versicolor' 'versicolor']
```

2.5 Summary and Outlook

We started this chapter with a discussion of model complexity, then discussed *generalization*, or learning a model that is able to perform well on new, previously unseen data. This led us to the concepts of underfitting, which describes a model that cannot capture the variations present in the training data, and overfitting, which describes a model that focuses too much on the training data and is not able to generalize to new data very well.

We then discussed a wide array of machine learning models for classification and regression, what their advantages and disadvantages are, and how to control model complexity for each of them. We saw that for many of the algorithms, setting the right parameters is important for good performance. Some of the algorithms are also sensitive to how we represent the input data, and in particular to how the features are scaled. Therefore, blindly applying an algorithm to a dataset without understanding the assumptions the model makes and the meanings of the parameter settings will rarely lead to an accurate model.

This chapter contains a lot of information about the algorithms, and it is not necessary for you to remember all of these details for the following chapters. However, some knowledge of the models described here—and which to use in a specific situation—is important for successfully applying machine learning in practice. Here is a quick summary of when to use each model:

Nearest neighbors
: For small datasets, good as a baseline, easy to explain.

Linear models
: Go-to as a first algorithm to try, good for very large datasets, good for very high-dimensional data.

Naive Bayes
: Only for classification. Even faster than linear models, good for very large datasets and high-dimensional data. Often less accurate than linear models.

Decision trees
: Very fast, don't need scaling of the data, can be visualized and easily explained.

Random forests
: Nearly always perform better than a single decision tree, very robust and powerful. Don't need scaling of data. Not good for very high-dimensional sparse data.

Gradient boosted decision trees
: Often slightly more accurate than random forests. Slower to train but faster to predict than random forests, and smaller in memory. Need more parameter tuning than random forests.

Support vector machines
: Powerful for medium-sized datasets of features with similar meaning. Require scaling of data, sensitive to parameters.

Neural networks
: Can build very complex models, particularly for large datasets. Sensitive to scaling of the data and to the choice of parameters. Large models need a long time to train.

When working with a new dataset, it is in general a good idea to start with a simple model, such as a linear model or a naive Bayes or nearest neighbors classifier, and see how far you can get. After understanding more about the data, you can consider moving to an algorithm that can build more complex models, such as random forests, gradient boosted decision trees, SVMs, or neural networks.

You should now be in a position where you have some idea of how to apply, tune, and analyze the models we discussed here. In this chapter, we focused on the binary classification case, as this is usually easiest to understand. Most of the algorithms presented have classification and regression variants, however, and all of the classification algorithms support both binary and multiclass classification. Try applying any of these algorithms to the built-in datasets in `scikit-learn`, like the `boston_housing` or `diabetes` datasets for regression, or the `digits` dataset for multiclass classification. Playing around with the algorithms on different datasets will give you a better feel for how long they need to train, how easy it is to analyze the models, and how sensitive they are to the representation of the data.

While we analyzed the consequences of different parameter settings for the algorithms we investigated, building a model that actually generalizes well to new data in production is a bit trickier than that. We will see how to properly adjust parameters and how to find good parameters automatically in Chapter 6.

First, though, we will dive in more detail into unsupervised learning and preprocessing in the next chapter.

CHAPTER 3

Unsupervised Learning and Preprocessing

The second family of machine learning algorithms that we will discuss is unsupervised learning algorithms. Unsupervised learning subsumes all kinds of machine learning where there is no known output, no teacher to instruct the learning algorithm. In unsupervised learning, the learning algorithm is just shown the input data and asked to extract knowledge from this data.

3.1 Types of Unsupervised Learning

We will look into two kinds of unsupervised learning in this chapter: transformations of the dataset and clustering.

Unsupervised transformations of a dataset are algorithms that create a new representation of the data which might be easier for humans or other machine learning algorithms to understand compared to the original representation of the data. A common application of unsupervised transformations is dimensionality reduction, which takes a high-dimensional representation of the data, consisting of many features, and finds a new way to represent this data that summarizes the essential characteristics with fewer features. A common application for dimensionality reduction is reduction to two dimensions for visualization purposes.

Another application for unsupervised transformations is finding the parts or components that "make up" the data. An example of this is topic extraction on collections of text documents. Here, the task is to find the unknown topics that are talked about in each document, and to learn what topics appear in each document. This can be useful for tracking the discussion of themes like elections, gun control, or pop stars on social media.

Clustering algorithms, on the other hand, partition data into distinct groups of similar items. Consider the example of uploading photos to a social media site. To allow you to organize your pictures, the site might want to group together pictures that show the same person. However, the site doesn't know which pictures show whom, and it doesn't know how many different people appear in your photo collection. A sensible approach would be to extract all the faces and divide them into groups of faces that look similar. Hopefully, these correspond to the same person, and the images can be grouped together for you.

3.2 Challenges in Unsupervised Learning

A major challenge in unsupervised learning is evaluating whether the algorithm learned something useful. Unsupervised learning algorithms are usually applied to data that does not contain any label information, so we don't know what the right output should be. Therefore, it is very hard to say whether a model "did well." For example, our hypothetical clustering algorithm could have grouped together all the pictures that show faces in profile and all the full-face pictures. This would certainly be a possible way to divide a collection of pictures of people's faces, but it's not the one we were looking for. However, there is no way for us to "tell" the algorithm what we are looking for, and often the only way to evaluate the result of an unsupervised algorithm is to inspect it manually.

As a consequence, unsupervised algorithms are used often in an exploratory setting, when a data scientist wants to understand the data better, rather than as part of a larger automatic system. Another common application for unsupervised algorithms is as a preprocessing step for supervised algorithms. Learning a new representation of the data can sometimes improve the accuracy of supervised algorithms, or can lead to reduced memory and time consumption.

Before we start with "real" unsupervised algorithms, we will briefly discuss some simple preprocessing methods that often come in handy. Even though preprocessing and scaling are often used in tandem with supervised learning algorithms, scaling methods don't make use of the supervised information, making them unsupervised.

3.3 Preprocessing and Scaling

In the previous chapter we saw that some algorithms, like neural networks and SVMs, are very sensitive to the scaling of the data. Therefore, a common practice is to adjust the features so that the data representation is more suitable for these algorithms. Often, this is a simple per-feature rescaling and shift of the data. The following code (Figure 3-1) shows a simple example:

In[1]:

```
mglearn.plots.plot_scaling()
```

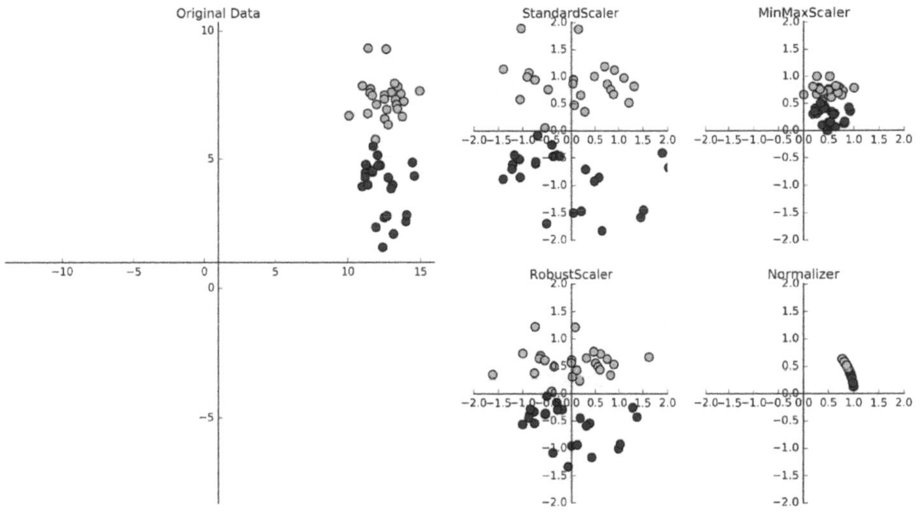

Figure 3-1. Different ways to rescale and preprocess a dataset

3.3.1 Different Kinds of Preprocessing

The first plot in Figure 3-1 shows a synthetic two-class classification dataset with two features. The first feature (the x-axis value) is between 10 and 15. The second feature (the y-axis value) is between around 1 and 9.

The following four plots show four different ways to transform the data that yield more standard ranges. The `StandardScaler` in `scikit-learn` ensures that for each feature the mean is 0 and the variance is 1, bringing all features to the same magnitude. However, this scaling does not ensure any particular minimum and maximum values for the features. The `RobustScaler` works similarly to the `StandardScaler` in that it ensures statistical properties for each feature that guarantee that they are on the same scale. However, the `RobustScaler` uses the median and quartiles,[1] instead of mean and variance. This makes the `RobustScaler` ignore data points that are very different from the rest (like measurement errors). These odd data points are also called *outliers*, and can lead to trouble for other scaling techniques.

The `MinMaxScaler`, on the other hand, shifts the data such that all features are exactly between 0 and 1. For the two-dimensional dataset this means all of the data is con-

1 The median of a set of numbers is the number *x* such that half of the numbers are smaller than *x* and half of the numbers are larger than *x*. The lower quartile is the number *x* such that one-fourth of the numbers are smaller than *x*, and the upper quartile is the number *x* such that one-fourth of the numbers are larger than *x*.

tained within the rectangle created by the x-axis between 0 and 1 and the y-axis between 0 and 1.

Finally, the `Normalizer` does a very different kind of rescaling. It scales each data point such that the feature vector has a Euclidean length of 1. In other words, it projects a data point on the circle (or sphere, in the case of higher dimensions) with a radius of 1. This means every data point is scaled by a different number (by the inverse of its length). This normalization is often used when only the direction (or angle) of the data matters, not the length of the feature vector.

3.3.2 Applying Data Transformations

Now that we've seen what the different kinds of transformations do, let's apply them using `scikit-learn`. We will use the `cancer` dataset that we saw in Chapter 2. Preprocessing methods like the scalers are usually applied before applying a supervised machine learning algorithm. As an example, say we want to apply the kernel SVM (`SVC`) to the `cancer` dataset, and use `MinMaxScaler` for preprocessing the data. We start by loading our dataset and splitting it into a training set and a test set (we need separate training and test sets to evaluate the supervised model we will build after the preprocessing):

In[2]:

```
from sklearn.datasets import load_breast_cancer
from sklearn.model_selection import train_test_split
cancer = load_breast_cancer()

X_train, X_test, y_train, y_test = train_test_split(cancer.data, cancer.target,
                                                    random_state=1)
print(X_train.shape)
print(X_test.shape)
```

Out[2]:

```
(426, 30)
(143, 30)
```

As a reminder, the dataset contains 569 data points, each represented by 30 measurements. We split the dataset into 426 samples for the training set and 143 samples for the test set.

As with the supervised models we built earlier, we first import the class that implements the preprocessing, and then instantiate it:

In[3]:

```
from sklearn.preprocessing import MinMaxScaler

scaler = MinMaxScaler()
```

We then fit the scaler using the `fit` method, applied to the training data. For the `MinMaxScaler`, the `fit` method computes the minimum and maximum value of each feature on the training set. In contrast to the classifiers and regressors of Chapter 2, the scaler is only provided with the data (`X_train`) when `fit` is called, and `y_train` is not used:

In[4]:

```
scaler.fit(X_train)
```

Out[4]:

```
MinMaxScaler(copy=True, feature_range=(0, 1))
```

To apply the transformation that we just learned—that is, to actually *scale* the training data—we use the `transform` method of the scaler. The `transform` method is used in `scikit-learn` whenever a model returns a new representation of the data:

In[5]:

```
# transform data
X_train_scaled = scaler.transform(X_train)
# print dataset properties before and after scaling
print("transformed shape: {}".format(X_train_scaled.shape))
print("per-feature minimum before scaling:\n {}".format(X_train.min(axis=0)))
print("per-feature maximum before scaling:\n {}".format(X_train.max(axis=0)))
print("per-feature minimum after scaling:\n {}".format(
    X_train_scaled.min(axis=0)))
print("per-feature maximum after scaling:\n {}".format(
    X_train_scaled.max(axis=0)))
```

Out[5]:

```
transformed shape: (426, 30)
per-feature minimum before scaling:
 [   6.981    9.71    43.79   143.5      0.053    0.019    0.       0.       0.106
   0.05     0.115    0.36     0.757    6.802    0.002    0.002    0.       0.
   0.01     0.001    7.93    12.02    50.41   185.2      0.071    0.027    0.
   0.       0.157    0.055]
per-feature maximum before scaling:
 [  28.11     39.28    188.5    2501.       0.163    0.287    0.427    0.201
    0.304    0.096    2.873    4.885   21.98    542.2      0.031    0.135
    0.396    0.053    0.061    0.03    36.04     49.54   251.2    4254.
    0.223    0.938    1.17     0.291    0.577    0.149]
per-feature minimum after scaling:
 [0. 0. 0. 0. 0. 0. 0. 0. 0. 0. 0. 0. 0. 0. 0. 0. 0. 0. 0. 0. 0. 0. 0. 0.
 0. 0. 0. 0. 0. 0.]
per-feature maximum after scaling:
 [1. 1. 1. 1. 1. 1. 1. 1. 1. 1. 1. 1. 1. 1. 1. 1. 1. 1. 1. 1. 1. 1. 1. 1.
 1. 1. 1. 1. 1. 1.]
```

The transformed data has the same shape as the original data—the features are simply shifted and scaled. You can see that all of the features are now between 0 and 1, as desired.

To apply the SVM to the scaled data, we also need to transform the test set. This is again done by calling the `transform` method, this time on `X_test`:

In[6]:

```
# transform test data
X_test_scaled = scaler.transform(X_test)
# print test data properties after scaling
print("per-feature minimum after scaling:\n{}".format(X_test_scaled.min(axis=0)))
print("per-feature maximum after scaling:\n{}".format(X_test_scaled.max(axis=0)))
```

Out[6]:

```
per-feature minimum after scaling:
[ 0.034  0.023  0.031  0.011  0.141  0.044  0.     0.     0.154 -0.006
 -0.001  0.006  0.004  0.001  0.039  0.011  0.     0.    -0.032  0.007
  0.027  0.058  0.02   0.009  0.109  0.026  0.     0.    -0.    -0.002]
per-feature maximum after scaling:
[0.958 0.815 0.956 0.894 0.811 1.22  0.88  0.933 0.932 1.037 0.427 0.498
 0.441 0.284 0.487 0.739 0.767 0.629 1.337 0.391 0.896 0.793 0.849 0.745
 0.915 1.132 1.07  0.924 1.205 1.631]
```

Maybe somewhat surprisingly, you can see that for the test set, after scaling, the minimum and maximum are not 0 and 1. Some of the features are even outside the 0–1 range! The explanation is that the `MinMaxScaler` (and all the other scalers) always applies exactly the same transformation to the training and the test set. This means the `transform` method always subtracts the training set minimum and divides by the training set range, which might be different from the minimum and range for the test set.

3.3.3 Scaling Training and Test Data the Same Way

It is important to apply exactly the same transformation to the training set and the test set for the supervised model to work on the test set. The following example (Figure 3-2) illustrates what would happen if we were to use the minimum and range of the test set instead:

In[7]:

```
from sklearn.datasets import make_blobs
# make synthetic data
X, _ = make_blobs(n_samples=50, centers=5, random_state=4, cluster_std=2)
# split it into training and test sets
X_train, X_test = train_test_split(X, random_state=5, test_size=.1)

# plot the training and test sets
fig, axes = plt.subplots(1, 3, figsize=(13, 4))
```

```
axes[0].scatter(X_train[:, 0], X_train[:, 1],
                c=mglearn.cm2(0), label="Training set", s=60)
axes[0].scatter(X_test[:, 0], X_test[:, 1], marker='^',
                c=mglearn.cm2(1), label="Test set", s=60)
axes[0].legend(loc='upper left')
axes[0].set_title("Original Data")

# scale the data using MinMaxScaler
scaler = MinMaxScaler()
scaler.fit(X_train)
X_train_scaled = scaler.transform(X_train)
X_test_scaled = scaler.transform(X_test)

# visualize the properly scaled data
axes[1].scatter(X_train_scaled[:, 0], X_train_scaled[:, 1],
                c=mglearn.cm2(0), label="Training set", s=60)
axes[1].scatter(X_test_scaled[:, 0], X_test_scaled[:, 1], marker='^',
                c=mglearn.cm2(1), label="Test set", s=60)
axes[1].set_title("Scaled Data")

# rescale the test set separately
# so test set min is 0 and test set max is 1
# DO NOT DO THIS! For illustration purposes only.
test_scaler = MinMaxScaler()
test_scaler.fit(X_test)
X_test_scaled_badly = test_scaler.transform(X_test)

# visualize wrongly scaled data
axes[2].scatter(X_train_scaled[:, 0], X_train_scaled[:, 1],
                c=mglearn.cm2(0), label="training set", s=60)
axes[2].scatter(X_test_scaled_badly[:, 0], X_test_scaled_badly[:, 1],
                marker='^', c=mglearn.cm2(1), label="test set", s=60)
axes[2].set_title("Improperly Scaled Data")

for ax in axes:
    ax.set_xlabel("Feature 0")
    ax.set_ylabel("Feature 1")
fig.tight_layout()
```

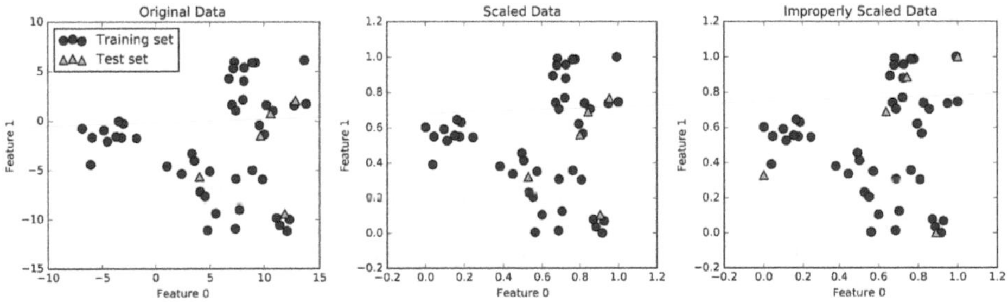

Figure 3-2. Effect of scaling training and test data shown on the left together (center) and separately (right)

The first panel is an unscaled two-dimensional dataset, with the training set shown as circles and the test set shown as triangles. The second panel is the same data, but scaled using the MinMaxScaler. Here, we called fit on the training set, and then called transform on the training and test sets. You can see that the dataset in the second panel looks identical to the first; only the ticks on the axes have changed. Now all the features are between 0 and 1. You can also see that the minimum and maximum feature values for the test data (the triangles) are not 0 and 1.

The third panel shows what would happen if we scaled the training set and test set separately. In this case, the minimum and maximum feature values for both the training and the test set are 0 and 1. But now the dataset looks different. The test points moved incongruously to the training set, as they were scaled differently. We changed the arrangement of the data in an arbitrary way. Clearly this is not what we want to do.

As another way to think about this, imagine your test set is a single point. There is no way to scale a single point correctly, to fulfill the minimum and maximum requirements of the MinMaxScaler. But the size of your test set should not change your processing.

Shortcuts and Efficient Alternatives

Often, you want to fit a model on some dataset, and then transform it. This is a very common task, which can often be computed more efficiently than by simply calling fit and then transform. For this use case, all models that have a transform method also have a fit_transform method. Here is an example using StandardScaler:

In[8]:

```
from sklearn.preprocessing import StandardScaler
scaler = StandardScaler()
# calling fit and transform in sequence (using method chaining)
X_scaled = scaler.fit(X_train).transform(X_train)
# same result, but more efficient computation
X_scaled_d = scaler.fit_transform(X_train)
```

While fit_transform is not necessarily more efficient for all models, it is still good practice to use this method when trying to transform the training set.

3.3.4 The Effect of Preprocessing on Supervised Learning

Now let's go back to the cancer dataset and see the effect of using the MinMaxScaler on learning the SVC (this is a different way of doing the same scaling we did in Chapter 2). First, let's fit the SVC on the original data again for comparison:

In[9]:

```
from sklearn.svm import SVC

X_train, X_test, y_train, y_test = train_test_split(cancer.data, cancer.target,
                                                    random_state=0)

svm = SVC(C=100)
svm.fit(X_train, y_train)
print("Test set accuracy: {:.2f}".format(svm.score(X_test, y_test)))
```

Out[9]:

```
Test set accuracy: 0.63
```

Now, let's scale the data using `MinMaxScaler` before fitting the `SVC`:

In[10]:

```
# preprocessing using 0-1 scaling
scaler = MinMaxScaler()
scaler.fit(X_train)
X_train_scaled = scaler.transform(X_train)
X_test_scaled = scaler.transform(X_test)

# learning an SVM on the scaled training data
svm.fit(X_train_scaled, y_train)

# scoring on the scaled test set
print("Scaled test set accuracy: {:.2f}".format(
    svm.score(X_test_scaled, y_test)))
```

Out[10]:

```
Scaled test set accuracy: 0.97
```

As we saw before, the effect of scaling the data is quite significant. Even though scaling the data doesn't involve any complicated math, it is good practice to use the scaling mechanisms provided by `scikit-learn` instead of reimplementing them yourself, as it's easy to make mistakes even in these simple computations.

You can also easily replace one preprocessing algorithm with another by changing the class you use, as all of the preprocessing classes have the same interface, consisting of the `fit` and `transform` methods:

In[11]:

```
# preprocessing using zero mean and unit variance scaling
from sklearn.preprocessing import StandardScaler
scaler = StandardScaler()
scaler.fit(X_train)
X_train_scaled = scaler.transform(X_train)
X_test_scaled = scaler.transform(X_test)
```

```
# learning an SVM on the scaled training data
svm.fit(X_train_scaled, y_train)

# scoring on the scaled test set
print("SVM test accuracy: {:.2f}".format(svm.score(X_test_scaled, y_test)))
```

Out[11]:

```
SVM test accuracy: 0.96
```

Now that we've seen how simple data transformations for preprocessing work, let's move on to more interesting transformations using unsupervised learning.

3.4 Dimensionality Reduction, Feature Extraction, and Manifold Learning

As we discussed earlier, transforming data using unsupervised learning can have many motivations. The most common motivations are visualization, compressing the data, and finding a representation that is more informative for further processing.

One of the simplest and most widely used algorithms for all of these is principal component analysis. We'll also look at two other algorithms: non-negative matrix factorization (NMF), which is commonly used for feature extraction, and t-SNE, which is commonly used for visualization using two-dimensional scatter plots.

3.4.1 Principal Component Analysis (PCA)

Principal component analysis is a method that rotates the dataset in a way such that the rotated features are statistically uncorrelated. This rotation is often followed by selecting only a subset of the new features, according to how important they are for explaining the data. The following example (Figure 3-3) illustrates the effect of PCA on a synthetic two-dimensional dataset:

In[12]:

```
mglearn.plots.plot_pca_illustration()
```

The first plot (top left) shows the original data points, colored to distinguish among them. The algorithm proceeds by first finding the direction of maximum variance, labeled "Component 1." This is the direction (or vector) in the data that contains most of the information, or in other words, the direction along which the features are most correlated with each other. Then, the algorithm finds the direction that contains the most information while being orthogonal (at a right angle) to the first direction. In two dimensions, there is only one possible orientation that is at a right angle, but in higher-dimensional spaces there would be (infinitely) many orthogonal directions. Although the two components are drawn as arrows, it doesn't really matter where the head and the tail are; we could have drawn the first component from the center up to the top left instead of down to the bottom right. The directions found using this process are called *principal components*, as they are the main directions of variance in the data. In general, there are as many principal components as original features.

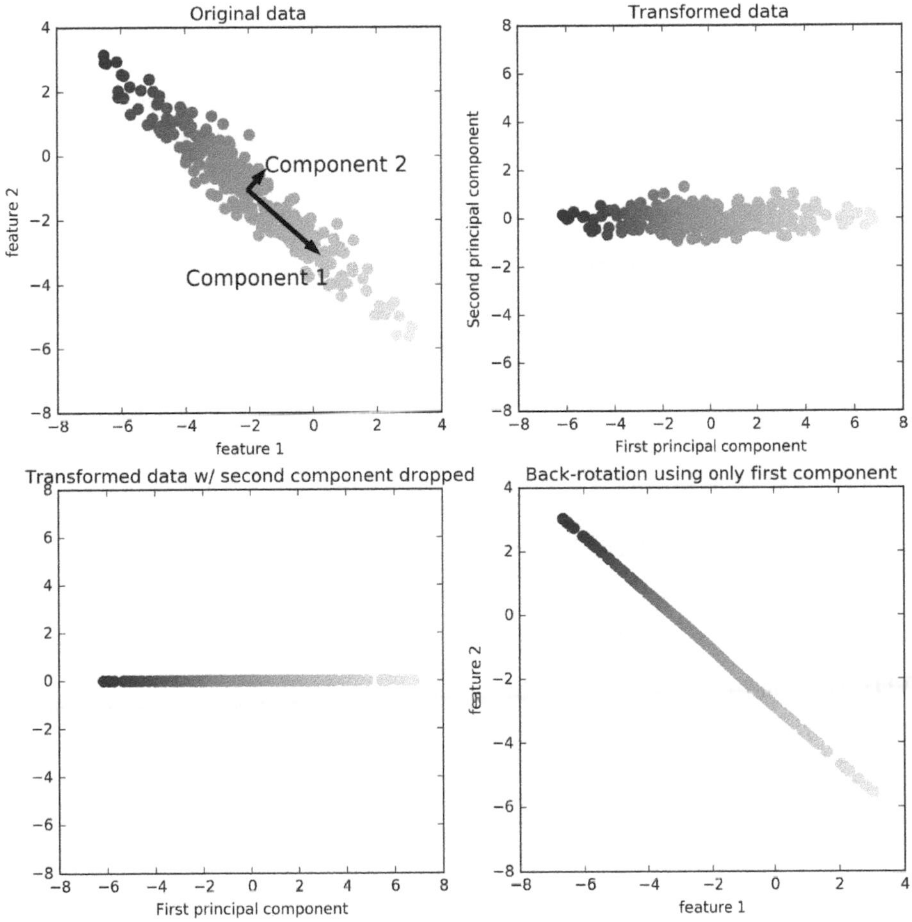

Figure 3-3. Transformation of data with PCA

The second plot (top right) shows the same data, but now rotated so that the first principal component aligns with the x-axis and the second principal component aligns with the y-axis. Before the rotation, the mean was subtracted from the data, so that the transformed data is centered around zero. In the rotated representation found by PCA, the two axes are uncorrelated, meaning that the correlation matrix of the data in this representation is zero except for the diagonal.

We can use PCA for dimensionality reduction by retaining only some of the principal components. In this example, we might keep only the first principal component, as shown in the third panel in Figure 3-3 (bottom left). This reduces the data from a two-dimensional dataset to a one-dimensional dataset. Note, however, that instead of keeping only one of the original features, we found the most interesting direction (top left to bottom right in the first panel) and kept this direction, the first principal component.

Finally, we can undo the rotation and add the mean back to the data. This will result in the data shown in the last panel in Figure 3-3. These points are in the original feature space, but we kept only the information contained in the first principal component. This transformation is sometimes used to remove noise effects from the data or visualize what part of the information is retained using the principal components.

Applying PCA to the cancer dataset for visualization

One of the most common applications of PCA is visualizing high-dimensional datasets. As we saw in Chapter 1, it is hard to create scatter plots of data that has more than two features. For the Iris dataset, we were able to create a pair plot (Figure 1-3 in Chapter 1) that gave us a partial picture of the data by showing us all the possible combinations of two features. But if we want to look at the Breast Cancer dataset, even using a pair plot is tricky. The breast cancer dataset has 30 features, which would result in 30 * 29 / 2 = 435 scatter plots (for just the upper triangle)! We'd never be able to look at all these plots in detail, let alone try to understand them.

There is an even simpler visualization we can use, though—computing histograms of each of the features for the two classes, benign and malignant cancer (Figure 3-4):

In[13]:

```
fig, axes = plt.subplots(15, 2, figsize=(10, 20))
malignant = cancer.data[cancer.target == 0]
benign = cancer.data[cancer.target == 1]

ax = axes.ravel()

for i in range(30):
    _, bins = np.histogram(cancer.data[:, i], bins=50)
    ax[i].hist(malignant[:, i], bins=bins, color=mglearn.cm3(0), alpha=.5)
    ax[i].hist(benign[:, i], bins=bins, color=mglearn.cm3(2), alpha=.5)
    ax[i].set_title(cancer.feature_names[i])
    ax[i].set_yticks(())
ax[0].set_xlabel("Feature magnitude")
ax[0].set_ylabel("Frequency")
ax[0].legend(["malignant", "benign"], loc="best")
fig.tight_layout()
```

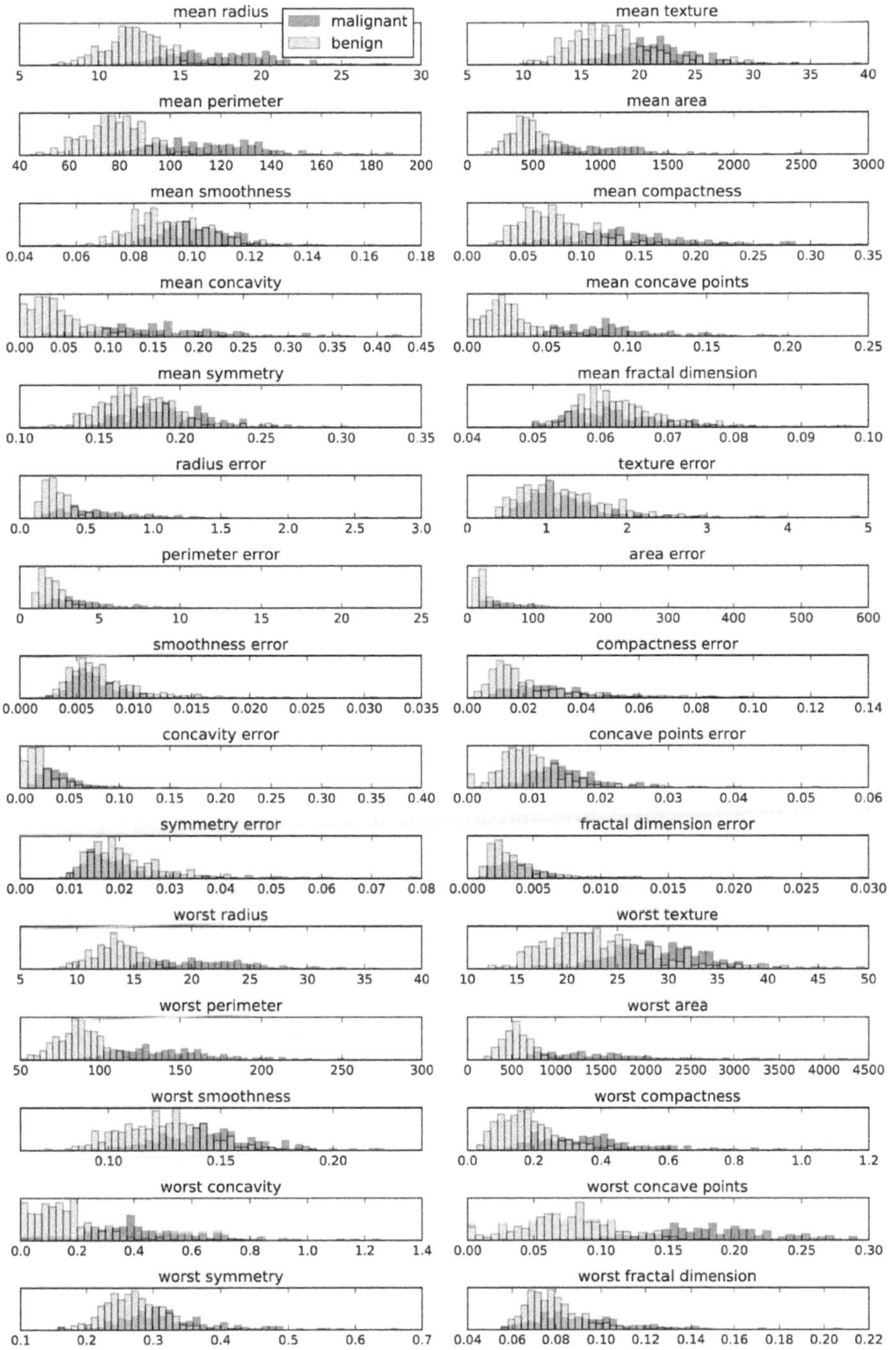

Figure 3-4. Per-class feature histograms on the Breast Cancer dataset

Here we create a histogram for each of the features, counting how often a data point appears with a feature in a certain range (called a *bin*). Each plot overlays two histograms, one for all of the points in the benign class and one for all the points in the malignant class. This gives us some idea of how each feature is distributed across the two classes, and allows us to venture a guess as to which features are better at distinguishing malignant and benign samples. For example, the feature "smoothness error" seems quite uninformative, because the two histograms mostly overlap, while the feature "worst concave points" seems quite informative, because the histograms are quite disjoint.

However, this plot doesn't show us anything about the interactions between variables and how these relate to the classes. Using PCA, we can capture the main interactions and get a slightly more complete picture. We can find the first two principal components, and visualize the data in this new two-dimensional space with a single scatter plot.

Before we apply PCA, we scale our data so that each feature has unit variance using `StandardScaler`:

In[14]:

```
from sklearn.datasets import load_breast_cancer
cancer = load_breast_cancer()

scaler = StandardScaler()
scaler.fit(cancer.data)
X_scaled = scaler.transform(cancer.data)
```

Learning the PCA transformation and applying it is as simple as applying a preprocessing transformation. We instantiate the PCA object, find the principal components by calling the `fit` method, and then apply the rotation and dimensionality reduction by calling `transform`. By default, `PCA` only rotates (and shifts) the data, but keeps all principal components. To reduce the dimensionality of the data, we need to specify how many components we want to keep when creating the `PCA` object:

In[15]:

```
from sklearn.decomposition import PCA
# keep the first two principal components of the data
pca = PCA(n_components=2)
# fit PCA model to breast cancer data
pca.fit(X_scaled)

# transform data onto the first two principal components
X_pca = pca.transform(X_scaled)
print("Original shape: {}".format(str(X_scaled.shape)))
print("Reduced shape: {}".format(str(X_pca.shape)))
```

Out[15]:

```
Original shape: (569, 30)
Reduced shape: (569, 2)
```

We can now plot the first two principal components (Figure 3-5):

In[16]:

```
# plot first vs. second principal component, colored by class
plt.figure(figsize=(8, 8))
mglearn.discrete_scatter(X_pca[:, 0], X_pca[:, 1], cancer.target)
plt.legend(cancer.target_names, loc="best")
plt.gca().set_aspect("equal")
plt.xlabel("First principal component")
plt.ylabel("Second principal component")
```

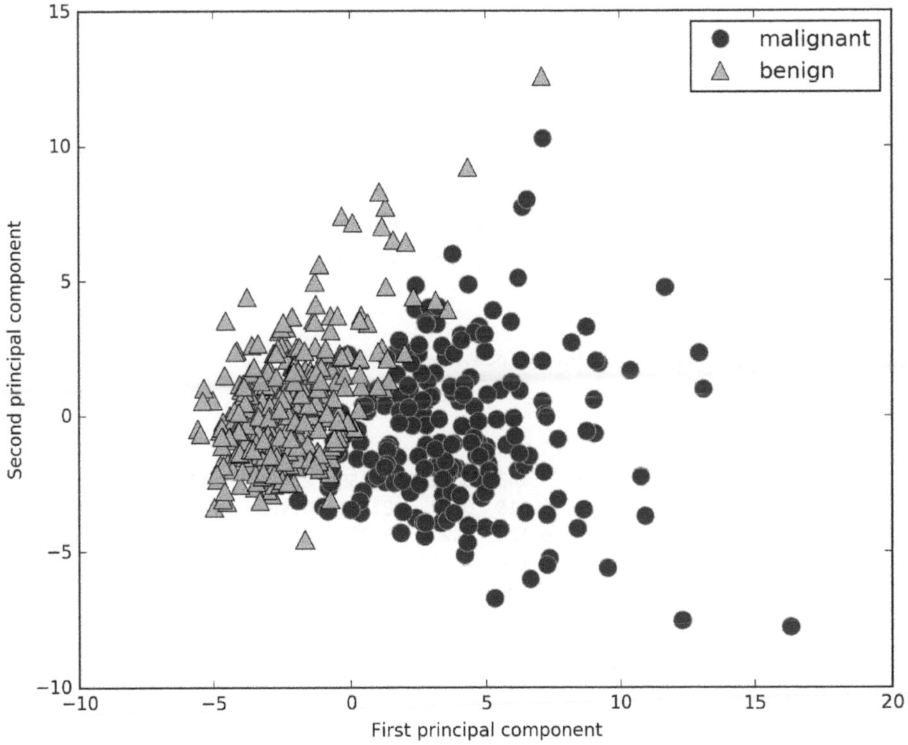

Figure 3-5. Two-dimensional scatter plot of the Breast Cancer dataset using the first two principal components

It is important to note that PCA is an unsupervised method, and does not use any class information when finding the rotation. It simply looks at the correlations in the data. For the scatter plot shown here, we plotted the first principal component against the second principal component, and then used the class information to color the points. You can see that the two classes separate quite well in this two-dimensional space. This leads us to believe that even a linear classifier (that would learn a line in this space) could do a reasonably good job at distinguishing the two classes. We can also see that the malignant points are more spread out than the benign points—something that we could already see a bit from the histograms in Figure 3-4.

A downside of PCA is that the two axes in the plot are often not very easy to interpret. The principal components correspond to directions in the original data, so they are combinations of the original features. However, these combinations are usually very complex, as we'll see shortly. The principal components themselves are stored in the `components_` attribute of the PCA object during fitting:

In[17]:

```
print("PCA component shape: {}".format(pca.components_.shape))
```

Out[17]:

```
PCA component shape: (2, 30)
```

Each row in `components_` corresponds to one principal component, and they are sorted by their importance (the first principal component comes first, etc.). The columns correspond to the original features attribute of the PCA in this example, "mean radius," "mean texture," and so on. Let's have a look at the content of `components_`:

In[18]:

```
print("PCA components:\n{}".format(pca.components_))
```

Out[18]:

```
PCA components:
[[ 0.219  0.104  0.228  0.221  0.143  0.239  0.258  0.261  0.138  0.064
   0.206  0.017  0.211  0.203  0.015  0.17   0.154  0.183  0.042  0.103
   0.228  0.104  0.237  0.225  0.128  0.21   0.229  0.251  0.123  0.132]
 [-0.234 -0.06  -0.215 -0.231  0.186  0.152  0.06  -0.035  0.19   0.367
  -0.106  0.09  -0.089 -0.152  0.204  0.233  0.197  0.13   0.184  0.28
  -0.22  -0.045 -0.2   -0.219  0.172  0.144  0.098 -0.008  0.142  0.275]]
```

We can also visualize the coefficients using a heat map (Figure 3-6), which might be easier to understand:

In[19]:

```
plt.matshow(pca.components_, cmap='viridis')
plt.yticks([0, 1], ["First component", "Second component"])
plt.colorbar()
plt.xticks(range(len(cancer.feature_names)),
           cancer.feature_names, rotation=60, ha='left')
plt.xlabel("Feature")
plt.ylabel("Principal components")
```

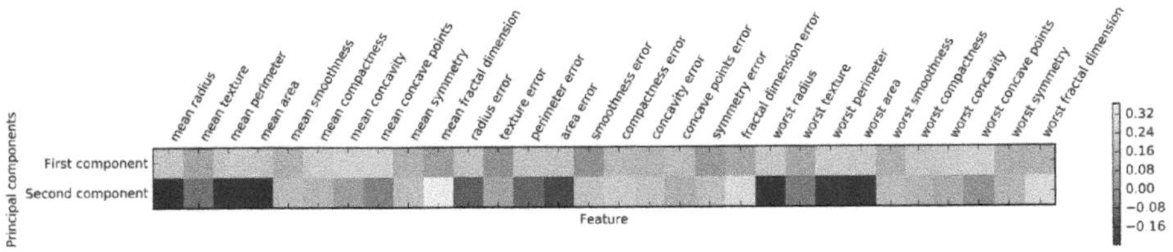

Figure 3-6. Heat map of the first two principal components on the Breast Cancer dataset

You can see that in the first component, all features have the same sign (it's positive, but as we mentioned earlier, it doesn't matter which direction the arrow points in). That means that there is a general correlation between all features. As one measurement is high, the others are likely to be high as well. The second component has mixed signs, and both of the components involve all of the 30 features. This mixing of all features is what makes explaining the axes in Figure 3-6 so tricky.

Eigenfaces for feature extraction

Another application of PCA that we mentioned earlier is feature extraction. The idea behind feature extraction is that it is possible to find a representation of your data that is better suited to analysis than the raw representation you were given. A great example of an application where feature extraction is helpful is with images. Images are made up of pixels, usually stored as red, green, and blue (RGB) intensities. Objects in images are usually made up of thousands of pixels, and only together are they meaningful.

We will give a very simple application of feature extraction on images using PCA, by working with face images from the Labeled Faces in the Wild dataset. This dataset contains face images of celebrities downloaded from the Internet, and it includes faces of politicians, singers, actors, and athletes from the early 2000s. We use grayscale versions of these images, and scale them down for faster processing. You can see some of the images in Figure 3-7:

In[20]:

```
from sklearn.datasets import fetch_lfw_people
people = fetch_lfw_people(min_faces_per_person=20, resize=0.7)
image_shape = people.images[0].shape

fig, axes = plt.subplots(2, 5, figsize=(15, 8),
                         subplot_kw={'xticks': (), 'yticks': ()})
for target, image, ax in zip(people.target, people.images, axes.ravel()):
    ax.imshow(image)
    ax.set_title(people.target_names[target])
```

Figure 3-7. Some images from the Labeled Faces in the Wild dataset

There are 3,023 images, each 87×65 pixels large, belonging to 62 different people:

In[21]:

```
print("people.images.shape: {}".format(people.images.shape))
print("Number of classes: {}".format(len(people.target_names)))
```

Out[21]:

```
people.images.shape: (3023, 87, 65)
Number of classes: 62
```

The dataset is a bit skewed, however, containing a lot of images of George W. Bush and Colin Powell, as you can see here:

In[22]:

```
# count how often each target appears
counts = np.bincount(people.target)
# print counts next to target names
for i, (count, name) in enumerate(zip(counts, people.target_names)):
    print("{0:25} {1:3}".format(name, count), end='   ')
    if (i + 1) % 3 == 0:
        print()
```

Out[22]:

```
Alejandro Toledo           39   Alvaro Uribe               35
Amelie Mauresmo            21   Andre Agassi               36
Angelina Jolie             20   Arnold Schwarzenegger      42
Atal Bihari Vajpayee       24   Bill Clinton               29
Carlos Menem               21   Colin Powell              236
David Beckham              31   Donald Rumsfeld           121
George W Bush             530   George Robertson           22
Gerhard Schroeder         109   Gloria Macapagal Arroyo    44
Gray Davis                 26   Guillermo Coria            30
Hamid Karzai               22   Hans Blix                  39
Hugo Chavez                71   Igor Ivanov                20
[...]                           [...]
Laura Bush                 41   Lindsay Davenport          22
Lleyton Hewitt             41   Luiz Inacio Lula da Silva  48
Mahmoud Abbas              29   Megawati Sukarnoputri      33
Michael Bloomberg          20   Naomi Watts                22
Nestor Kirchner            37   Paul Bremer                20
Pete Sampras               22   Recep Tayyip Erdogan       30
Ricardo Lagos              27   Roh Moo-hyun               32
Rudolph Giuliani           26   Saddam Hussein             23
Serena Williams            52   Silvio Berlusconi          33
Tiger Woods                23   Tom Daschle                25
Tom Ridge                  33   Tony Blair                144
Vicente Fox                32   Vladimir Putin             49
Winona Ryder               24
```

To make the data less skewed, we will only take up to 50 images of each person (otherwise, the feature extraction would be overwhelmed by the likelihood of George W. Bush):

In[23]:

```
mask = np.zeros(people.target.shape, dtype=np.bool)
for target in np.unique(people.target):
    mask[np.where(people.target == target)[0][:50]] = 1

X_people = people.data[mask]
y_people = people.target[mask]

# scale the grayscale values to be between 0 and 1
# instead of 0 and 255 for better numeric stability
X_people = X_people / 255.
```

A common task in face recognition is to ask if a previously unseen face belongs to a known person from a database. This has applications in photo collection, social media, and security applications. One way to solve this problem would be to build a classifier where each person is a separate class. However, there are usually many different people in face databases, and very few images of the same person (i.e., very few training examples per class). That makes it hard to train most classifiers. Additionally, you often want to be able to add new people easily, without needing to retrain a large model.

A simple solution is to use a one-nearest-neighbor classifier that looks for the most similar face image to the face you are classifying. This classifier could in principle work with only a single training example per class. Let's take a look at how well `KNeighborsClassifier` does here:

In[24]:

```
from sklearn.neighbors import KNeighborsClassifier
# split the data into training and test sets
X_train, X_test, y_train, y_test = train_test_split(
    X_people, y_people, stratify=y_people, random_state=0)
# build a KNeighborsClassifier using one neighbor
knn = KNeighborsClassifier(n_neighbors=1)
knn.fit(X_train, y_train)
print("Test set score of 1-nn: {:.2f}".format(knn.score(X_test, y_test)))
```

Out[24]:

```
Test set score of 1-nn: 0.27
```

We obtain an accuracy of 26.6%, which is not actually that bad for a 62-class classification problem (random guessing would give you around 1/62 = 1.6% accuracy), but is also not great. We only correctly identify a person every fourth time.

This is where PCA comes in. Computing distances in the original pixel space is quite a bad way to measure similarity between faces. When using a pixel representation to compare two images, we compare the grayscale value of each individual pixel to the value of the pixel in the corresponding position in the other image. This representation is quite different from how humans would interpret the image of a face, and it is hard to capture the facial features using this raw representation. For example, using pixel distances means that shifting a face by one pixel to the right corresponds to a drastic change, with a completely different representation. We hope that using distances along principal components can improve our accuracy. Here, we enable the *whitening* option of PCA, which rescales the principal components to have the same scale. This is the same as using `StandardScaler` after the transformation. Reusing the data from Figure 3-3 again, whitening corresponds to not only rotating the data, but also rescaling it so that the center panel is a circle instead of an ellipse (see Figure 3-8):

In[25]:

```
mglearn.plots.plot_pca_whitening()
```

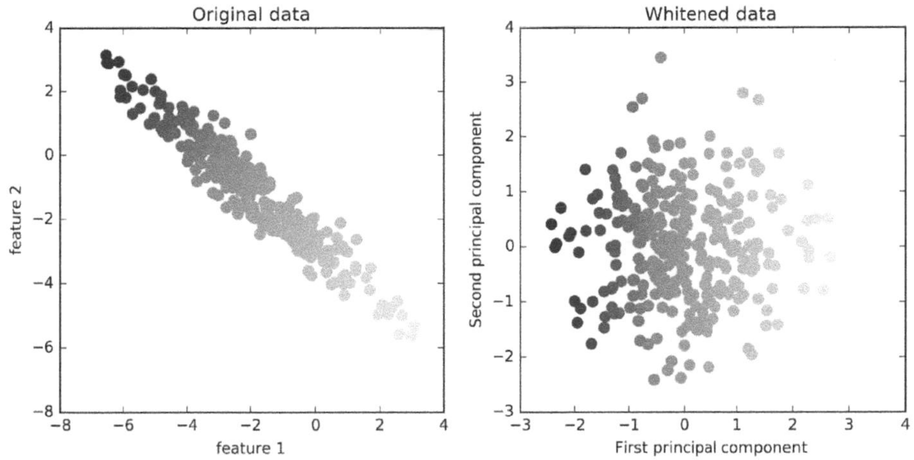

Figure 3-8. Transformation of data with PCA using whitening

We fit the PCA object to the training data and extract the first 100 principal components. Then we transform the training and test data:

In[26]:

```
pca = PCA(n_components=100, whiten=True, random_state=0).fit(X_train)
X_train_pca = pca.transform(X_train)
X_test_pca = pca.transform(X_test)

print("X_train_pca.shape: {}".format(X_train_pca.shape))
```

Out[26]:

```
X_train_pca.shape: (1547, 100)
```

The new data has 100 features, the first 100 principal components. Now, we can use the new representation to classify our images using a one-nearest-neighbors classifier:

In[27]:

```
knn = KNeighborsClassifier(n_neighbors=1)
knn.fit(X_train_pca, y_train)
print("Test set accuracy: {:.2f}".format(knn.score(X_test_pca, y_test)))
```

Out[27]:

```
Test set accuracy: 0.36
```

Our accuracy improved quite significantly, from 26.6% to 35.7%, confirming our intuition that the principal components might provide a better representation of the data.

For image data, we can also easily visualize the principal components that are found. Remember that components correspond to directions in the input space. The input space here is 87×65-pixel grayscale images, so directions within this space are also 87×65-pixel grayscale images.

Let's look at the first couple of principal components (Figure 3-9):

In[28]:

```
print("pca.components_.shape: {}".format(pca.components_.shape))
```

Out[28]:

```
pca.components_.shape: (100, 5655)
```

In[29]:

```
fig, axes = plt.subplots(3, 5, figsize=(15, 12),
                         subplot_kw={'xticks': (), 'yticks': ()})
for i, (component, ax) in enumerate(zip(pca.components_, axes.ravel())):
    ax.imshow(component.reshape(image_shape),
              cmap='viridis')
    ax.set_title("{}. component".format((i + 1)))
```

While we certainly cannot understand all aspects of these components, we can guess which aspects of the face images some of the components are capturing. The first component seems to mostly encode the contrast between the face and the background, the second component encodes differences in lighting between the right and the left half of the face, and so on. While this representation is slightly more semantic than the raw pixel values, it is still quite far from how a human might perceive a face. As the PCA model is based on pixels, the alignment of the face (the position of eyes, chin, and nose) and the lighting both have a strong influence on how similar two images are in their pixel representation. But alignment and lighting are probably not what a human would perceive first. When asking people to rate similarity of faces, they are more likely to use attributes like age, gender, facial expression, and hair style, which are attributes that are hard to infer from the pixel intensities. It's important to keep in mind that algorithms often interpret data (particularly visual data, such as images, which humans are very familiar with) quite differently from how a human would.

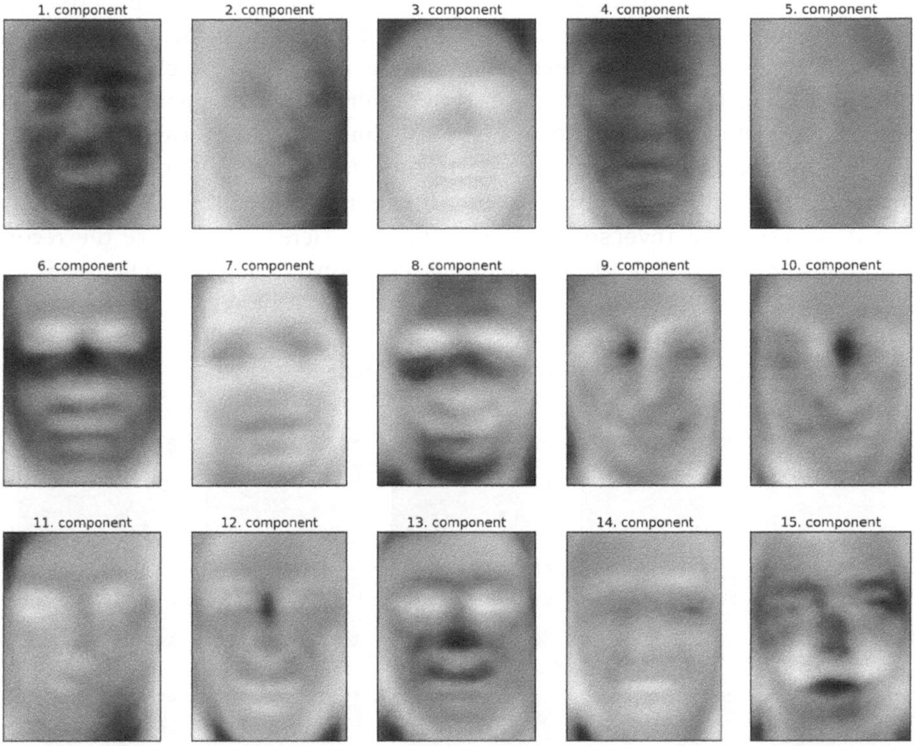

Figure 3-9. Component vectors of the first 15 principal components of the faces dataset

Let's come back to the specific case of PCA, though. We introduced the PCA transformation as rotating the data and then dropping the components with low variance. Another useful interpretation is to try to find some numbers (the new feature values after the PCA rotation) so that we can express the test points as a weighted sum of the principal components (see Figure 3-10).

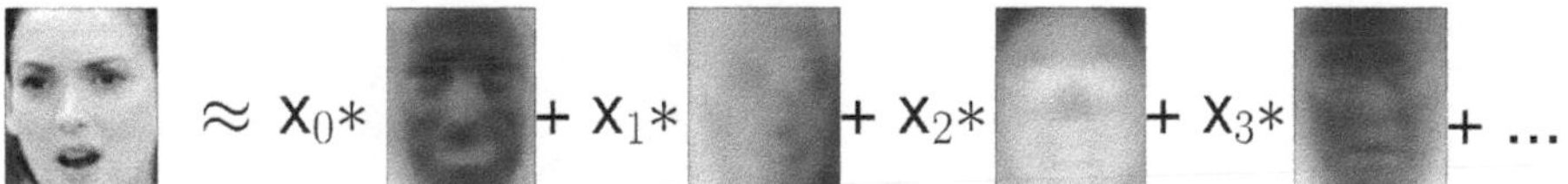

Figure 3-10. Schematic view of PCA as decomposing an image into a weighted sum of components

Here, x_0, x_1, and so on are the coefficients of the principal components for this data point; in other words, they are the representation of the image in the rotated space.

Another way we can try to understand what a PCA model is doing is by looking at the reconstructions of the original data using only some components. In Figure 3-3, after dropping the second component and arriving at the third panel, we undid the rotation and added the mean back to obtain new points in the original space with the second component removed, as shown in the last panel. We can do a similar transformation for the faces by reducing the data to only some principal components and then rotating back into the original space. This return to the original feature space can be done using the `inverse_transform` method. Here, we visualize the reconstruction of some faces using 10, 50, 100, or 500 components (Figure 3-11):

In[30]:

```
mglearn.plots.plot_pca_faces(X_train, X_test, image_shape)
```

Figure 3-11. Reconstructing three face images using increasing numbers of principal components

You can see that when we use only the first 10 principal components, only the essence of the picture, like the face orientation and lighting, is captured. By using more and more principal components, more and more details in the image are preserved. This corresponds to extending the sum in Figure 3-10 to include more and more terms. Using as many components as there are pixels would mean that we would not discard any information after the rotation, and we would reconstruct the image perfectly.

We can also try to use PCA to visualize all the faces in the dataset in a scatter plot using the first two principal components (Figure 3-12), with classes given by who is shown in the image, similarly to what we did for the cancer dataset:

In[31]:

```
mglearn.discrete_scatter(X_train_pca[:, 0], X_train_pca[:, 1], y_train)
plt.xlabel("First principal component")
plt.ylabel("Second principal component")
```

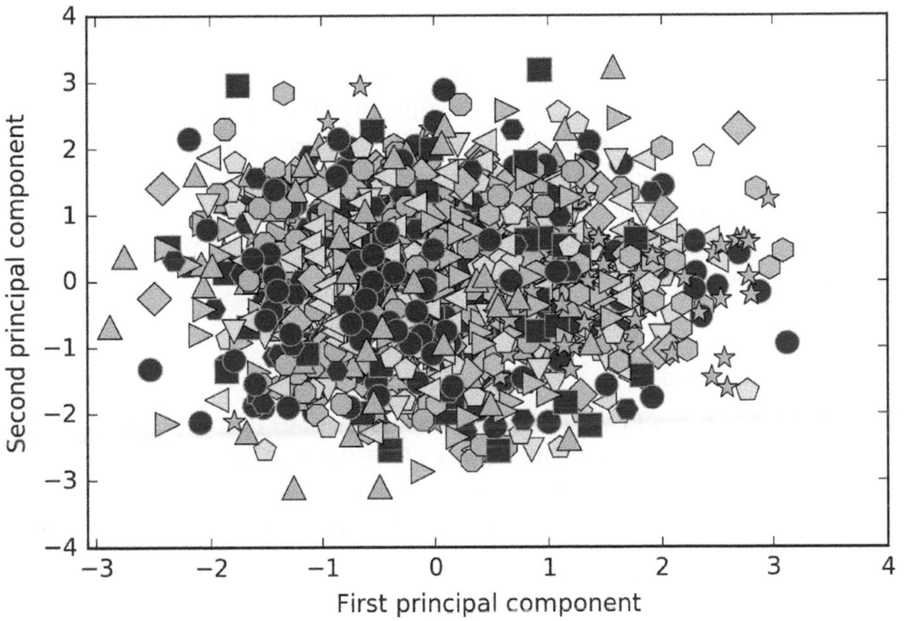

Figure 3-12. Scatter plot of the faces dataset using the first two principal components (see Figure 3-5 for the corresponding image for the cancer dataset)

As you can see, when we use only the first two principal components the whole data is just a big blob, with no separation of classes visible. This is not very surprising, given that even with 10 components, as shown earlier in Figure 3-11, PCA only captures very rough characteristics of the faces.

3.4.2 Non-Negative Matrix Factorization (NMF)

Non-negative matrix factorization is another unsupervised learning algorithm that aims to extract useful features. It works similarly to PCA and can also be used for dimensionality reduction. As in PCA, we are trying to write each data point as a weighted sum of some components, as illustrated in Figure 3-10. But whereas in PCA we wanted components that were orthogonal and that explained as much variance of the data as possible, in NMF, we want the components and the coefficients to be non-negative; that is, we want both the components and the coefficients to be greater than or equal to zero. Consequently, this method can only be applied to data where each feature is non-negative, as a non-negative sum of non-negative components cannot become negative.

The process of decomposing data into a non-negative weighted sum is particularly helpful for data that is created as the addition (or overlay) of several independent sources, such as an audio track of multiple people speaking, or music with many instruments. In these situations, NMF can identify the original components that make up the combined data. Overall, NMF leads to more interpretable components than PCA, as negative components and coefficients can lead to hard-to-interpret cancellation effects. The eigenfaces in Figure 3-9, for example, contain both positive and negative parts, and as we mentioned in the description of PCA, the sign is actually arbitrary. Before we apply NMF to the face dataset, let's briefly revisit the synthetic data.

Applying NMF to synthetic data

In contrast to when using PCA, we need to ensure that our data is positive for NMF to be able to operate on the data. This means where the data lies relative to the origin (0, 0) actually matters for NMF. Therefore, you can think of the non-negative components that are extracted as directions from (0, 0) toward the data.

The following example (Figure 3-13) shows the results of NMF on the two-dimensional toy data:

In[32]:

```
mglearn.plots.plot_nmf_illustration()
```

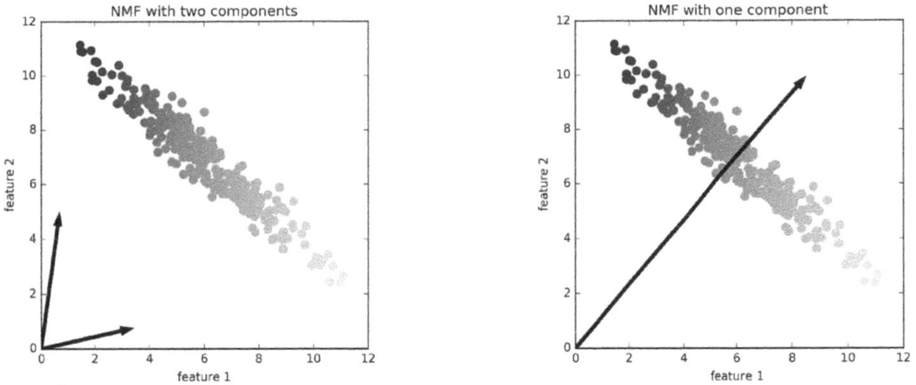

Figure 3-13. Components found by non-negative matrix factorization with two components (left) and one component (right)

For NMF with two components, as shown on the left, it is clear that all points in the data can be written as a positive combination of the two components. If there are enough components to perfectly reconstruct the data (as many components as there are features), the algorithm will choose directions that point toward the extremes of the data.

If we only use a single component, NMF creates a component that points toward the mean, as pointing there best explains the data. You can see that in contrast with PCA, reducing the number of components not only removes some directions, but creates an entirely different set of components! Components in NMF are also not ordered in any specific way, so there is no "first non-negative component": all components play an equal part.

NMF uses a random initialization, which might lead to different results depending on the random seed. In relatively simple cases such as the synthetic data with two components, where all the data can be explained perfectly, the randomness has little effect (though it might change the order or scale of the components). In more complex situations, there might be more drastic changes.

Applying NMF to face images

Now, let's apply NMF to the Labeled Faces in the Wild dataset we used earlier. The main parameter of NMF is how many components we want to extract. Usually this is lower than the number of input features (otherwise, the data could be explained by making each pixel a separate component).

First, let's inspect how the number of components impacts how well the data can be reconstructed using NMF (Figure 3-14):

In[33]:

```
mglearn.plots.plot_nmf_faces(X_train, X_test, image_shape)
```

Figure 3-14. Reconstructing three face images using increasing numbers of components found by NMF

The quality of the back-transformed data is similar to when using PCA, but slightly worse. This is expected, as PCA finds the optimum directions in terms of reconstruction. NMF is usually not used for its ability to reconstruct or encode data, but rather for finding interesting patterns within the data.

As a first look into the data, let's try extracting only a few components (say, 15). Figure 3-15 shows the result:

In[34]:

```
from sklearn.decomposition import NMF
nmf = NMF(n_components=15, random_state=0)
nmf.fit(X_train)
X_train_nmf = nmf.transform(X_train)
X_test_nmf = nmf.transform(X_test)

fig, axes = plt.subplots(3, 5, figsize=(15, 12),
                         subplot_kw={'xticks': (), 'yticks': ()})
for i, (component, ax) in enumerate(zip(nmf.components_, axes.ravel())):
    ax.imshow(component.reshape(image_shape))
    ax.set_title("{}. component".format(i))
```

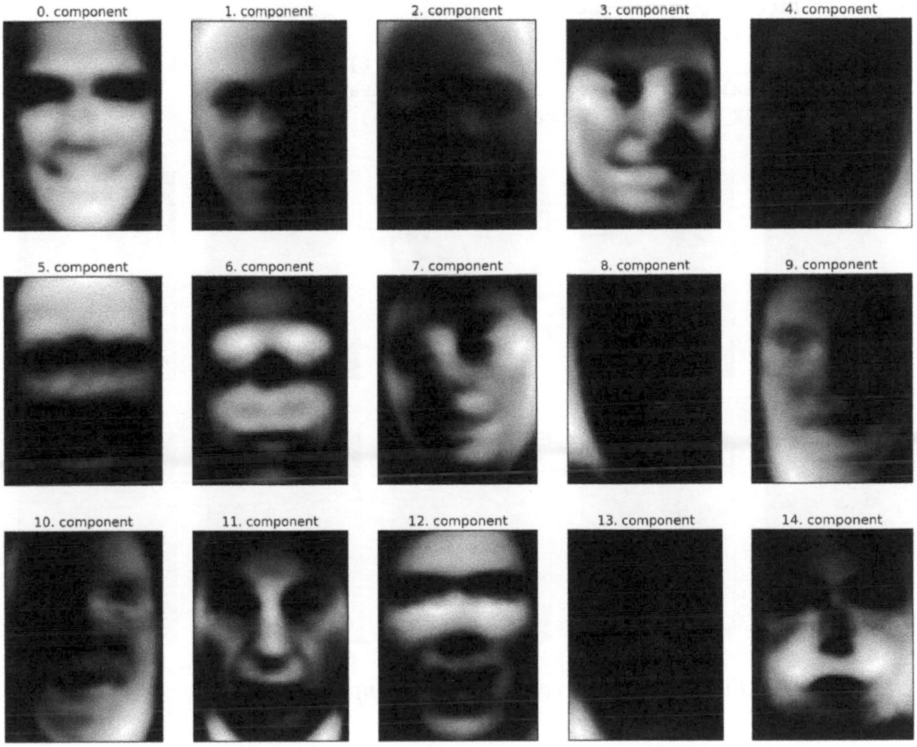

Figure 3-15. The components found by NMF on the faces dataset when using 15 components

These components are all positive, and so resemble prototypes of faces much more so than the components shown for PCA in Figure 3-9. For example, one can clearly see that component 3 shows a face rotated somewhat to the right, while component 7 shows a face somewhat rotated to the left. Let's look at the images for which these components are particularly strong, shown in Figures 3-16 and 3-17:

In[35]:

```
compn = 3
# sort by 3rd component, plot first 10 images
inds = np.argsort(X_train_nmf[:, compn])[::-1]
fig, axes = plt.subplots(2, 5, figsize=(15, 8),
                         subplot_kw={'xticks': (), 'yticks': ()})
fig.suptitle("Large component 3")
for i, (ind, ax) in enumerate(zip(inds, axes.ravel())):
    ax.imshow(X_train[ind].reshape(image_shape))

compn = 7
# sort by 7th component, plot first 10 images
inds = np.argsort(X_train_nmf[:, compn])[::-1]
fig.suptitle("Large component 7")
fig, axes = plt.subplots(2, 5, figsize=(15, 8),
                         subplot_kw={'xticks': (), 'yticks': ()})
for i, (ind, ax) in enumerate(zip(inds, axes.ravel())):
    ax.imshow(X_train[ind].reshape(image_shape))
```

Figure 3-16. Faces that have a large coefficient for component 3

Figure 3-17. Faces that have a large coefficient for component 7

As expected, faces that have a high coefficient for component 3 are faces looking to the right (Figure 3-16), while faces with a high coefficient for component 7 are looking to the left (Figure 3-17). As mentioned earlier, extracting patterns like these works best for data with additive structure, including audio, gene expression, and text data. Let's walk through one example on synthetic data to see what this might look like.

Let's say we are interested in a signal that is a combination of three different sources (Figure 3-18):

In[36]:

```
S = mglearn.datasets.make_signals()
plt.figure(figsize=(6, 1))
plt.plot(S, '-')
plt.xlabel("Time")
plt.ylabel("Signal")
```

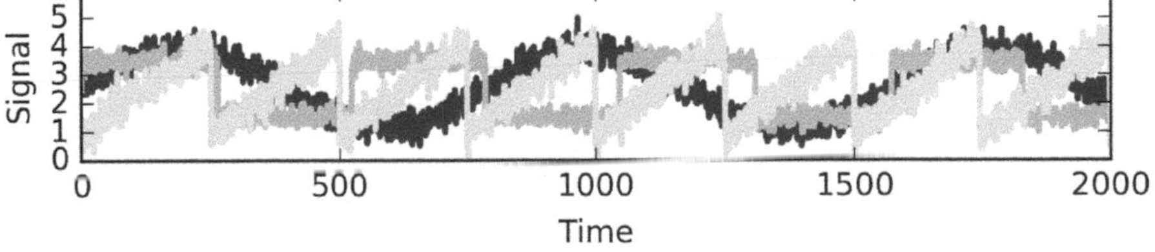

Figure 3-18. Original signal sources

Unfortunately we cannot observe the original signals, but only an additive mixture of all three of them. We want to recover the decomposition of the mixed signal into the original components. We assume that we have many different ways to observe the mixture (say 100 measurement devices), each of which provides us with a series of measurements:

In[37]:

```
# mix data into a 100-dimensional state
A = np.random.RandomState(0).uniform(size=(100, 3))
X = np.dot(S, A.T)
print("Shape of measurements: {}".format(X.shape))
```

Out[37]:

```
Shape of measurements: (2000, 100)
```

We can use NMF to recover the three signals:

In[38]:

```
nmf = NMF(n_components=3, random_state=42)
S_ = nmf.fit_transform(X)
print("Recovered signal shape: {}".format(S_.shape))
```

Out[38]:

```
Recovered signal shape: (2000, 3)
```

For comparison, we also apply PCA:

In[39]:

```
pca = PCA(n_components=3)
H = pca.fit_transform(X)
```

Figure 3-19 shows the signal activity that was discovered by NMF and PCA:

In[40]:

```
models = [X, S, S_, H]
names = ['Observations (first three measurements)',
         'True sources',
         'NMF recovered signals',
         'PCA recovered signals']

fig, axes = plt.subplots(4, figsize=(8, 4), gridspec_kw={'hspace': .5},
                         subplot_kw={'xticks': (), 'yticks': ()})

for model, name, ax in zip(models, names, axes):
    ax.set_title(name)
    ax.plot(model[:, :3], '-')
```

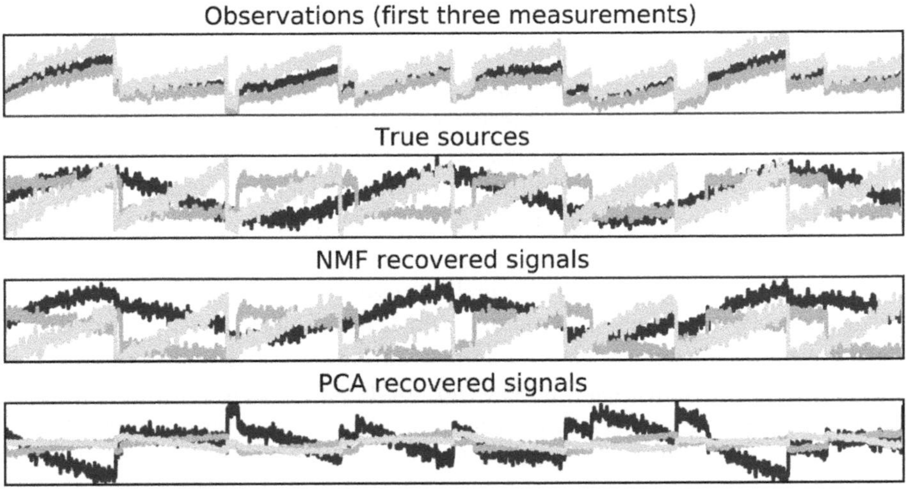

Figure 3-19. Recovering mixed sources using NMF and PCA

The figure includes 3 of the 100 measurements from the mixed measurements `X` for reference. As you can see, NMF did a reasonable job of discovering the original sources, while PCA failed and used the first component to explain the majority of the variation in the data. Keep in mind that the components produced by NMF have no natural ordering. In this example, the ordering of the NMF components is the same as in the original signal (see the shading of the three curves), but this is purely accidental.

There are many other algorithms that can be used to decompose each data point into a weighted sum of a fixed set of components, as PCA and NMF do. Discussing all of them is beyond the scope of this book, and describing the constraints made on the components and coefficients often involves probability theory. If you are interested in this kind of pattern extraction, we recommend that you study the sections of the `scikit_learn` user guide on independent component analysis (ICA), factor analysis (FA), and sparse coding (dictionary learning), all of which you can find on the page about decomposition methods (*http://scikit-learn.org/stable/modules/decomposition.html*).

3.4.3 Manifold Learning with t-SNE

While PCA is often a good first approach for transforming your data so that you might be able to visualize it using a scatter plot, the nature of the method (applying a rotation and then dropping directions) limits its usefulness, as we saw with the scatter plot of the Labeled Faces in the Wild dataset. There is a class of algorithms for visualization called *manifold learning algorithms* that allow for much more complex mappings, and often provide better visualizations. A particularly useful one is the t-SNE algorithm.

Manifold learning algorithms are mainly aimed at visualization, and so are rarely used to generate more than two new features. Some of them, including t-SNE, compute a new representation of the training data, but don't allow transformations of new data. This means these algorithms cannot be applied to a test set: rather, they can only transform the data they were trained for. Manifold learning can be useful for exploratory data analysis, but is rarely used if the final goal is supervised learning. The idea behind t-SNE is to find a two-dimensional representation of the data that preserves the distances between points as best as possible. t-SNE starts with a random two-dimensional representation for each data point, and then tries to make points that are close in the original feature space closer, and points that are far apart in the original feature space farther apart. t-SNE puts more emphasis on points that are close by, rather than preserving distances between far-apart points. In other words, it tries to preserve the information indicating which points are neighbors to each other.

We will apply the t-SNE manifold learning algorithm on a dataset of handwritten digits that is included in `scikit-learn`.[2] Each data point in this dataset is an 8×8 grayscale image of a handwritten digit between 0 and 9. Figure 3-20 shows an example image for each class:

In[41]:

```
from sklearn.datasets import load_digits
digits = load_digits()

fig, axes = plt.subplots(2, 5, figsize=(10, 5),
                         subplot_kw={'xticks':(), 'yticks': ()})
for ax, img in zip(axes.ravel(), digits.images):
    ax.imshow(img)
```

2 Not to be confused with the much larger MNIST dataset.

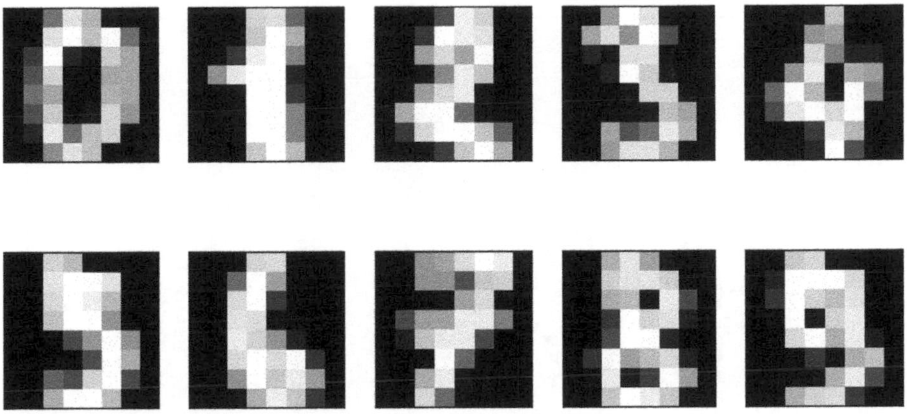

Figure 3-20. Example images from the digits dataset

Let's use PCA to visualize the data reduced to two dimensions. We plot the first two principal components, and represent each sample with a digit corresponding to its class (see Figure 3-21):

In[42]:

```
# build a PCA model
pca = PCA(n_components=2)
pca.fit(digits.data)
# transform the digits data onto the first two principal components
digits_pca = pca.transform(digits.data)
colors = ["#476A2A", "#7851B8", "#BD3430", "#4A2D4E", "#875525",
          "#A83683", "#4E655E", "#853541", "#3A3120", "#535D8E"]
plt.figure(figsize=(10, 10))
plt.xlim(digits_pca[:, 0].min(), digits_pca[:, 0].max())
plt.ylim(digits_pca[:, 1].min(), digits_pca[:, 1].max())
for i in range(len(digits.data)):
    # actually plot the digits as text instead of using scatter
    plt.text(digits_pca[i, 0], digits_pca[i, 1], str(digits.target[i]),
             color = colors[digits.target[i]],
             fontdict={'weight': 'bold', 'size': 9})
plt.xlabel("First principal component")
plt.ylabel("Second principal component")
```

Here, we actually used the true digit classes as glyphs, to show which class is where. The digits zero, six, and four are relatively well separated using the first two principal components, though they still overlap. Most of the other digits overlap significantly.

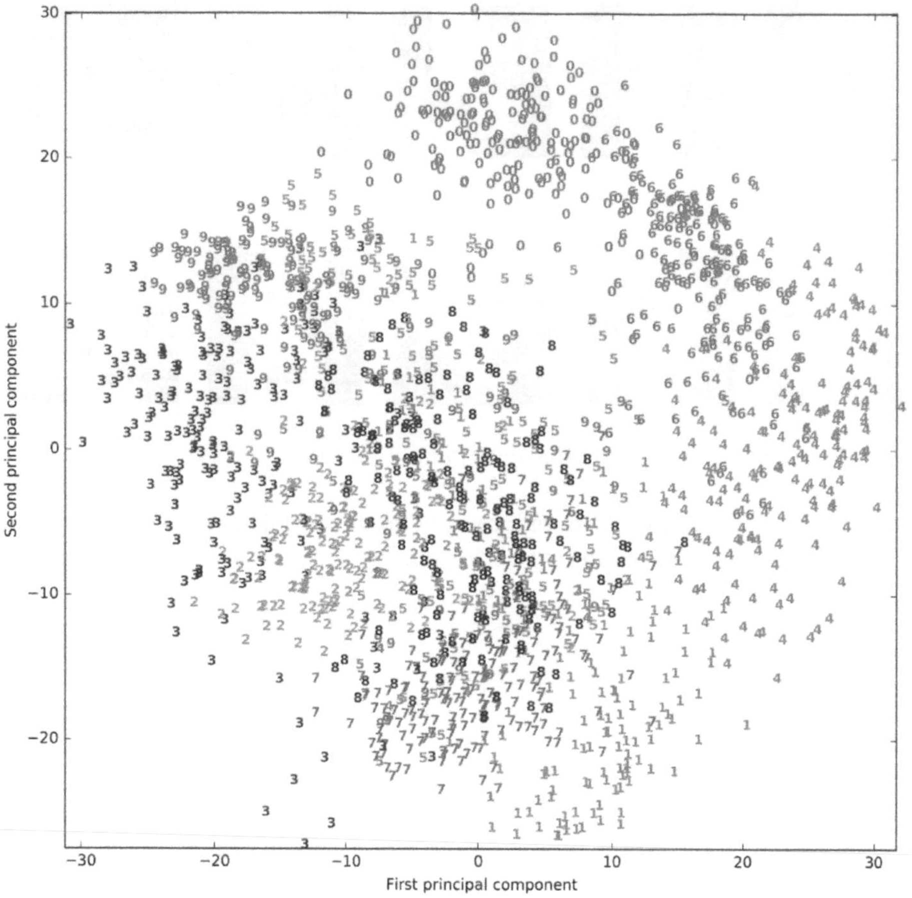

Figure 3-21. Scatter plot of the digits dataset using the first two principal components

Let's apply t-SNE to the same dataset, and compare the results. As t-SNE does not support transforming new data, the `TSNE` class has no `transform` method. Instead, we can call the `fit_transform` method, which will build the model and immediately return the transformed data (see Figure 3-22):

In[43]:

```
from sklearn.manifold import TSNE
tsne = TSNE(random_state=42)
# use fit_transform instead of fit, as TSNE has no transform method
digits_tsne = tsne.fit_transform(digits.data)
```

In[44]:

```
plt.figure(figsize=(10, 10))
plt.xlim(digits_tsne[:, 0].min(), digits_tsne[:, 0].max() + 1)
plt.ylim(digits_tsne[:, 1].min(), digits_tsne[:, 1].max() + 1)
for i in range(len(digits.data)):
    # actually plot the digits as text instead of using scatter
    plt.text(digits_tsne[i, 0], digits_tsne[i, 1], str(digits.target[i]),
             color = colors[digits.target[i]],
             fontdict={'weight': 'bold', 'size': 9})
plt.xlabel("t-SNE feature 0")
plt.ylabel("t-SNE feature 1")
```

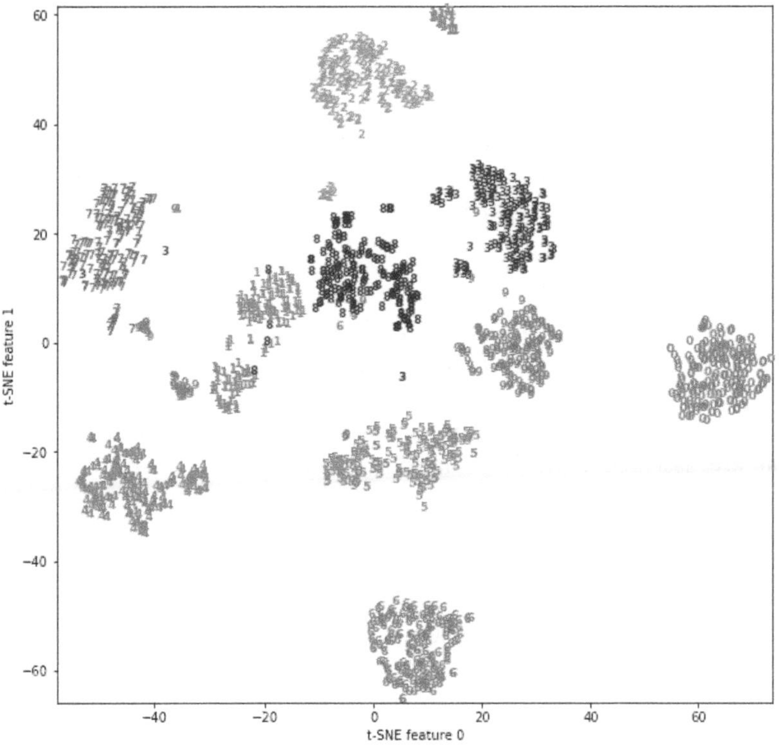

Figure 3-22. Scatter plot of the digits dataset using two components found by t-SNE

The result of t-SNE is quite remarkable. All the classes are quite clearly separated. The ones and nines are somewhat split up, but most of the classes form a single dense group. Keep in mind that this method has no knowledge of the class labels: it is completely unsupervised. Still, it can find a representation of the data in two dimensions that clearly separates the classes, based solely on how close points are in the original space.

The t-SNE algorithm has some tuning parameters, though it often works well with the default settings. You can try playing with `perplexity` and `early_exaggeration`, but the effects are usually minor.

3.5 Clustering

As we described earlier, *clustering* is the task of partitioning the dataset into groups, called clusters. The goal is to split up the data in such a way that points within a single cluster are very similar and points in different clusters are different. Similarly to classification algorithms, clustering algorithms assign (or predict) a number to each data point, indicating which cluster a particular point belongs to.

3.5.1 k-Means Clustering

k-means clustering is one of the simplest and most commonly used clustering algorithms. It tries to find *cluster centers* that are representative of certain regions of the data. The algorithm alternates between two steps: assigning each data point to the closest cluster center, and then setting each cluster center as the mean of the data points that are assigned to it. The algorithm is finished when the assignment of instances to clusters no longer changes. The following example (Figure 3-23) illustrates the algorithm on a synthetic dataset:

In[45]:

```
mglearn.plots.plot_kmeans_algorithm()
```

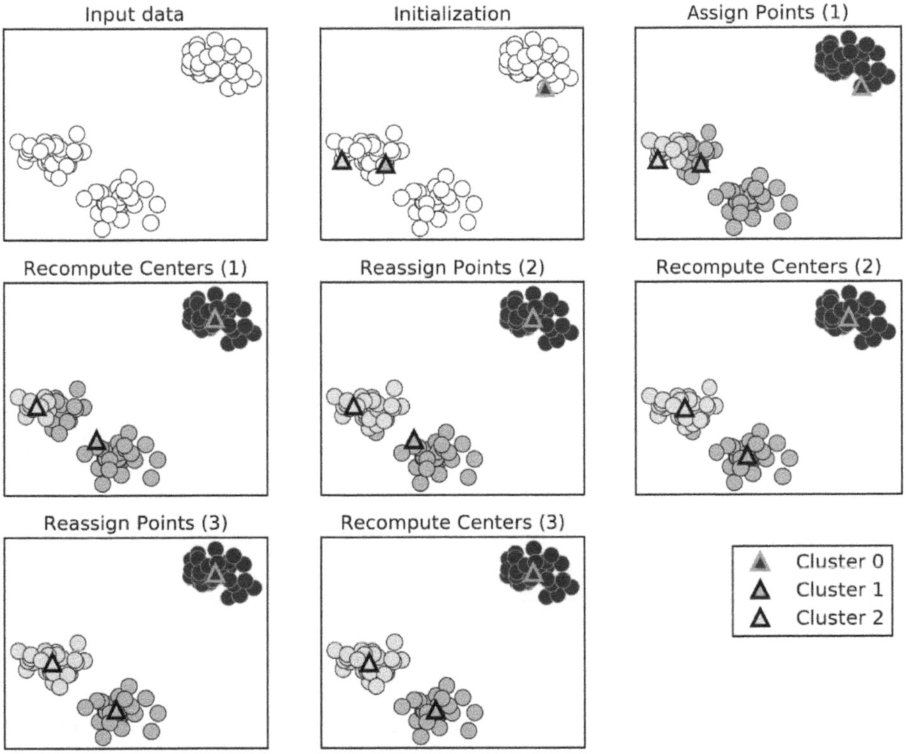

Figure 3-23. Input data and three steps of the k-means algorithm

Cluster centers are shown as triangles, while data points are shown as circles. Colors indicate cluster membership. We specified that we are looking for three clusters, so the algorithm was initialized by declaring three data points randomly as cluster centers (see "Initialization"). Then the iterative algorithm starts. First, each data point is assigned to the cluster center it is closest to (see "Assign Points (1)"). Next, the cluster centers are updated to be the mean of the assigned points (see "Recompute Centers (1)"). Then the process is repeated two more times. After the third iteration, the assignment of points to cluster centers remained unchanged, so the algorithm stops.

Given new data points, *k*-means will assign each to the closest cluster center. The next example (Figure 3-24) shows the boundaries of the cluster centers that were learned in Figure 3-23:

In[46]:

```
mglearn.plots.plot_kmeans_boundaries()
```

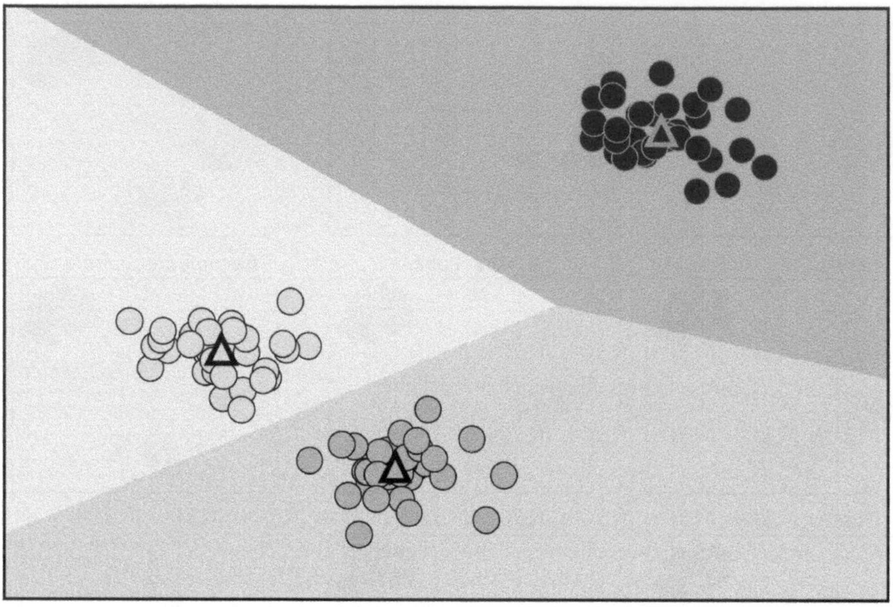

Figure 3-24. Cluster centers and cluster boundaries found by the k-means algorithm

Applying *k*-means with `scikit-learn` is quite straightforward. Here, we apply it to the synthetic data that we used for the preceding plots. We instantiate the `KMeans` class, and set the number of clusters we are looking for.[3] Then we call the `fit` method with the data:

In[47]:

```
from sklearn.datasets import make_blobs
from sklearn.cluster import KMeans

# generate synthetic two-dimensional data
X, y = make_blobs(random_state=1)

# build the clustering model
kmeans = KMeans(n_clusters=3)
kmeans.fit(X)
```

During the algorithm, each training data point in `X` is assigned a cluster label. You can find these labels in the `kmeans.labels_` attribute:

3 If you don't provide `n_clusters`, it is set to 8 by default. There is no particular reason why you should use this value.

In[48]:

```
print("Cluster memberships:\n{}".format(kmeans.labels_))
```

Out[48]:

```
Cluster memberships:
[0 2 2 2 1 1 1 2 0 0 2 2 1 0 1 1 1 0 2 2 1 2 1 0 2 1 1 0 0 1 0 0 1 0 2 1 2
 2 2 1 1 2 0 2 2 1 0 0 0 0 2 1 1 1 0 1 2 2 0 0 2 1 1 2 2 1 0 1 0 2 2 2 1 0
 0 2 1 1 0 2 0 2 2 1 0 0 0 0 2 0 1 0 0 2 2 1 1 0 1 0]
```

As we asked for three clusters, the clusters are numbered 0 to 2.

You can also assign cluster labels to new points, using the `predict` method. Each new point is assigned to the closest cluster center when predicting, but the existing model is not changed. Running `predict` on the training set returns the same result as `labels_`:

In[49]:

```
print(kmeans.predict(X))
```

Out[49]:

```
[0 2 2 2 1 1 1 2 0 0 2 2 1 0 1 1 1 0 2 2 1 2 1 0 2 1 1 0 0 1 0 0 1 0 2 1 2
 2 2 1 1 2 0 2 2 1 0 0 0 0 2 1 1 1 0 1 2 2 0 0 2 1 1 2 2 1 0 1 0 2 2 2 1 0
 0 2 1 1 0 2 0 2 2 1 0 0 0 0 2 0 1 0 0 2 2 1 1 0 1 0]
```

You can see that clustering is somewhat similar to classification, in that each item gets a label. However, there is no ground truth, and consequently the labels themselves have no *a priori* meaning. Let's go back to the example of clustering face images that we discussed before. It might be that the cluster 3 found by the algorithm contains only faces of your friend Bela. You can only know that after you look at the pictures, though, and the number 3 is arbitrary. The only information the algorithm gives you is that all faces labeled as 3 are similar.

For the clustering we just computed on the two-dimensional toy dataset, that means that we should not assign any significance to the fact that one group was labeled 0 and another one was labeled 1. Running the algorithm again might result in a different numbering of clusters because of the random nature of the initialization.

Here is a plot of this data again (Figure 3-25). The cluster centers are stored in the `cluster_centers_` attribute, and we plot them as triangles:

In[50]:

```
mglearn.discrete_scatter(X[:, 0], X[:, 1], kmeans.labels_, markers='o')
mglearn.discrete_scatter(
    kmeans.cluster_centers_[:, 0], kmeans.cluster_centers_[:, 1], [0, 1, 2],
    markers='^', markeredgewidth=2)
```

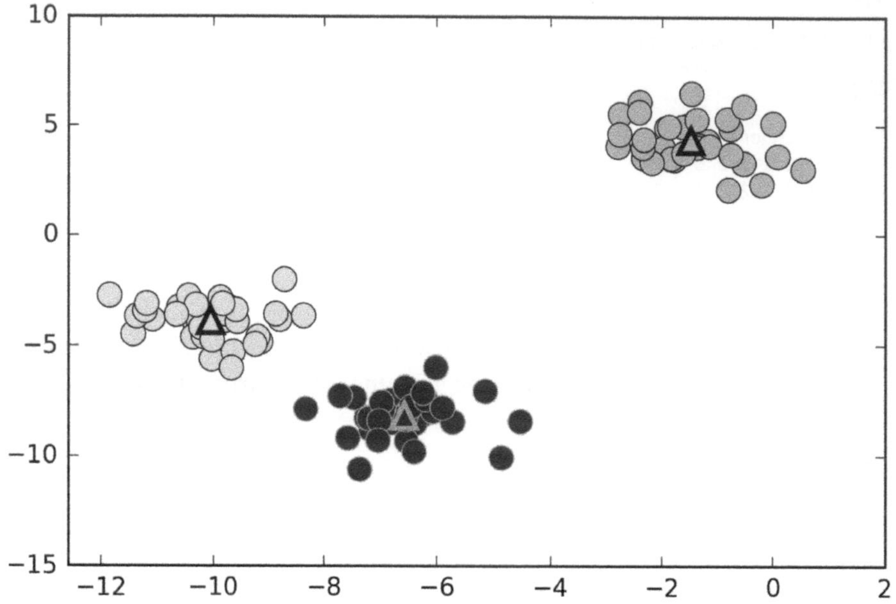

Figure 3-25. Cluster assignments and cluster centers found by k-means with three clusters

We can also use more or fewer cluster centers (Figure 3-26):

In[51]:

```
fig, axes = plt.subplots(1, 2, figsize=(10, 5))

# using two cluster centers:
kmeans = KMeans(n_clusters=2)
kmeans.fit(X)
assignments = kmeans.labels_

mglearn.discrete_scatter(X[:, 0], X[:, 1], assignments, ax=axes[0])

# using five cluster centers:
kmeans = KMeans(n_clusters=5)
kmeans.fit(X)
assignments = kmeans.labels_

mglearn.discrete_scatter(X[:, 0], X[:, 1], assignments, ax=axes[1])
```

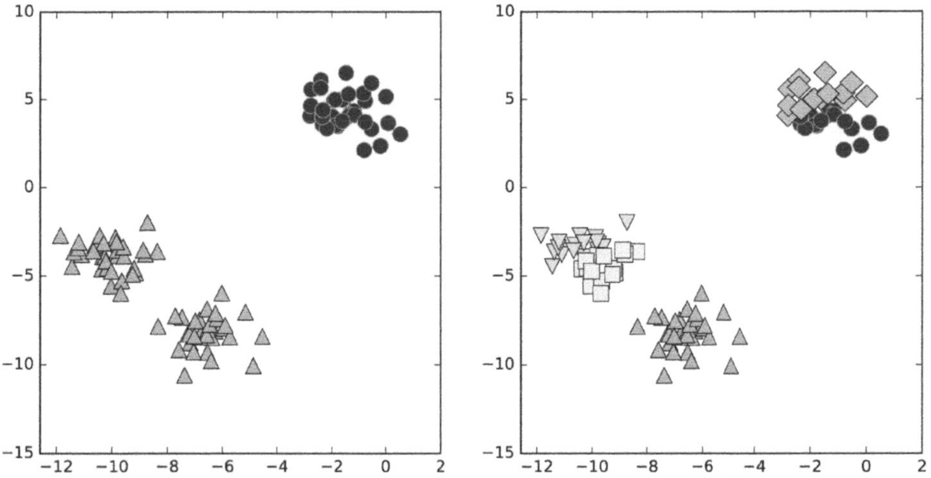

Figure 3-26. Cluster assignments found by k-means using two clusters (left) and five clusters (right)

Failure cases of k-means

Even if you know the "right" number of clusters for a given dataset, *k*-means might not always be able to recover them. Each cluster is defined solely by its center, which means that each cluster is a convex shape. As a result of this, *k*-means can only capture relatively simple shapes. *k*-means also assumes that all clusters have the same "diameter" in some sense; it always draws the boundary between clusters to be exactly in the middle between the cluster centers. That can sometimes lead to surprising results, as shown in Figure 3-27:

In[52]:

```
X_varied, y_varied = make_blobs(n_samples=200,
                                cluster_std=[1.0, 2.5, 0.5],
                                random_state=170)
y_pred = KMeans(n_clusters=3, random_state=0).fit_predict(X_varied)

mglearn.discrete_scatter(X_varied[:, 0], X_varied[:, 1], y_pred)
plt.legend(["cluster 0", "cluster 1", "cluster 2"], loc='best')
plt.xlabel("Feature 0")
plt.ylabel("Feature 1")
```

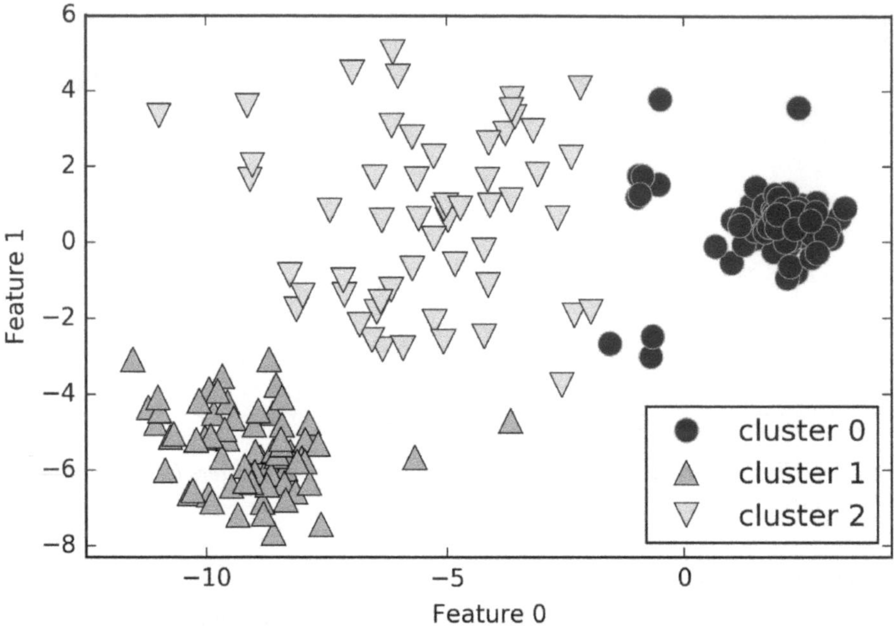

Figure 3-27. Cluster assignments found by k-means when clusters have different densities

One might have expected the dense region in the lower left to be the first cluster, the dense region in the upper right to be the second, and the less dense region in the center to be the third. Instead, both cluster 0 and cluster 1 have some points that are far away from all the other points in these clusters that "reach" toward the center.

k-means also assumes that all directions are equally important for each cluster. The following plot (Figure 3-28) shows a two-dimensional dataset where there are three clearly separated parts in the data. However, these groups are stretched toward the diagonal. As *k*-means only considers the distance to the nearest cluster center, it can't handle this kind of data:

In[53]:

```
# generate some random cluster data
X, y = make_blobs(random_state=170, n_samples=600)
rng = np.random.RandomState(74)

# transform the data to be stretched
transformation = rng.normal(size=(2, 2))
X = np.dot(X, transformation)
```

```
# cluster the data into three clusters
kmeans = KMeans(n_clusters=3)
kmeans.fit(X)
y_pred = kmeans.predict(X)

# plot the cluster assignments and cluster centers
mglearn.discrete_scatter(X[:, 0], X[:, 1], kmeans.labels_, markers='o')
mglearn.discrete_scatter(
    kmeans.cluster_centers_[:, 0], kmeans.cluster_centers_[:, 1], [0, 1, 2],
    markers='^', markeredgewidth=2)
plt.xlabel("Feature 0")
plt.ylabel("Feature 1")
```

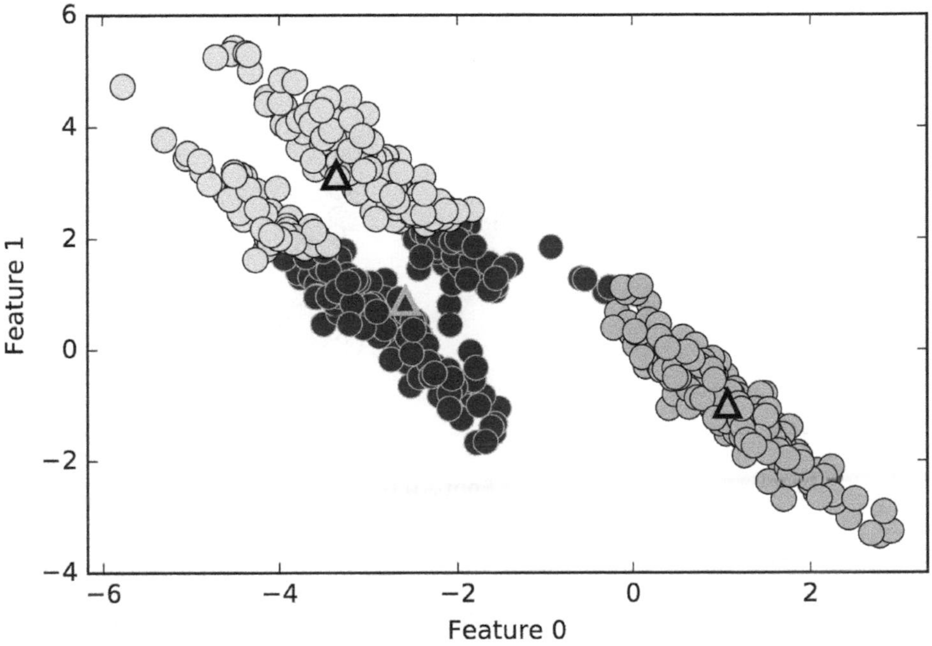

Figure 3-28. k-means fails to identify nonspherical clusters

k-means also performs poorly if the clusters have more complex shapes, like the two_moons data we encountered in Chapter 2 (see Figure 3-29):

In[54]:

```
# generate synthetic two_moons data (with less noise this time)
from sklearn.datasets import make_moons
X, y = make_moons(n_samples=200, noise=0.05, random_state=0)

# cluster the data into two clusters
kmeans = KMeans(n_clusters=2)
kmeans.fit(X)
y_pred = kmeans.predict(X)
```

```
# plot the cluster assignments and cluster centers
plt.scatter(X[:, 0], X[:, 1], c=y_pred, cmap=mglearn.cm2, s=60, edgecolor='k')
plt.scatter(kmeans.cluster_centers_[:, 0], kmeans.cluster_centers_[:, 1],
            marker='^', c=[mglearn.cm2(0), mglearn.cm2(1)], s=100, linewidth=2,
            edgecolor='k')
plt.xlabel("Feature 0")
plt.ylabel("Feature 1")
```

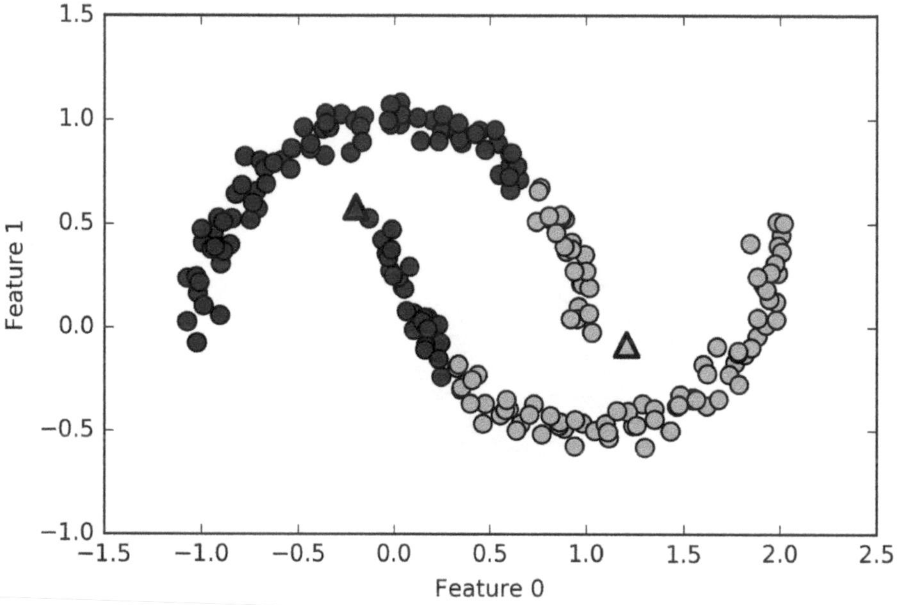

Figure 3-29. k-means fails to identify clusters with complex shapes

Here, we would hope that the clustering algorithm can discover the two half-moon shapes. However, this is not possible using the *k*-means algorithm.

Vector quantization, or seeing k-means as decomposition

Even though *k*-means is a clustering algorithm, there are interesting parallels between *k*-means and the decomposition methods like PCA and NMF that we discussed earlier. You might remember that PCA tries to find directions of maximum variance in the data, while NMF tries to find additive components, which often correspond to "extremes" or "parts" of the data (see Figure 3-13). Both methods tried to express the data points as a sum over some components. *k*-means, on the other hand, tries to represent each data point using a cluster center. You can think of that as each point being represented using only a single component, which is given by the cluster center. This view of *k*-means as a decomposition method, where each point is represented using a single component, is called *vector quantization*.

Let's do a side-by-side comparison of PCA, NMF, and *k*-means, showing the components extracted (Figure 3-30), as well as reconstructions of faces from the test set using 100 components (Figure 3-31). For *k*-means, the reconstruction is the closest cluster center found on the training set:

In[55]:

```
X_train, X_test, y_train, y_test = train_test_split(
    X_people, y_people, stratify=y_people, random_state=0)
nmf = NMF(n_components=100, random_state=0)
nmf.fit(X_train)
pca = PCA(n_components=100, random_state=0)
pca.fit(X_train)
kmeans = KMeans(n_clusters=100, random_state=0)
kmeans.fit(X_train)

X_reconstructed_pca = pca.inverse_transform(pca.transform(X_test))
X_reconstructed_kmeans = kmeans.cluster_centers_[kmeans.predict(X_test)]
X_reconstructed_nmf = np.dot(nmf.transform(X_test), nmf.components_)
```

In[56]:

```
fig, axes = plt.subplots(3, 5, figsize=(8, 8),
                         subplot_kw={'xticks': (), 'yticks': ()})
fig.suptitle("Extracted Components")
for ax, comp_kmeans, comp_pca, comp_nmf in zip(
        axes.T, kmeans.cluster_centers_, pca.components_, nmf.components_):
    ax[0].imshow(comp_kmeans.reshape(image_shape))
    ax[1].imshow(comp_pca.reshape(image_shape), cmap='viridis')
    ax[2].imshow(comp_nmf.reshape(image_shape))

axes[0, 0].set_ylabel("kmeans")
axes[1, 0].set_ylabel("pca")
axes[2, 0].set_ylabel("nmf")

fig, axes = plt.subplots(4, 5, subplot_kw={'xticks': (), 'yticks': ()},
                         figsize=(8, 8))
fig.suptitle("Reconstructions")
for ax, orig, rec_kmeans, rec_pca, rec_nmf in zip(
        axes.T, X_test, X_reconstructed_kmeans, X_reconstructed_pca,
        X_reconstructed_nmf):

    ax[0].imshow(orig.reshape(image_shape))
    ax[1].imshow(rec_kmeans.reshape(image_shape))
    ax[2].imshow(rec_pca.reshape(image_shape))
    ax[3].imshow(rec_nmf.reshape(image_shape))

axes[0, 0].set_ylabel("original")
axes[1, 0].set_ylabel("kmeans")
axes[2, 0].set_ylabel("pca")
axes[3, 0].set_ylabel("nmf")
```

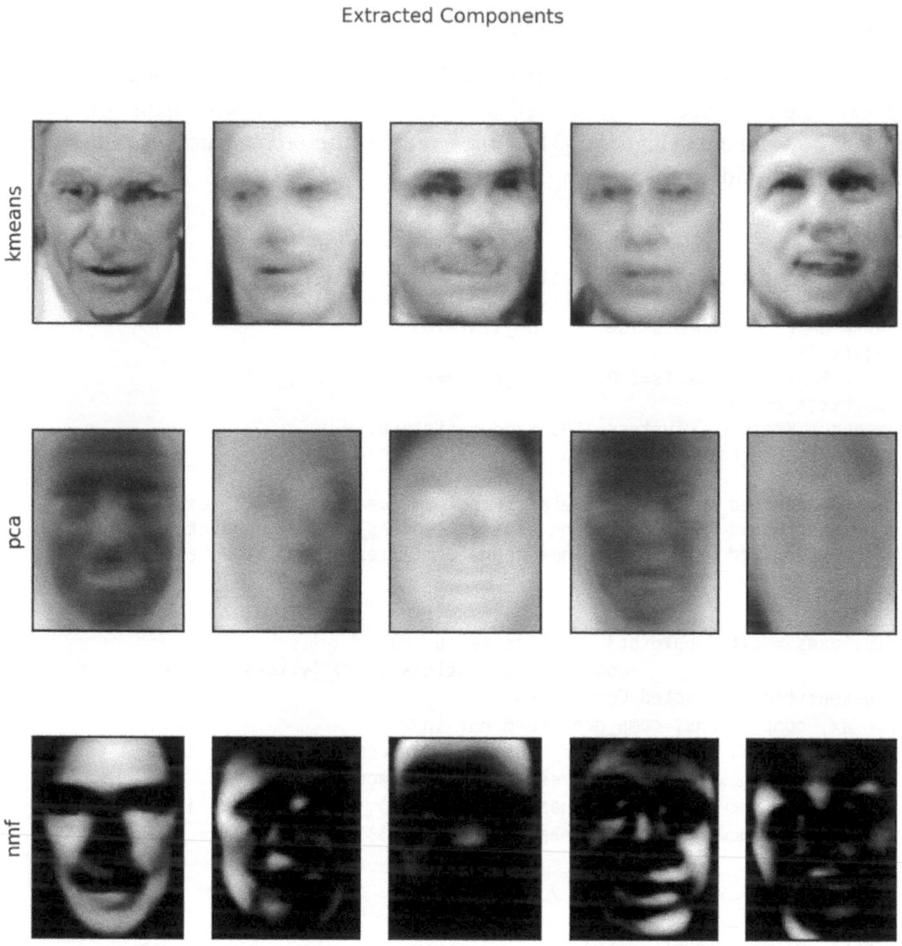

Figure 3-30. Comparing k-means cluster centers to components found by PCA and NMF

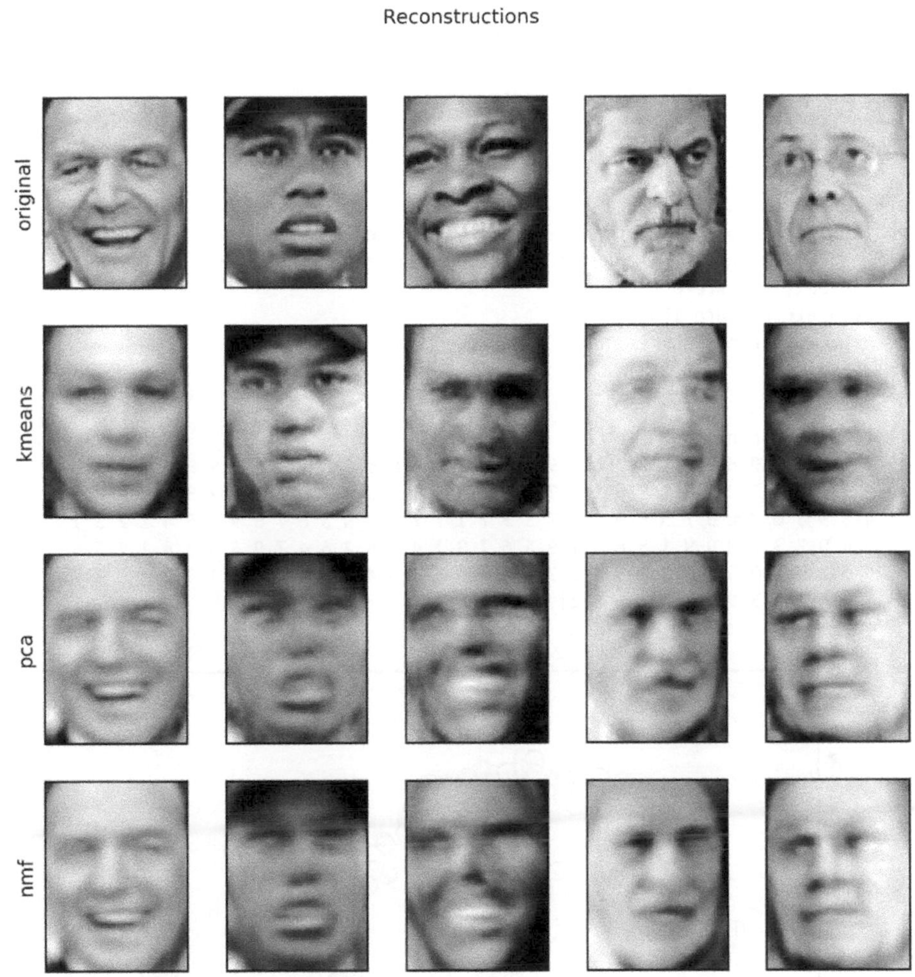

Figure 3-31. Comparing image reconstructions using k-means, PCA, and NMF with 100 components (or cluster centers)—k-means uses only a single cluster center per image

An interesting aspect of vector quantization using *k*-means is that we can use many more clusters than input dimensions to encode our data. Let's go back to the `two_moons` data. Using PCA or NMF, there is nothing much we can do to this data, as it lives in only two dimensions. Reducing it to one dimension with PCA or NMF would completely destroy the structure of the data. But we can find a more expressive representation with *k*-means, by using more cluster centers (see Figure 3-32):

In[57]:

```
X, y = make_moons(n_samples=200, noise=0.05, random_state=0)

kmeans = KMeans(n_clusters=10, random_state=0)
kmeans.fit(X)
y_pred = kmeans.predict(X)

plt.scatter(X[:, 0], X[:, 1], c=y_pred, s=60, cmap='Paired')
plt.scatter(kmeans.cluster_centers_[:, 0], kmeans.cluster_centers_[:, 1], s=60,
            marker='^', c=range(kmeans.n_clusters), linewidth=2, cmap='Paired')
plt.xlabel("Feature 0")
plt.ylabel("Feature 1")
print("Cluster memberships:\n{}".format(y_pred))
```

Out[57]:

```
Cluster memberships:
[9 2 5 4 2 7 9 6 9 6 1 0 2 6 1 9 3 0 3 1 7 6 8 6 8 5 2 7 5 8 9 8 6 5 3 7 0
 9 4 5 0 1 3 5 2 8 9 1 5 6 1 0 7 4 6 3 3 6 3 8 0 4 2 9 6 4 8 2 8 4 0 4 0 5
 6 4 5 9 3 0 7 8 0 7 5 8 9 8 0 7 3 9 7 1 7 2 2 0 4 5 6 7 8 9 4 5 4 1 2 3 1
 8 8 4 9 2 3 7 0 9 9 1 5 8 5 1 9 5 6 7 9 1 4 0 6 2 6 4 7 9 5 5 3 8 1 9 5 6
 3 5 0 2 9 3 0 8 6 0 3 3 5 6 3 2 0 2 3 0 2 6 3 4 4 1 5 6 7 1 1 3 2 4 7 2 7
 3 8 6 4 1 4 3 9 9 5 1 7 5 8 2]
```

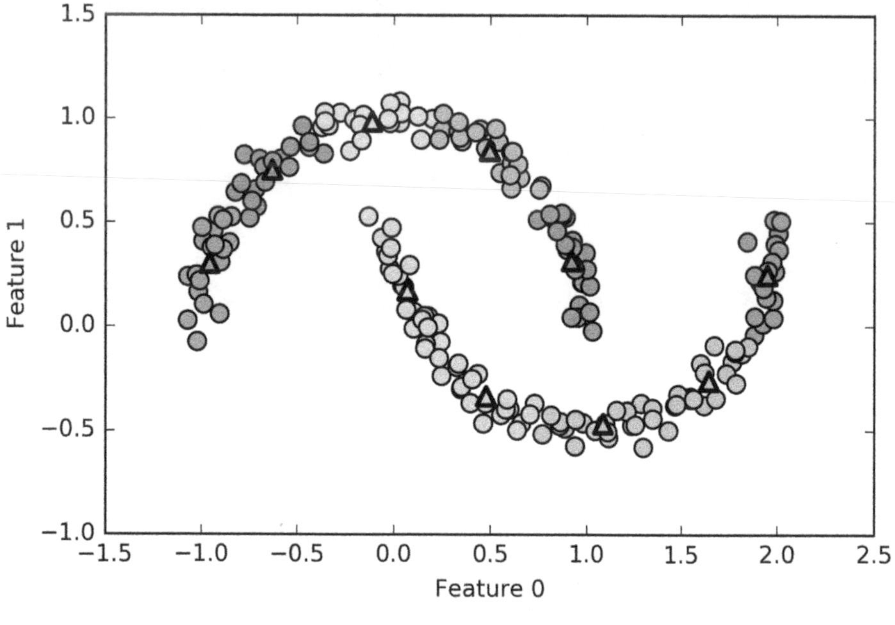

Figure 3-32. Using many k-means clusters to cover the variation in a complex dataset

We used 10 cluster centers, which means each point is now assigned a number between 0 and 9. We can see this as the data being represented using 10 components (that is, we have 10 new features), with all features being 0, apart from the one that represents the cluster center the point is assigned to. Using this 10-dimensional representation, it would now be possible to separate the two half-moon shapes using a linear model, which would not have been possible using the original two features. It is also possible to get an even more expressive representation of the data by using the distances to each of the cluster centers as features. This can be accomplished using the `transform` method of `kmeans`:

In[58]:

```
distance_features = kmeans.transform(X)
print("Distance feature shape: {}".format(distance_features.shape))
print("Distance features:\n{}".format(distance_features))
```

Out[58]:

```
Distance feature shape: (200, 10)
Distance features:
[[0.922 1.466 1.14  ... 1.166 1.039 0.233]
 [1.142 2.517 0.12  ... 0.707 2.204 0.983]
 [0.788 0.774 1.749 ... 1.971 0.716 0.944]
 ...
 [0.446 1.106 1.49  ... 1.791 1.032 0.812]
 [1.39  0.798 1.981 ... 1.978 0.239 1.058]
 [1.149 2.454 0.045 ... 0.572 2.113 0.882]]
```

k-means is a very popular algorithm for clustering, not only because it is relatively easy to understand and implement, but also because it runs relatively quickly. *k*-means scales easily to large datasets, and `scikit-learn` even includes a more scalable variant in the `MiniBatchKMeans` class, which can handle very large datasets.

One of the drawbacks of *k*-means is that it relies on a random initialization, which means the outcome of the algorithm depends on a random seed. By default, `scikit-learn` runs the algorithm 10 times with 10 different random initializations, and returns the best result.[4] Further downsides of *k*-means are the relatively restrictive assumptions made on the shape of clusters, and the requirement to specify the number of clusters you are looking for (which might not be known in a real-world application).

Next, we will look at two more clustering algorithms that improve upon these properties in some ways.

4 In this case, "best" means that the sum of variances of the clusters is small.

3.5.2 Agglomerative Clustering

Agglomerative clustering refers to a collection of clustering algorithms that all build upon the same principles: the algorithm starts by declaring each point its own cluster, and then merges the two most similar clusters until some stopping criterion is satisfied. The stopping criterion implemented in `scikit-learn` is the number of clusters, so similar clusters are merged until only the specified number of clusters are left. There are several *linkage* criteria that specify how exactly the "most similar cluster" is measured. This measure is always defined between two existing clusters.

The following three choices are implemented in `scikit-learn`:

`ward`
: The default choice, `ward` picks the two clusters to merge such that the variance within all clusters increases the least. This often leads to clusters that are relatively equally sized.

`average`
: `average` linkage merges the two clusters that have the smallest average distance between all their points.

`complete`
: `complete` linkage (also known as maximum linkage) merges the two clusters that have the smallest maximum distance between their points.

`ward` works on most datasets, and we will use it in our examples. If the clusters have very dissimilar numbers of members (if one is much bigger than all the others, for example), `average` or `complete` might work better.

The following plot (Figure 3-33) illustrates the progression of agglomerative clustering on a two-dimensional dataset, looking for three clusters:

In[59]:

```
mglearn.plots.plot_agglomerative_algorithm()
```

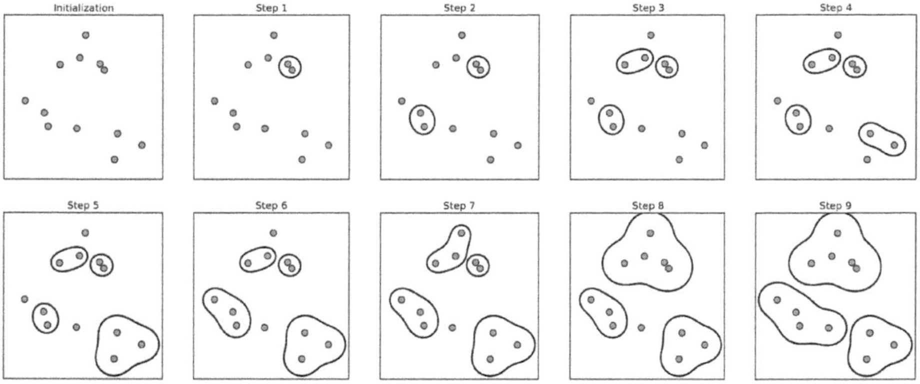

Figure 3-33. Agglomerative clustering iteratively joins the two closest clusters

Initially, each point is its own cluster. Then, in each step, the two clusters that are closest are merged. In the first four steps, two single-point clusters are picked and these are joined into two-point clusters. In step 5, one of the two-point clusters is extended to a third point, and so on. In step 9, there are only three clusters remaining. As we specified that we are looking for three clusters, the algorithm then stops.

Let's have a look at how agglomerative clustering performs on the simple three-cluster data we used here. Because of the way the algorithm works, agglomerative clustering cannot make predictions for new data points. Therefore, `AgglomerativeClustering` has no `predict` method. To build the model and get the cluster memberships on the training set, use the `fit_predict` method instead.[5] The result is shown in Figure 3-34:

In[60]:

```
from sklearn.cluster import AgglomerativeClustering
X, y = make_blobs(random_state=1)

agg = AgglomerativeClustering(n_clusters=3)
assignment = agg.fit_predict(X)

mglearn.discrete_scatter(X[:, 0], X[:, 1], assignment)
plt.legend(["Cluster 0", "Cluster 1", "Cluster 2"], loc="best")
plt.xlabel("Feature 0")
plt.ylabel("Feature 1")
```

5 We could also use the `labels_` attribute, as we did for *k*-means.

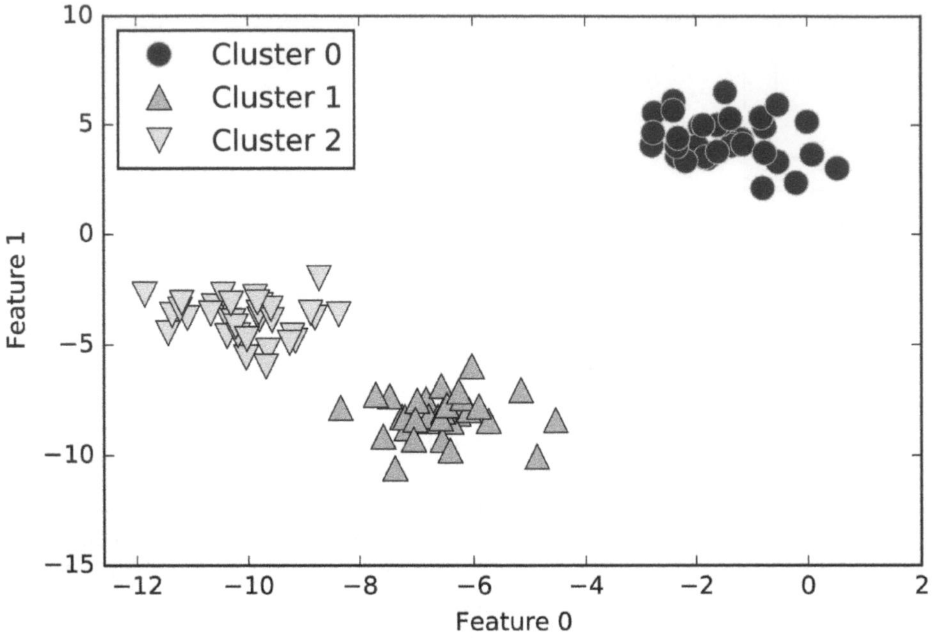

Figure 3-34. Cluster assignment using agglomerative clustering with three clusters

As expected, the algorithm recovers the clustering perfectly. While the `scikit-learn` implementation of agglomerative clustering requires you to specify the number of clusters you want the algorithm to find, agglomerative clustering methods provide some help with choosing the right number, which we will discuss next.

Hierarchical clustering and dendrograms

Agglomerative clustering produces what is known as a *hierarchical clustering*. The clustering proceeds iteratively, and every point makes a journey from being a single point cluster to belonging to some final cluster. Each intermediate step provides a clustering of the data (with a different number of clusters). It is sometimes helpful to look at all possible clusterings jointly. The next example (Figure 3-35) shows an overlay of all the possible clusterings shown in Figure 3-33, providing some insight into how each cluster breaks up into smaller clusters:

In[61]:

```
mglearn.plots.plot_agglomerative()
```

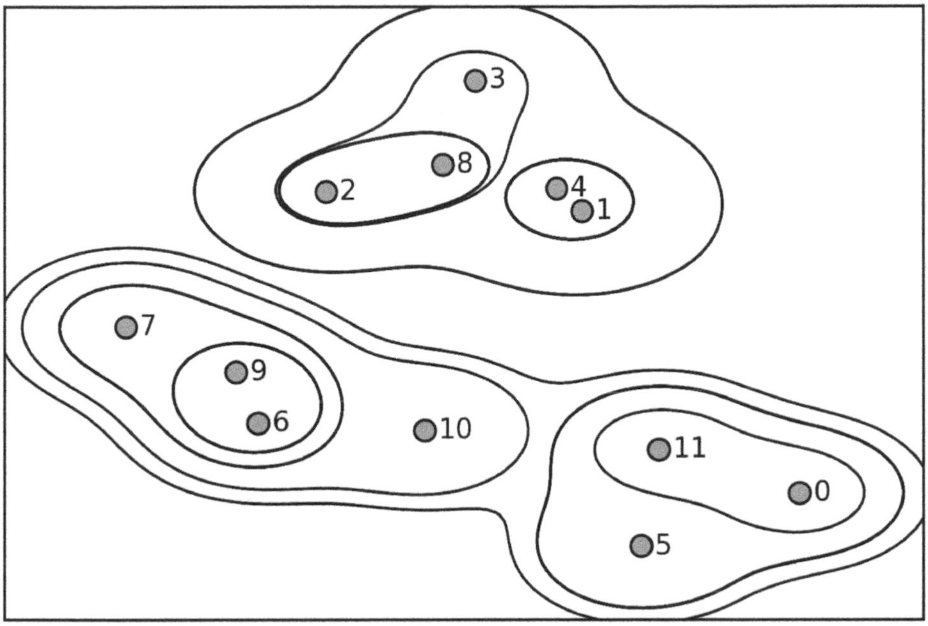

Figure 3-35. Hierarchical cluster assignment (shown as lines) generated with agglomerative clustering, with numbered data points (cf. Figure 3-36)

While this visualization provides a very detailed view of the hierarchical clustering, it relies on the two-dimensional nature of the data and therefore cannot be used on datasets that have more than two features. There is, however, another tool to visualize hierarchical clustering, called a *dendrogram*, that can handle multidimensional datasets.

Unfortunately, `scikit-learn` currently does not have the functionality to draw dendrograms. However, you can generate them easily using SciPy. The SciPy clustering algorithms have a slightly different interface to the `scikit-learn` clustering algorithms. SciPy provides a function that takes a data array `X` and computes a *linkage array*, which encodes hierarchical cluster similarities. We can then feed this linkage array into the scipy `dendrogram` function to plot the dendrogram (Figure 3-36):

In[62]:

```
# Import the dendrogram function and the ward clustering function from SciPy
from scipy.cluster.hierarchy import dendrogram, ward

X, y = make_blobs(random_state=0, n_samples=12)
# Apply the ward clustering to the data array X
# The SciPy ward function returns an array that specifies the distances
# bridged when performing agglomerative clustering
linkage_array = ward(X)
```

```
# Now we plot the dendrogram for the linkage_array containing the distances
# between clusters
dendrogram(linkage_array)

# Mark the cuts in the tree that signify two or three clusters
ax = plt.gca()
bounds = ax.get_xbound()
ax.plot(bounds, [7.25, 7.25], '--', c='k')
ax.plot(bounds, [4, 4], '--', c='k')

ax.text(bounds[1], 7.25, ' two clusters', va='center', fontdict={'size': 15})
ax.text(bounds[1], 4, ' three clusters', va='center', fontdict={'size': 15})
plt.xlabel("Sample index")
plt.ylabel("Cluster distance")
```

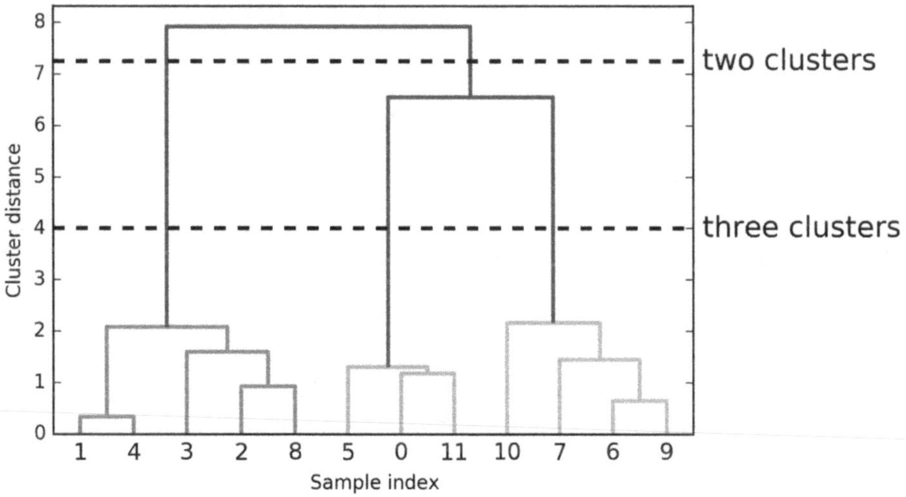

Figure 3-36. Dendrogram of the clustering shown in Figure 3-35 with lines indicating splits into two and three clusters

The dendrogram shows data points as points on the bottom (numbered from 0 to 11). Then, a tree is plotted with these points (representing single-point clusters) as the leaves, and a new node parent is added for each two clusters that are joined.

Reading from bottom to top, the data points 1 and 4 are joined first (as you could see in Figure 3-33). Next, points 6 and 9 are joined into a cluster, and so on. At the top level, there are two branches, one consisting of points 11, 0, 5, 10, 7, 6, and 9, and the other consisting of points 1, 4, 3, 2, and 8. These correspond to the two largest clusters in the lefthand side of the plot.

The y-axis in the dendrogram doesn't just specify when in the agglomerative algorithm two clusters get merged. The length of each branch also shows how far apart the merged clusters are. The longest branches in this dendrogram are the three lines that are marked by the dashed line labeled "three clusters." That these are the longest branches indicates that going from three to two clusters meant merging some very far-apart points. We see this again at the top of the chart, where merging the two remaining clusters into a single cluster again bridges a relatively large distance.

Unfortunately, agglomerative clustering still fails at separating complex shapes like the `two_moons` dataset. But the same is not true for the next algorithm we will look at, DBSCAN.

3.5.3 DBSCAN

Another very useful clustering algorithm is DBSCAN (which stands for "density-based spatial clustering of applications with noise"). The main benefits of DBSCAN are that it does not require the user to set the number of clusters *a priori*, it can capture clusters of complex shapes, and it can identify points that are not part of any cluster. DBSCAN is somewhat slower than agglomerative clustering and *k*-means, but still scales to relatively large datasets.

DBSCAN works by identifying points that are in "crowded" regions of the feature space, where many data points are close together. These regions are referred to as *dense* regions in feature space. The idea behind DBSCAN is that clusters form dense regions of data, separated by regions that are relatively empty.

Points that are within a dense region are called *core samples* (or core points), and they are defined as follows. There are two parameters in DBSCAN: `min_samples` and `eps`. If there are at least `min_samples` many data points within a distance of `eps` to a given data point, that data point is classified as a core sample. Core samples that are closer to each other than the distance `eps` are put into the same cluster by DBSCAN.

The algorithm works by picking an arbitrary point to start with. It then finds all points with distance `eps` or less from that point. If there are less than `min_samples` points within distance `eps` of the starting point, this point is labeled as *noise*, meaning that it doesn't belong to any cluster. If there are more than `min_samples` points within a distance of `eps`, the point is labeled a core sample and assigned a new cluster label. Then, all neighbors (within `eps`) of the point are visited. If they have not been assigned a cluster yet, they are assigned the new cluster label that was just created. If they are core samples, their neighbors are visited in turn, and so on. The cluster grows until there are no more core samples within distance `eps` of the cluster. Then another point that hasn't yet been visited is picked, and the same procedure is repeated.

In the end, there are three kinds of points: core points, points that are within distance eps of core points (called *boundary points*), and noise. When the DBSCAN algorithm is run on a particular dataset multiple times, the clustering of the core points is always the same, and the same points will always be labeled as noise. However, a boundary point might be neighbor to core samples of more than one cluster. Therefore, the cluster membership of boundary points depends on the order in which points are visited. Usually there are only few boundary points, and this slight dependence on the order of points is not important.

Let's apply DBSCAN on the synthetic dataset we used to demonstrate agglomerative clustering. Like agglomerative clustering, DBSCAN does not allow predictions on new test data, so we will use the fit_predict method to perform clustering and return the cluster labels in one step:

In[63]:

```
from sklearn.cluster import DBSCAN
X, y = make_blobs(random_state=0, n_samples=12)

dbscan = DBSCAN()
clusters = dbscan.fit_predict(X)
print("Cluster memberships:\n{}".format(clusters))
```

Out[63]:

```
Cluster memberships:
[-1 -1 -1 -1 -1 -1 -1 -1 -1 -1 -1 -1]
```

As you can see, all data points were assigned the label -1, which stands for noise. This is a consequence of the default parameter settings for eps and min_samples, which are not tuned for small toy datasets. The cluster assignments for different values of min_samples and eps are shown below, and visualized in Figure 3-37:

In[64]:

```
mglearn.plots.plot_dbscan()
```

Out[64]:

```
min_samples: 2 eps: 1.000000  cluster: [-1  0  0 -1  0 -1  1  1  0  1 -1 -1]
min_samples: 2 eps: 1.500000  cluster: [0 1 1 1 1 0 2 2 1 2 2 0]
min_samples: 2 eps: 2.000000  cluster: [0 1 1 1 1 0 0 0 1 0 0 0]
min_samples: 2 eps: 3.000000  cluster: [0 0 0 0 0 0 0 0 0 0 0 0]
min_samples: 3 eps: 1.000000  cluster: [-1  0  0 -1  0 -1  1  1  0  1 -1 -1]
min_samples: 3 eps: 1.500000  cluster: [0 1 1 1 1 0 2 2 1 2 2 0]
min_samples: 3 eps: 2.000000  cluster: [0 1 1 1 1 0 0 0 1 0 0 0]
min_samples: 3 eps: 3.000000  cluster: [0 0 0 0 0 0 0 0 0 0 0 0]
min_samples: 5 eps: 1.000000  cluster: [-1 -1 -1 -1 -1 -1 -1 -1 -1 -1 -1 -1]
min_samples: 5 eps: 1.500000  cluster: [-1  0  0  0  0 -1 -1 -1  0 -1 -1 -1]
min_samples: 5 eps: 2.000000  cluster: [-1  0  0  0  0 -1 -1 -1  0 -1 -1 -1]
min_samples: 5 eps: 3.000000  cluster: [0 0 0 0 0 0 0 0 0 0 0 0]
```

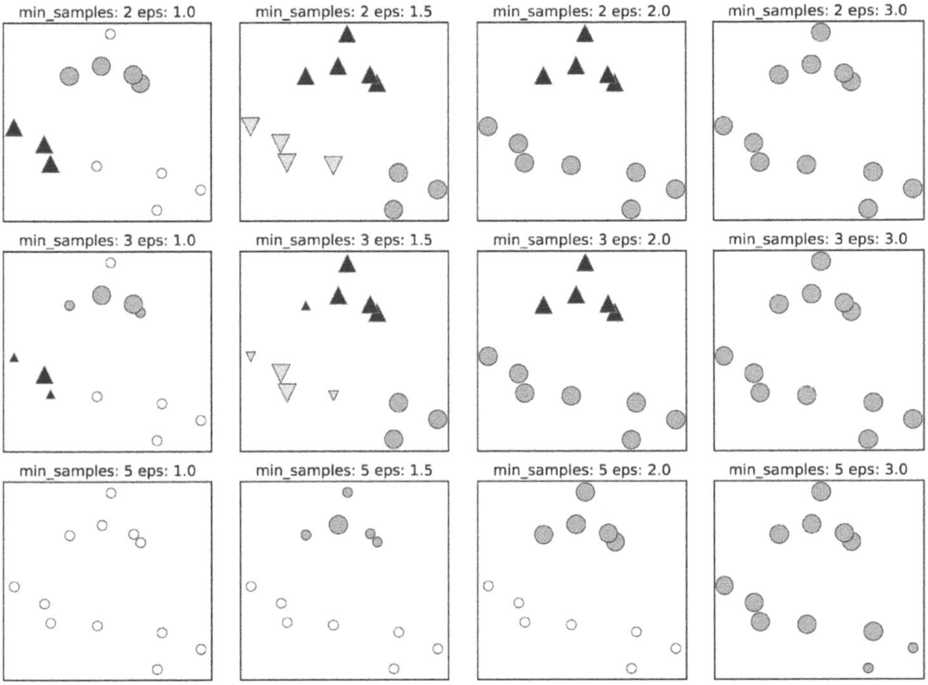

Figure 3-37. Cluster assignments found by DBSCAN with varying settings for the min_samples and eps parameters

In this plot, points that belong to clusters are solid, while the noise points are shown in white. Core samples are shown as large markers, while boundary points are displayed as smaller markers. Increasing `eps` (going from left to right in the figure) means that more points will be included in a cluster. This makes clusters grow, but might also lead to multiple clusters joining into one. Increasing `min_samples` (going from top to bottom in the figure) means that fewer points will be core points, and more points will be labeled as noise.

The parameter `eps` is somewhat more important, as it determines what it means for points to be "close." Setting `eps` to be very small will mean that no points are core samples, and may lead to all points being labeled as noise. Setting `eps` to be very large will result in all points forming a single cluster.

The `min_samples` setting mostly determines whether points in less dense regions will be labeled as outliers or as their own clusters. If you increase `min_samples`, anything that would have been a cluster with less than `min_samples` many samples will now be labeled as noise. `min_samples` therefore determines the minimum cluster size. You can see this very clearly in Figure 3-37, when going from `min_samples=3` to `min_samples=5` with `eps=1.5`. With `min_samples=3`, there are three clusters: one of four points, one of five points, and one of three points. Using `min_samples=5`, the two smaller clusters (with three and four points) are now labeled as noise, and only the cluster with five samples remains.

While DBSCAN doesn't require setting the number of clusters explicitly, setting `eps` implicitly controls how many clusters will be found. Finding a good setting for `eps` is sometimes easier after scaling the data using `StandardScaler` or `MinMaxScaler`, as using these scaling techniques will ensure that all features have similar ranges.

Figure 3-38 shows the result of running DBSCAN on the `two_moons` dataset. The algorithm actually finds the two half-circles and separates them using the default settings:

In[65]:

```
X, y = make_moons(n_samples=200, noise=0.05, random_state=0)

# rescale the data to zero mean and unit variance
scaler = StandardScaler()
scaler.fit(X)
X_scaled = scaler.transform(X)

dbscan = DBSCAN()
clusters = dbscan.fit_predict(X_scaled)
# plot the cluster assignments
plt.scatter(X_scaled[:, 0], X_scaled[:, 1], c=clusters, cmap=mglearn.cm2, s=60)
plt.xlabel("Feature 0")
plt.ylabel("Feature 1")
```

As the algorithm produced the desired number of clusters (two), the parameter settings seem to work well. If we decrease `eps` to `0.2` (from the default of `0.5`), we will get eight clusters, which is clearly too many. Increasing `eps` to `0.7` results in a single cluster.

When using DBSCAN, you need to be careful about handling the returned cluster assignments. The use of `-1` to indicate noise might result in unexpected effects when using the cluster labels to index another array.

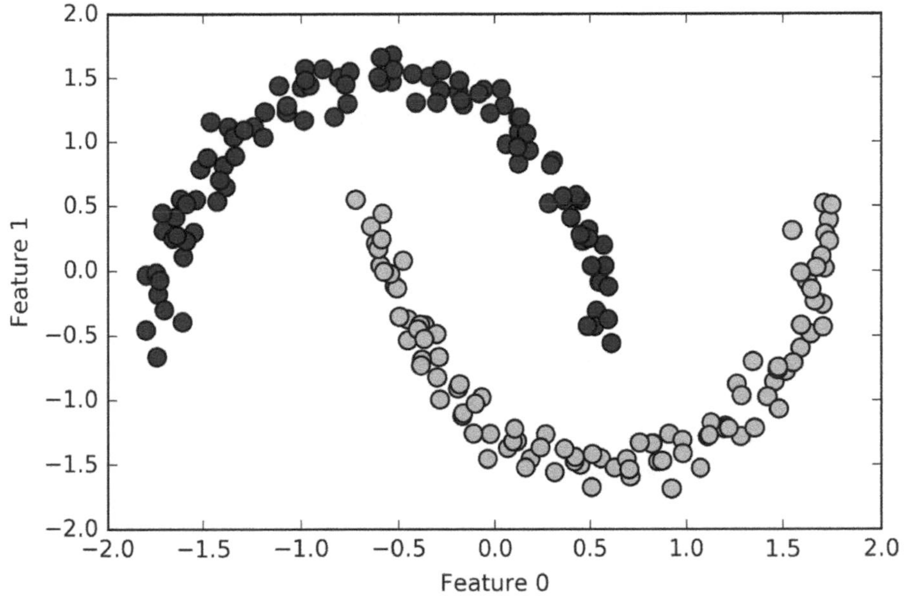

Figure 3-38. Cluster assignment found by DBSCAN using the default value of eps=0.5

3.5.4 Comparing and Evaluating Clustering Algorithms

One of the challenges in applying clustering algorithms is that it is very hard to assess how well an algorithm worked, and to compare outcomes between different algorithms. After talking about the algorithms behind *k*-means, agglomerative clustering, and DBSCAN, we will now compare them on some real-world datasets.

Evaluating clustering with ground truth

There are metrics that can be used to assess the outcome of a clustering algorithm relative to a ground truth clustering, the most important ones being the *adjusted rand index* (ARI) and *normalized mutual information* (NMI), which both provide a quantitative measure with an optimum of 1 and a value of 0 for unrelated clusterings (though the ARI can become negative).

Here, we compare the *k*-means, agglomerative clustering, and DBSCAN algorithms using ARI. We also include what it looks like when we randomly assign points to two clusters for comparison (see Figure 3-39):

In[66]:

```
from sklearn.metrics.cluster import adjusted_rand_score
X, y = make_moons(n_samples=200, noise=0.05, random_state=0)

# rescale the data to zero mean and unit variance
scaler = StandardScaler()
scaler.fit(X)
X_scaled = scaler.transform(X)

fig, axes = plt.subplots(1, 4, figsize=(15, 3),
                         subplot_kw={'xticks': (), 'yticks': ()})

# make a list of algorithms to use
algorithms = [KMeans(n_clusters=2), AgglomerativeClustering(n_clusters=2),
              DBSCAN()]

# create a random cluster assignment for reference
random_state = np.random.RandomState(seed=0)
random_clusters = random_state.randint(low=0, high=2, size=len(X))

# plot random assignment
axes[0].scatter(X_scaled[:, 0], X_scaled[:, 1], c=random_clusters,
                cmap=mglearn.cm3, s=60)
axes[0].set_title("Random assignment - ARI: {:.2f}".format(
        adjusted_rand_score(y, random_clusters)))

for ax, algorithm in zip(axes[1:], algorithms):
    # plot the cluster assignments and cluster centers
    clusters = algorithm.fit_predict(X_scaled)
    ax.scatter(X_scaled[:, 0], X_scaled[:, 1], c=clusters,
               cmap=mglearn.cm3, s=60)
    ax.set_title("{} - ARI: {:.2f}".format(algorithm.__class__.__name__,
                                           adjusted_rand_score(y, clusters)))
```

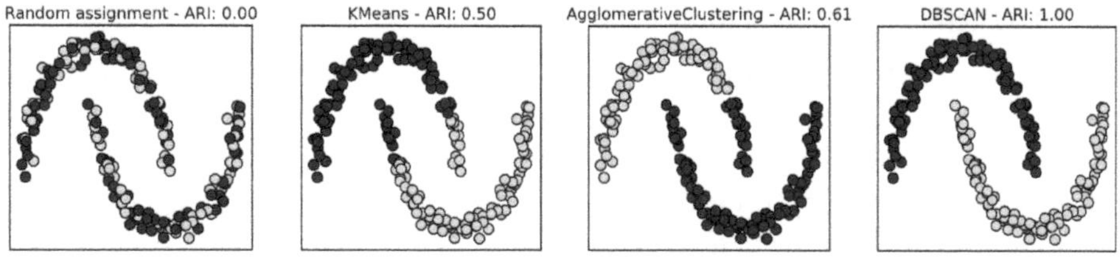

Figure 3-39. Comparing random assignment, k-means, agglomerative clustering, and DBSCAN on the two_moons dataset using the supervised ARI score

The adjusted rand index provides intuitive results, with a random cluster assignment having a score of 0 and DBSCAN (which recovers the desired clustering perfectly) having a score of 1.

A common mistake when evaluating clustering in this way is to use `accuracy_score` instead of `adjusted_rand_score`, `normalized_mutual_info_score`, or some other clustering metric. The problem in using accuracy is that it requires the assigned cluster labels to exactly match the ground truth. However, the cluster labels themselves are meaningless—the only thing that matters is which points are in the same cluster:

In[67]:

```
from sklearn.metrics import accuracy_score

# these two labelings of points correspond to the same clustering
clusters1 = [0, 0, 1, 1, 0]
clusters2 = [1, 1, 0, 0, 1]
# accuracy is zero, as none of the labels are the same
print("Accuracy: {:.2f}".format(accuracy_score(clusters1, clusters2)))
# adjusted rand score is 1, as the clustering is exactly the same
print("ARI: {:.2f}".format(adjusted_rand_score(clusters1, clusters2)))
```

Out[67]:

```
Accuracy: 0.00
ARI: 1.00
```

Evaluating clustering without ground truth

Although we have just shown one way to evaluate clustering algorithms, in practice, there is a big problem with using measures like ARI. When applying clustering algorithms, there is usually no ground truth to which to compare the results. If we knew the right clustering of the data, we could use this information to build a supervised model like a classifier. Therefore, using metrics like ARI and NMI usually only helps in developing algorithms, not in assessing success in an application.

There are scoring metrics for clustering that don't require ground truth, like the *silhouette coefficient*. However, these often don't work well in practice. The silhouette score computes the compactness of a cluster, where higher is better, with a perfect score of 1. While compact clusters are good, compactness doesn't allow for complex shapes.

Here is an example comparing the outcome of *k*-means, agglomerative clustering, and DBSCAN on the `two-moons` dataset using the silhouette score (Figure 3-40):

In[68]:

```
from sklearn.metrics.cluster import silhouette_score

X, y = make_moons(n_samples=200, noise=0.05, random_state=0)
# rescale the data to zero mean and unit variance
scaler = StandardScaler()
scaler.fit(X)
X_scaled = scaler.transform(X)
```

```
fig, axes = plt.subplots(1, 4, figsize=(15, 3),
                         subplot_kw={'xticks': (), 'yticks': ()})

# create a random cluster assignment for reference
random_state = np.random.RandomState(seed=0)
random_clusters = random_state.randint(low=0, high=2, size=len(X))

# plot random assignment
axes[0].scatter(X_scaled[:, 0], X_scaled[:, 1], c=random_clusters,
                cmap=mglearn.cm3, s=60)
axes[0].set_title("Random assignment: {:.2f}".format(
    silhouette_score(X_scaled, random_clusters)))

algorithms = [KMeans(n_clusters=2), AgglomerativeClustering(n_clusters=2),
              DBSCAN()]

for ax, algorithm in zip(axes[1:], algorithms):
    clusters = algorithm.fit_predict(X_scaled)
    # plot the cluster assignments and cluster centers
    ax.scatter(X_scaled[:, 0], X_scaled[:, 1], c=clusters, cmap=mglearn.cm3,
               s=60)
    ax.set_title("{} : {:.2f}".format(algorithm.__class__.__name__,
                                      silhouette_score(X_scaled, clusters)))
```

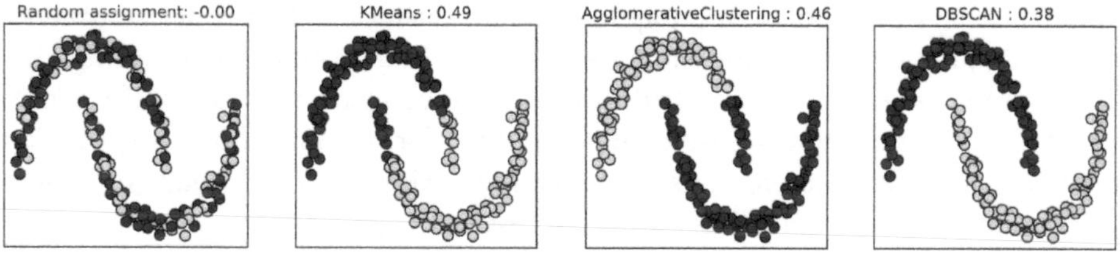

Figure 3-40. Comparing random assignment, k-means, agglomerative clustering, and DBSCAN on the two_moons dataset using the unsupervised silhouette score—the more intuitive result of DBSCAN has a lower silhouette score than the assignments found by k-means

As you can see, *k*-means gets the highest silhouette score, even though we might prefer the result produced by DBSCAN. A slightly better strategy for evaluating clusters is using *robustness-based* clustering metrics. These run an algorithm after adding some noise to the data, or using different parameter settings, and compare the outcomes. The idea is that if many algorithm parameters and many perturbations of the data return the same result, it is likely to be trustworthy. Unfortunately, this strategy is not implemented in `scikit-learn` at the time of writing.

Even if we get a very robust clustering, or a very high silhouette score, we still don't know if there is any semantic meaning in the clustering, or whether the clustering reflects an aspect of the data that we are interested in. Let's go back to the example of face images. We hope to find groups of similar faces—say, men and women, or old people and young people, or people with beards and without. Let's say we cluster the data into two clusters, and all algorithms agree about which points should be clustered together. We still don't know if the clusters that are found correspond in any way to the concepts we are interested in. It could be that they found side views versus front views, or pictures taken at night versus pictures taken during the day, or pictures taken with iPhones versus pictures taken with Android phones. The only way to know whether the clustering corresponds to anything we are interested in is to analyze the clusters manually.

Comparing algorithms on the faces dataset

Let's apply the *k*-means, DBSCAN, and agglomerative clustering algorithms to the Labeled Faces in the Wild dataset, and see if any of them find interesting structure. We will use the eigenface representation of the data, as produced by `PCA(whiten=True)`, with 100 components:

In[69]:

```
# extract eigenfaces from lfw data and transform data
from sklearn.decomposition import PCA
pca = PCA(n_components=100, whiten=True, random_state=0)
X_pca = pca.fit_transform(X_people)
```

We saw earlier that this is a more semantic representation of the face images than the raw pixels. It will also make computation faster. A good exercise would be for you to run the following experiments on the original data, without PCA, and see if you find similar clusters.

Analyzing the faces dataset with DBSCAN. We will start by applying DBSCAN, which we just discussed:

In[70]:

```
# apply DBSCAN with default parameters
dbscan = DBSCAN()
labels = dbscan.fit_predict(X_pca)
print("Unique labels: {}".format(np.unique(labels)))
```

Out[70]:

```
Unique labels: [-1]
```

We see that all the returned labels are –1, so all of the data was labeled as "noise" by DBSCAN. There are two things we can change to help this: we can make `eps` higher, to expand the neighborhood of each point, and set `min_samples` lower, to consider smaller groups of points as clusters. Let's try changing `min_samples` first:

In[71]:

```
dbscan = DBSCAN(min_samples=3)
labels = dbscan.fit_predict(X_pca)
print("Unique labels: {}".format(np.unique(labels)))
```

Out[71]:

```
Unique labels: [-1]
```

Even when considering groups of three points, everything is labeled as noise. So, we need to increase `eps`:

In[72]:

```
dbscan = DBSCAN(min_samples=3, eps=15)
labels = dbscan.fit_predict(X_pca)
print("Unique labels: {}".format(np.unique(labels)))
```

Out[72]:

```
Unique labels: [-1  0]
```

Using a much larger `eps` of `15`, we get only a single cluster and noise points. We can use this result to find out what the "noise" looks like compared to the rest of the data. To understand better what's happening, let's look at how many points are noise, and how many points are inside the cluster:

In[73]:

```
# Count number of points in all clusters and noise.
# bincount doesn't allow negative numbers, so we need to add 1.
# The first number in the result corresponds to noise points.
print("Number of points per cluster: {}".format(np.bincount(labels + 1)))
```

Out[73]:

```
Number of points per cluster: [  27 2036]
```

There are very few noise points—only 27—so we can look at all of them (see Figure 3-41):

In[74]:

```
noise = X_people[labels==-1]

fig, axes = plt.subplots(3, 9, subplot_kw={'xticks': (), 'yticks': ()},
                         figsize=(12, 4))
for image, ax in zip(noise, axes.ravel()):
    ax.imshow(image.reshape(image_shape), vmin=0, vmax=1)
```

Figure 3-41. Samples from the faces dataset labeled as noise by DBSCAN

Comparing these images to the random sample of face images from Figure 3-7, we can guess why they were labeled as noise: the fifth image in the first row shows a person drinking from a glass, there are images of people wearing hats, and in the last image there's a hand in front of the person's face. The other images contain odd angles or crops that are too close or too wide.

This kind of analysis—trying to find "the odd one out"—is called *outlier detection*. If this was a real application, we might try to do a better job of cropping images, to get more homogeneous data. There is little we can do about people in photos sometimes wearing hats, drinking, or holding something in front of their faces, but it's good to know that these are issues in the data that any algorithm we might apply needs to handle.

If we want to find more interesting clusters than just one large one, we need to set `eps` smaller, somewhere between `15` and `0.5` (the default). Let's have a look at what different values of `eps` result in:

In[75]:

```
for eps in [1, 3, 5, 7, 9, 11, 13]:
    print("\neps={}".format(eps))
    dbscan = DBSCAN(eps=eps, min_samples=3)
    labels = dbscan.fit_predict(X_pca)
    print("Number of clusters: {}".format(len(np.unique(labels))))
    print("Cluster sizes: {}".format(np.bincount(labels + 1)))
```

Out[75]:

```
eps=1
Number of clusters: 1
Cluster sizes: [2063]

eps=3
Number of clusters: 1
Cluster sizes: [2063]
```

```
eps=5
Number of clusters: 1
Cluster sizes: [2063]

eps=7
Number of clusters: 14
Cluster sizes: [2006   4   6   6   6   9   3   3   4   3   3   3   3   4]

eps=9
Number of clusters: 4
Cluster sizes: [1269  788    3    3]

eps=11
Number of clusters: 2
Cluster sizes: [ 430 1633]

eps=13
Number of clusters: 2
Cluster sizes: [ 112 1951]
```

For low settings of `eps`, all points are labeled as noise. For `eps=7`, we get many noise points and many smaller clusters. For `eps=9` we still get many noise points, but we get one big cluster and some smaller clusters. Starting from `eps=11`, we get only one large cluster and noise.

What is interesting to note is that there is never more than one large cluster. At most, there is one large cluster containing most of the points, and some smaller clusters. This indicates that there are not two or three different kinds of face images in the data that are very distinct, but rather that all images are more or less equally similar to (or dissimilar from) the rest.

The results for `eps=7` look most interesting, with many small clusters. We can investigate this clustering in more detail by visualizing all of the points in each of the 13 small clusters (Figure 3-42):

In[76]:

```
dbscan = DBSCAN(min_samples=3, eps=7)
labels = dbscan.fit_predict(X_pca)

for cluster in range(max(labels) + 1):
    mask = labels == cluster
    n_images =  np.sum(mask)
    fig, axes = plt.subplots(1, n_images, figsize=(n_images * 1.5, 4),
                             subplot_kw={'xticks': (), 'yticks': ()})
    for image, label, ax in zip(X_people[mask], y_people[mask], axes):

        ax.imshow(image.reshape(image_shape), vmin=0, vmax=1)
        ax.set_title(people.target_names[label].split()[-1])
```

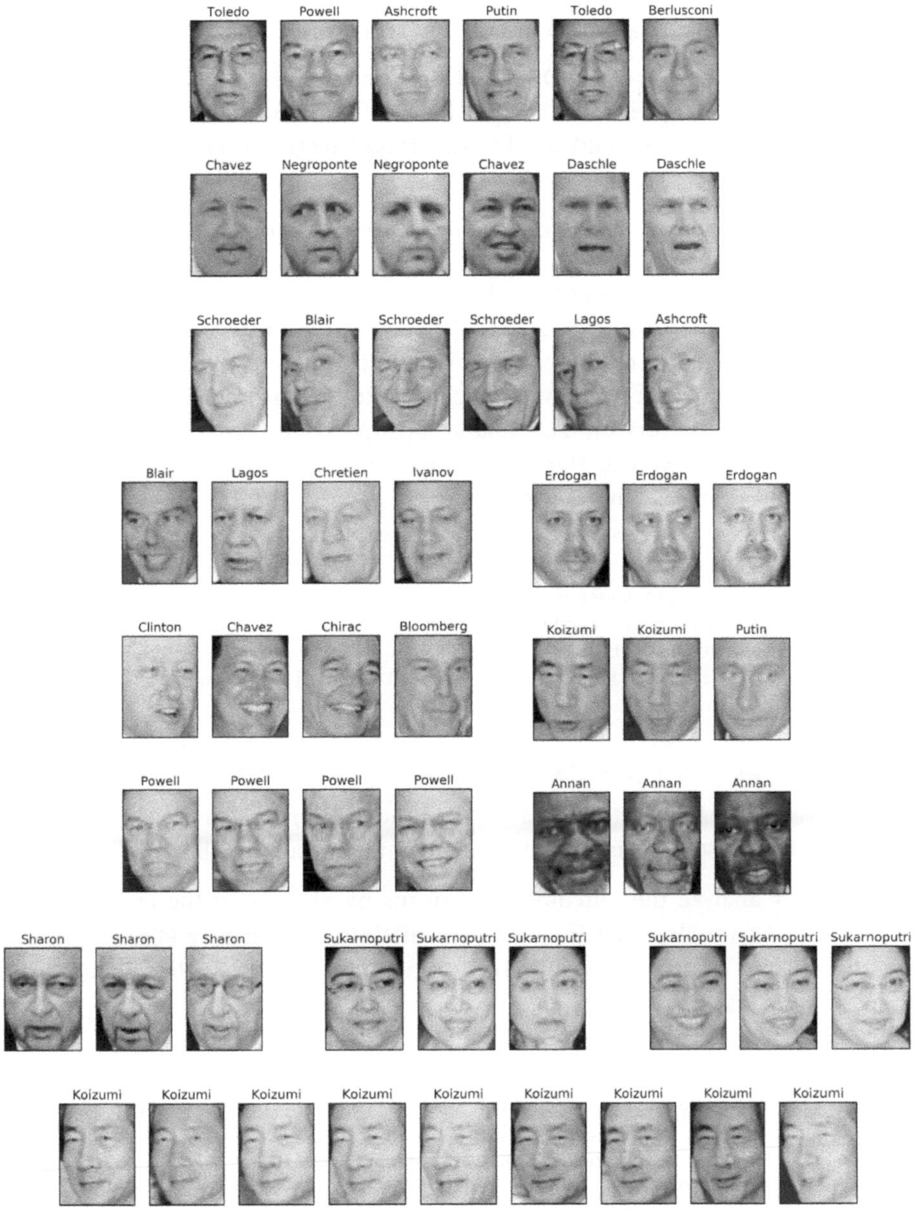

Figure 3-42. Clusters found by DBSCAN with eps=7

Some of the clusters correspond to people with very distinct faces (within this dataset), such as Sharon or Koizumi. Within each cluster, the orientation of the face is also quite fixed, as well as the facial expression. Some of the clusters contain faces of multiple people, but they share a similar orientation and expression.

This concludes our analysis of the DBSCAN algorithm applied to the faces dataset. As you can see, we are doing a manual analysis here, different from the much more automatic search approach we could use for supervised learning based on R^2 score or accuracy.

Let's move on to applying *k*-means and agglomerative clustering.

Analyzing the faces dataset with k-means. We saw that it was not possible to create more than one big cluster using DBSCAN. Agglomerative clustering and *k*-means are much more likely to create clusters of even size, but we do need to set a target number of clusters. We could set the number of clusters to the known number of people in the dataset, though it is very unlikely that an unsupervised clustering algorithm will recover them. Instead, we can start with a low number of clusters, like 10, which might allow us to analyze each of the clusters:

In[77]:

```
# extract clusters with k-means
km = KMeans(n_clusters=10, random_state=0)
labels_km = km.fit_predict(X_pca)
print("Cluster sizes k-means: {}".format(np.bincount(labels_km)))
```

Out[77]:

```
Cluster sizes k-means: [269 128 170 186 386 222 237  64 253 148]
```

As you can see, *k*-means clustering partitioned the data into relatively similarly sized clusters from 64 to 386. This is quite different from the result of DBSCAN.

We can further analyze the outcome of *k*-means by visualizing the cluster centers (Figure 3-43). As we clustered in the representation produced by `PCA`, we need to rotate the cluster centers back into the original space to visualize them, using `pca.inverse_transform`:

In[78]:

```
fig, axes = plt.subplots(2, 5, subplot_kw={'xticks': (), 'yticks': ()},
                         figsize=(12, 4))
for center, ax in zip(km.cluster_centers_, axes.ravel()):
    ax.imshow(pca.inverse_transform(center).reshape(image_shape),
              vmin=0, vmax=1)
```

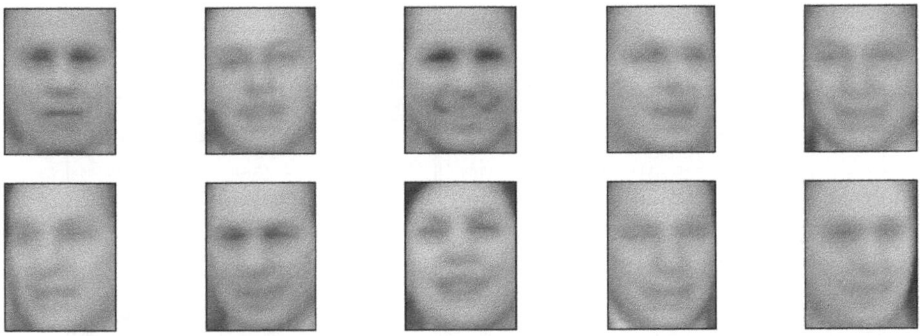

Figure 3-43. Cluster centers found by k-means when setting the number of clusters to 10

The cluster centers found by *k*-means are very smooth versions of faces. This is not very surprising, given that each center is an average of 64 to 386 face images. Working with a reduced PCA representation adds to the smoothness of the images (compared to the faces reconstructed using 100 PCA dimensions in Figure 3-11). The clustering seems to pick up on different orientations of the face, different expressions (the third cluster center seems to show a smiling face), and the presence of shirt collars (see the second-to-last cluster center).

For a more detailed view, in Figure 3-44 we show for each cluster center the five most typical images in the cluster (the images assigned to the cluster that are closest to the cluster center) and the five most atypical images in the cluster (the images assigned to the cluster that are furthest from the cluster center):

In[79]:

```
mglearn.plots.plot_kmeans_faces(km, pca, X_pca, X_people,
                                y_people, people.target_names)
```

Figure 3-44. Sample images for each cluster found by k-means—the cluster centers are on the left, followed by the five closest points to each center and the five points that are assigned to the cluster but are furthest away from the center

Figure 3-44 confirms our intuition about smiling faces for the third cluster, and also the importance of orientation for the other clusters. The "atypical" points are not very similar to the cluster centers, though, and their assignment seems somewhat arbitrary. This can be attributed to the fact that *k*-means partitions all the data points and doesn't have a concept of "noise" points, as DBSCAN does. Using a larger number of clusters, the algorithm could find finer distinctions. However, adding more clusters makes manual inspection even harder.

Analyzing the faces dataset with agglomerative clustering. Now, let's look at the results of agglomerative clustering:

In[80]:

```
# extract clusters with ward agglomerative clustering
agglomerative = AgglomerativeClustering(n_clusters=10)
labels_agg = agglomerative.fit_predict(X_pca)
print("Cluster sizes agglomerative clustering: {}".format(
    np.bincount(labels_agg)))
```

Out[80]:

```
Cluster sizes agglomerative clustering: [255 623  86 102 122 199 265  26 230 155]
```

Agglomerative clustering also produces relatively equally sized clusters, with cluster sizes between 26 and 623. These are more uneven than those produced by *k*-means, but much more even than the ones produced by DBSCAN.

We can compute the ARI to measure whether the two partitions of the data given by agglomerative clustering and *k*-means are similar:

In[81]:

```
print("ARI: {:.2f}".format(adjusted_rand_score(labels_agg, labels_km)))
```

Out[81]:

```
ARI: 0.13
```

An ARI of only 0.13 means that the two clusterings `labels_agg` and `labels_km` have little in common. This is not very surprising, given the fact that points further away from the cluster centers seem to have little in common for *k*-means.

Next, we might want to plot the dendrogram (Figure 3-45). We'll limit the depth of the tree in the plot, as branching down to the individual 2,063 data points would result in an unreadably dense plot:

In[82]:

```
linkage_array = ward(X_pca)
# now we plot the dendrogram for the linkage_array
# containing the distances between clusters
plt.figure(figsize=(20, 5))
dendrogram(linkage_array, p=7, truncate_mode='level', no_labels=True)
plt.xlabel("Sample index")
plt.ylabel("Cluster distance")
```

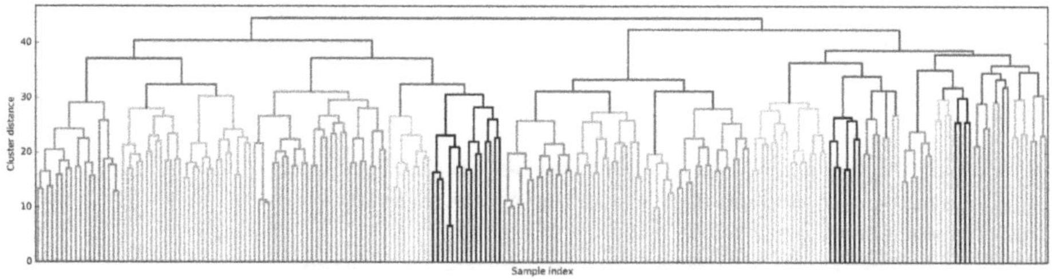

Figure 3-45. Dendrogram of agglomerative clustering on the faces dataset

Creating 10 clusters, we cut across the tree at the very top, where there are 10 vertical lines. In the dendrogram for the toy data shown in Figure 3-36, you could see by the length of the branches that two or three clusters might capture the data appropriately. For the faces data, there doesn't seem to be a very natural cutoff point. There are some branches that represent more distinct groups, but there doesn't appear to be a particular number of clusters that is a good fit. This is not surprising, given the result of DBSCAN that we observed earlier, which tried to cluster all points together.

Let's visualize the 10 clusters, as we did for *k*-means earlier (Figure 3-46). Note that there is no notion of cluster center in agglomerative clustering (though we could compute the mean), and we simply show the first couple of points in each cluster. We show the number of points in each cluster to the left of the first image:

In[83]:

```
n_clusters = 10
for cluster in range(n_clusters):
    mask = labels_agg == cluster
    fig, axes = plt.subplots(1, 10, subplot_kw={'xticks': (), 'yticks': ()},
                             figsize=(15, 8))
    axes[0].set_ylabel(np.sum(mask))
    for image, label, asdf, ax in zip(X_people[mask], y_people[mask],
                                      labels_agg[mask], axes):
        ax.imshow(image.reshape(image_shape), vmin=0, vmax=1)
        ax.set_title(people.target_names[label].split()[-1],
                     fontdict={'fontsize': 9})
```

Figure 3-46. Random images from the clusters generated by In[82]—each row corresponds to one cluster; the number to the left lists the number of images in each cluster

While some of the clusters seem to have a semantic theme, many of them are too large to be actually homogeneous. To get more homogeneous clusters, we can run the algorithm again, this time with 40 clusters, and pick out some of the clusters that are particularly interesting (Figure 3-47):

In[84]:

```
# extract clusters with ward agglomerative clustering
agglomerative = AgglomerativeClustering(n_clusters=40)
labels_agg = agglomerative.fit_predict(X_pca)
print("cluster sizes agglomerative clustering: {}".format(np.bincount(labels_agg)))

n_clusters = 40
for cluster in [10, 13, 19, 22, 36]: # hand-picked "interesting" clusters
    mask = labels_agg == cluster
    fig, axes = plt.subplots(1, 15, subplot_kw={'xticks': (), 'yticks': ()},
                             figsize=(15, 8))
    cluster_size = np.sum(mask)
    axes[0].set_ylabel("#{}: {}".format(cluster, cluster_size))
    for image, label, asdf, ax in zip(X_people[mask], y_people[mask],
                                      labels_agg[mask], axes):
        ax.imshow(image.reshape(image_shape), vmin=0, vmax=1)
        ax.set_title(people.target_names[label].split()[-1],
                     fontdict={'fontsize': 9})
    for i in range(cluster_size, 15):
        axes[i].set_visible(False)
```

Out[84]:

```
cluster sizes agglomerative clustering:
 [ 58  80  79  40 222  50  55  78 172  28  26  34  14  11  60  66 152  27
   47  31  54   5   8  56   3   5   8  18  22  82  37  89  28  24  41  40
   21  10 113  69]
```

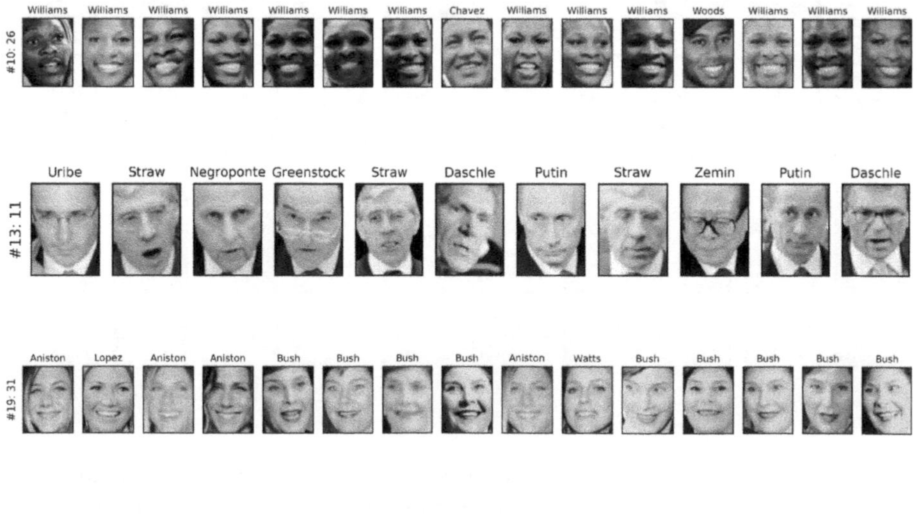

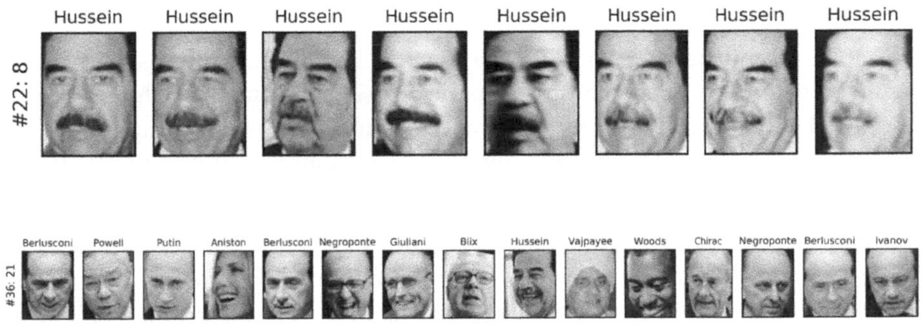

Figure 3-47. Images from selected clusters found by agglomerative clustering when setting the number of clusters to 40—the text to the left shows the index of the cluster and the total number of points in the cluster

Here, the clustering seems to have picked up on "dark skinned and smiling," "collared shirt," "smiling woman," "Hussein," and "high forehead." We could also find these highly similar clusters using the dendrogram, if we did more a detailed analysis.

3.5.5 Summary of Clustering Methods

This section has shown that applying and evaluating clustering is a highly qualitative procedure, and often most helpful in the exploratory phase of data analysis. We looked at three clustering algorithms: *k*-means, DBSCAN, and agglomerative clustering. All three have a way of controlling the granularity of clustering. *k*-means and agglomerative clustering allow you to specify the number of desired clusters, while DBSCAN lets you define proximity using the `eps` parameter, which indirectly influences cluster size. All three methods can be used on large, real-world datasets, are relatively easy to understand, and allow for clustering into many clusters.

Each of the algorithms has somewhat different strengths. *k*-means allows for a characterization of the clusters using the cluster means. It can also be viewed as a decomposition method, where each data point is represented by its cluster center. DBSCAN allows for the detection of "noise points" that are not assigned any cluster, and it can help automatically determine the number of clusters. In contrast to the other two methods, it allow for complex cluster shapes, as we saw in the `two_moons` example. DBSCAN sometimes produces clusters of very differing size, which can be a strength or a weakness. Agglomerative clustering can provide a whole hierarchy of possible partitions of the data, which can be easily inspected via dendrograms.

3.6 Summary and Outlook

This chapter introduced a range of unsupervised learning algorithms that can be applied for exploratory data analysis and preprocessing. Having the right representation of the data is often crucial for supervised or unsupervised learning to succeed, and preprocessing and decomposition methods play an important part in data preparation.

Decomposition, manifold learning, and clustering are essential tools to further your understanding of your data, and can be the only ways to make sense of your data in the absence of supervision information. Even in a supervised setting, exploratory tools are important for a better understanding of the properties of the data. Often it is hard to quantify the usefulness of an unsupervised algorithm, though this shouldn't deter you from using them to gather insights from your data. With these methods under your belt, you are now equipped with all the essential learning algorithms that machine learning practitioners use every day.

We encourage you to try clustering and decomposition methods both on two-dimensional toy data and on real-world datasets included in `scikit-learn`, like the `digits`, `iris`, and `cancer` datasets.

Summary of the Estimator Interface

Let's briefly review the API that we introduced in Chapters 2 and 3. All algorithms in `scikit-learn`, whether preprocessing, supervised learning, or unsupervised learning algorithms, are implemented as classes. These classes are called *estimators* in `scikit-learn`. To apply an algorithm, you first have to instantiate an object of the particular class:

In[85]:

```
from sklearn.linear_model import LogisticRegression
logreg = LogisticRegression()
```

The estimator class contains the algorithm, and also stores the model that is learned from data using the algorithm.

You should set any parameters of the model when constructing the model object. These parameters include regularization, complexity control, number of clusters to find, etc. All estimators have a `fit` method, which is used to build the model. The `fit` method always requires as its first argument the data `X`, represented as a NumPy array or a SciPy sparse matrix, where each row represents a single data point. The data `X` is always assumed to be a NumPy array or SciPy sparse matrix that has continuous (floating-point) entries. Supervised algorithms also require a `y` argument, which is a one-dimensional NumPy array containing target values for regression or classification (i.e., the known output labels or responses).

There are two main ways to apply a learned model in `scikit-learn`. To create a prediction in the form of a new output like `y`, you use the `predict` method. To create a new representation of the input data `X`, you use the `transform` method. Table 3-1 summarizes the use cases of the `predict` and `transform` methods.

Table 3-1. scikit-learn API summary

`estimator.fit(x_train, [y_train])`	
`estimator.predict(X_test)`	`estimator.transform(X_test)`
Classification	Preprocessing
Regression	Dimensionality reduction
Clustering	Feature extraction
	Feature selection

Additionally, all supervised models have a `score(X_test, y_test)` method that allows an evaluation of the model. In Table 3-1, `X_train` and `y_train` refer to the training data and training labels, while `X_test` refers to the test data and test labels (if applicable).

CHAPTER 4

Representing Data and Engineering Features

So far, we've assumed that our data comes in as a two-dimensional array of floating-point numbers, where each column is a *continuous feature* that describes the data points. For many applications, this is not how the data is collected. A particularly common type of feature is the *categorical features*. Also known as *discrete features*, these are usually not numeric. The distinction between categorical features and continuous features is analogous to the distinction between classification and regression, only on the input side rather than the output side. Examples of continuous features that we have seen are pixel brightnesses and size measurements of plant flowers. Examples of categorical features are the brand of a product, the color of a product, or the department (books, clothing, hardware) it is sold in. These are all properties that can describe a product, but they don't vary in a continuous way. A product belongs either in the clothing department or in the books department. There is no middle ground between books and clothing, and no natural order for the different categories (books is not greater or less than clothing, hardware is not between books and clothing, etc.).

Regardless of the types of features your data consists of, how you represent them can have an enormous effect on the performance of machine learning models. We saw in Chapters 2 and 3 that scaling of the data is important. In other words, if you don't rescale your data (say, to unit variance), then it makes a difference whether you represent a measurement in centimeters or inches. We also saw in Chapter 2 that it can be helpful to *augment* your data with additional features, like adding interactions (products) of features or more general polynomials.

The question of how to represent your data best for a particular application is known as *feature engineering*, and it is one of the main tasks of data scientists and machine learning practitioners trying to solve real-world problems. Representing your data in the right way can have a bigger influence on the performance of a supervised model than the exact parameters you choose.

In this chapter, we will first go over the important and very common case of categorical features, and then give some examples of helpful transformations for specific combinations of features and models.

4.1 Categorical Variables

As an example, we will use the dataset of adult incomes in the United States, derived from the 1994 census database. The task of the `adult` dataset is to predict whether a worker has an income of over $50,000 or under $50,000. The features in this dataset include the workers' ages, how they are employed (self employed, private industry employee, government employee, etc.), their education, their gender, their working hours per week, occupation, and more. Table 4-1 shows the first few entries in the dataset.

Table 4-1. The first few entries in the adult dataset

	age	workclass	education	gender	hours-per-week	occupation	income
0	39	State-gov	Bachelors	Male	40	Adm-clerical	<=50K
1	50	Self-emp-not-inc	Bachelors	Male	13	Exec-managerial	<=50K
2	38	Private	HS-grad	Male	40	Handlers-cleaners	<=50K
3	53	Private	11th	Male	40	Handlers-cleaners	<=50K
4	28	Private	Bachelors	Female	40	Prof-specialty	<=50K
5	37	Private	Masters	Female	40	Exec-managerial	<=50K
6	49	Private	9th	Female	16	Other-service	<=50K
7	52	Self-emp-not-inc	HS-grad	Male	45	Exec-managerial	>50K
8	31	Private	Masters	Female	50	Prof-specialty	>50K
9	42	Private	Bachelors	Male	40	Exec-managerial	>50K
10	37	Private	Some-college	Male	80	Exec-managerial	>50K

The task is phrased as a classification task with the two classes being income `<=50k` and `>50k`. It would also be possible to predict the exact income, and make this a regression task. However, that would be much more difficult, and the 50K division is interesting to understand on its own.

In this dataset, `age` and `hours-per-week` are continuous features, which we know how to treat. The `workclass`, `education`, `sex`, and `occupation` features are categorical, however. All of them come from a fixed list of possible values, as opposed to a range, and denote a qualitative property, as opposed to a quantity.

As a starting point, let's say we want to learn a logistic regression classifier on this data. We know from Chapter 2 that a logistic regression makes predictions, $\hat{y}$, using the following formula:

$$\hat{y} = w[0] * x[0] + w[1] * x[1] + ... + w[p] * x[p] + b > 0$$

where $w[i]$ and b are coefficients learned from the training set and $x[i]$ are the input features. This formula makes sense when $x[i]$ are numbers, but not when $x[2]$ is `"Masters"` or `"Bachelors"`. Clearly we need to represent our data in some different way when applying logistic regression. The next section will explain how we can overcome this problem.

4.1.1 One-Hot-Encoding (Dummy Variables)

By far the most common way to represent categorical variables is using the *one-hot-encoding* or *one-out-of-N encoding*, also known as *dummy variables*. The idea behind dummy variables is to replace a categorical variable with one or more new features that can have the values 0 and 1. The values 0 and 1 make sense in the formula for linear binary classification (and for all other models in `scikit-learn`), and we can represent any number of categories by introducing one new feature per category, as described here.

Let's say for the `workclass` feature we have possible values of `"Government Employee"`, `"Private Employee"`, `"Self Employed"`, and `"Self Employed Incorporated"`. To encode these four possible values, we create four new features, called `"Government Employee"`, `"Private Employee"`, `"Self Employed"`, and `"Self Employed Incorporated"`. A feature is 1 if `workclass` for this person has the corresponding value and 0 otherwise, so exactly one of the four new features will be 1 for each data point. This is why this is called one-hot or one-out-of-N encoding.

The principle is illustrated in Table 4-2. A single feature is encoded using four new features. When using this data in a machine learning algorithm, we would drop the original `workclass` feature and only keep the 0–1 features.

Table 4-2. Encoding the workclass feature using one-hot encoding

workclass	Government Employee	Private Employee	Self Employed	Self Employed Incorporated
Government Employee	1	0	0	0
Private Employee	0	1	0	0
Self Employed	0	0	1	0
Self Employed Incorporated	0	0	0	1

The one-hot encoding we use is quite similar, but not identical, to the dummy coding used in statistics. For simplicity, we encode each category with a different binary feature. In statistics, it is common to encode a categorical feature with k different possible values into k–1 features (the last one is represented as all zeros). This is done to simplify the analysis (more technically, this will avoid making the data matrix rank-deficient).

There are two ways to convert your data to a one-hot encoding of categorical variables, using either `pandas` or `scikit-learn`. Let's see how we can do it using pandas. We start by loading the data using `pandas` from a comma-separated values (CSV) file:

In[1]:

```
import os
# The file has no headers naming the columns, so we pass header=None
# and provide the column names explicitly in "names"
adult_path = os.path.join(mglearn.datasets.DATA_PATH, "adult.data")
data = pd.read_csv(
    adult_path, header=None, index_col=False,
    names=['age', 'workclass', 'fnlwgt', 'education',  'education-num',
           'marital-status', 'occupation', 'relationship', 'race', 'gender',
           'capital-gain', 'capital-loss', 'hours-per-week', 'native-country',
           'income'])
# For illustration purposes, we only select some of the columns
data = data[['age', 'workclass', 'education', 'gender', 'hours-per-week',
             'occupation', 'income']]
# IPython.display allows nice output formatting within the Jupyter notebook
display(data.head())
```

Table 4-3 shows the result.

Table 4-3. The first five rows of the adult dataset

	age	workclass	education	gender	hours-per-week	occupation	income
0	39	State-gov	Bachelors	Male	40	Adm-clerical	<=50K
1	50	Self-emp-not-inc	Bachelors	Male	13	Exec-managerial	<=50K
2	38	Private	HS-grad	Male	40	Handlers-cleaners	<=50K
3	53	Private	11th	Male	40	Handlers-cleaners	<=50K
4	28	Private	Bachelors	Female	40	Prof-specialty	<=50K

Checking string-encoded categorical data

After reading a dataset like this, it is often good to first check if a column actually contains meaningful categorical data. When working with data that was input by humans (say, users on a website), there might not be a fixed set of categories, and differences in spelling and capitalization might require preprocessing. For example, it might be that some people specified gender as "male" and some as "man," and we might want to represent these two inputs using the same category. A good way to check the contents of a column is using the `value_counts` method of a `pandas` `Series` (the type of a single column in a `DataFrame`), to show us what the unique values are and how often they appear:

In[2]:

```
print(data.gender.value_counts())
```

Out[2]:

```
 Male      21790
 Female    10771
Name: gender, dtype: int64
```

We can see that there are exactly two values for gender in this dataset, `Male` and `Female`, meaning the data is already in a good format to be represented using one-hot-encoding. In a real application, you should look at all columns and check their values. We will skip this here for brevity's sake.

There is a very simple way to encode the data in `pandas`, using the `get_dummies` function. The `get_dummies` function automatically transforms all columns that have object type (like strings) or are categorical (which is a special `pandas` concept that we haven't talked about yet):

In[3]:

```
print("Original features:\n", list(data.columns), "\n")
data_dummies = pd.get_dummies(data)
print("Features after get_dummies:\n", list(data_dummies.columns))
```

Out[3]:

```
Original features:
 ['age', 'workclass', 'education', 'gender', 'hours-per-week', 'occupation',
  'income']

Features after get_dummies:
 ['age', 'hours-per-week', 'workclass_ ?', 'workclass_ Federal-gov',
  'workclass_ Local-gov', 'workclass_ Never-worked', 'workclass_ Private',
  'workclass_ Self-emp-inc', 'workclass_ Self-emp-not-inc',
  'workclass_ State-gov', 'workclass_ Without-pay', 'education_ 10th',
  'education_ 11th', 'education_ 12th', 'education_ 1st-4th',
  ...
  'education_ Preschool', 'education_ Prof-school', 'education_ Some-college',
  'gender_ Female', 'gender_ Male', 'occupation_ ?',
  'occupation_ Adm-clerical', 'occupation_ Armed-Forces',
  'occupation_ Craft-repair', 'occupation_ Exec-managerial',
  'occupation_ Farming-fishing', 'occupation_ Handlers-cleaners',
  ...
  'occupation_ Tech-support', 'occupation_ Transport-moving',
  'income_ <=50K', 'income_ >50K']
```

You can see that the continuous features `age` and `hours-per-week` were not touched, while the categorical features were expanded into one new feature for each possible value:

In[4]:

```
data_dummies.head()
```

Out[4]:

	age	hours-per-week	workclass_ ?	workclass_ Federal-gov	workclass_ Local-gov	...	occupation_ Tech-support	occupation_ Transport-moving	income_ <=50K	income_ >50K
0	39	40	0.0	0.0	0.0	...	0.0	0.0	1.0	0.0
1	50	13	0.0	0.0	0.0	...	0.0	0.0	1.0	0.0
2	38	40	0.0	0.0	0.0	...	0.0	0.0	1.0	0.0
3	53	40	0.0	0.0	0.0	...	0.0	0.0	1.0	0.0
4	28	40	0.0	0.0	0.0	...	0.0	0.0	1.0	0.0

```
5 rows × 46 columns
```

We can now use the `values` attribute to convert the `data_dummies DataFrame` into a NumPy array, and then train a machine learning model on it. Be careful to separate the target variable (which is now encoded in two `income` columns) from the data before training a model. Including the output variable, or some derived property of the output variable, into the feature representation is a very common mistake in building supervised machine learning models.

> Be careful: column indexing in `pandas` includes the end of the range, so `'age':'occupation_ Transport-moving'` is inclusive of `occupation_ Transport-moving`. This is different from slicing a NumPy array, where the end of a range is not included: for example, `np.arange(11)[0:10]` doesn't include the entry with index 10.

In this case, we extract only the columns containing features—that is, all columns from `age` to `occupation_ Transport-moving`. This range contains all the features but not the target:

In[5]:

```
features = data_dummies.loc[:, 'age':'occupation_ Transport-moving']
# Extract NumPy arrays
X = features.values
y = data_dummies['income_ >50K'].values
print("X.shape: {}  y.shape: {}".format(X.shape, y.shape))
```

Out[5]:

```
X.shape: (32561, 44)  y.shape: (32561,)
```

Now the data is represented in a way that `scikit-learn` can work with, and we can proceed as usual:

In[6]:

```
from sklearn.linear_model import LogisticRegression
from sklearn.model_selection import train_test_split
X_train, X_test, y_train, y_test = train_test_split(X, y, random_state=0)
logreg = LogisticRegression()
logreg.fit(X_train, y_train)
print("Test score: {:.2f}".format(logreg.score(X_test, y_test)))
```

Out[6]:

```
Test score: 0.81
```

In this example, we called `get_dummies` on a `DataFrame` containing both the training and the test data. This is important to ensure categorical values are represented in the same way in the training set and the test set.

Imagine we have the training and test sets in two different `DataFrame`s. If the `"Private Employee"` value for the `workclass` feature does not appear in the test set, `pandas` will assume there are only three possible values for this feature and will create only three new dummy features. Now our training and test sets have different numbers of features, and we can't apply the model we learned on the training set to the test set anymore. Even worse, imagine the `workclass` feature has the values `"Government Employee"` and `"Private Employee"` in the training set, and `"Self Employed"` and `"Self Employed Incorporated"` in the test set. In both cases, `pandas` will create two new dummy features, so the encoded `DataFrame`s will have the same number of features. However, the two dummy features have entirely different meanings in the training and test sets. The column that means `"Government Employee"` for the training set would encode `"Self Employed"` for the test set.

If we built a machine learning model on this data it would work very badly, because it would assume the columns mean the same things (because they are in the same position) when in fact they mean very different things. To fix this, either call `get_dummies` on a `DataFrame` that contains both the training and the test data points, or make sure that the column names are the same for the training and test sets after calling `get_dummies`, to ensure they have the same semantics.

4.1.2 Numbers Can Encode Categoricals

In the example of the adult dataset, the categorical variables were encoded as strings. On the one hand, that opens up the possibility of spelling errors, but on the other hand, it clearly marks a variable as categorical. Often, whether for ease of storage or because of the way the data is collected, categorical variables are encoded as integers. For example, imagine the census data in the adult dataset was collected using a questionnaire, and the answers for workclass were recorded as 0 (first box ticked), 1 (second box ticked), 2 (third box ticked), and so on. Now the column will contain numbers from 0 to 8, instead of strings like "Private", and it won't be immediately obvious to someone looking at the table representing the dataset whether they should treat this variable as continuous or categorical. Knowing that the numbers indicate employment status, however, it is clear that these are very distinct states and should not be modeled by a single continuous variable.

> Categorical features are often encoded using integers. That they are numbers doesn't mean that they should necessarily be treated as continuous features. It is not always clear whether an integer feature should be treated as continuous or discrete (and one-hot-encoded). If there is no ordering between the semantics that are encoded (like in the workclass example), the feature must be treated as discrete. For other cases, like five-star ratings, the better encoding depends on the particular task and data and which machine learning algorithm is used.

The get_dummies function in pandas treats all numbers as continuous and will not create dummy variables for them. To illustrate, let's create a DataFrame object with two columns corresponding to two different categorical features, one represented as a string and one as an integer.

In[7]:

```
# create a DataFrame with an integer feature and a categorical string feature
demo_df = pd.DataFrame({'Integer Feature': [0, 1, 2, 1],
                        'Categorical Feature': ['socks', 'fox', 'socks', 'box']})
display(demo_df)
```

Table 4-4 shows the result.

Table 4-4. DataFrame containing categorical string features and integer features

	Categorical Feature	Integer Feature
0	socks	0
1	fox	1
2	socks	2
3	box	1

Using `get_dummies` will only encode the string feature and will not change the integer feature, as you can see in Table 4-5:

In[8]:

```
display(pd.get_dummies(demo_df))
```

Table 4-5. One-hot-encoded version of the data from Table 4-4, leaving the integer feature unchanged

	Integer Feature	Categorical Feature_box	Categorical Feature_fox	Categorical Feature_socks
0	0	0.0	0.0	1.0
1	1	0.0	1.0	0.0
2	2	0.0	0.0	1.0
3	1	1.0	0.0	0.0

If you want dummy variables to be created for the "Integer Feature" column, you can explicitly list the columns you want to encode using the `columns` parameter. Then, both features will be treated as categorical (see Table 4-6):

In[9]:

```
demo_df['Integer Feature'] = demo_df['Integer Feature'].astype(str)
display(pd.get_dummies(demo_df, columns=['Integer Feature', 'Categorical Feature']))
```

Table 4-6. One-hot encoding of the data shown in Table 4-4, encoding the integer and string features

	Integer Feature_0	Integer Feature_1	Integer Feature_2	Categorical Feature_box	Categorical Feature_fox	Categorical Feature_socks
0	1.0	0.0	0.0	0.0	0.0	1.0
1	0.0	1.0	0.0	0.0	1.0	0.0
2	0.0	0.0	1.0	0.0	0.0	1.0
3	0.0	1.0	0.0	1.0	0.0	0.0

4.2 OneHotEncoder and ColumnTransformer: Categorical Variables with scikit-learn

As mentioned before, scikit-learn can also perform one-hot-encoding. Using scikit-learn has the advantage of making it easy to treat training and test set in a consistent way. One-hot-encoding is implemented in the OneHotEncoder class[1] Notably, the OneHotEncoder applies the encoding to all input columns:

In[10]:

```
from sklearn.preprocessing import OneHotEncoder
# Setting sparse=False means OneHotEncode will return a numpy array,
# not a sparse matrix
ohe = OneHotEncoder(sparse=False)
print(ohe.fit_transform(demo_df))
```

Out[10]:

```
[[1. 0. 0. 0. 0. 1.]
 [0. 1. 0. 0. 1. 0.]
 [0. 0. 1. 0. 0. 1.]
 [0. 1. 0. 1. 0. 0.]]
```

You can see that both the string and integer feature were transformed. As usual for scikit-learn, the output is not a DataFrame, so there are no column names. To obtain the correspondence of the transformed features to the original categorical variables, we can use the get_feature_names method:

In[11]:

```
print(ohe.get_feature_names())
```

Out[11]:

```
['x0_0' 'x0_1' 'x0_2' 'x1_box' 'x1_fox' 'x1_socks']
```

There, the first three columns correspond to the values 0, 1, and 2 of the first original feature (called x0 here), while the last three columns correspond to the values box, fox, and socks for the second original feature (called x1 here).

In most applications, some features are categorical and some are continuous, so OneHotEncoder is not directly applicable, as it assumes all features are categorical. This is where the ColumnTransformer class comes in handy: it allows you to apply different transformations to different columns in the input data. This is incredibly useful, since continuous and categorical features need very different kinds of preprocessing.

1 This class underwent significant changes in version 0.20.0, so make sure you have the current version of scikit-learn.

Let's go back to the example of the adult census data we considered earlier:

In[12]:

```
display(data.head())
```

Out[12]:

```
[cols=",,,,,,,",options="header",]
|=======================================================================
| |age |workclass |education |gender |hours-per-week |occupation |income
|0 |39 |State-gov |Bachelors |Male |40 |Adm-clerical |<=50K
|1 |50 |Self-emp-not-inc |Bachelors |Male |13 |Exec-managerial |<=50K
|2 |38 |Private |HS-grad |Male |40 |Handlers-cleaners |<=50K
|3 |53 |Private |11th |Male |40 |Handlers-cleaners |<=50K
|4 |28 |Private |Bachelors |Female |40 |Prof-specialty |<=50K
|=======================================================================
```

To apply, say, a linear model to this dataset to predict income, in addition to applying one-hot-encoding to the categorical variables, we might also want to scale the continuous variables `age` and `hours-per-week`. This is exactly what `ColumnTransformer` can do for us. Each transformation in the column transformer is specified by a name (we will see later why this is useful), a transformer object, and the columns this transformer should be applied to. The columns can be specified using column names, integer indices, or boolean masks. Each transformer is applied to the corresponding columns, and the result of the transformations are concatenated (horizontally). For the example earlier, using column names the specification looks like this:

In[13]:

```
from sklearn.compose import ColumnTransformer
from sklearn.preprocessing import StandardScaler

ct = ColumnTransformer(
    [("scaling", StandardScaler(), ['age', 'hours-per-week']),
     ("onehot", OneHotEncoder(sparse=False),
     ['workclass', 'education', 'gender', 'occupation'])])
```

Now we can use the `ColumnTransformer` object as we would any other `scikit-learn` transformation, using `fit` and `transform`. So let's build a linear model as before, but this time include scaling of the continuous variables. Note that we are calling `train_test_split` on the `DataFrame` containing the features, not on a NumPy array. We need to preserve the column names so that they can be used in the `ColumnTransformer`.

In[14]:

```
from sklearn.linear_model import LogisticRegression
from sklearn.model_selection import train_test_split
# get all columns apart from income for the features
data_features = data.drop("income", axis=1)
```

```
# split dataframe and income
X_train, X_test, y_train, y_test = train_test_split(
    data_features, data.income, random_state=0)

ct.fit(X_train)
X_train_trans = ct.transform(X_train)
print(X_train_trans.shape)
```

Out[14]:

```
(24420, 44)
```

You can see that we obtained 44 features, the same as when we used `pd.get_dummies` before, except that we also scaled the continuous features. Now we can build a `LogisticRegression` model:

In[15]:

```
logreg = LogisticRegression()
logreg.fit(X_train_trans, y_train)

X_test_trans = ct.transform(X_test)
print("Test score: {:.2f}".format(logreg.score(X_test_trans, y_test)))
```

Out[15]:

```
Test score: 0.81
```

In this case, scaling the data didn't make a difference, but encapsulating all of the preprocessing inside a transformer has additional benefits that we will discuss later. You can access the steps inside the `ColumnTransformer` via the `named_transformers_` attribute:

In[16]:

```
ct.named_transformers_.onehot
```

Out[16]:

```
OneHotEncoder(categorical_features=None, categories=None,
       dtype=<class 'numpy.float64'>, handle_unknown='error',
       n_values=None, sparse=False)
```

4.3 Convenient ColumnTransformer creation with make_columntransformer

Creating a `ColumnTransformer` using the syntax described earlier is sometimes a bit cumbersome, and we often don't need user-specified names for each step. There is a convenience function (`make_columntransformer`) that will create a `ColumnTransformer` for us and automatically name each step based on its class. The syntax for `make_columntransformer` is as follows:

In[17]:

```
from sklearn.compose import make_column_transformer
ct = make_column_transformer(
    (['age', 'hours-per-week'], StandardScaler()),
    (['workclass', 'education', 'gender', 'occupation'], OneHotEncoder(sparse=False)))
```

A disadavantage of using the `ColumnTransformer` is that in version 0.20 it is not yet possible to readily find which input columns correspond to which output columns of the column transformer in all cases.

4.4 Binning, Discretization, Linear Models, and Trees

The best way to represent data depends not only on the semantics of the data, but also on the kind of model you are using. Linear models and tree-based models (such as decision trees, gradient boosted trees, and random forests), two large and very commonly used families, have very different properties when it comes to how they work with different feature representations. Let's go back to the `wave` regression dataset that we used in Chapter 2. It has only a single input feature. Here is a comparison of a linear regression model and a decision tree regressor on this dataset (see Figure 4-1):

In[18]:

```
from sklearn.linear_model import LinearRegression
from sklearn.tree import DecisionTreeRegressor

X, y = mglearn.datasets.make_wave(n_samples=120)
line = np.linspace(-3, 3, 1000, endpoint=False).reshape(-1, 1)

reg = DecisionTreeRegressor(min_samples_leaf=3).fit(X, y)
plt.plot(line, reg.predict(line), label="decision tree")

reg = LinearRegression().fit(X, y)
plt.plot(line, reg.predict(line), label="linear regression")

plt.plot(X[:, 0], y, 'o', c='k')
plt.ylabel("Regression output")
plt.xlabel("Input feature")
plt.legend(loc="best")
```

As you know, linear models can only model linear relationships, which are lines in the case of a single feature. The decision tree can build a much more complex model of the data. However, this is strongly dependent on the representation of the data. One way to make linear models more powerful on continuous data is to use *binning* (also known as *discretization*) of the feature to split it up into multiple features, as described here.

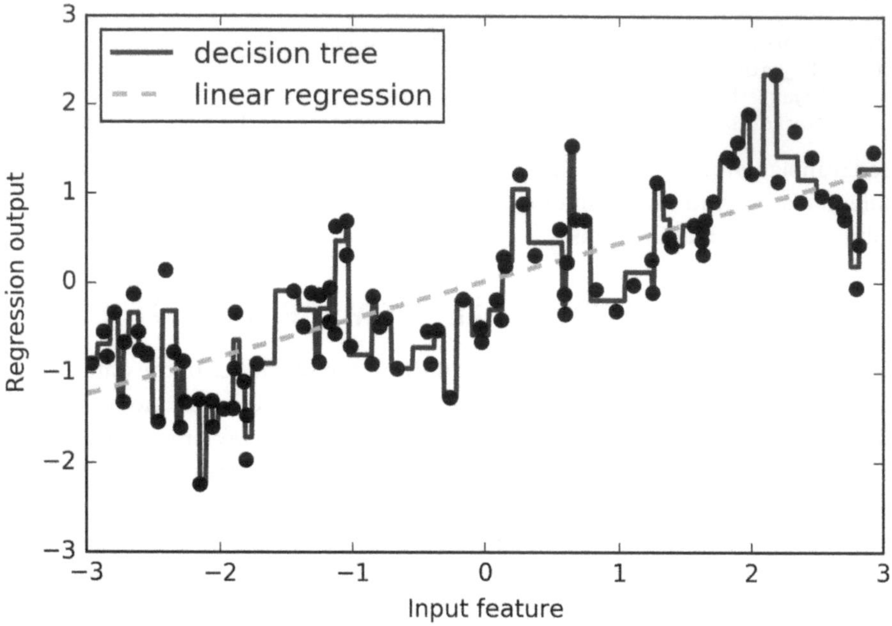

Figure 4-1. Comparing linear regression and a decision tree on the wave dataset

We imagine a partition of the input range for the feature (in this case, the numbers from –3 to 3) into a fixed number of *bins*—say, 10. A data point will then be represented by which bin it falls into. There are several ways to define the edges of the bins; for example, giving them uniform width (making the bin edges equidistant) or using quantiles of the data (i.e., having smaller bins where there's more data). Both of these strategies are implemented in the `KBinsDiscretizer`:

In[19]:

```
from sklearn.preprocessing import KBinsDiscretizer
```

In[20]:

```
kb = KBinsDiscretizer(n_bins=10, strategy='uniform')
kb.fit(X)
print("bin edges: \n", kb.bin_edges_)
```

Out[20]:

```
bin edges:
 [array([-2.967, -2.378, -1.789, -1.2  , -0.612, -0.023,  0.566,  1.155,
        1.744,  2.333,  2.921])]
```

Here, the first bin contains all data points with feature values from -2.967 (the smallest value in the data) to -2.378, the second bin contains all points with feature values from -2.378 to -1.789, and so on. KBinsDiscretizer can be applied to multiple features at the same time, and the bin_edges_ contain the edges per feature. This is why they are a list of length one in this case.

Using transform, we can encode each data point by which bin it falls into. By default, KBinDiscretizer applies one-hot-encoding to the bins, so there is one new feature per bin, and it produces a sparse matrix. Because we specified 10 bins, the transformed data is ten-dimensional.

In[21]:

```
X_binned = kb.transform(X)
X_binned
```

Out[21]:

```
<120x10 sparse matrix of type '<class 'numpy.float64'>'
        with 120 stored elements in Compressed Sparse Row format>
```

We can convert the sparse matrix to a dense array and compare the data points to their encoding:

In[22]:

```
print(X[:10])
X_binned.toarray()[:10]
```

Out[22]:

```
[[-0.753]
 [ 2.704]
 [ 1.392]
 [ 0.592]
 [-2.064]
 [-2.064]
 [-2.651]
 [ 2.197]
 [ 0.607]
 [ 1.248]]

array([[0., 0., 0., 1., 0., 0., 0., 0., 0., 0.],
       [0., 0., 0., 0., 0., 0., 0., 0., 0., 1.],
       [0., 0., 0., 0., 0., 0., 0., 1., 0., 0.],
       [0., 0., 0., 0., 0., 0., 1., 0., 0., 0.],
       [0., 1., 0., 0., 0., 0., 0., 0., 0., 0.],
       [0., 1., 0., 0., 0., 0., 0., 0., 0., 0.],
       [1., 0., 0., 0., 0., 0., 0., 0., 0., 0.],
       [0., 0., 0., 0., 0., 0., 0., 0., 1., 0.],
       [0., 0., 0., 0., 0., 0., 1., 0., 0., 0.],
       [0., 0., 0., 0., 0., 0., 0., 1., 0., 0.]])
```

We can see that the first data point with value -0.753 was put in the 4th bin, the second data point with value 2.704 was put in the 10th bin, and so on.

What we did here is transform the single continuous input feature in the wave dataset into a one-hot encoded categorical feature which encodes which bin a data point is in. You can forego the one-hot-encoding by specifying encode='ordinal' though that is usually less useful. To make things easier for demonstration purposes, we will use encode='onehot-dense' which uses dense one-hot encoding so we can directly print all features.

In[23]:

```
kb = KBinsDiscretizer(n_bins=10, strategy='uniform', encode='onehot-dense')
kb.fit(X)
X_binned = kb.transform(X)
```

Now we build a new linear regression model and a new decision tree model on the one-hot-encoded data. The result is visualized in Figure 4-2, together with the bin boundaries, shown as dotted black lines:

In[24]:

```
line_binned = kb.transform(line)

reg = LinearRegression().fit(X_binned, y)
plt.plot(line, reg.predict(line_binned), label='linear regression binned')

reg = DecisionTreeRegressor(min_samples_split=3).fit(X_binned, y)
plt.plot(line, reg.predict(line_binned), label='decision tree binned')
plt.plot(X[:, 0], y, 'o', c='k')
plt.vlines(kb.bin_edges_[0], -3, 3, linewidth=1, alpha=.2)
plt.legend(loc="best")
plt.ylabel("Regression output")
plt.xlabel("Input feature")
```

The dashed line and solid line are exactly on top of each other, meaning the linear regression model and the decision tree make exactly the same predictions. For each bin, they predict a constant value. As features are constant within each bin, any model must predict the same value for all points within a bin. Comparing what the models learned before binning the features and after, we see that the linear model became much more flexible, because it now has a different value for each bin, while the decision tree model got much less flexible. Binning features generally has no beneficial effect for tree-based models, as these models can learn to split up the data anywhere. In a sense, that means decision trees can learn whatever binning is most useful for predicting on this data. Additionally, decision trees look at multiple features at once, while binning is usually done on a per-feature basis. However, the linear model benefited greatly in expressiveness from the transformation of the data.

If there are good reasons to use a linear model for a particular dataset—say, because it is very large and high-dimensional, but some features have nonlinear relations with the output—binning can be a great way to increase modeling power.

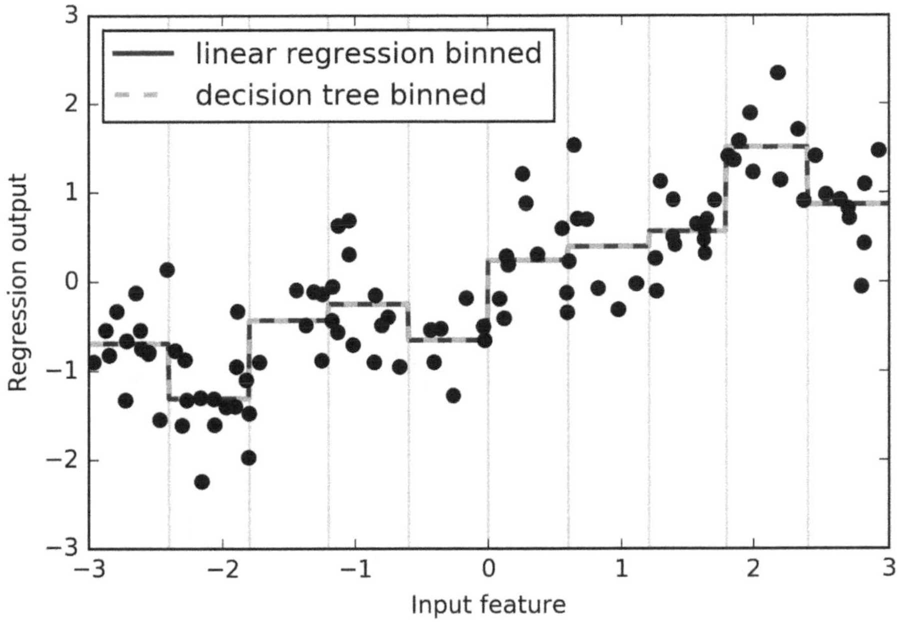

Figure 4-2. Comparing linear regression and decision tree regression on binned features

4.5 Interactions and Polynomials

Another way to enrich a feature representation, particularly for linear models, is adding *interaction features* and *polynomial features* of the original data. This kind of feature engineering is often used in statistical modeling, but it's also common in many practical machine learning applications.

As a first example, look again at Figure 4-2. The linear model learned a constant value for each bin in the wave dataset. We know, however, that linear models can learn not only offsets, but also slopes. One way to add a slope to the linear model on the binned data is to add the original feature (the x-axis in the plot) back in. This leads to an 11-dimensional dataset, as seen in Figure 4-3:

In[25]:

```
X_combined = np.hstack([X, X_binned])
print(X_combined.shape)
```

Out[25]:

```
(120, 11)
```

In[26]:

```
reg = LinearRegression().fit(X_combined, y)

line_combined = np.hstack([line, line_binned])
plt.plot(line, reg.predict(line_combined), label='linear regression combined')

plt.vlines(kb.bin_edges_[0], -3, 3, linewidth=1, alpha=.2)
plt.legend(loc="best")
plt.ylabel("Regression output")
plt.xlabel("Input feature")
plt.plot(X[:, 0], y, 'o', c='k')
```

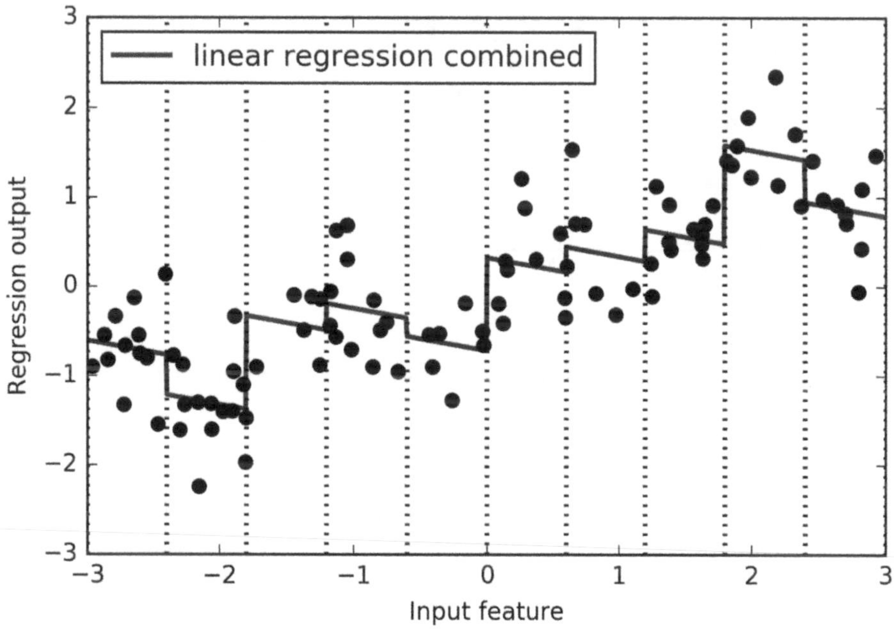

Figure 4-3. Linear regression using binned features and a single global slope

In this example, the model learned an offset for each bin, together with a slope. The learned slope is downward, and shared across all the bins—there is a single x-axis feature, which has a single slope. Because the slope is shared across all bins, it doesn't seem to be very helpful. We would rather have a separate slope for each bin! We can achieve this by adding an interaction or product feature that indicates which bin a data point is in *and* where it lies on the x-axis. This feature is a product of the bin indicator and the original feature. Let's create this dataset:

In[27]:

```
X_product = np.hstack([X_binned, X * X_binned])
print(X_product.shape)
```

Out[27]:

```
(120, 20)
```

The dataset now has 20 features: the indicators for which bin a data point is in, and a product of the original feature and the bin indicator. You can think of the product feature as a separate copy of the x-axis feature for each bin. It is the original feature within the bin, and zero everywhere else. Figure 4-4 shows the result of the linear model on this new representation:

In[28]:

```
reg = LinearRegression().fit(X_product, y)

line_product = np.hstack([line_binned, line * line_binned])
plt.plot(line, reg.predict(line_product), label='linear regression product')

plt.vlines(kb.bin_edges_[0], -3, 3, linewidth=1, alpha=.2)

plt.plot(X[:, 0], y, 'o', c='k')
plt.ylabel("Regression output")
plt.xlabel("Input feature")
plt.legend(loc="best")
```

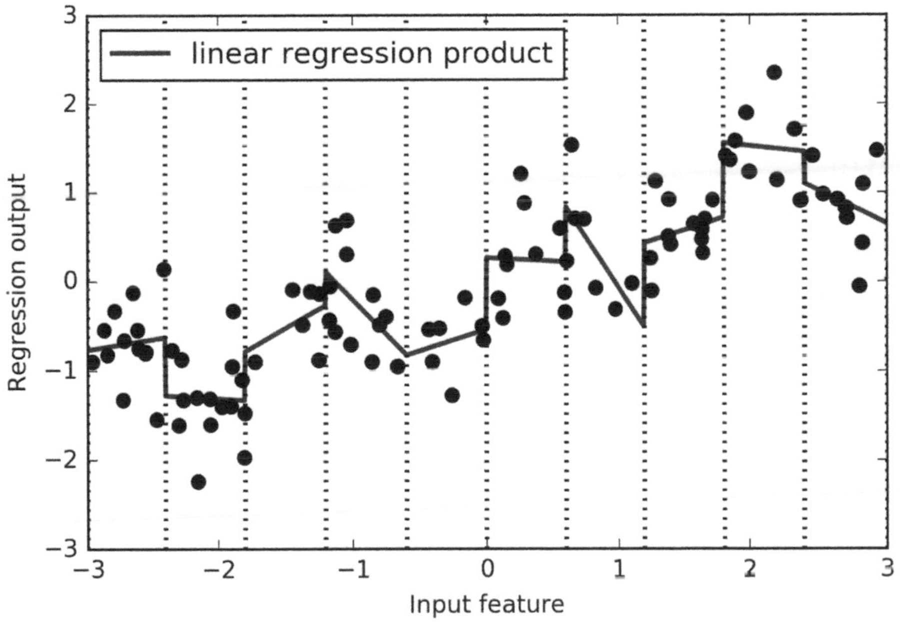

Figure 4-4. Linear regression with a separate slope per bin

As you can see, now each bin has its own offset and slope in this model.

Using binning is one way to expand a continuous feature. Another one is to use *polynomials* of the original features. For a given feature `x`, we might want to consider `x ** 2`, `x ** 3`, `x ** 4`, and so on. This is implemented in `PolynomialFeatures` in the `preprocessing` module:

In[29]:

```
from sklearn.preprocessing import PolynomialFeatures

# include polynomials up to x ** 10:
# the default "include_bias=True" adds a feature that's constantly 1
poly = PolynomialFeatures(degree=10, include_bias=False)
poly.fit(X)
X_poly = poly.transform(X)
```

Using a degree of 10 yields 10 features:

In[30]:

```
print("X_poly.shape: {}".format(X_poly.shape))
```

Out[30]:

```
X_poly.shape: (120, 10)
```

Let's compare the entries of `X_poly` to those of `X`:

In[31]:

```
print("Entries of X:\n{}".format(X[:5]))
print("Entries of X_poly:\n{}".format(X_poly[:5]))
```

Out[31]:

```
Entries of X:
[[-0.753]
 [ 2.704]
 [ 1.392]
 [ 0.592]
 [-2.064]]
Entries of X_poly:
[[   -0.753     0.567    -0.427     0.321    -0.242     0.182    -0.137
      0.103    -0.078     0.058]
 [    2.704     7.313    19.777    53.482   144.632   391.125  1057.714
   2860.36   7735.232 20918.278]
 [    1.392     1.938     2.697     3.754     5.226     7.274    10.125
     14.094    19.618    27.307]
 [    0.592     0.35      0.207     0.123     0.073     0.043     0.025
      0.015     0.009     0.005]
 [   -2.064     4.26     -8.791    18.144   -37.448    77.289  -159.516
    329.222  -679.478  1402.367]]
```

You can obtain the semantics of the features by calling the `get_feature_names` method, which provides the exponent for each feature:

In[32]:

```
print("Polynomial feature names:\n{}".format(poly.get_feature_names()))
```

Out[32]:

```
Polynomial feature names:
['x0', 'x0^2', 'x0^3', 'x0^4', 'x0^5', 'x0^6', 'x0^7', 'x0^8', 'x0^9', 'x0^10']
```

You can see that the first column of `X_poly` corresponds exactly to `X`, while the other columns are the powers of the first entry. It's interesting to see how large some of the values can get. The second row has entries above 20,000, orders of magnitude different from the rest.

Using polynomial features together with a linear regression model yields the classical model of *polynomial regression* (see Figure 4-5):

In[33]:

```
reg = LinearRegression().fit(X_poly, y)

line_poly = poly.transform(line)
plt.plot(line, reg.predict(line_poly), label='polynomial linear regression')
plt.plot(X[:, 0], y, 'o', c='k')
plt.ylabel("Regression output")
plt.xlabel("Input feature")
plt.legend(loc="best")
```

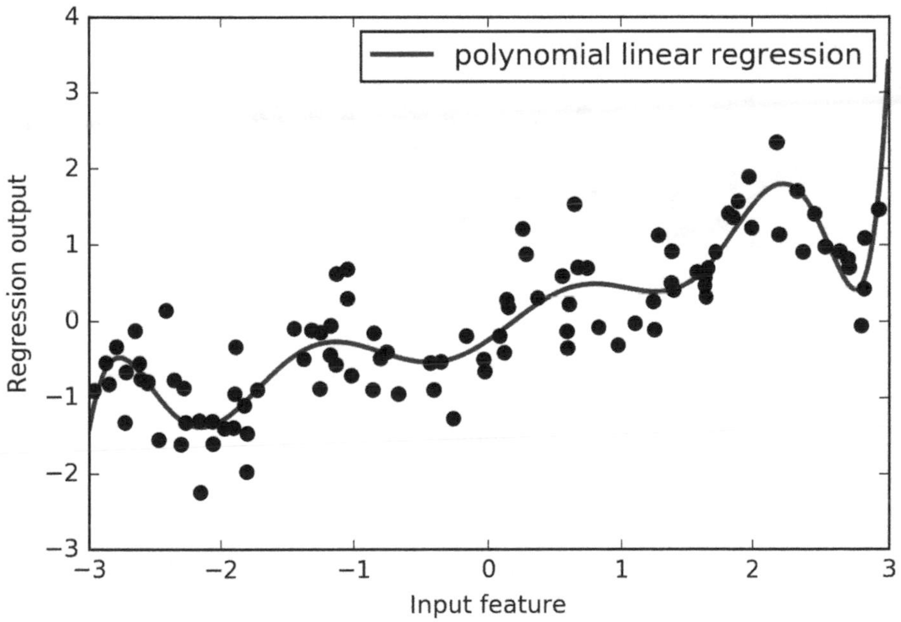

Figure 4-5. Linear regression with tenth-degree polynomial features

As you can see, polynomial features yield a very smooth fit on this one-dimensional data. However, polynomials of high degree tend to behave in extreme ways on the boundaries or in regions with little data.

As a comparison, here is a kernel SVM model learned on the original data, without any transformation (see Figure 4-6):

In[34]:

```
from sklearn.svm import SVR

for gamma in [1, 10]:
    svr = SVR(gamma=gamma).fit(X, y)
    plt.plot(line, svr.predict(line), label='SVR gamma={}'.format(gamma))

plt.plot(X[:, 0], y, 'o', c='k')
plt.ylabel("Regression output")
plt.xlabel("Input feature")
plt.legend(loc="best")
```

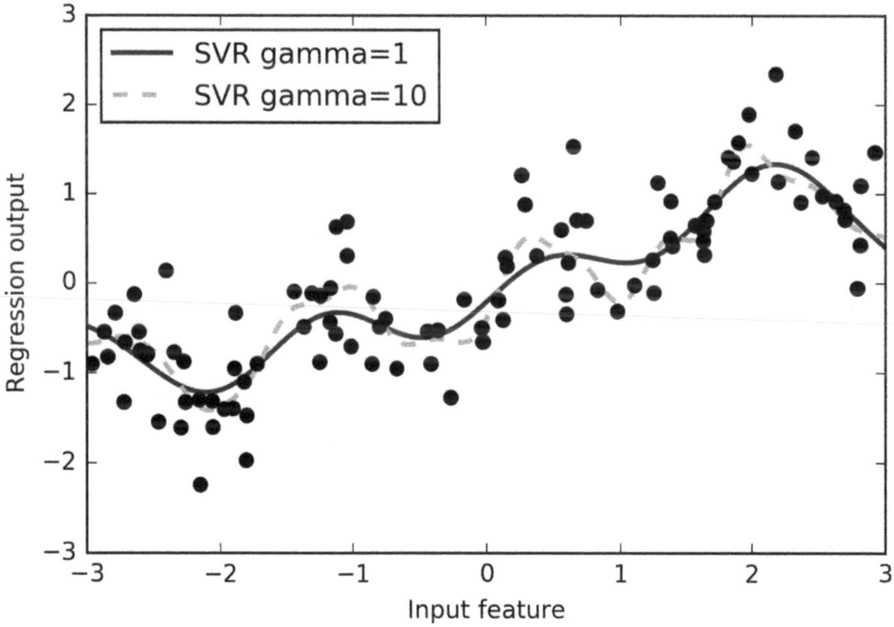

Figure 4-6. Comparison of different gamma parameters for an SVM with RBF kernel

Using a more complex model, a kernel SVM, we are able to learn a similarly complex prediction to the polynomial regression without an explicit transformation of the features.

As a more realistic application of interactions and polynomials, let's look again at the Boston Housing dataset. We already used polynomial features on this dataset in Chapter 2. Now let's have a look at how these features were constructed, and at how much the polynomial features help. First we load the data, and rescale it to be between 0 and 1 using `MinMaxScaler`:

In[35]:

```
from sklearn.datasets import load_boston
from sklearn.model_selection import train_test_split
from sklearn.preprocessing import MinMaxScaler

boston = load_boston()
X_train, X_test, y_train, y_test = train_test_split(
    boston.data, boston.target, random_state=0)

# rescale data
scaler = MinMaxScaler()
X_train_scaled = scaler.fit_transform(X_train)
X_test_scaled = scaler.transform(X_test)
```

Now, we extract polynomial features and interactions up to a degree of 2:

In[36]:

```
poly = PolynomialFeatures(degree=2).fit(X_train_scaled)
X_train_poly = poly.transform(X_train_scaled)
X_test_poly = poly.transform(X_test_scaled)
print("X_train.shape: {}".format(X_train.shape))
print("X_train_poly.shape: {}".format(X_train_poly.shape))
```

Out[36]:

```
X_train.shape: (379, 13)
X_train_poly.shape: (379, 105)
```

The data originally had 13 features, which were expanded into 105 interaction features. These new features represent all possible interactions between two different original features, as well as the square of each original feature. `degree=2` here means that we look at all features that are the product of up to two original features. The exact correspondence between input and output features can be found using the `get_feature_names` method:

In[37]:

```
print("Polynomial feature names:\n{}".format(poly.get_feature_names()))
```

Out[37]:

```
Polynomial feature names:
['1', 'x0', 'x1', 'x2', 'x3', 'x4', 'x5', 'x6', 'x7', 'x8', 'x9', 'x10',
'x11', 'x12', 'x0^2', 'x0 x1', 'x0 x2', 'x0 x3', 'x0 x4', 'x0 x5', 'x0 x6',
'x0 x7', 'x0 x8', 'x0 x9', 'x0 x10', 'x0 x11', 'x0 x12', 'x1^2', 'x1 x2',
```

```
'x1 x3', 'x1 x4', 'x1 x5', 'x1 x6', 'x1 x7', 'x1 x8', 'x1 x9', 'x1 x10',
'x1 x11', 'x1 x12', 'x2^2', 'x2 x3', 'x2 x4', 'x2 x5', 'x2 x6', 'x2 x7',
'x2 x8', 'x2 x9', 'x2 x10', 'x2 x11', 'x2 x12', 'x3^2', 'x3 x4', 'x3 x5',
'x3 x6', 'x3 x7', 'x3 x8', 'x3 x9', 'x3 x10', 'x3 x11', 'x3 x12', 'x4^2',
'x4 x5', 'x4 x6', 'x4 x7', 'x4 x8', 'x4 x9', 'x4 x10', 'x4 x11', 'x4 x12',
'x5^2', 'x5 x6', 'x5 x7', 'x5 x8', 'x5 x9', 'x5 x10', 'x5 x11', 'x5 x12',
'x6^2', 'x6 x7', 'x6 x8', 'x6 x9', 'x6 x10', 'x6 x11', 'x6 x12', 'x7^2',
'x7 x8', 'x7 x9', 'x7 x10', 'x7 x11', 'x7 x12', 'x8^2', 'x8 x9', 'x8 x10',
'x8 x11', 'x8 x12', 'x9^2', 'x9 x10', 'x9 x11', 'x9 x12', 'x10^2', 'x10 x11',
'x10 x12', 'x11^2', 'x11 x12', 'x12^2']
```

The first new feature is a constant feature, called "1" here. The next 13 features are the original features (called "x0" to "x12"). Then follows the first feature squared ("x0^2") and combinations of the first and the other features.

Let's compare the performance using Ridge on the data with and without interactions:

In[38]:

```
from sklearn.linear_model import Ridge
ridge = Ridge().fit(X_train_scaled, y_train)
print("Score without interactions: {:.3f}".format(
    ridge.score(X_test_scaled, y_test)))
ridge = Ridge().fit(X_train_poly, y_train)
print("Score with interactions: {:.3f}".format(
    ridge.score(X_test_poly, y_test)))
```

Out[38]:

```
Score without interactions: 0.621
Score with interactions: 0.753
```

Clearly, the interactions and polynomial features gave us a good boost in performance when using Ridge. When using a more complex model like a random forest, the story is a bit different, though:

In[39]:

```
from sklearn.ensemble import RandomForestRegressor
rf = RandomForestRegressor(n_estimators=100).fit(X_train_scaled, y_train)
print("Score without interactions: {:.3f}".format(
    rf.score(X_test_scaled, y_test)))
rf = RandomForestRegressor(n_estimators=100).fit(X_train_poly, y_train)
print("Score with interactions: {:.3f}".format(rf.score(X_test_poly, y_test)))
```

Out[39]:

```
Score without interactions: 0.798
Score with interactions: 0.765
```

You can see that even without additional features, the random forest beats the performance of Ridge. Adding interactions and polynomials actually decreases performance slightly.

4.6 Univariate Nonlinear Transformations

We just saw that adding squared or cubed features can help linear models for regression. There are other transformations that often prove useful for transforming certain features: in particular, applying mathematical functions like log, exp, or sin. While tree-based models only care about the ordering of the features, linear models and neural networks are very tied to the scale and distribution of each feature, and if there is a nonlinear relation between the feature and the target, that becomes hard to model —particularly in regression. The functions log and exp can help by adjusting the relative scales in the data so that they can be captured better by a linear model or neural network. We saw an application of that in Chapter 2 with the memory price data. The sin and cos functions can come in handy when dealing with data that encodes periodic patterns.

Most models work best when each feature (and in regression also the target) is loosely Gaussian distributed—that is, a histogram of each feature should have something resembling the familiar "bell curve" shape. Using transformations like log and exp is a hacky but simple and efficient way to achieve this. A particularly common case when such a transformation can be helpful is when dealing with integer count data. By count data, we mean features like "how often did user A log in?" Counts are never negative, and often follow particular statistical patterns. We are using a synthetic dataset of counts here that has properties similar to those you can find in the wild. The features are all integer-valued, while the response is continuous:

In[40]:

```
rnd = np.random.RandomState(0)
X_org = rnd.normal(size=(1000, 3))
w = rnd.normal(size=3)

X = rnd.poisson(10 * np.exp(X_org))
y = np.dot(X_org, w)
```

Let's look at the first 10 entries of the first feature. All are integer values and positive, but apart from that it's hard to make out a particular pattern.

If we count the appearance of each value, the distribution of values becomes clearer:

In[41]:

```
print("Number of feature appearances:\n{}".format(np.bincount(X[:, 0])))
```

Out[41]:

```
Number of feature appearances:
[28 38 68 48 61 59 45 56 37 40 35 34 36 26 23 26 27 21 23 23 18 21 10  9 17
  9  7 14 12  7  3  8  4  5  5  3  4  2  4  1  1  3  2  5  3  8  2  5  2  1
  2  3  3  2  2  3  3  0  1  2  1  0  0  3  1  0  0  0  1  3  0  1  0  2  0
  1  1  0  0  0  0  1  0  0  2  2  0  1  1  0  0  0  0  1  1  0  0  0  0  0
  0  0  1  0  0  0  0  0  1  1  0  0  1  0  0  0  0  0  0  0  1  0  0  0  0
  1  0  0  0  0  0  0  0  0  0  0  0  0  0  1]
```

The value 2 seems to be the most common, with 68 appearances (`bincount` always starts at 0), and the counts for higher values fall quickly. However, there are some very high values, like 84 and 85, that are appearing twice. We visualize the counts in Figure 4-7:

In[42]:

```
bins = np.bincount(X[:, 0])
plt.bar(range(len(bins)), bins, color='grey')
plt.ylabel("Number of appearances")
plt.xlabel("Value")
```

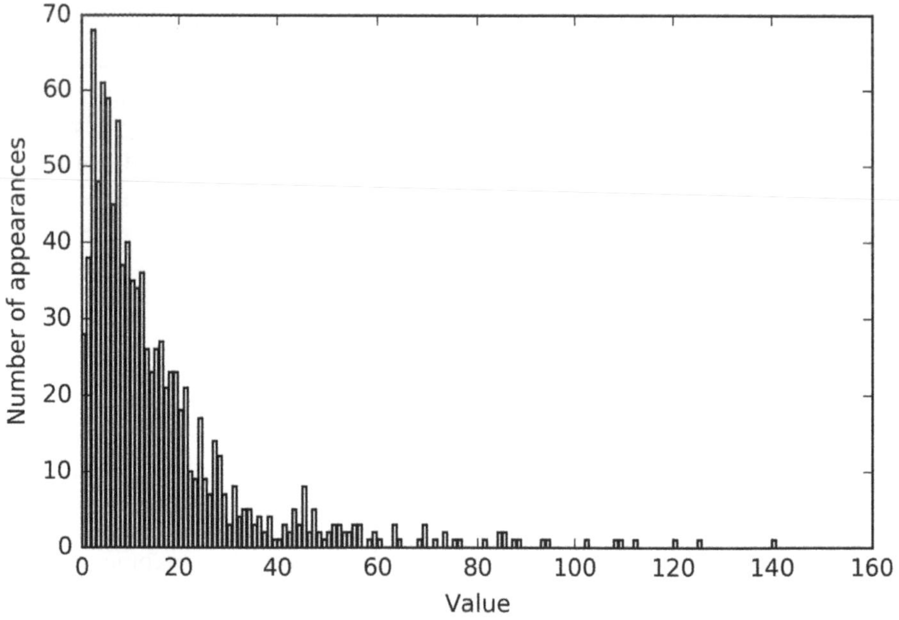

Figure 4-7. Histogram of feature values for X[0]

Features `X[:, 1]` and `X[:, 2]` have similar properties. This kind of distribution of values (many small ones and a few very large ones) is very common in practice.[2] However, it is something most linear models can't handle very well. Let's try to fit a ridge regression to this model:

In[43]:

```
from sklearn.linear_model import Ridge
X_train, X_test, y_train, y_test = train_test_split(X, y, random_state=0)
score = Ridge().fit(X_train, y_train).score(X_test, y_test)
print("Test score: {:.3f}".format(score))
```

Out[43]:

```
Test score: 0.622
```

As you can see from the relatively low R^2 score, `Ridge` was not able to really capture the relationship between `X` and `y`. Applying a logarithmic transformation can help, though. Because the value 0 appears in the data (and the logarithm is not defined at 0), we can't actually just apply `log`, but we have to compute `log(X + 1)`:

In[44]:

```
X_train_log = np.log(X_train + 1)
X_test_log = np.log(X_test + 1)
```

After the transformation, the distribution of the data is less asymmetrical and doesn't have very large outliers anymore (see Figure 4-8):

In[45]:

```
plt.hist(X_train_log[:, 0], bins=25, color='gray')
plt.ylabel("Number of appearances")
plt.xlabel("Value")
```

2 This is a Poisson distribution, which is quite fundamental to count data.

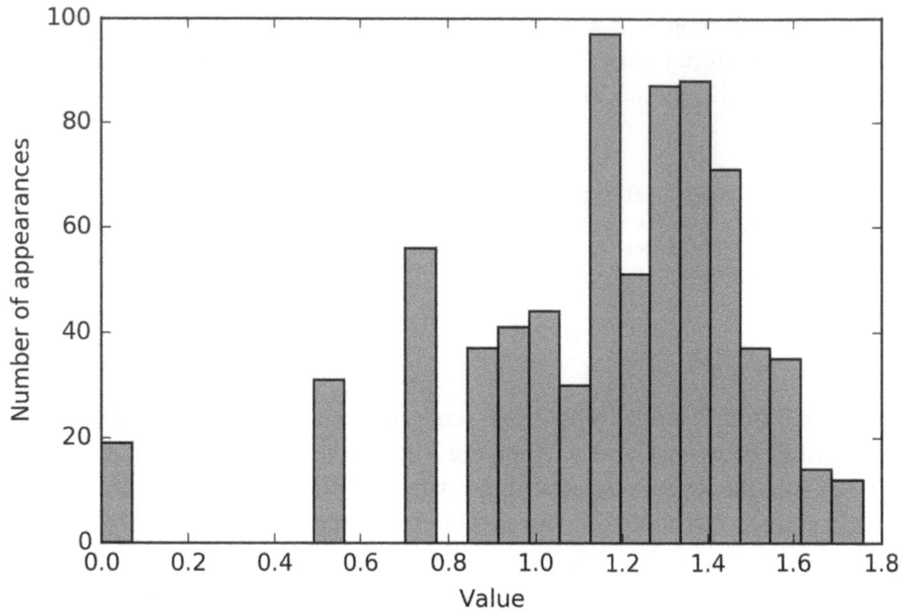

Figure 4-8. Histogram of feature values for X[0] after logarithmic transformation

Building a ridge model on the new data provides a much better fit:

In[46]:

```
score = Ridge().fit(X_train_log, y_train).score(X_test_log, y_test)
print("Test score: {:.3f}".format(score))
```

Out[46]:

```
Test score: 0.875
```

Finding the transformation that works best for each combination of dataset and model is somewhat of an art. In this example, all the features had the same properties. This is rarely the case in practice, and usually only a subset of the features should be transformed, or sometimes each feature needs to be transformed in a different way. As we mentioned earlier, these kinds of transformations are irrelevant for tree-based models but might be essential for linear models. Sometimes it is also a good idea to transform the target variable `y` in regression. Trying to predict counts (say, number of orders) is a fairly common task, and using the `log(y + 1)` transformation often helps.[3]

3 This is a very crude approximation of using Poisson regression, which would be the proper solution from a probabilistic standpoint.

As you saw in the previous examples, binning, polynomials, and interactions can have a huge influence on how models perform on a given dataset. This is particularly true for less complex models like linear models and naive Bayes models. Tree-based models, on the other hand, are often able to discover important interactions themselves, and don't require transforming the data explicitly most of the time. Other models, like SVMs, nearest neighbors, and neural networks, might sometimes benefit from using binning, interactions, or polynomials, but the implications there are usually much less clear than in the case of linear models.

4.7 Automatic Feature Selection

With so many ways to create new features, you might get tempted to increase the dimensionality of the data way beyond the number of original features. However, adding more features makes all models more complex, and so increases the chance of overfitting. When adding new features, or with high-dimensional datasets in general, it can be a good idea to reduce the number of features to only the most useful ones, and discard the rest. This can lead to simpler models that generalize better. But how can you know how good each feature is? There are three basic strategies: *univariate statistics*, *model-based selection*, and *iterative selection*. We will discuss all three of them in detail. All of these methods are supervised methods, meaning they need the target for fitting the model. This means we need to split the data into training and test sets, and fit the feature selection only on the training part of the data.

4.7.1 Univariate Statistics

In univariate statistics, we compute whether there is a statistically significant relationship between each feature and the target. Then the features that are related with the highest confidence are selected. In the case of classification, this is also known as *analysis of variance* (ANOVA). A key property of these tests is that they are *univariate*, meaning that they only consider each feature individually. Consequently, a feature will be discarded if it is only informative when combined with another feature. Univariate tests are often very fast to compute, and don't require building a model. On the other hand, they are completely independent of the model that you might want to apply after the feature selection.

To use univariate feature selection in `scikit-learn`, you need to choose a test, usually either `f_classif` (the default) for classification or `f_regression` for regression, and a method to discard features based on the *p*-values determined in the test. All methods for discarding parameters use a threshold to discard all features with too high a *p*-value (which means they are unlikely to be related to the target). The methods differ in how they compute this threshold, with the simplest ones being `SelectKBest`, which selects a fixed number k of features, and `SelectPercentile`, which selects a fixed percentage of features. Let's apply the feature selection for classification on the cancer dataset. To make the task a bit harder, we'll add some noninformative noise features to the data. We expect the feature selection to be able to identify the features that are noninformative and remove them:

In[47]:

```
from sklearn.datasets import load_breast_cancer
from sklearn.feature_selection import SelectPercentile
from sklearn.model_selection import train_test_split

cancer = load_breast_cancer()

# get deterministic random numbers
rng = np.random.RandomState(42)
noise = rng.normal(size=(len(cancer.data), 50))
# add noise features to the data
# the first 30 features are from the dataset, the next 50 are noise
X_w_noise = np.hstack([cancer.data, noise])

X_train, X_test, y_train, y_test = train_test_split(
    X_w_noise, cancer.target, random_state=0, test_size=.5)
# use f_classif (the default) and SelectPercentile to select 50% of features
select = SelectPercentile(percentile=50)
select.fit(X_train, y_train)
# transform training set
X_train_selected = select.transform(X_train)

print("X_train.shape: {}".format(X_train.shape))
print("X_train_selected.shape: {}".format(X_train_selected.shape))
```

Out[47]:

```
X_train.shape: (284, 80)
X_train_selected.shape: (284, 40)
```

As you can see, the number of features was reduced from 80 to 40 (50 percent of the original number of features). We can find out which features have been selected using the `get_support` method, which returns a Boolean mask of the selected features (visualized in Figure 4-9):

In[48]:

```
mask = select.get_support()
print(mask)
# visualize the mask -- black is True, white is False
plt.matshow(mask.reshape(1, -1), cmap='gray_r')
plt.xlabel("Sample index")
plt.yticks(())
```

Out[48]:

```
[ True  True  True  True  True  True  True  True  True False  True False
  True  True  True  True  True  True False False  True  True  True  True
```

```
 True  True  True  True  True  True False False False  True False  True
False False  True False False False False  True False False  True False
False  True False  True False False False False False False  True False
 True False False False False  True False  True False False False False
 True  True False  True False False False False]
```

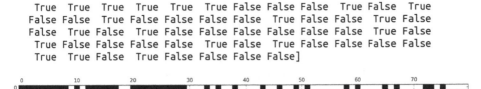

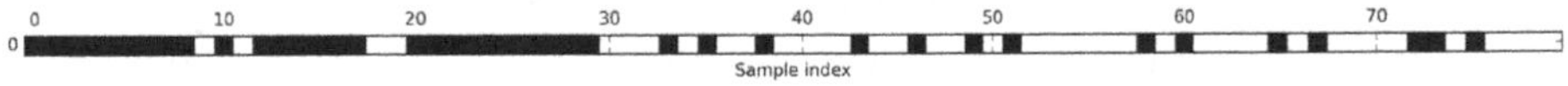

Figure 4-9. Features selected by `SelectPercentile`

As you can see from the visualization of the mask, most of the selected features are the original features, and most of the noise features were removed. However, the recovery of the original features is not perfect. Let's compare the performance of logistic regression on all features against the performance using only the selected features:

In[49]:

```
from sklearn.linear_model import LogisticRegression

# transform test data
X_test_selected = select.transform(X_test)

lr = LogisticRegression()
lr.fit(X_train, y_train)
print("Score with all features: {:.3f}".format(lr.score(X_test, y_test)))
lr.fit(X_train_selected, y_train)
print("Score with only selected features: {:.3f}".format(
    lr.score(X_test_selected, y_test)))
```

Out[49]:

```
Score with all features: 0.930
Score with only selected features: 0.940
```

In this case, removing the noise features improved performance, even though some of the original features were lost. This was a very simple synthetic example, and outcomes on real data are usually mixed. Univariate feature selection can still be very helpful, though, if there is such a large number of features that building a model on them is infeasible, or if you suspect that many features are completely uninformative.

4.7.2 Model-Based Feature Selection

Model-based feature selection uses a supervised machine learning model to judge the importance of each feature, and keeps only the most important ones. The supervised model that is used for feature selection doesn't need to be the same model that is used for the final supervised modeling. The feature selection model needs to provide some measure of importance for each feature, so that they can be ranked by this measure. Decision trees and decision tree–based models provide a `feature_importances_` attribute, which directly encodes the importance of each feature. Linear models have coefficients, which can also be used to capture feature importances by considering the absolute values. As we saw in Chapter 2, linear models with L1 penalty learn sparse coefficients, which only use a small subset of features. This can be viewed as a form of feature selection for the model itself, but can also be used as a preprocessing step to select features for another model. In contrast to univariate selection, model-based selection considers all features at once, and so can capture interactions (if the model can capture them). To use model-based feature selection, we need to use the `SelectFromModel` transformer:

In[50]:

```
from sklearn.feature_selection import SelectFromModel
from sklearn.ensemble import RandomForestClassifier
select = SelectFromModel(
    RandomForestClassifier(n_estimators=100, random_state=42),
    threshold="median")
```

The `SelectFromModel` class selects all features that have an importance measure of the feature (as provided by the supervised model) greater than the provided threshold. To get a comparable result to what we got with univariate feature selection, we used the median as a threshold, so that half of the features will be selected. We use a random forest classifier with 100 trees to compute the feature importances. This is a quite complex model and much more powerful than using univariate tests. Now let's actually fit the model:

In[51]:

```
select.fit(X_train, y_train)
X_train_l1 = select.transform(X_train)
print("X_train.shape: {}".format(X_train.shape))
print("X_train_l1.shape: {}".format(X_train_l1.shape))
```

Out[51]:

```
X_train.shape: (284, 80)
X_train_l1.shape: (284, 40)
```

Again, we can have a look at the features that were selected (Figure 4-10):

In[52]:

```
mask = select.get_support()
# visualize the mask -- black is True, white is False
plt.matshow(mask.reshape(1, -1), cmap='gray_r')
plt.xlabel("Sample index")
plt.yticks(())
```

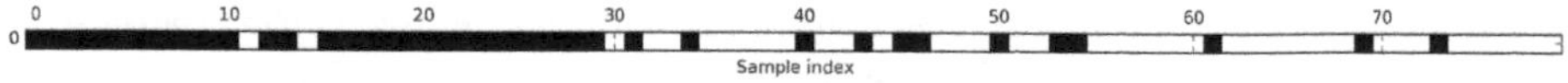

Figure 4-10. Features selected by SelectFromModel using the RandomForestClassifier

This time, all but two of the original features were selected. Because we specified to select 40 features, some of the noise features are also selected. Let's take a look at the performance:

In[53]:

```
X_test_l1 = select.transform(X_test)
score = LogisticRegression().fit(X_train_l1, y_train).score(X_test_l1, y_test)
print("Test score: {:.3f}".format(score))
```

Out[53]:

```
Test score: 0.951
```

With the better feature selection, we also gained some improvements here.

4.7.3 Iterative Feature Selection

In univariate testing we used no model, while in model-based selection we used a single model to select features. In iterative feature selection, a series of models are built, with varying numbers of features. There are two basic methods: starting with no features and adding features one by one until some stopping criterion is reached, or starting with all features and removing features one by one until some stopping criterion is reached. Because a series of models are built, these methods are much more computationally expensive than the methods we discussed previously. One particular method of this kind is *recursive feature elimination* (RFE), which starts with all features, builds a model, and discards the least important feature according to the model. Then a new model is built using all but the discarded feature, and so on until only a prespecified number of features are left. For this to work, the model used for selection needs to provide some way to determine feature importance, as was the case for the model-based selection. Here, we use the same random forest model that we used earlier, and get the results shown in Figure 4-11:

In[54]:

```
from sklearn.feature_selection import RFE
select = RFE(RandomForestClassifier(n_estimators=100, random_state=42),
             n_features_to_select=40)

select.fit(X_train, y_train)
# visualize the selected features:
mask = select.get_support()
plt.matshow(mask.reshape(1, -1), cmap='gray_r')
plt.xlabel("Sample index")
plt.yticks(())
```

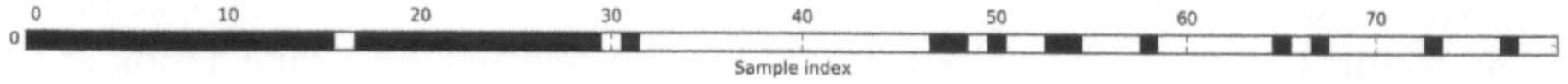

Figure 4-11. Features selected by recursive feature elimination with the random forest classifier model

The feature selection got better compared to the univariate and model-based selection, but one feature was still missed. Running this code also takes significantly longer than that for the model-based selection, because a random forest model is trained 40 times, once for each feature that is dropped. Let's test the accuracy of the logistic regression model when using RFE for feature selection:

In[55]:

```
X_train_rfe = select.transform(X_train)
X_test_rfe = select.transform(X_test)

score = LogisticRegression().fit(X_train_rfe, y_train).score(X_test_rfe, y_test)
print("Test score: {:.3f}".format(score))
```

Out[55]:

```
Test score: 0.951
```

We can also use the model used inside the RFE to make predictions. This uses only the feature set that was selected:

In[56]:

```
print("Test score: {:.3f}".format(select.score(X_test, y_test)))
```

Out[56]:

```
Test score: 0.951
```

Here, the performance of the random forest used inside the RFE is the same as that achieved by training a logistic regression model on top of the selected features. In other words, once we've selected the right features, the linear model performs as well as the random forest.

If you are unsure when selecting what to use as input to your machine learning algorithms, automatic feature selection can be quite helpful. It is also great for reducing the amount of features needed—for example, to speed up prediction or to allow for more interpretable models. In most real-world cases, applying feature selection is unlikely to provide large gains in performance. However, it is still a valuable tool in the toolbox of the feature engineer.

4.8 Utilizing Expert Knowledge

Feature engineering is often an important place to use *expert knowledge* for a particular application. While the purpose of machine learning in many cases is to avoid having to create a set of expert-designed rules, that doesn't mean that prior knowledge of the application or domain should be discarded. Often, domain experts can help in identifying useful features that are much more informative than the initial representation of the data. Imagine you work for a travel agency and want to predict flight prices. Let's say you have a record of prices together with dates, airlines, start locations, and destinations. A machine learning model might be able to build a decent model from that. Some important factors in flight prices, however, cannot be learned. For example, flights are usually more expensive during peak vacation months and around holidays. While the dates of some holidays (like Christmas) are fixed, and their effect can therefore be learned from the date, others might depend on the phases of the moon (like Hanukkah and Easter) or be set by authorities (like school holidays). These events cannot be learned from the data if each flight is only recorded using the (Gregorian) date. However, it is easy to add a feature that encodes whether a flight was on, preceding, or following a public or school holiday. In this way, prior knowledge about the nature of the task can be encoded in the features to aid a machine learning algorithm. Adding a feature does not force a machine learning algorithm to use it, and even if the holiday information turns out to be noninformative for flight prices, augmenting the data with this information doesn't hurt.

We'll now look at one particular case of using expert knowledge—though in this case it might be more rightfully called "common sense." The task is predicting bicycle rentals in front of Andreas's house.

In New York, Citi Bike operates a network of bicycle rental stations with a subscription system. The stations are all over the city and provide a convenient way to get around. Bike rental data is made public in an anonymized form (*https://www.citibikenyc.com/system-data*) and has been analyzed in various ways. The task we want to solve is to predict for a given time and day how many people will rent a bike in front of Andreas's house—so he knows if any bikes will be left for him.

We first load the data for August 2015 for this particular station as a `pandas DataFrame`. We resample the data into three-hour intervals to obtain the main trends for each day:

In[57]:

```
citibike = mglearn.datasets.load_citibike()
```

In[58]:

```
print("Citi Bike data:\n{}".format(citibike.head()))
```

Out[58]:

```
Citi Bike data:
starttime
2015-08-01 00:00:00     3
2015-08-01 03:00:00     0
2015-08-01 06:00:00     9
2015-08-01 09:00:00    41
2015-08-01 12:00:00    39
Freq: 3H, Name: one, dtype: int64
```

The following example shows a visualization of the rental frequencies for the whole month (Figure 4-12):

In[59]:

```
plt.figure(figsize=(10, 3))
xticks = pd.date_range(start=citibike.index.min(), end=citibike.index.max(),
                       freq='D')
plt.xticks(xticks.astype("int"), xticks.strftime("%a %m-%d"), rotation=90, ha="left")
plt.plot(citibike, linewidth=1)
plt.xlabel("Date")
plt.ylabel("Rentals")
```

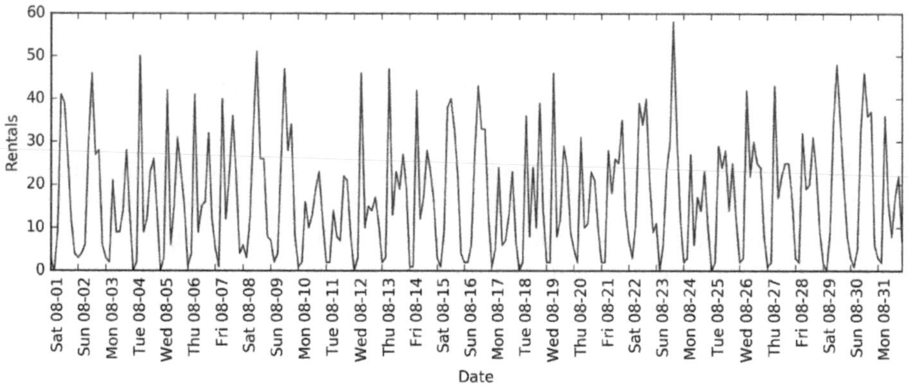

Figure 4-12. Number of bike rentals over time for a selected Citi Bike station

Looking at the data, we can clearly distinguish day and night for each 24-hour interval. The patterns for weekdays and weekends also seem to be quite different. When evaluating a prediction task on a time series like this, we usually want to *learn from the past* and *predict for the future*. This means when doing a split into a training and a test set, we want to use all the data up to a certain date as the training set and all the data past that date as the test set. This is how we would usually use time series prediction: given everything that we know about rentals in the past, what do we think will happen tomorrow? We will use the first 184 data points, corresponding to the first 23 days, as our training set, and the remaining 64 data points, corresponding to the remaining 8 days, as our test set.

The only feature that we are using in our prediction task is the date and time when a particular number of rentals occurred. So, the input feature is the date and time—say, `2015-08-01 00:00:00`—and the output is the number of rentals in the following three hours (three in this case, according to our `DataFrame`).

A (surprisingly) common way that dates are stored on computers is using POSIX time, which is the number of seconds since January 1970 00:00:00 (aka the beginning of Unix time). As a first try, we can use this single integer feature as our data representation:

In[60]:

```
# extract the target values (number of rentals)
y = citibike.values
# convert to POSIX time by dividing by 10**9
X = citibike.index.astype("int64").values.reshape(-1, 1) // 10**9
```

We first define a function to split the data into training and test sets, build the model, and visualize the result:

In[61]:

```
# use the first 184 data points for training, and the rest for testing
n_train = 184

# function to evaluate and plot a regressor on a given feature set
def eval_on_features(features, target, regressor):
    # split the given features into a training and a test set
    X_train, X_test = features[:n_train], features[n_train:]
    # also split the target array
    y_train, y_test = target[:n_train], target[n_train:]
    regressor.fit(X_train, y_train)
    print("Test-set R^2: {:.2f}".format(regressor.score(X_test, y_test)))
    y_pred = regressor.predict(X_test)
    y_pred_train = regressor.predict(X_train)
    plt.figure(figsize=(10, 3))

    plt.xticks(range(0, len(X), 8), xticks.strftime("%a %m-%d"), rotation=90,
               ha="left")

    plt.plot(range(n_train), y_train, label="train")
    plt.plot(range(n_train, len(y_test) + n_train), y_test, '-', label="test")
    plt.plot(range(n_train), y_pred_train, '--', label="prediction train")

    plt.plot(range(n_train, len(y_test) + n_train), y_pred, '--',
             label="prediction test")
    plt.legend(loc=(1.01, 0))
    plt.xlabel("Date")
    plt.ylabel("Rentals")
```

We saw earlier that random forests require very little preprocessing of the data, which makes this seem like a good model to start with. We use the POSIX time feature X and pass a random forest regressor to our eval_on_features function. Figure 4-13 shows the result:

In[62]:

```
from sklearn.ensemble import RandomForestRegressor
regressor = RandomForestRegressor(n_estimators=100, random_state=0)
eval_on_features(X, y, regressor)
```

Out[62]:

```
Test-set R^2: -0.04
```

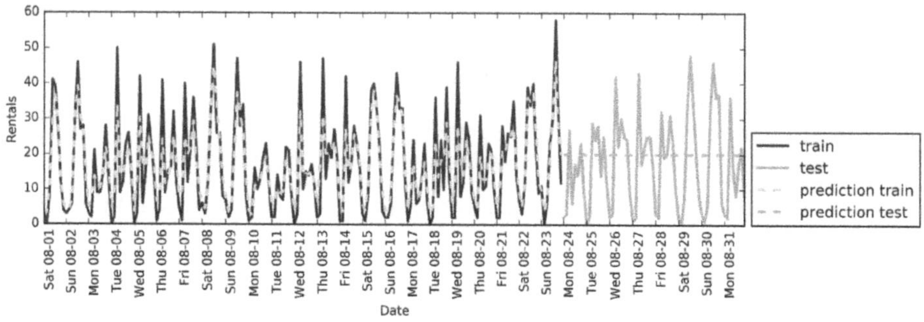

Figure 4-13. Predictions made by a random forest using only the POSIX time

The predictions on the training set are quite good, as is usual for random forests. However, for the test set, a constant line is predicted. The R^2 is –0.04, which means that we learned nothing. What happened?

The problem lies in the combination of our feature and the random forest. The value of the POSIX time feature for the test set is outside of the range of the feature values in the training set: the points in the test set have timestamps that are later than all the points in the training set. Trees, and therefore random forests, cannot *extrapolate* to feature ranges outside the training set. The result is that the model simply predicts the target value of the closest point in the training set—which is the last time it observed any data.

Clearly we can do better than this. This is where our "expert knowledge" comes in. From looking at the rental figures in the training data, two factors seem to be very important: the time of day and the day of the week. So, let's add these two features. We can't really learn anything from the POSIX time, so we drop that feature. First, let's use only the hour of the day. As Figure 4-14 shows, now the predictions have the same pattern for each day of the week:

In[63]:

```
X_hour = citibike.index.hour.values.reshape(-1, 1)
eval_on_features(X_hour, y, regressor)
```

Out[63]:

```
Test-set R^2: 0.60
```

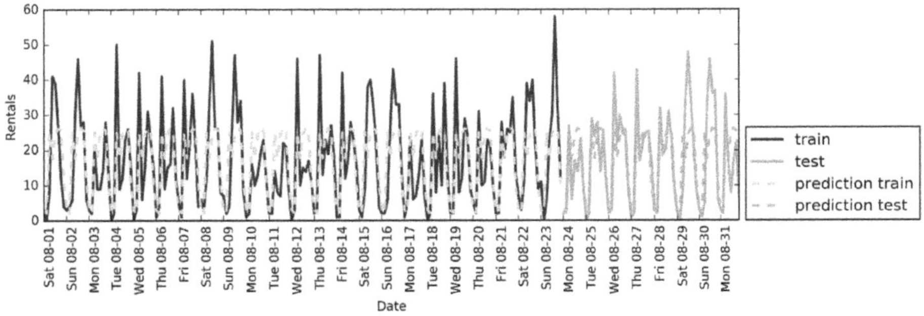

Figure 4-14. Predictions made by a random forest using only the hour of the day

The R^2 is already much better, but the predictions clearly miss the weekly pattern. Now let's also add the day of the week (see Figure 4-15):

In[64]:

```
X_hour_week = np.hstack([citibike.index.dayofweek.values.reshape(-1, 1),
                         citibike.index.hour.values.reshape(-1, 1)])
eval_on_features(X_hour_week, y, regressor)
```

Out[64]:

```
Test-set R^2: 0.84
```

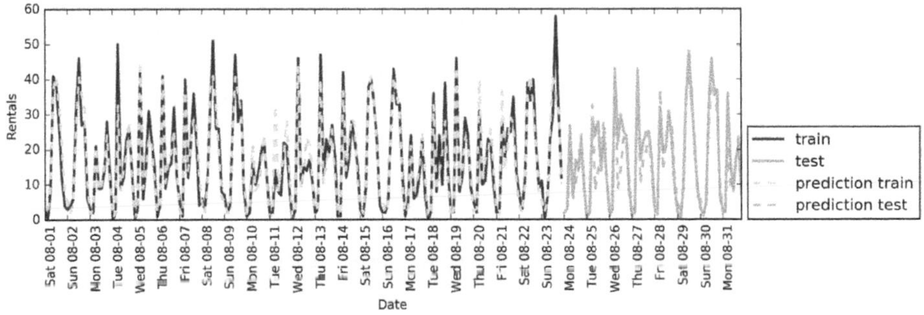

Figure 4-15. Predictions with a random forest using day of week and hour of day features

Now we have a model that captures the periodic behavior by considering the day of week and time of day. It has an R^2 of 0.84, and shows pretty good predictive performance. What this model likely is learning is the mean number of rentals for each combination of weekday and time of day from the first 23 days of August. This actually does not require a complex model like a random forest, so let's try with a simpler model, `LinearRegression` (see Figure 4-16):

In[65]:

```
from sklearn.linear_model import LinearRegression
eval_on_features(X_hour_week, y, LinearRegression())
```

Out[65]:

```
Test-set R^2: 0.13
```

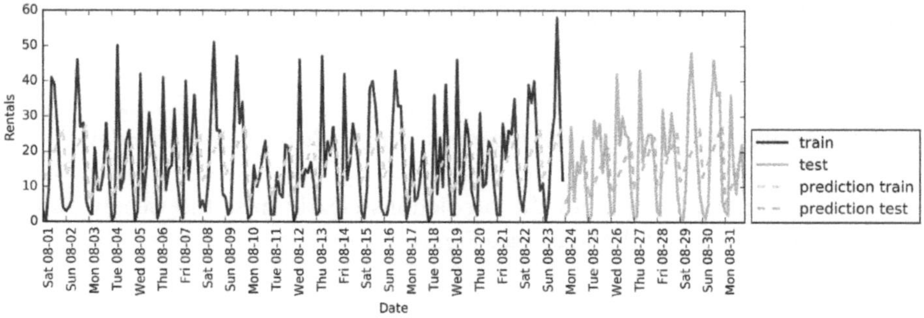

Figure 4-16. Predictions made by linear regression using day of week and hour of day as features

`LinearRegression` works much worse, and the periodic pattern looks odd. The reason for this is that we encoded day of week and time of day using integers, which are interpreted as continuous variables. Therefore, the linear model can only learn a linear function of the time of day—and it learned that later in the day, there are more rentals. However, the patterns are much more complex than that. We can capture this by interpreting the integers as categorical variables, by transforming them using `OneHotEncoder` (see Figure 4-17):

In[66]:

```
enc = OneHotEncoder()
X_hour_week_onehot = enc.fit_transform(X_hour_week).toarray()
```

In[67]:

```
eval_on_features(X_hour_week_onehot, y, Ridge())
```

Out[67]:

```
Test-set R^2: 0.62
```

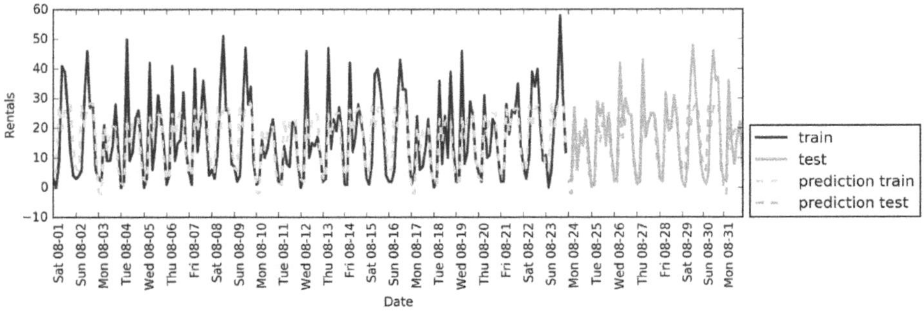

Figure 4-17. Predictions made by linear regression using a one-hot encoding of hour of day and day of week

This gives us a much better match than the continuous feature encoding. Now the linear model learns one coefficient for each day of the week, and one coefficient for each time of the day. That means that the "time of day" pattern is shared over all days of the week, though.

Using interaction features, we can allow the model to learn one coefficient for each combination of day and time of day (see Figure 4-18):

In[68]:

```
poly_transformer = PolynomialFeatures(degree=2, interaction_only=True,
                                      include_bias=False)
X_hour_week_onehot_poly = poly_transformer.fit_transform(X_hour_week_onehot)
lr = Ridge()
eval_on_features(X_hour_week_onehot_poly, y, lr)
```

Out[68]:

```
Test-set R^2: 0.85
```

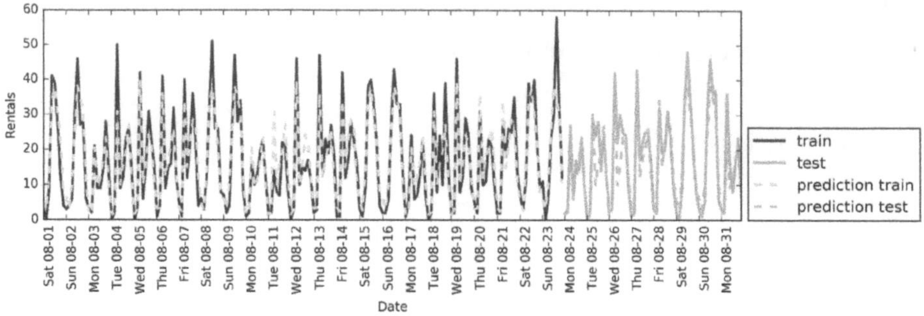

Figure 4-18. Predictions made by linear regression using a product of the day of week and hour of day features

This transformation finally yields a model that performs similarly well to the random forest. A big benefit of this model is that it is very clear what is learned: one coefficient for each day and time. We can simply plot the coefficients learned by the model, something that would not be possible for the random forest.

First, we create feature names for the hour and day features:

In[69]:

```
hour = ["%02d:00" % i for i in range(0, 24, 3)]
day = ["Mon", "Tue", "Wed", "Thu", "Fri", "Sat", "Sun"]
features =  day + hour
```

Then we name all the interaction features extracted by `PolynomialFeatures`, using the `get_feature_names` method, and keep only the features with nonzero coefficients:

In[70]:

```
features_poly = poly_transformer.get_feature_names(features)
features_nonzero = np.array(features_poly)[lr.coef_ != 0]
coef_nonzero = lr.coef_[lr.coef_ != 0]
```

Now we can visualize the coefficients learned by the linear model, as seen in Figure 4-19:

In[71]:

```
plt.figure(figsize=(15, 2))
plt.plot(coef_nonzero, 'o')
plt.xticks(np.arange(len(coef_nonzero)), features_nonzero, rotation=90)
plt.xlabel("Feature name")
plt.ylabel("Feature magnitude")
```

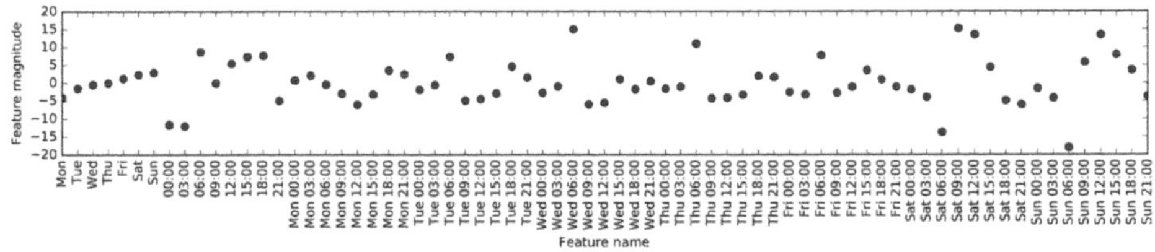

Figure 4-19. Coefficients of the linear regression model using a product of hour and day

4.9 Summary and Outlook

In this chapter, we discussed how to deal with different data types (in particular, with categorical variables). We emphasized the importance of representing data in a way that is suitable for the machine learning algorithm—for example, by one-hot-encoding categorical variables. We also discussed the importance of engineering new features, and the possibility of utilizing expert knowledge in creating derived features from your data. In particular, linear models might benefit greatly from generating new features via binning and adding polynomials and interactions, while more complex, nonlinear models like random forests and SVMs might be able to learn more complex tasks without explicitly expanding the feature space. In practice, the features that are used (and the match between features and method) is often the most important piece in making a machine learning approach work well.

Now that you have a good idea of how to represent your data in an appropriate way and which algorithm to use for which task, the next chapter will focus on evaluating the performance of machine learning models and selecting the right parameter settings.

CHAPTER 5
Model Evaluation and Improvement

Having discussed the fundamentals of supervised and unsupervised learning, and having explored a variety of machine learning algorithms, we will now dive more deeply into evaluating models and selecting parameters.

We will focus on the supervised methods, regression and classification, as evaluating and selecting models in unsupervised learning is often a very qualitative process (as we saw in Chapter 3).

To evaluate our supervised models, so far we have split our dataset into a training set and a test set using the `train_test_split` function, built a model on the training set by calling the `fit` method, and evaluated it on the test set using the `score` method, which for classification computes the fraction of correctly classified samples. Here's an example of that process:

In[1]:

```
from sklearn.datasets import make_blobs
from sklearn.linear_model import LogisticRegression
from sklearn.model_selection import train_test_split

# create a synthetic dataset
X, y = make_blobs(random_state=0)
# split data and labels into a training and a test set
X_train, X_test, y_train, y_test = train_test_split(X, y, random_state=0)
# instantiate a model and fit it to the training set
logreg = LogisticRegression().fit(X_train, y_train)
# evaluate the model on the test set
print("Test set score: {:.2f}".format(logreg.score(X_test, y_test)))
```

Out[1]:

```
Test set score: 0.88
```

Remember, the reason we split our data into training and test sets is that we are interested in measuring how well our model *generalizes* to new, previously unseen data. We are not interested in how well our model fit the training set, but rather in how well it can make predictions for data that was not observed during training.

In this chapter, we will expand on two aspects of this evaluation. We will first introduce cross-validation, a more robust way to assess generalization performance, and discuss methods to evaluate classification and regression performance that go beyond the default measures of accuracy and R^2 provided by the `score` method.

We will also discuss *grid search*, an effective method for adjusting the parameters in supervised models for the best generalization performance.

5.1 Cross-Validation

Cross-validation is a statistical method of evaluating generalization performance that is more stable and thorough than using a split into a training and a test set. In cross-validation, the data is instead split repeatedly and multiple models are trained. The most commonly used version of cross-validation is *k-fold cross-validation*, where *k* is a user-specified number, usually 5 or 10. When performing five-fold cross-validation, the data is first partitioned into five parts of (approximately) equal size, called *folds*. Next, a sequence of models is trained. The first model is trained using the first fold as the test set, and the remaining folds (2–5) are used as the training set. The model is built using the data in folds 2–5, and then the accuracy is evaluated on fold 1. Then another model is built, this time using fold 2 as the test set and the data in folds 1, 3, 4, and 5 as the training set. This process is repeated using folds 3, 4, and 5 as test sets. For each of these five *splits* of the data into training and test sets, we compute the accuracy. In the end, we have collected five accuracy values. The process is illustrated in Figure 5-1:

In[2]:

```
mglearn.plots.plot_cross_validation()
```

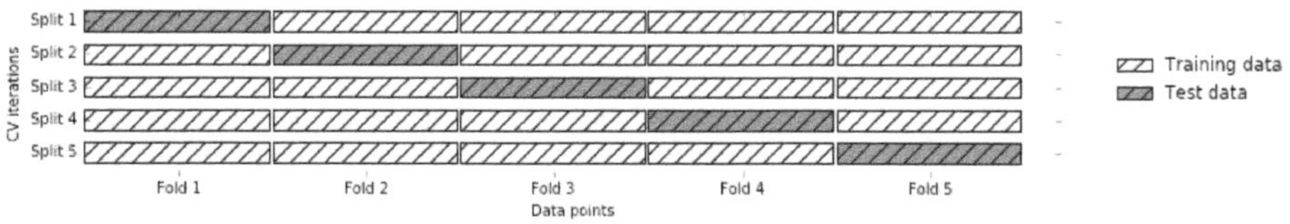

Figure 5-1. Data splitting in five-fold cross-validation

Usually, the first fifth of the data is the first fold, the second fifth of the data is the second fold, and so on.

5.1.1 Cross-Validation in scikit-learn

Cross-validation is implemented in `scikit-learn` using the `cross_val_score` function from the `model_selection` module. The parameters of the `cross_val_score` function are the model we want to evaluate, the training data, and the ground-truth labels. Let's evaluate `LogisticRegression` on the `iris` dataset:

In[3]:

```
from sklearn.model_selection import cross_val_score
from sklearn.datasets import load_iris
from sklearn.linear_model import LogisticRegression

iris = load_iris()
logreg = LogisticRegression()

scores = cross_val_score(logreg, iris.data, iris.target)
print("Cross-validation scores: {}".format(scores))
```

Out[3]:

```
Cross-validation scores: [0.961 0.922 0.958]
```

Here, `cross_val_score` performed three-fold cross-validation and therefore returned three scores. By default, `cross_val_score` performs three-fold cross-validation in earlier versions of `scikit-learn`, and will perform five-fold cross-validation by default (starting with `scikit-learn` 0.22). We can change the number of folds used by changing the cv parameter:

In[4]:

```
scores = cross_val_score(logreg, iris.data, iris.target, cv=5)
print("Cross-validation scores: {}".format(scores))
```

Out[4]:

```
Cross-validation scores: [1.    0.967 0.933 0.9   1.   ]
```

It's recommended to use at least five-fold cross-validation. A common way to summarize the cross-validation accuracy is to compute the mean:

In[5]:

```
print("Average cross-validation score: {:.2f}".format(scores.mean()))
```

Out[5]:

```
Average cross-validation score: 0.96
```

Using the mean cross-validation we can conclude that we expect the model to be around 96% accurate on average. Looking at all five scores produced by the five-fold cross-validation, we can also conclude that there is a relatively high variance in the accuracy between folds, ranging from 100% accuracy to 90% accuracy. This could imply that the model is very dependent on the particular folds used for training, but it could also just be a consequence of the small size of the dataset. There is a second function you can use for cross-validation, called `cross_validate`. It has a similar interface to `cross_val_score`, but returns a dictionary containing training and test times (and optionally the training score, in addition to the test scores) for each split:

In[6]:

```
from sklearn.model_selection import cross_validate
res = cross_validate(logreg, iris.data, iris.target, cv=5,
                     return_train_score=True)
display(res)
```

Out[6]:

```
{'fit_time': array([0.002, 0.002, 0.002, 0.001, 0.002]),
 'score_time': array([0.   , 0.   , 0.001, 0.001, 0.001]),
 'test_score': array([1.   , 0.967, 0.933, 0.9  , 1.   ]),
 'train_score': array([0.95 , 0.967, 0.967, 0.975, 0.958])}
```

Using pandas, we can nicely display these results and compute summaries:

In[7]:

```
res_df = pd.DataFrame(res)
display(res_df)
print("Mean times and scores:\n", res_df.mean())
```

Out[7]:

```
[cols=",,,,",options="header",]
|===============================================
| |fit_time |score_time |test_score |train_score
|0 |1.50e-03 |4.62e-04 |1.00 |0.95
|1 |1.58e-03 |4.99e-04 |0.97 |0.97
|2 |1.60e-03 |6.45e-04 |0.93 |0.97
|3 |1.49e-03 |5.19e-04 |0.90 |0.97
|4 |1.54e-03 |1.06e-03 |1.00 |0.96
|===============================================

Mean times and scores:
 fit_time       1.54e-03
score_time     6.37e-04
test_score     9.60e-01
train_score    9.63e-01
dtype: float64
```

5.1.2 Benefits of Cross-Validation

There are several benefits to using cross-validation instead of a single split into a training and a test set. First, remember that `train_test_split` performs a random split of the data. Imagine that we are "lucky" when randomly splitting the data, and all examples that are hard to classify end up in the training set. In that case, the test set will only contain "easy" examples, and our test set accuracy will be unrealistically high. Conversely, if we are "unlucky," we might have randomly put all the hard-to-classify examples in the test set and consequently obtain an unrealistically low score. However, when using cross-validation, each example will be in the test set exactly once: each example is in one of the folds, and each fold is the test set once. Therefore, the model needs to generalize well to all of the samples in the dataset for all of the cross-validation scores (and their mean) to be high.

Having multiple splits of the data also provides some information about how sensitive our model is to the selection of the training dataset. For the `iris` dataset, we saw accuracies between 90% and 100%. This is quite a range, and it provides us with an idea about how the model might perform in the worst case and best case scenarios when applied to new data.

Another benefit of cross-validation as compared to using a single split of the data is that we use our data more effectively. When using `train_test_split`, we usually use 75% of the data for training and 25% of the data for evaluation. When using five-fold cross-validation, in each iteration we can use four-fifths of the data (80%) to fit the model. When using 10-fold cross-validation, we can use nine-tenths of the data (90%) to fit the model. More data will usually result in more accurate models.

The main disadvantage of cross-validation is increased computational cost. As we are now training *k* models instead of a single model, cross-validation will be roughly *k* times slower than doing a single split of the data.

> It is important to keep in mind that cross-validation is not a way to build a model that can be applied to new data. Cross-validation does not return a model. When calling `cross_val_score`, multiple models are built internally, but the purpose of cross-validation is only to evaluate how well a given algorithm will generalize when trained on a specific dataset.

5.1.3 Stratified k-Fold Cross-Validation and Other Strategies

Splitting the dataset into *k* folds by starting with the first one-*k*-th part of the data, as described in the previous section, might not always be a good idea. For example, let's have a look at the `iris` dataset:

In[8]:

```
from sklearn.datasets import load_iris
iris = load_iris()
print("Iris labels:\n{}".format(iris.target))
```

Out[8]:

```
Iris labels:
[0 0 0 0 0 0 0 0 0 0 0 0 0 0 0 0 0 0 0 0 0 0 0 0 0 0 0 0 0 0 0 0 0 0 0 0 0
 0 0 0 0 0 0 0 0 0 0 0 0 0 1 1 1 1 1 1 1 1 1 1 1 1 1 1 1 1 1 1 1 1 1 1 1 1
 1 1 1 1 1 1 1 1 1 1 1 1 1 1 1 1 1 1 1 1 1 1 1 1 1 1 2 2 2 2 2 2 2 2 2 2 2
 2 2 2 2 2 2 2 2 2 2 2 2 2 2 2 2 2 2 2 2 2 2 2 2 2 2 2 2 2 2 2 2 2 2 2 2 2
 2 2]
```

As you can see, the first third of the data is the class 0, the second third is the class 1, and the last third is the class 2. Imagine doing three-fold cross-validation on this dataset. The first fold would be only class 0, so in the first split of the data, the test set would be only class 0, and the training set would be only classes 1 and 2. As the classes in training and test sets would be different for all three splits, the three-fold cross-validation accuracy would be zero on this dataset. That is not very helpful, as we can do much better than 0% accuracy on `iris`.

As the simple *k*-fold strategy fails here, `scikit-learn` does not use it for classification, but rather uses *stratified k-fold cross-validation*. In stratified cross-validation, we split the data such that the proportions between classes are the same in each fold as they are in the whole dataset, as illustrated in Figure 5-2:

In[9]:

```
mglearn.plots.plot_stratified_cross_validation()
```

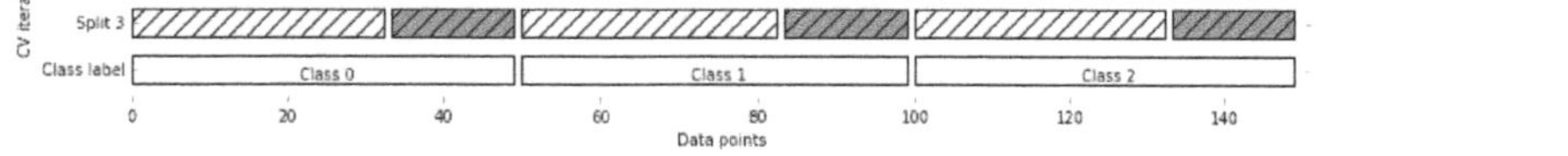

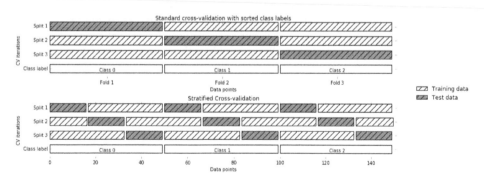

Figure 5-2. Comparison of standard cross-validation and stratified cross-validation when the data is ordered by class label

For example, if 90% of your samples belong to class A and 10% of your samples belong to class B, then stratified cross-validation ensures that in each fold, 90% of samples belong to class A and 10% of samples belong to class B.

It is usually a good idea to use stratified *k*-fold cross-validation instead of *k*-fold cross-validation to evaluate a classifier, because it results in more reliable estimates of generalization performance. In the case of only 10% of samples belonging to class B, using standard *k*-fold cross-validation it might easily happen that one fold only contains samples of class A. Using this fold as a test set would not be very informative about the overall performance of the classifier.

For regression, `scikit-learn` uses the standard *k*-fold cross-validation by default. It would be possible to also try to make each fold representative of the different values the regression target has, but this is not a commonly used strategy and would be surprising to most users.

More control over cross-validation

We saw earlier that we can adjust the number of folds that are used in `cross_val_score` using the `cv` parameter. However, `scikit-learn` allows for much finer control over what happens during the splitting of the data by providing a *cross-validation splitter* as the `cv` parameter. For most use cases, the defaults of *k*-fold cross-validation for regression and stratified *k*-fold for classification work well, but there are some cases where you might want to use a different strategy. Say, for example, we want to use the standard *k*-fold cross-validation on a classification dataset to reproduce someone else's results. To do this, we first have to import the `KFold` splitter class from the `model_selection` module and instantiate it with the number of folds we want to use:

In[10]:

```
from sklearn.model_selection import KFold
kfold = KFold(n_splits=5)
```

Then, we can pass the `kfold` splitter object as the `cv` parameter to `cross_val_score`:

In[11]:

```
print("Cross-validation scores:\n{}".format(
      cross_val_score(logreg, iris.data, iris.target, cv=kfold)))
```

Out[11]:

```
Cross-validation scores:
[1.    0.933 0.433 0.967 0.433]
```

This way, we can verify that it is indeed a really bad idea to use three-fold (nonstratified) cross-validation on the `iris` dataset:

In[12]:

```
kfold = KFold(n_splits=3)
print("Cross-validation scores:\n{}".format(
    cross_val_score(logreg, iris.data, iris.target, cv=kfold)))
```

Out[12]:

```
Cross-validation scores:
[0. 0. 0.]
```

Remember: each fold corresponds to one of the classes in the `iris` dataset, and so nothing can be learned. Another way to resolve this problem is to shuffle the data instead of stratifying the folds, to remove the ordering of the samples by label. We can do that by setting the `shuffle` parameter of `KFold` to `True`. If we shuffle the data, we also need to fix the `random_state` to get a reproducible shuffling. Otherwise, each run of `cross_val_score` would yield a different result, as each time a different split would be used (this might not be a problem, but can be surprising). Shuffling the data before splitting it yields a much better result:

In[13]:

```
kfold = KFold(n_splits=3, shuffle=True, random_state=0)
print("Cross-validation scores:\n{}".format(
    cross_val_score(logreg, iris.data, iris.target, cv=kfold)))
```

Out[13]:

```
Cross-validation scores:
[0.9  0.96 0.96]
```

Leave-one-out cross-validation

Another frequently used cross-validation method is *leave-one-out*. You can think of leave-one-out cross-validation as *k*-fold cross-validation where each fold is a single sample. For each split, you pick a single data point to be the test set. This can be very time consuming, particularly for large datasets, but sometimes provides better estimates on small datasets:

In[14]:

```
from sklearn.model_selection import LeaveOneOut
loo = LeaveOneOut()
scores = cross_val_score(logreg, iris.data, iris.target, cv=loo)
print("Number of cv iterations: ", len(scores))
print("Mean accuracy: {:.2f}".format(scores.mean()))
```

Out[14]:

```
Number of cv iterations:  150
Mean accuracy: 0.95
```

Shuffle-split cross-validation

Another, very flexible strategy for cross-validation is *shuffle-split cross-validation*. In shuffle-split cross-validation, each split samples `train_size` many points for the training set and `test_size` many (disjoint) point for the test set. This splitting is repeated `n_splits` times. Figure 5-3 illustrates running four iterations of splitting a dataset consisting of 10 points, with a training set of 5 points and test sets of 2 points each (you can use integers for `train_size` and `test_size` to use absolute sizes for these sets, or floating-point numbers to use fractions of the whole dataset):

In[15]:

```
mglearn.plots.plot_shuffle_split()
```

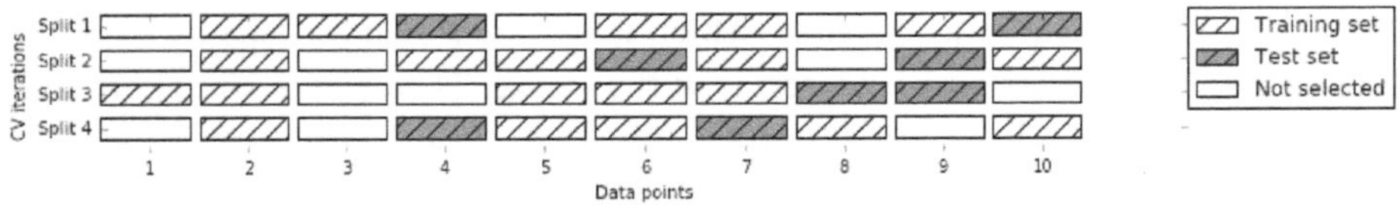

Figure 5-3. ShuffleSplit with 10 points, train_size=5, test_size=2, and n_splits=4

The following code splits the dataset into 50% training set and 50% test set for 10 iterations:

In[16]:

```
from sklearn.model_selection import ShuffleSplit
shuffle_split = ShuffleSplit(test_size=.5, train_size=.5, n_splits=10)
scores = cross_val_score(logreg, iris.data, iris.target, cv=shuffle_split)
print("Cross-validation scores:\n{}".format(scores))
```

Out[16]:

```
Cross-validation scores:
[0.973 0.92  0.96  0.96  0.893 0.947 0.88  0.893 0.947 0.947]
```

Shuffle-split cross-validation allows for control over the number of iterations independently of the training and test sizes, which can sometimes be helpful. It also allows for using only part of the data in each iteration, by providing `train_size` and `test_size` settings that don't add up to one. Subsampling the data in this way can be useful for experimenting with large datasets.

There is also a stratified variant of `ShuffleSplit`, aptly named `StratifiedShuffleSplit`, which can provide more reliable results for classification tasks.

Cross-validation with groups

Another very common setting for cross-validation is when there are groups in the data that are highly related. Say you want to build a system to recognize emotions from pictures of faces, and you collect a dataset of pictures of 100 people where each person is captured multiple times, showing various emotions. The goal is to build a classifier that can correctly identify emotions of people not in the dataset. You could use the default stratified cross-validation to measure the performance of a classifier here. However, it is likely that pictures of the same person will be in both the training and the test set. It will be much easier for a classifier to detect emotions in a face that is part of the training set, compared to a completely new face. To accurately evaluate the generalization to new faces, we must therefore ensure that the training and test sets contain images of different people.

To achieve this, we can use `GroupKFold`, which takes an array of `groups` as argument that we can use to indicate which person is in the image. The `groups` array here indicates groups in the data that should not be split when creating the training and test sets, and should not be confused with the class label.

This example of groups in the data is common in medical applications, where you might have multiple samples from the same patient, but are interested in generalizing to new patients. Similarly, in speech recognition, you might have multiple recordings of the same speaker in your dataset, but are interested in recognizing speech of new speakers.

The following is an example of using a synthetic dataset with a grouping given by the `groups` array. The dataset consists of 12 data points, and for each of the data points, `groups` specifies which group (think patient) the point belongs to. The groups specify that there are four groups, and the first three samples belong to the first group, the next four samples belong to the second group, and so on:

In[17]:

```
from sklearn.model_selection import GroupKFold
# create synthetic dataset
X, y = make_blobs(n_samples=12, random_state=0)
# assume the first three samples belong to the same group,
# then the next four, etc.
groups = [0, 0, 0, 1, 1, 1, 1, 2, 2, 3, 3, 3]
scores = cross_val_score(logreg, X, y, groups, cv=GroupKFold(n_splits=3))
print("Cross-validation scores:\n{}".format(scores))
```

Out[17]:

```
Cross-validation scores:
[0.75  0.8   0.667]
```

The samples don't need to be ordered by group; we just did this for illustration purposes. The splits that are calculated based on these labels are visualized in Figure 5-4.

As you can see, for each split, each group is either entirely in the training set or entirely in the test set:

In[18]:

```
mglearn.plots.plot_group_kfold()
```

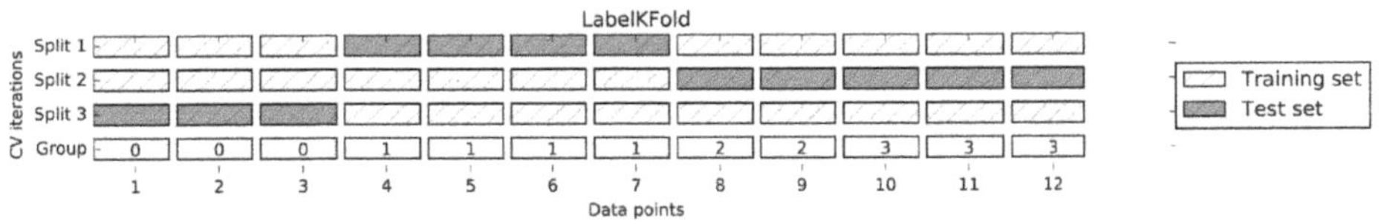

Figure 5-4. Label-dependent splitting with GroupKFold

There are more splitting strategies for cross-validation in `scikit-learn`, which allow for an even greater variety of use cases (you can find these in the `scikit-learn` user guide (*http://scikit-learn.org/stable/modules/cross_validation.html*)). However, the standard `KFold`, `StratifiedKFold`, and `GroupKFold` are by far the most commonly used ones.

5.2 Grid Search

Now that we know how to evaluate how well a model generalizes, we can take the next step and improve the model's generalization performance by tuning its parameters. We discussed the parameter settings of many of the algorithms in `scikit-learn` in Chapters 2 and 3, and it is important to understand what the parameters mean before trying to adjust them. Finding the values of the important parameters of a model (the ones that provide the best generalization performance) is a tricky task, but necessary for almost all models and datasets. Because it is such a common task, there are standard methods in `scikit-learn` to help you with it. The most commonly used method is *grid search*, which basically means trying all possible combinations of the parameters of interest.

Consider the case of a kernel SVM with an RBF (radial basis function) kernel, as implemented in the `SVC` class. As we discussed in Chapter 2, there are two important parameters: the kernel bandwidth, `gamma`, and the regularization parameter, `C`. Say we want to try the values `0.001`, `0.01`, `0.1`, `1`, `10`, and `100` for the parameter `C`, and the same for `gamma`. Because we have six different settings for `C` and `gamma` that we want to try, we have 36 combinations of parameters in total. Looking at all possible combinations creates a table (or grid) of parameter settings for the SVM, as shown here:

	C = 0.001	C = 0.01	...	C = 10
gamma=0.001	SVC(C=0.001, gamma=0.001)	SVC(C=0.01, gamma=0.001)	...	SVC(C=10, gamma=0.001)
gamma=0.01	SVC(C=0.001, gamma=0.01)	SVC(C=0.01, gamma=0.01)	...	SVC(C=10, gamma=0.01)
...	...	...	...	...
gamma=100	SVC(C=0.001, gamma=100)	SVC(C=0.01, gamma=100)	...	SVC(C=10, gamma=100)

5.2.1 Simple Grid Search

We can implement a simple grid search just as for loops over the two parameters, training and evaluating a classifier for each combination:

In[19]:

```
# naive grid search implementation
from sklearn.svm import SVC
X_train, X_test, y_train, y_test = train_test_split(
    iris.data, iris.target, random_state=0)
print("Size of training set: {}   size of test set: {}".format(
      X_train.shape[0], X_test.shape[0]))

best_score = 0

for gamma in [0.001, 0.01, 0.1, 1, 10, 100]:
    for C in [0.001, 0.01, 0.1, 1, 10, 100]:
        # for each combination of parameters, train an SVC
        svm = SVC(gamma=gamma, C=C)
        svm.fit(X_train, y_train)
        # evaluate the SVC on the test set
        score = svm.score(X_test, y_test)
        # if we got a better score, store the score and parameters
        if score > best_score:
            best_score = score
            best_parameters = {'C': C, 'gamma': gamma}

print("Best score: {:.2f}".format(best_score))
print("Best parameters: {}".format(best_parameters))
```

Out[19]:

```
Size of training set: 112   size of test set: 38
Best score: 0.97
Best parameters: {'C': 100, 'gamma': 0.001}
```

5.2.2 The Danger of Overfitting the Parameters and the Validation Set

Given this result, we might be tempted to report that we found a model that performs with 97% accuracy on our dataset. However, this claim could be overly optimistic (or just wrong), for the following reason: we tried many different parameters and selected the one with best accuracy on the test set, but this accuracy won't necessarily carry over to new data. Because we used the test data to adjust the parameters, we can no longer use it to assess how good the model is. This is the same reason we needed to split the data into training and test sets in the first place; we need an independent dataset to evaluate, one that was not used to create the model.

One way to resolve this problem is to split the data again, so we have three sets: the training set to build the model, the validation (or development) set to select the parameters of the model, and the test set to evaluate the performance of the selected parameters. Figure 5-5 shows what this looks like:

In[20]:

```
mglearn.plots.plot_threefold_split()
```

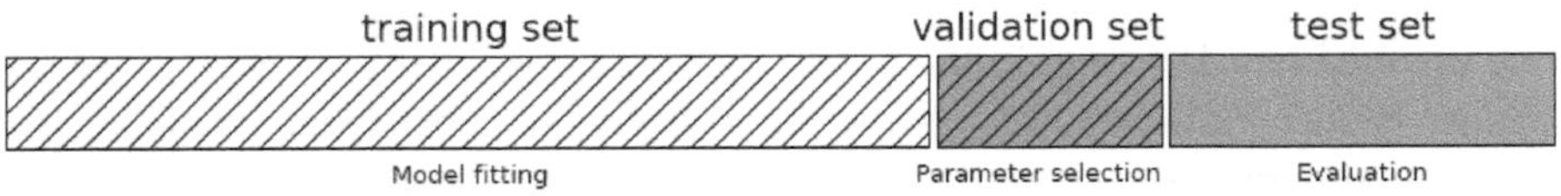

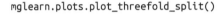

Figure 5-5. A threefold split of data into training set, validation set, and test set

After selecting the best parameters using the validation set, we can rebuild a model using the parameter settings we found, but now training on both the training data and the validation data. This way, we can use as much data as possible to build our model. This leads to the following implementation:

In[21]:

```
from sklearn.svm import SVC
# split data into train+validation set and test set
X_trainval, X_test, y_trainval, y_test = train_test_split(
    iris.data, iris.target, random_state=0)
# split train+validation set into training and validation sets
X_train, X_valid, y_train, y_valid = train_test_split(
    X_trainval, y_trainval, random_state=1)
print("Size of training set: {}   size of validation set: {}   size of test set:"
      " {}\n".format(X_train.shape[0], X_valid.shape[0], X_test.shape[0]))

best_score = 0

for gamma in [0.001, 0.01, 0.1, 1, 10, 100]:
    for C in [0.001, 0.01, 0.1, 1, 10, 100]:
        # for each combination of parameters, train an SVC
        svm = SVC(gamma=gamma, C=C)
        svm.fit(X_train, y_train)
        # evaluate the SVC on the validation set
        score = svm.score(X_valid, y_valid)
        # if we got a better score, store the score and parameters
        if score > best_score:
            best_score = score
```

```
            best_parameters = {'C': C, 'gamma': gamma}

# rebuild a model on the combined training and validation set,
# and evaluate it on the test set
svm = SVC(**best_parameters)
svm.fit(X_trainval, y_trainval)
test_score = svm.score(X_test, y_test)
print("Best score on validation set: {:.2f}".format(best_score))
print("Best parameters: ", best_parameters)
print("Test set score with best parameters: {:.2f}".format(test_score))
```

Out[21]:

```
Size of training set: 84   size of validation set: 28   size of test set: 38

Best score on validation set: 0.96
Best parameters:  {'C': 10, 'gamma': 0.001}
Test set score with best parameters: 0.92
```

The best score on the validation set is 96%: slightly lower than before, probably because we used less data to train the model (`X_train` is smaller now because we split our dataset twice). However, the score on the test set—the score that actually tells us how well we generalize—is even lower, at 92%. So we can only claim to classify new data 92% correctly, not 97% correctly as we thought before!

The distinction between the training set, validation set, and test set is fundamentally important to applying machine learning methods in practice. Any choices made based on the test set accuracy "leak" information from the test set into the model. Therefore, it is important to keep a separate test set, which is only used for the final evaluation. It is good practice to do all exploratory analysis and model selection using the combination of a training and a validation set, and reserve the test set for a final evaluation—this is even true for exploratory visualization. Strictly speaking, evaluating more than one model on the test set and choosing the better of the two will result in an overly optimistic estimate of how accurate the model is.

5.2.3 Grid Search with Cross-Validation

While the method of splitting the data into a training, a validation, and a test set that we just saw is workable, and relatively commonly used, it is quite sensitive to how exactly the data is split. From the output of the previous code snippet we can see that grid search selects `'C': 10, 'gamma': 0.001` as the best parameters, while the output of the code in the previous section selects `'C': 100, 'gamma': 0.001` as the best parameters. For a better estimate of the generalization performance, instead of using a single split into a training and a validation set, we can use cross-validation to evaluate the performance of each parameter combination. This method can be coded up as follows:

In[22]:

```
for gamma in [0.001, 0.01, 0.1, 1, 10, 100]:
    for C in [0.001, 0.01, 0.1, 1, 10, 100]:
        # for each combination of parameters,
        # train an SVC
        svm = SVC(gamma=gamma, C=C)
        # perform cross-validation
        scores = cross_val_score(svm, X_trainval, y_trainval, cv=5)
        # compute mean cross-validation accuracy
        score = np.mean(scores)
        # if we got a better score, store the score and parameters
        if score > best_score:
            best_score = score
            best_parameters = {'C': C, 'gamma': gamma}
# rebuild a model on the combined training and validation set
svm = SVC(**best_parameters)
svm.fit(X_trainval, y_trainval)
```

To evaluate the accuracy of the SVM using a particular setting of `C` and `gamma` using five-fold cross-validation, we need to train 36 * 5 = 180 models. As you can imagine, the main downside of the use of cross-validation is the time it takes to train all these models.

The following visualization (Figure 5-6) illustrates how the best parameter setting is selected in the preceding code:

In[23]:

```
mglearn.plots.plot_cross_val_selection()
```

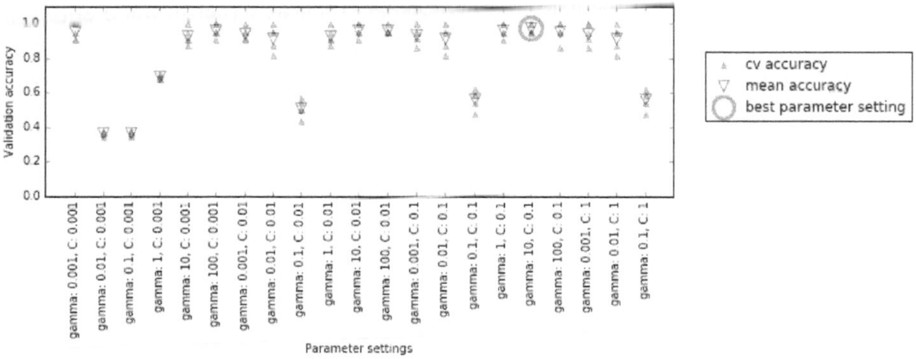

Figure 5-6. Results of grid search with cross-validation

For each parameter setting (only a subset is shown), five accuracy values are computed, one for each split in the cross-validation. Then the mean validation accuracy is computed for each parameter setting. The parameters with the highest mean validation accuracy are chosen, marked by the circle.

As we said earlier, cross-validation is a way to evaluate a given algorithm on a specific dataset. However, it is often used in conjunction with parameter search methods like grid search. For this reason, many people use the term *cross-validation* colloquially to refer to grid search with cross-validation.

The overall process of splitting the data, running the grid search, and evaluating the final parameters is illustrated in Figure 5-7:

In[24]:

```
mglearn.plots.plot_grid_search_overview()
```

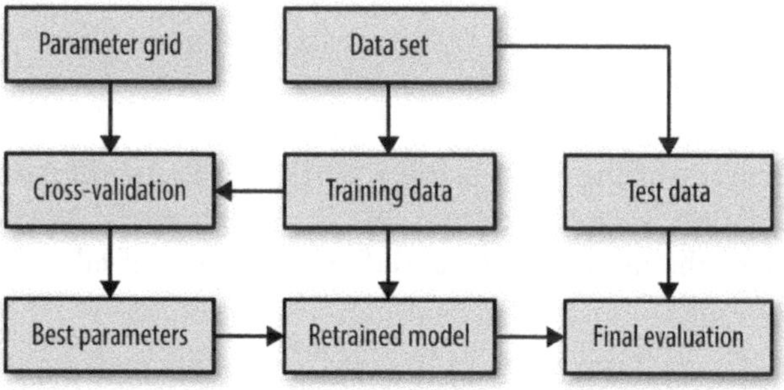

Figure 5-7. Overview of the process of parameter selection and model evaluation with GridSearchCV

Because grid search with cross-validation is such a commonly used method to adjust parameters, `scikit-learn` provides the `GridSearchCV` class, which implements it in the form of an estimator. To use the `GridSearchCV` class, you first need to specify the parameters you want to search over using a dictionary. `GridSearchCV` will then perform all the necessary model fits. The keys of the dictionary are the names of parameters we want to adjust (as given when constructing the model—in this case, `C` and `gamma`), and the values are the parameter settings we want to try out. Trying the values `0.001`, `0.01`, `0.1`, `1`, `10`, and `100` for `C` and `gamma` translates to the following dictionary:

In[25]:

```
param_grid = {'C': [0.001, 0.01, 0.1, 1, 10, 100],
              'gamma': [0.001, 0.01, 0.1, 1, 10, 100]}
print("Parameter grid:\n{}".format(param_grid))
```

Out[25]:

```
Parameter grid:
{'C': [0.001, 0.01, 0.1, 1, 10, 100], 'gamma': [0.001, 0.01, 0.1, 1, 10, 100]}
```

We can now instantiate the GridSearchCV class with the model (SVC), the parameter grid to search (param_grid), and the cross-validation strategy we want to use (say, five-fold stratified cross-validation):

In[26]:

```
from sklearn.model_selection import GridSearchCV
from sklearn.svm import SVC
grid_search = GridSearchCV(SVC(), param_grid, cv=5,
                           return_train_score=True)
```

GridSearchCV will use cross-validation in place of the split into a training and validation set that we used before. However, we still need to split the data into a training and a test set, to avoid overfitting the parameters:

In[27]:

```
X_train, X_test, y_train, y_test = train_test_split(
    iris.data, iris.target, random_state=0)
```

The grid_search object that we created behaves just like a classifier; we can call the standard methods fit, predict, and score on it.[1] However, when we call fit, it will run cross-validation for each combination of parameters we specified in param_grid:

In[28]:

```
grid_search.fit(X_train, y_train)
```

Fitting the GridSearchCV object not only searches for the best parameters, but also automatically fits a new model on the whole training dataset with the parameters that yielded the best cross-validation performance. What happens in fit is therefore equivalent to the result of the In[21] code we saw at the beginning of this section. The GridSearchCV class provides a very convenient interface to access the retrained model using the predict and score methods. To evaluate how well the best found parameters generalize, we can call score on the test set:

In[29]:

```
print("Test set score: {:.2f}".format(grid_search.score(X_test, y_test)))
```

Out[29]:

```
Test set score: 0.97
```

Choosing the parameters using cross-validation, we actually found a model that achieves 97% accuracy on the test set. The important thing here is that we *did not use the test set* to choose the parameters. The parameters that were found are stored in the

1 A scikit-learn estimator that is created using another estimator is called a *meta-estimator*. GridSearchCV is the most commonly used meta-estimator, but we will see more later.

best_params_ attribute, and the best cross-validation accuracy (the mean accuracy over the different splits for this parameter setting) is stored in best_score_:

In[30]:

```
print("Best parameters: {}".format(grid_search.best_params_))
print("Best cross-validation score: {:.2f}".format(grid_search.best_score_))
```

Out[30]:

```
Best parameters: {'C': 100, 'gamma': 0.01}
Best cross-validation score: 0.97
```

> Again, be careful not to confuse best_score_ with the generalization performance of the model as computed by the score method on the test set. Using the score method (or evaluating the output of the predict method) employs a model *trained on the whole training set*. The best_score_ attribute stores the mean cross-validation accuracy, with *cross-validation performed on the training set*.

Sometimes it is helpful to have access to the actual model that was found—for example, to look at coefficients or feature importances. You can access the model with the best parameters trained on the whole training set using the best_estimator_ attribute:

In[31]:

```
print("Best estimator:\n{}".format(grid_search.best_estimator_))
```

Out[31]:

```
Best estimator:
SVC(C=100, cache_size=200, class_weight=None, coef0=0.0,
  decision_function_shape='ovr', degree=3, gamma=0.01, kernel='rbf',
  max_iter=-1, probability=False, random_state=None, shrinking=True,
  tol=0.001, verbose=False)
```

Because grid_search itself has predict and score methods, using best_estimator_ is not needed to make predictions or evaluate the model.

Analyzing the result of cross-validation

It is often helpful to visualize the results of cross-validation, to understand how the model generalization depends on the parameters we are searching. As grid searches are quite computationally expensive to run, often it is a good idea to start with a relatively coarse and small grid. We can then inspect the results of the cross-validated grid search, and possibly expand our search. The results of a grid search can be found in the cv_results_ attribute, which is a dictionary storing all aspects of the search. It contains a lot of details, as you can see in the following output, and is best looked at after converting it to a pandas `DataFrame`:

In[32]:

```
import pandas as pd
# convert to DataFrame
results = pd.DataFrame(grid_search.cv_results_)
# show the first 5 rows
display(results.head())
```

Out[32]:

```
     param_C   param_gamma   params                              mean_test_score
0    0.001     0.001         {'C': 0.001, 'gamma': 0.001}           0.366
1    0.001      0.01         {'C': 0.001, 'gamma': 0.01}            0.366
2    0.001       0.1         {'C': 0.001, 'gamma': 0.1}             0.366
3    0.001         1         {'C': 0.001, 'gamma': 1}               0.366
4    0.001        10         {'C': 0.001, 'gamma': 10}              0.366

       rank_test_score  split0_test_score  split1_test_score  split2_test_score
0                22             0.375              0.347              0.363
1                22             0.375              0.347              0.363
2                22             0.375              0.347              0.363
3                22             0.375              0.347              0.363
4                22             0.375              0.347              0.363

       split3_test_score  split4_test_score  std_test_score
0           0.363              0.380              0.011
1           0.363              0.380              0.011
2           0.363              0.380              0.011
3           0.363              0.380              0.011
4           0.363              0.380              0.011
```

Each row in `results` corresponds to one particular parameter setting. For each setting, the results of all cross-validation splits are recorded, as well as the mean and standard deviation over all splits. As we were searching a two-dimensional grid of parameters (`C` and `gamma`), this is best visualized as a heat map (Figure 5-8). First we extract the mean validation scores, then we reshape the scores so that the axes correspond to `C` and `gamma`:

In[33]:

```
scores = np.array(results.mean_test_score).reshape(6, 6)

# plot the mean cross-validation scores
mglearn.tools.heatmap(scores, xlabel='gamma', xticklabels=param_grid['gamma'],
                      ylabel='C', yticklabels=param_grid['C'], cmap="viridis")
```

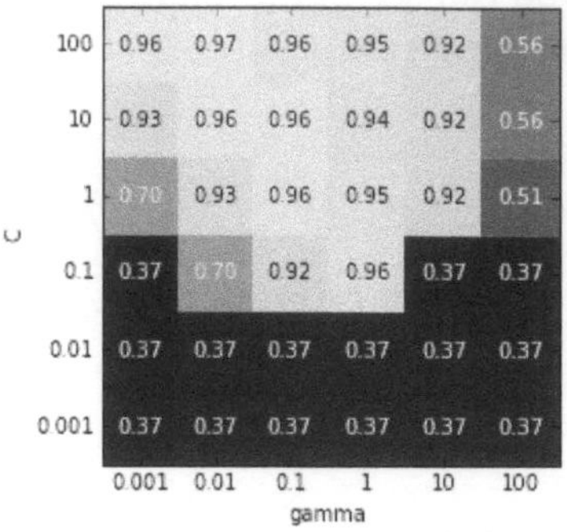

Figure 5-8. Heat map of mean cross-validation score as a function of C and gamma

Each point in the heat map corresponds to one run of cross-validation, with a particular parameter setting. The color encodes the cross-validation accuracy, with light colors meaning high accuracy and dark colors meaning low accuracy. You can see that `SVC` is very sensitive to the setting of the parameters. For many of the parameter settings, the accuracy is around 40%, which is quite bad; for other settings the accuracy is around 96%. We can take away from this plot several things. First, the parameters we adjusted are *very important* for obtaining good performance. Both parameters (`C` and `gamma`) matter a lot, as adjusting them can change the accuracy from 40% to 96%. Additionally, the ranges we picked for the parameters are ranges in which we see significant changes in the outcome. It's also important to note that the ranges for the parameters are large enough: the optimum values for each parameter are not on the edges of the plot.

Now let's look at some plots (shown in Figure 5-9) where the result is less ideal, because the search ranges were not chosen properly:

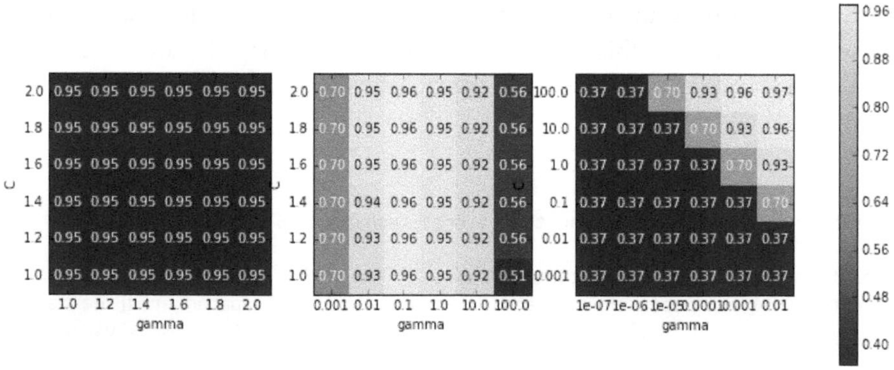

Figure 5-9. Heat map visualizations of misspecified search grids

In[34]:

```
fig, axes = plt.subplots(1, 3, figsize=(13, 5))

param_grid_linear = {'C': np.linspace(1, 2, 6),
                     'gamma':  np.linspace(1, 2, 6)}

param_grid_one_log = {'C': np.linspace(1, 2, 6),
                      'gamma':  np.logspace(-3, 2, 6)}

param_grid_range = {'C': np.logspace(-3, 2, 6),
                    'gamma':  np.logspace(-7, -2, 6)}

for param_grid, ax in zip([param_grid_linear, param_grid_one_log,
                           param_grid_range], axes):
    grid_search = GridSearchCV(SVC(), param_grid, cv=5)
    grid_search.fit(X_train, y_train)
    scores = grid_search.cv_results_['mean_test_score'].reshape(6, 6)

    # plot the mean cross-validation scores
    scores_image = mglearn.tools.heatmap(
        scores, xlabel='gamma', ylabel='C', xticklabels=param_grid['gamma'],
        yticklabels=param_grid['C'], cmap="viridis", ax=ax)

plt.colorbar(scores_image, ax=axes.tolist())
```

The first panel shows no changes at all, with a constant color over the whole parameter grid. In this case, this is caused by improper scaling and range of the parameters `C` and `gamma`. However, if no change in accuracy is visible over the different parameter settings, it could also be that a parameter is just not important at all. It is usually good to try very extreme values first, to see if there are any changes in the accuracy as a result of changing a parameter.

The second panel shows a vertical stripe pattern. This indicates that only the setting of the `gamma` parameter makes any difference. This could mean that the `gamma` parameter is searching over interesting values but the `C` parameter is not—or it could mean the `C` parameter is not important.

The third panel shows changes in both `C` and `gamma`. However, we can see that in the entire bottom left of the plot, nothing interesting is happening. We can probably exclude the very small values from future grid searches. The optimum parameter setting is at the top right. As the optimum is in the border of the plot, we can expect that there might be even better values beyond this border, and we might want to change our search range to include more parameters in this region.

Tuning the parameter grid based on the cross-validation scores is perfectly fine, and a good way to explore the importance of different parameters. However, you should not test different parameter ranges on the final test set—as we discussed earlier, evaluation of the test set should happen only once we know exactly what model we want to use.

Search over spaces that are not grids

In some cases, trying all possible combinations of all parameters as GridSearchCV usually does, is not a good idea. For example, SVC has a kernel parameter, and depending on which kernel is chosen, other parameters will be relevant. If kernel='linear', the model is linear, and only the C parameter is used. If kernel='rbf', both the C and gamma parameters are used (but not other parameters like degree). In this case, searching over all possible combinations of C, gamma, and kernel wouldn't make sense: if kernel='linear', gamma is not used, and trying different values for gamma would be a waste of time. To deal with these kinds of "conditional" parameters, GridSearchCV allows the param_grid to be a *list of dictionaries*. Each dictionary in the list is expanded into an independent grid. A possible grid search involving kernel and parameters could look like this:

In[35]:

```
param_grid = [{'kernel': ['rbf'],
               'C': [0.001, 0.01, 0.1, 1, 10, 100],
               'gamma': [0.001, 0.01, 0.1, 1, 10, 100]},
              {'kernel': ['linear'],
               'C': [0.001, 0.01, 0.1, 1, 10, 100]}]
print("List of grids:\n{}".format(param_grid))
```

Out[35]:

```
List of grids:
[{'kernel': ['rbf'], 'C': [0.001, 0.01, 0.1, 1, 10, 100],
  'gamma': [0.001, 0.01, 0.1, 1, 10, 100]},
 {'kernel': ['linear'], 'C': [0.001, 0.01, 0.1, 1, 10, 100]}]
```

In the first grid, the kernel parameter is always set to 'rbf' (note that the entry for kernel is a list of length one), and both the C and gamma parameters are varied. In the second grid, the kernel parameter is always set to linear, and only C is varied. Now let's apply this more complex parameter search:

In[36]:

```
grid_search = GridSearchCV(SVC(), param_grid, cv=5,
                           return_train_score=True)
grid_search.fit(X_train, y_train)
print("Best parameters: {}".format(grid_search.best_params_))
print("Best cross-validation score: {:.2f}".format(grid_search.best_score_))
```

Out[36]:

```
Best parameters: {'C': 100, 'gamma': 0.01, 'kernel': 'rbf'}
Best cross-validation score: 0.97
```

Let's look at the `cv_results_` again. As expected, if `kernel` is `'linear'`, then only `C` is varied:

In[37]:

```
results = pd.DataFrame(grid_search.cv_results_)
# we display the transposed table so that it better fits on the page:
display(results.T)
```

Out[37]:

	0	1	2	3	...	38	39	40	41
param_C	0.001	0.001	0.001	0.001	...	0.1	1	10	100
param_gamma	0.001	0.01	0.1	1	...	NaN	NaN	NaN	NaN
param_kernel	rbf	rbf	rbf	rbf	...	linear	linear	linear	linear
params	{*C*: 0.001, *kernel*: *rbf*, *gamma*: 0.001}	{*C*: 0.001, *kernel*: *rbf*, *gamma*: 0.01}	{*C*: 0.001, *kernel*: *rbf*, *gamma*: 0.1}	{*C*: 0.001, *kernel*: *rbf*, *gamma*: 1}	...	{*C*: 0.1, *kernel*: *linear*}	{*C*: 1, *kernel*: *linear*}	{*C*: 10, *kernel*: *linear*}	{*C*: 100, *kernel*: *linear*}
mean_test_score	0.37	0.37	0.37	0.37	...	0.95	0.97	0.96	0.96
rank_test_score	27	27	27	27	...	11	1	3	3
split0_test_score	0.38	0.38	0.38	0.38	...	0.96	1	0.96	0.96
split1_test_score	0.35	0.35	0.35	0.35	...	0.91	0.96	1	1
split2_test_score	0.36	0.36	0.36	0.36	...	1	1	1	1
split3_test_score	0.36	0.36	0.36	0.36	...	0.91	0.95	0.91	0.91
split4_test_score	0.38	0.38	0.38	0.38	...	0.95	0.95	0.95	0.95
std_test_score	0.011	0.011	0.011	0.011	...	0.033	0.022	0.034	0.034

```
12 rows × 42 columns
```

Using different cross-validation strategies with grid search

Similarly to `cross_val_score`, `GridSearchCV` uses stratified *k*-fold cross-validation by default for classification, and *k*-fold cross-validation for regression. However, you can also pass any cross-validation splitter, as described in "More control over cross-validation" on page 263, as the `cv` parameter in `GridSearchCV`. In particular, to get only a single split into a training and a validation set, you can use `ShuffleSplit` or `StratifiedShuffleSplit` with `n_splits=1`. This might be helpful for very large datasets, or very slow models.

Nested cross-validation

In the preceding examples, we went from using a single split of the data into training, validation, and test sets to splitting the data into training and test sets and then performing cross-validation on the training set. But when using `GridSearchCV` as described earlier, we still have a single split of the data into training and test sets, which might make our results unstable and make us depend too much on this single split of the data. We can go a step further, and instead of splitting the original data into training and test sets once, use multiple splits of cross-validation. This will result in what is called *nested cross-validation*. In nested cross-validation, there is an outer loop over splits of the data into training and test sets. For each of them, a grid search is run (which might result in different best parameters for each split in the outer loop). Then, for each outer split, the test set score using the best settings is reported.

The result of this procedure is a list of scores—not a model, and not a parameter setting. The scores tell us how well a model generalizes, given the best parameters found by grid search. As it doesn't provide a model that can be used on new data, nested cross-validation is rarely used when looking for a predictive model to apply to future data. However, it can be useful for evaluating how well a given model works on a particular dataset.

Implementing nested cross-validation in `scikit-learn` is straightforward. We call `cross_val_score` with an instance of `GridSearchCV` as the model:

In[38]:

```
param_grid = {'C': [0.001, 0.01, 0.1, 1, 10, 100],
              'gamma': [0.001, 0.01, 0.1, 1, 10, 100]}
scores = cross_val_score(GridSearchCV(SVC(), param_grid, cv=5),
                         iris.data, iris.target, cv=5)
print("Cross-validation scores: ", scores)
print("Mean cross-validation score: ", scores.mean())
```

Out[38]:

```
Cross-validation scores:  [0.967 1.    0.967 0.967 1.   ]
Mean cross-validation score:  0.98
```

The result of our nested cross-validation can be summarized as "`SVC` can achieve 98% mean cross-validation accuracy on the `iris` dataset"—nothing more and nothing less.

Here, we used stratified five-fold cross-validation in both the inner and the outer loop. As our `param_grid` contains 36 combinations of parameters, this results in a whopping 36 * 5 * 5 = 900 models being built, making nested cross-validation a very expensive procedure. Here, we used the same cross-validation splitter in the inner and the outer loop; however, this is not necessary and you can use any combination of cross-validation strategies in the inner and outer loops. It can be a bit tricky to understand what is happening in the single line given above, and it can be helpful to visualize it as `for` loops, as done in the following simplified implementation:

In[39]:

```
def nested_cv(X, y, inner_cv, outer_cv, Classifier, parameter_grid):
    outer_scores = []
    # for each split of the data in the outer cross-validation
    # (split method returns indices of training and test parts)
    for training_samples, test_samples in outer_cv.split(X, y):
        # find best parameter using inner cross-validation
        best_parms = {}
        best_score = -np.inf
        # iterate over parameters
        for parameters in parameter_grid:
            # accumulate score over inner splits
            cv_scores = []
            # iterate over inner cross-validation
            for inner_train, inner_test in inner_cv.split(
                    X[training_samples], y[training_samples]):
                # build classifier given parameters and training data
                clf = Classifier(**parameters)
                clf.fit(X[inner_train], y[inner_train])
                # evaluate on inner test set
                score = clf.score(X[inner_test], y[inner_test])
                cv_scores.append(score)
            # compute mean score over inner folds
            mean_score = np.mean(cv_scores)
            if mean_score > best_score:
                # if better than so far, remember parameters
                best_score = mean_score
                best_params = parameters
        # build classifier on best parameters using outer training set
        clf = Classifier(**best_params)
        clf.fit(X[training_samples], y[training_samples])
        # evaluate
        outer_scores.append(clf.score(X[test_samples], y[test_samples]))
    return np.array(outer_scores)
```

Now, let's run this function on the iris dataset:

In[40]:

```
from sklearn.model_selection import ParameterGrid, StratifiedKFold
scores = nested_cv(iris.data, iris.target, StratifiedKFold(5),
                   StratifiedKFold(5), SVC, ParameterGrid(param_grid))
print("Cross-validation scores: {}".format(scores))
```

Out[40]:

```
Cross-validation scores: [0.967 1.    0.967 0.967 1.   ]
```

Parallelizing cross-validation and grid search

While running a grid search over many parameters and on large datasets can be computationally challenging, it is also *embarrassingly parallel*. This means that building a model using a particular parameter setting on a particular cross-validation split can be done completely independently from the other parameter settings and models. This makes grid search and cross-validation ideal candidates for parallelization over multiple CPU cores or over a cluster. You can make use of multiple cores in `GridSearchCV` and `cross_val_score` by setting the `n_jobs` parameter to the number of CPU cores you want to use. You can set `n_jobs=-1` to use all available cores.

Setting `n_jobs` in both the model and `GridSearchCV` is supported since `scikit-learn` 0.20.0, but is not well tested yet. If your dataset and model are very large, it might be that using many cores uses up too much memory, and you should monitor your memory usage when building large models in parallel.

It is also possible to parallelize grid search and cross-validation over multiple machines in a cluster by using the distributed computing package `dask`. See *http://distributed.dask.org/en/latest/joblib.html* for more details.

5.3 Evaluation Metrics and Scoring

So far, we have evaluated classification performance using accuracy (the fraction of correctly classified samples) and regression performance using R^2. However, these are only two of the many possible ways to summarize how well a supervised model performs on a given dataset. In practice, these evaluation metrics might not be appropriate for your application, and it is important to choose the right metric when selecting between models and adjusting parameters.

5.3.1 Keep the End Goal in Mind

When selecting a metric, you should always have the end goal of the machine learning application in mind. In practice, we are usually interested not just in making accurate predictions, but in using these predictions as part of a larger decision-making process. Before picking a machine learning metric, you should think about the high-level goal of the application, often called the *business metric*. The consequences of choosing a particular algorithm for a machine learning application are called the *business impact*.[2] Maybe the high-level goal is avoiding traffic accidents, or decreasing the number of hospital admissions. It could also be getting more users for your website, or having users spend more money in your shop. When choosing a model or adjusting parameters, you should pick the model or parameter values that have the most positive influence on the business metric. Often this is hard, as assess-

2 We ask scientifically minded readers to excuse the commercial language in this section. Not losing track of the end goal is equally important in science, though the authors are not aware of a similar phrase to "business impact" being used in that realm.

ing the business impact of a particular model might require putting it in production in a real-life system.

In the early stages of development, and for adjusting parameters, it is often infeasible to put models into production just for testing purposes, because of the high business or personal risks that can be involved. Imagine evaluating the pedestrian avoidance capabilities of a self-driving car by just letting it drive around, without verifying it first; if your model is bad, pedestrians will be in trouble! Therefore we often need to find some surrogate evaluation procedure, using an evaluation metric that is easier to compute. For example, we could test classifying images of pedestrians against non-pedestrians and measure accuracy. Keep in mind that this is only a surrogate, and it pays off to find the closest metric to the original business goal that is feasible to evaluate. This closest metric should be used whenever possible for model evaluation and selection. The result of this evaluation might not be a single number—the consequence of your algorithm could be that you have 10% more customers, but each customer will spend 15% less—but it should capture the expected business impact of choosing one model over another.

In this section, we will first discuss metrics for the important special case of binary classification, then turn to multiclass classification and finally regression.

5.3.2 Metrics for Binary Classification

Binary classification is arguably the most common and conceptually simple application of machine learning in practice. However, there are still a number of caveats in evaluating even this simple task. Before we dive into alternative metrics, let's have a look at the ways in which measuring accuracy might be misleading. Remember that for binary classification, we often speak of a *positive* class and a *negative* class, with the understanding that the positive class is the one we are looking for.

Kinds of errors

Often, accuracy is not a good measure of predictive performance, as the number of mistakes we make does not contain all the information we are interested in. Imagine an application to screen for the early detection of cancer using an automated test. If the test is negative, the patient will be assumed healthy, while if the test is positive, the patient will undergo additional screening. Here, we would call a positive test (an indication of cancer) the positive class, and a negative test the negative class. We can't assume that our model will always work perfectly, and it will make mistakes. For any application, we need to ask ourselves what the consequences of these mistakes might be in the real world.

One possible mistake is that a healthy patient will be classified as positive, leading to additional testing. This leads to some costs and an inconvenience for the patient (and possibly some mental distress). An incorrect positive prediction is called a *false posi-*

tive. The other possible mistake is that a sick patient will be classified as negative, and will not receive further tests and treatment. The undiagnosed cancer might lead to serious health issues, and could even be fatal. A mistake of this kind—an incorrect negative prediction—is called a *false negative*. In statistics, a false positive is also known as *type I error*, and a false negative as *type II error*. We will stick to "false negative" and "false positive," as they are more explicit and easier to remember. In the cancer diagnosis example, it is clear that we want to avoid false negatives as much as possible, while false positives can be viewed as more of a minor nuisance.

While this is a particularly drastic example, the consequence of false positives and false negatives are rarely the same. In commercial applications, it might be possible to assign dollar values to both kinds of mistakes, which would allow measuring the error of a particular prediction in dollars, instead of accuracy. This might be much more meaningful for making business decisions on which model to use.

Imbalanced datasets

Types of errors play an important role when one of two classes is much more frequent than the other one. This is very common in practice; a good example is click-through prediction, where each data point represents an "impression," an item that was shown to a user. This item might be an ad, or a related story, or a related person to follow on a social media site. The goal is to predict whether, if shown a particular item, a user will click on it (indicating they are interested). Most things users are shown on the Internet (in particular, ads) will not result in a click. You might need to show a user 100 ads or articles before they find something interesting enough to click on. This results in a dataset where for each 99 "no click" data points, there is 1 "clicked" data point; in other words, 99% of the samples belong to the "no click" class. Datasets in which one class is much more frequent than the other are often called *imbalanced datasets*, or *datasets with imbalanced classes*. In reality, imbalanced data is the norm, and it is rare that the events of interest have equal or even similar frequency in the data.

Now let's say you build a classifier that is 99% accurate on the click prediction task. What does that tell you? 99% accuracy sounds impressive, but this doesn't take the class imbalance into account. You can achieve 99% accuracy without building a machine learning model, by always predicting "no click." On the other hand, even with imbalanced data, a 99% accurate model could in fact be quite good. However, accuracy doesn't allow us to distinguish the constant "no click" model from a potentially good model.

To illustrate, we'll create a 9:1 imbalanced dataset from the `digits` dataset, by classifying the digit 9 against the nine other classes:

In[41]:

```
from sklearn.datasets import load_digits

digits = load_digits()
y = digits.target == 9

X_train, X_test, y_train, y_test = train_test_split(
    digits.data, y, random_state=0)
```

We can use the `DummyClassifier` to always predict the majority class (here "not nine") to see how uninformative accuracy can be:

In[42]:

```
from sklearn.dummy import DummyClassifier
dummy_majority = DummyClassifier(strategy='most_frequent').fit(X_train, y_train)
pred_most_frequent = dummy_majority.predict(X_test)
print("Unique predicted labels: {}".format(np.unique(pred_most_frequent)))
print("Test score: {:.2f}".format(dummy_majority.score(X_test, y_test)))
```

Out[42]:

```
Unique predicted labels: [False]
Test score: 0.90
```

We obtained close to 90% accuracy without learning anything. This might seem striking, but think about it for a minute. Imagine someone telling you their model is 90% accurate. You might think they did a very good job. But depending on the problem, that might be possible by just predicting one class! Let's compare this against using an actual classifier:

In[43]:

```
from sklearn.tree import DecisionTreeClassifier
tree = DecisionTreeClassifier(max_depth=2).fit(X_train, y_train)
pred_tree = tree.predict(X_test)
print("Test score: {:.2f}".format(tree.score(X_test, y_test)))
```

Out[43]:

```
Test score: 0.92
```

According to accuracy, the `DecisionTreeClassifier` is only slightly better than the constant predictor. This could indicate either that something is wrong with how we used `DecisionTreeClassifier`, or that accuracy is in fact not a good measure here.

For comparison purposes, let's evaluate two more classifiers, `LogisticRegression` and the default `DummyClassifier`, which makes random predictions but produces classes with the same proportions as in the training set:

In[44]:

```
from sklearn.linear_model import LogisticRegression

dummy = DummyClassifier().fit(X_train, y_train)
pred_dummy = dummy.predict(X_test)
print("dummy score: {:.2f}".format(dummy.score(X_test, y_test)))

logreg = LogisticRegression(C=0.1).fit(X_train, y_train)
pred_logreg = logreg.predict(X_test)
print("logreg score: {:.2f}".format(logreg.score(X_test, y_test)))
```

Out[44]:

```
dummy score: 0.80
logreg score: 0.98
```

The dummy classifier that produces random output is clearly the worst of the lot (according to accuracy), while `LogisticRegression` produces very good results. However, even the random classifier yields over 80% accuracy. This makes it very hard to judge which of these results is actually helpful. The problem here is that accuracy is an inadequate measure for quantifying predictive performance in this imbalanced setting. For the rest of this chapter, we will explore alternative metrics that provide better guidance in selecting models. In particular, we would like to have metrics that tell us how much better a model is than making "most frequent" predictions or random predictions, as they are computed in `pred_most_frequent` and `pred_dummy`. If we use a metric to assess our models, it should definitely be able to weed out these nonsense predictions.

Confusion matrices

One of the most comprehensive ways to represent the result of evaluating binary classification is using confusion matrices. Let's inspect the predictions of `LogisticRegression` from the previous section using the `confusion_matrix` function. We already stored the predictions on the test set in `pred_logreg`:

In[45]:

```
from sklearn.metrics import confusion_matrix

confusion = confusion_matrix(y_test, pred_logreg)
print("Confusion matrix:\n{}".format(confusion))
```

Out[45]:

```
Confusion matrix:
[[401   2]
 [  8  39]]
```

The output of `confusion_matrix` is a two-by-two array, where the rows correspond to the true classes and the columns correspond to the predicted classes. Each entry counts how often a sample that belongs to the class corresponding to the row (here, "not nine" and "nine") was classified as the class corresponding to the column. The following plot (Figure 5-10) illustrates this meaning:

In[46]:

```
mglearn.plots.plot_confusion_matrix_illustration()
```

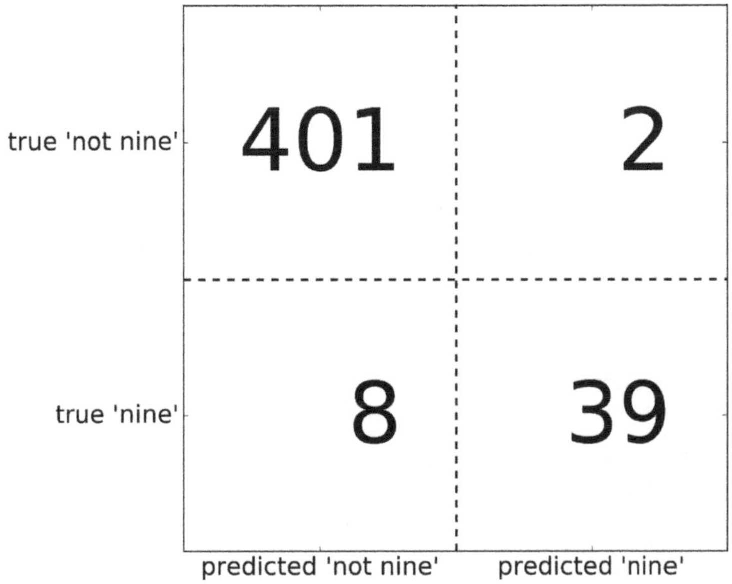

Figure 5-10. Confusion matrix of the "nine vs. rest" classification task

Entries on the main diagonal[3] of the confusion matrix correspond to correct classifications, while other entries tell us how many samples of one class got mistakenly classified as another class.

If we declare "a nine" the positive class, we can relate the entries of the confusion matrix with the terms *false positive* and *false negative* that we introduced earlier. To complete the picture, we call correctly classified samples belonging to the positive class *true positives* and correctly classified samples belonging to the negative class *true negatives*. These terms are usually abbreviated FP, FN, TP, and TN and lead to the following interpretation for the confusion matrix (Figure 5-11):

In[47]:

```
mglearn.plots.plot_binary_confusion_matrix()
```

3 The main diagonal of a two-dimensional array or matrix A is `A[i, i]`.

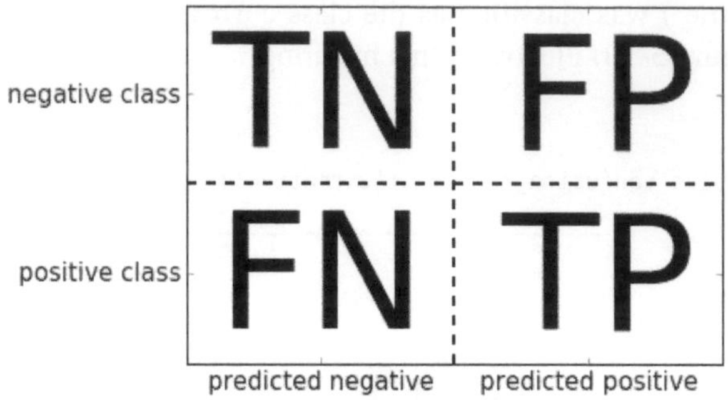

Figure 5-11. Confusion matrix for binary classification

Now let's use the confusion matrix to compare the models we fitted earlier (the two dummy models, the decision tree, and the logistic regression):

In[48]:

```
print("Most frequent class:")
print(confusion_matrix(y_test, pred_most_frequent))
print("\nDummy model:")
print(confusion_matrix(y_test, pred_dummy))
print("\nDecision tree:")
print(confusion_matrix(y_test, pred_tree))
print("\nLogistic Regression")
print(confusion_matrix(y_test, pred_logreg))
```

Out[48]:

```
Most frequent class:
[[403   0]
 [ 47   0]]

Dummy model:
[[361  42]
 [ 43   4]]

Decision tree:
[[390  13]
 [ 24  23]]

Logistic Regression
[[401   2]
 [  8  39]]
```

Looking at the confusion matrix, it is quite clear that something is wrong with `pred_most_frequent`, because it always predicts the same class. `pred_dummy`, on the other hand, has a very small number of true positives (4), particularly compared to the number of false negatives and false positives—there are many more false positives than true positives! The predictions made by the decision tree make much more sense than the dummy predictions, even though the accuracy was nearly the same. Finally, we can see that logistic regression does better than `pred_tree` in all aspects: it has more true positives and true negatives while having fewer false positives and false negatives. From this comparison, it is clear that only the decision tree and the logistic regression give reasonable results, and that the logistic regression works better than the tree on all accounts. However, inspecting the full confusion matrix is a bit cumbersome, and while we gained a lot of insight from looking at all aspects of the matrix, the process was very manual and qualitative. There are several ways to summarize the information in the confusion matrix, which we will discuss next.

Relation to accuracy. We already saw one way to summarize the result in the confusion matrix—by computing accuracy, which can be expressed as:

$$\text{Accuracy} = \frac{\text{TP+TN}}{\text{TP+TN + FP + FN}}$$

In other words, accuracy is the number of correct predictions (TP and TN) divided by the number of all samples (all entries of the confusion matrix summed up).

Precision, recall, and f-score. There are several other ways to summarize the confusion matrix, with the most common ones being precision and recall. *Precision* measures how many of the samples predicted as positive are actually positive:

$$\text{Precision} = \frac{\text{TP}}{\text{TP+FP}}$$

Precision is used as a performance metric when the goal is to limit the number of false positives. As an example, imagine a model for predicting whether a new drug will be effective in treating a disease in clinical trials. Clinical trials are notoriously expensive, and a pharmaceutical company will only want to run an experiment if it is very sure that the drug will actually work. Therefore, it is important that the model does not produce many false positives—in other words, that it has a high precision. Precision is also known as *positive predictive value* (PPV).

Recall, on the other hand, measures how many of the positive samples are captured by the positive predictions:

$$\text{Recall} = \frac{\text{TP}}{\text{TP+FN}}$$

Recall is used as performance metric when we need to identify all positive samples; that is, when it is important to avoid false negatives. The cancer diagnosis example from earlier in this chapter is a good example for this: it is important to find all people that are sick, possibly including healthy patients in the prediction. Other names for recall are *sensitivity*, *hit rate*, or *true positive rate* (TPR).

There is a trade-off between optimizing recall and optimizing precision. You can trivially obtain a perfect recall if you predict all samples to belong to the positive class—there will be no false negatives, and no true negatives either. However, predicting all samples as positive will result in many false positives, and therefore the precision will be very low. On the other hand, if you find a model that predicts only the single data point it is most sure about as positive and the rest as negative, then precision will be perfect (assuming this data point is in fact positive), but recall will be very bad.

> Precision and recall are only two of many classification measures derived from TP, FP, TN, and FN. You can find a great summary of all the measures on Wikipedia (*https://en.wikipedia.org/wiki/Sensitivity_and_specificity*). In the machine learning community, precision and recall are arguably the most commonly used measures for binary classification, but other communities might use other related metrics.

So, while precision and recall are very important measures, looking at only one of them will not provide you with the full picture. One way to summarize them is the *f-score* or *f-measure*, which is with the harmonic mean of precision and recall:

$$F = 2 \cdot \frac{\text{precision} \cdot \text{recall}}{\text{precision} + \text{recall}}$$

This particular variant is also known as the f_1-score. As it takes precision and recall into account, it can be a better measure than accuracy on imbalanced binary classification datasets. Let's run it on the predictions for the "nine vs. rest" dataset that we computed earlier. Here, we will assume that the "nine" class is the positive class (it is labeled as `True` while the rest is labeled as `False`), so the positive class is the minority class:

In[49]:

```
from sklearn.metrics import f1_score
print("f1 score most frequent: {:.2f}".format(
    f1_score(y_test, pred_most_frequent)))
print("f1 score dummy: {:.2f}".format(f1_score(y_test, pred_dummy)))
print("f1 score tree: {:.2f}".format(f1_score(y_test, pred_tree)))
print("f1 score logistic regression: {:.2f}".format(
    f1_score(y_test, pred_logreg)))
```

Out[49]:

```
f1 score most frequent: 0.00
f1 score dummy: 0.10
f1 score tree: 0.55
f1 score logistic regression: 0.89
```

We can note two things here. First, we get an error message for the `most_frequent` prediction, as there were no predictions of the positive class (which makes the denominator in the *f*-score zero). Also, we can see a pretty strong distinction between the dummy predictions and the tree predictions, which wasn't clear when looking at accuracy alone. Using the *f*-score for evaluation, we summarized the predictive performance again in one number. However, the *f*-score seems to capture our intuition of what makes a good model much better than accuracy did. A disadvantage of the *f*-score, however, is that it is harder to interpret and explain than accuracy.

If we want a more comprehensive summary of precision, recall, and f_1-score, we can use the `classification_report` convenience function to compute all three at once, and print them in a nice format:

In[50]:

```
from sklearn.metrics import classification_report
print(classification_report(y_test, pred_most_frequent,
                            target_names=["not nine", "nine"]))
```

Out[50]:

```
              precision    recall  f1-score   support

    not nine       0.90      1.00      0.94       403
        nine       0.00      0.00      0.00        47

   micro avg       0.90      0.90      0.90       450
   macro avg       0.45      0.50      0.47       450
weighted avg       0.80      0.90      0.85       450
```

The `classification_report` function produces one line per class (here, `True` and `False`) and reports precision, recall, and *f*-score with this class as the positive class. Before, we assumed the minority "nine" class was the positive class. If we change the positive class to "not nine," we can see from the output of `classification_report` that we obtain an *f*-score of 0.94 with the `most_frequent` model. Furthermore, for the "not nine" class we have a recall of 1, as we classified all samples as "not nine." The last column next to the *f*-score provides the *support* of each class, which simply means the number of samples in this class according to the ground truth.

Three additional rows in the classification report show averages of the precision, recall, and f_1-score. The macro average simply computes the average across the classes, while the weighted average computes a weighted average, weighted by the number of samples in the class. Because they are averages over both classes, these metrics don't require a notion of positive class, and in contrast to just looking at precision or just looking at recall for the positive class, averaging over both classes provides a meaningful metric in a single number. Here are two more reports, one for the dummy classifier and one for the logistic regression:

In[51]:

```
print(classification_report(y_test, pred_dummy,
                            target_names=["not nine", "nine"]))
```

Out[51]:

```
              precision    recall  f1-score   support

    not nine       0.90      0.89      0.90       403
        nine       0.17      0.19      0.18        47

   micro avg       0.82      0.82      0.82       450
   macro avg       0.54      0.54      0.54       450
weighted avg       0.83      0.82      0.82       450
```

In[52]:

```
print(classification_report(y_test, pred_logreg,
                            target_names=["not nine", "nine"]))
```

Out[52]:

```
              precision    recall  f1-score   support

    not nine       0.98      1.00      0.99       403
        nine       0.95      0.83      0.89        47

   micro avg       0.98      0.98      0.98       450
   macro avg       0.97      0.91      0.94       450
weighted avg       0.98      0.98      0.98       450
```

As you may notice when looking at the reports, the differences between the dummy models and a very good model are not as clear any more. Picking which class is declared the positive class has a big impact on the metrics. While the *f*-score for the dummy classification is 0.10 (vs. 0.89 for the logistic regression) on the "nine" class, for the "not nine" class it is 0.91 vs. 0.99, which both seem like reasonable results. Looking at all the numbers together paints a pretty accurate picture, though, and we can clearly see the superiority of the logistic regression model.

Taking uncertainty into account

The confusion matrix and the classification report provide a very detailed analysis of a particular set of predictions. However, the predictions themselves already threw away a lot of information that is contained in the model. As we discussed in Chapter 2, most classifiers provide a `decision_function` or a `predict_proba` method to assess degrees of certainty about predictions. Making predictions can be seen as thresholding the output of `decision_function` or `predict_proba` at a certain fixed point—in binary classification we use 0 for the decision function and 0.5 for `predict_proba`.

The following is an example of an imbalanced binary classification task, with 400 points in the negative class classified against 50 points in the positive class. The training data is shown on the left in Figure 5-12. We train a kernel SVM model on this data, and the plots to the right of the training data illustrate the values of the decision function as a heat map. You can see a black circle in the plot in the top center, which denotes the threshold of the `decision_function` being exactly zero. Points inside this circle will be classified as the positive class, and points outside as the negative class:

In[53]:

```
X, y = make_blobs(n_samples=(400, 50), cluster_std=[7.0, 2], random_state=22)
X_train, X_test, y_train, y_test = train_test_split(X, y, random_state=0)
svc = SVC(gamma=.05).fit(X_train, y_train)
```

In[54]:

```
mglearn.plots.plot_decision_threshold()
```

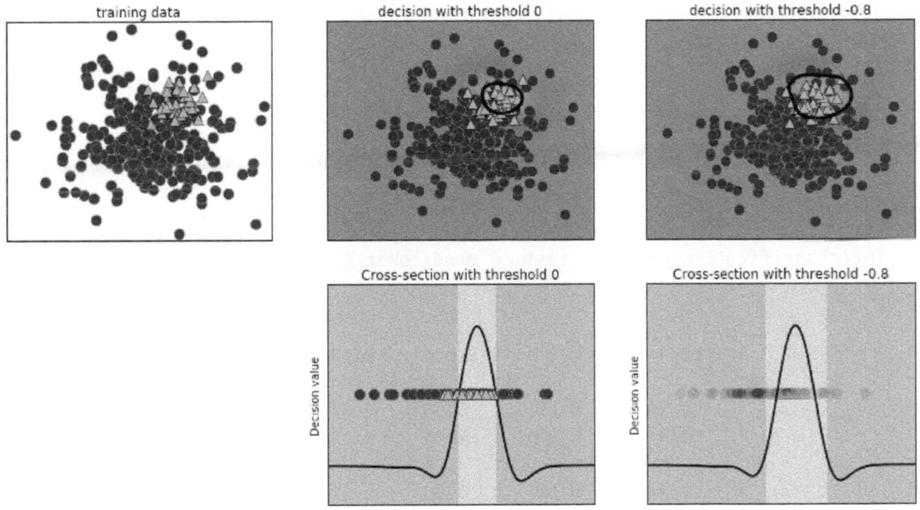

Figure 5-12. Heatmap of the decision function and the impact of changing the decision threshold

We can use the `classification_report` function to evaluate precision and recall for both classes:

In[55]:

```
print(classification_report(y_test, svc.predict(X_test)))
```

Out[55]:

```
              precision    recall  f1-score   support

           0       0.97      0.89      0.93       104
           1       0.35      0.67      0.46         9

   micro avg       0.88      0.88      0.88       113
   macro avg       0.66      0.78      0.70       113
weighted avg       0.92      0.88      0.89       113
```

For class 1, we get a fairly small precision, and recall is mixed. Because class 0 is so much larger, the classifier focuses on getting class 0 right, and not the smaller class 1.

Let's assume in our application it is more important to have a high recall for class 1, as in the cancer screening example earlier. This means we are willing to risk more false positives (false class 1) in exchange for more true positives (which will increase the recall). The predictions generated by `svc.predict` really do not fulfill this requirement, but we can adjust the predictions to focus on a higher recall of class 1 by changing the decision threshold away from 0. By default, points with a `decision_function` value greater than 0 will be classified as class 1. We want *more* points to be classified as class 1, so we need to *decrease* the threshold:

In[56]:

```
y_pred_lower_threshold = svc.decision_function(X_test) > -.8
```

Let's look at the classification report for this prediction:

In[57]:

```
print(classification_report(y_test, y_pred_lower_threshold))
```

Out[57]:

```
              precision    recall  f1-score   support

           0       1.00      0.82      0.90       104
           1       0.32      1.00      0.49         9

   micro avg       0.83      0.83      0.83       113
   macro avg       0.66      0.91      0.69       113
weighted avg       0.95      0.83      0.87       113
```

As expected, the recall of class 1 went up, and the precision went down. We are now classifying a larger region of space as class 1, as illustrated in the top-right panel of Figure 5-12. If you value precision over recall or the other way around, or you data is heavily imbalanced, changing the decision threshold is the easiest way to obtain better results. As the `decision_function` can have arbitrary ranges, it is hard to provide a rule of thumb regarding how to pick a threshold. If you do set a threshold, you need to be careful not to do so using the test set. As with any other parameter, setting a decision threshold on the test set is likely to yield overly optimistic results. Use a validation set or cross-validation instead.

> For simplicity, we changed the threshold value based on test set results in the code above. In practice, you need to use a hold-out validation set, not the test set. As with any other parameter, setting a decision threshold on the test set is likely to yield overly optimistic results. Use a validation set or cross-validation instead.

Picking a threshold for models that implement the `predict_proba` method can be easier, as the output of `predict_proba` is on a fixed 0 to 1 scale, and models probabilities. By default, the threshold of 0.5 means that if the model is more than 50% "sure" that a point is of the positive class, it will be classified as such. Increasing the threshold means that the model needs to be more confident to make a positive decision (and less confident to make a negative decision). While working with probabilities may be more intuitive than working with arbitrary thresholds, not all models provide realistic models of uncertainty (a `DecisionTree` that is grown to its full depth is always 100% sure of its decisions, even though it might often be wrong). This relates to the concept of *calibration*: a calibrated model is a model that provides an accurate measure of its uncertainty. Discussing calibration in detail is beyond the scope of this book, but you can find more details in the paper "Predicting Good Probabilities with Supervised Learning" (*http://www.machinelearning.org/proceedings/icml2005/papers/079_GoodProbabilities_NiculescuMizilCaruana.pdf*) by Alexandru Niculescu-Mizil and Rich Caruana.

Precision-recall curves and ROC curves

As we just discussed, changing the threshold that is used to make a classification decision in a model is a way to adjust the trade-off of precision and recall for a given classifier. Maybe you want to miss less than 10% of positive samples, meaning a desired recall of 90%. This decision depends on the application, and it should be driven by business goals. Once a particular goal is set—say, a particular recall or precision value for a class—a threshold can be set appropriately. It is always possible to set a threshold to fulfill a particular target, like 90% recall. The hard part is to develop a model that still has reasonable precision with this threshold—if you classify everything as positive, you will have 100% recall, but your model will be useless.

Setting a requirement on a classifier like 90% recall is often called setting the *operating point*. Fixing an operating point is often helpful in business settings to make performance guarantees to customers or other groups inside your organization.

Often, when developing a new model, it is not entirely clear what the operating point will be. For this reason, and to understand a modeling problem better, it is instructive to look at all possible thresholds, or all possible trade-offs of precision and recall *at once*. This is possible using a tool called the *precision-recall curve*. You can find the function to compute the precision-recall curve in the `sklearn.metrics` module. It needs the ground truth labeling and predicted uncertainties, created via either `decision_function` or `predict_proba`:

In[58]:

```
from sklearn.metrics import precision_recall_curve
precision, recall, thresholds = precision_recall_curve(
    y_test, svc.decision_function(X_test))
```

The `precision_recall_curve` function returns a list of precision and recall values for all possible thresholds (all values that appear in the decision function) in sorted order, so we can plot a curve, as seen in Figure 5-13:

In[59]:

```
# Use more data points for a smoother curve
X, y = make_blobs(n_samples=(4000, 500), cluster_std=[7.0, 2], random_state=22)
X_train, X_test, y_train, y_test = train_test_split(X, y, random_state=0)
svc = SVC(gamma=.05).fit(X_train, y_train)
precision, recall, thresholds = precision_recall_curve(
    y_test, svc.decision_function(X_test))
# find threshold closest to zero
close_zero = np.argmin(np.abs(thresholds))
plt.plot(precision[close_zero], recall[close_zero], 'o', markersize=10,
         label="threshold zero", fillstyle="none", c='k', mew=2)

plt.plot(precision, recall, label="precision recall curve")
plt.xlabel("Precision")
plt.ylabel("Recall")
plt.legend(loc="best")
```

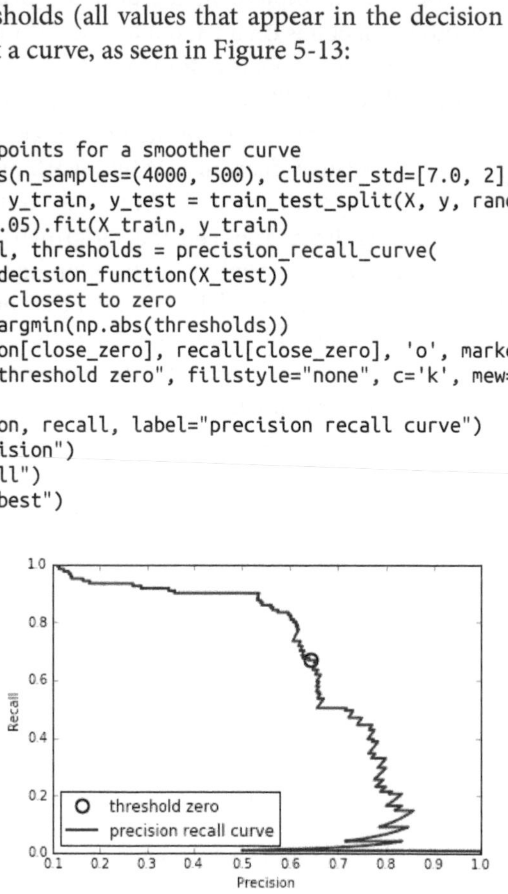

Figure 5-13. Precision recall curve for SVC(gamma=0.05)

Each point along the curve in Figure 5-13 corresponds to a possible threshold of the decision_function. We can see, for example, that we can achieve a recall of 0.4 at a precision of about 0.75. The black circle marks the point that corresponds to a threshold of 0, the default threshold for decision_function. This point is the trade-off that is chosen when calling the predict method.

The closer a curve stays to the upper-right corner, the better the classifier. A point at the upper right means high precision *and* high recall for the same threshold. The curve starts at the top-left corner, corresponding to a very low threshold, classifying everything as the positive class. Raising the threshold moves the curve toward higher precision, but also lower recall. Raising the threshold more and more, we get to a situation where most of the points classified as being positive are true positives, leading to a very high precision but lower recall. The more the model keeps recall high as precision goes up, the better.

Looking at this particular curve a bit more, we can see that with this model it is possible to get a precision of up to around 0.5 with very high recall. If we want a much higher precision, we have to sacrifice a lot of recall. In other words, on the left the curve is relatively flat, meaning that recall does not go down a lot when we require increased precision. For precision greater than 0.5, each gain in precision costs us a lot of recall.

Different classifiers can work well in different parts of the curve—that is, at different operating points. Let's compare the SVM we trained to a random forest trained on the same dataset. The RandomForestClassifier doesn't have a decision_function, only predict_proba. The precision_recall_curve function expects as its second argument a certainty measure for the positive class (class 1), so we pass the probability of a sample being class 1—that is, rf.predict_proba(X_test)[:, 1]. The default threshold for predict_proba in binary classification is 0.5, so this is the point we marked on the curve (see Figure 5-14):

In[60]:

```
from sklearn.ensemble import RandomForestClassifier

rf = RandomForestClassifier(n_estimators=100, random_state=0, max_features=2)
rf.fit(X_train, y_train)

# RandomForestClassifier has predict_proba, but not decision_function
precision_rf, recall_rf, thresholds_rf = precision_recall_curve(
    y_test, rf.predict_proba(X_test)[:, 1])

plt.plot(precision, recall, label="svc")

plt.plot(precision[close_zero], recall[close_zero], 'o', markersize=10,
         label="threshold zero svc", fillstyle="none", c='k', mew=2)
```

```
plt.plot(precision_rf, recall_rf, label="rf")

close_default_rf = np.argmin(np.abs(thresholds_rf - 0.5))
plt.plot(precision_rf[close_default_rf], recall_rf[close_default_rf], '^', c='k',
         markersize=10, label="threshold 0.5 rf", fillstyle="none", mew=2)
plt.xlabel("Precision")
plt.ylabel("Recall")
plt.legend(loc="best")
```

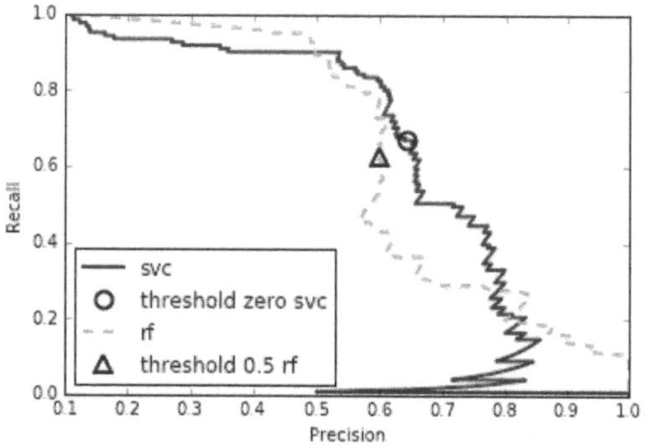

Figure 5-14. Comparing precision recall curves of SVM and random forest

From the comparison plot we can see that the random forest performs better at the extremes, for very high recall or very high precision requirements. Around the middle (approximately precision=0.7), the SVM performs better. If we only looked at the f_1-score to compare overall performance, we would have missed these subtleties. The f_1-score only captures one point on the precision-recall curve, the one given by the default threshold:

In[61]:

```
print("f1_score of random forest: {:.3f}".format(
    f1_score(y_test, rf.predict(X_test))))
print("f1_score of svc: {:.3f}".format(f1_score(y_test, svc.predict(X_test))))
```

Out[61]:

```
f1_score of random forest: 0.610
f1_score of svc: 0.656
```

Comparing two precision-recall curves provides a lot of detailed insight, but is a fairly manual process. For automatic model comparison, we might want to summarize the information contained in the curve, without limiting ourselves to a particular threshold or operating point. One particular way to summarize the precision-recall curve is by computing the integral or area under the curve of the precision-recall curve, also known as the *average precision*.[4] You can use the average_precision_score function to compute the average precision. Because we need to compute the precision-recall curve and consider multiple thresholds, the result of decision_function or predict_proba needs to be passed to average_precision_score, not the result of predict:

In[62]:

```
from sklearn.metrics import average_precision_score
ap_rf = average_precision_score(y_test, rf.predict_proba(X_test)[:, 1])
ap_svc = average_precision_score(y_test, svc.decision_function(X_test))
print("Average precision of random forest: {:.3f}".format(ap_rf))
print("Average precision of svc: {:.3f}".format(ap_svc))
```

Out[62]:

```
Average precision of random forest: 0.666
Average precision of svc: 0.663
```

When averaging over all possible thresholds, we see that the random forest and SVC perform similarly well, with the random forest even slightly ahead. This is quite different from the result we got from f1_score earlier. Because average precision is the area under a curve that goes from 0 to 1, average precision always returns a value between 0 (worst) and 1 (best). The average precision of a classifier that assigns decision_function at random is the fraction of positive samples in the dataset.

Receiver operating characteristics (ROC) and AUC

There is another tool that is commonly used to analyze the behavior of classifiers at different thresholds: the *receiver operating characteristics curve*, or *ROC curve* for short. Similar to the precision-recall curve, the ROC curve considers all possible thresholds for a given classifier, but instead of reporting precision and recall, it shows the *false positive rate* (FPR) against the *true positive rate* (TPR). Recall that the true positive rate is simply another name for recall, while the false positive rate is the fraction of false positives out of all negative samples:

$$\text{FPR} = \frac{\text{FP}}{\text{FP+TN}}$$

The ROC curve can be computed using the roc_curve function (see Figure 5-15):

4 There are some minor technical differences between the area under the precision-recall curve and average precision. However, this explanation conveys the general idea.

In[63]:

```
from sklearn.metrics import roc_curve
fpr, tpr, thresholds = roc_curve(y_test, svc.decision_function(X_test))

plt.plot(fpr, tpr, label="ROC Curve")
plt.xlabel("FPR")
plt.ylabel("TPR (recall)")
# find threshold closest to zero
close_zero = np.argmin(np.abs(thresholds))
plt.plot(fpr[close_zero], tpr[close_zero], 'o', markersize=10,
         label="threshold zero", fillstyle="none", c='k', mew=2)
plt.legend(loc=4)
```

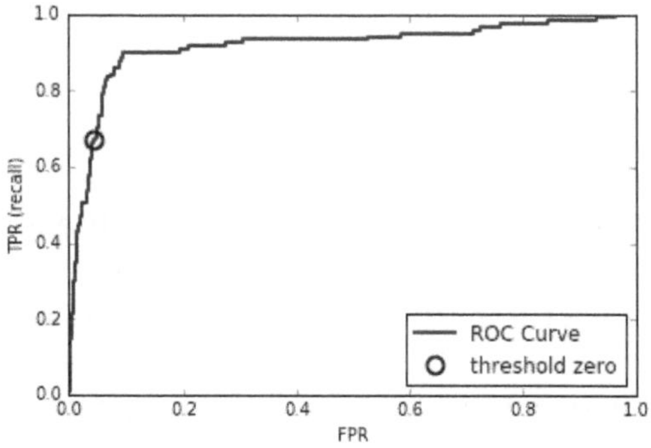

Figure 5-15. ROC curve for SVM

For the ROC curve, the ideal curve is close to the top left: you want a classifier that produces a *high recall* while keeping a *low false positive rate*. Compared to the default threshold of 0, the curve shows that we can achieve a significantly higher recall (around 0.9) while only increasing the FPR slightly. The point closest to the top left might be a better operating point than the one chosen by default. Again, be aware that choosing a threshold should not be done on the test set, but on a separate validation set.

You can find a comparison of the random forest and the SVM using ROC curves in Figure 5-16:

In[64]:

```
fpr_rf, tpr_rf, thresholds_rf = roc_curve(y_test, rf.predict_proba(X_test)[:, 1])

plt.plot(fpr, tpr, label="ROC Curve SVC")
plt.plot(fpr_rf, tpr_rf, label="ROC Curve RF")

plt.xlabel("FPR")
plt.ylabel("TPR (recall)")
plt.plot(fpr[close_zero], tpr[close_zero], 'o', markersize=10,
```

```
        label="threshold zero SVC", fillstyle="none", c='k', mew=2)
close_default_rf = np.argmin(np.abs(thresholds_rf - 0.5))
plt.plot(fpr_rf[close_default_rf], tpr[close_default_rf], '^', markersize=10,
         label="threshold 0.5 RF", fillstyle="none", c='k', mew=2)

plt.legend(loc=4)
```

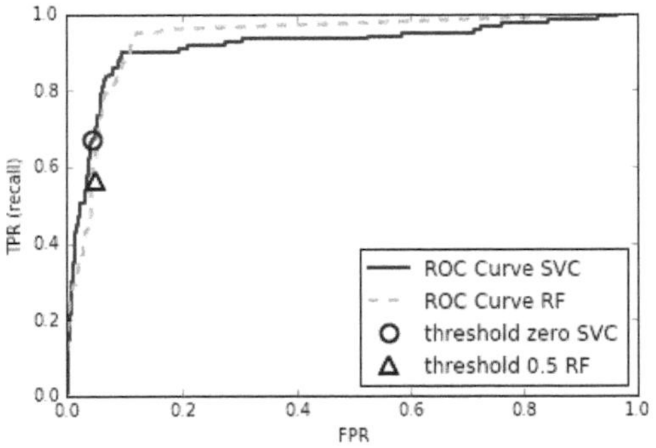

Figure 5-16. Comparing ROC curves for SVM and random forest

As for the precision-recall curve, we often want to summarize the ROC curve using a single number, the area under the curve (this is commonly just referred to as the AUC, and it is understood that the curve in question is the ROC curve). We can compute the area under the ROC curve using the `roc_auc_score` function:

In[65]:

```
from sklearn.metrics import roc_auc_score
rf_auc = roc_auc_score(y_test, rf.predict_proba(X_test)[:, 1])
svc_auc = roc_auc_score(y_test, svc.decision_function(X_test))
print("AUC for Random Forest: {:.3f}".format(rf_auc))
print("AUC for SVC: {:.3f}".format(svc_auc))
```

Out[65]:

```
AUC for Random Forest: 0.937
AUC for SVC: 0.916
```

Comparing the random forest and SVM using the AUC score, we find that the random forest performs quite a bit better than the SVM. Recall that because AUC is the area under a curve that goes from 0 to 1, AUC always returns a value between 0 (worst) and 1 (best). Predicting randomly always produces an AUC of 0.5, no matter how imbalanced the classes in a dataset are. This makes AUC a much better metric for imbalanced classification problems than accuracy. The AUC can be interpreted as evaluating the *ranking* of positive samples. It's equivalent to the probability that a randomly picked point of the positive class will have a higher score according to the classifier than a randomly picked point from the negative class. So, a perfect AUC of 1 means that all positive points have a higher score than all negative points. For classification problems with imbalanced classes, using AUC for model selection is often much more meaningful than using accuracy.

Let's go back to the problem we studied earlier of classifying all nines in the `digits` dataset versus all other digits. We will classify the dataset with an SVM with three different settings of the kernel bandwidth, `gamma` (see Figure 5-17):

In[66]:

```
y = digits.target == 9

X_train, X_test, y_train, y_test = train_test_split(
    digits.data, y, random_state=0)

plt.figure()

for gamma in [1, 0.05, 0.01]:
    svc = SVC(gamma=gamma).fit(X_train, y_train)
    accuracy = svc.score(X_test, y_test)
    auc = roc_auc_score(y_test, svc.decision_function(X_test))
    fpr, tpr, _ = roc_curve(y_test , svc.decision_function(X_test))
    print("gamma = {:.2f}  accuracy = {:.2f}  AUC = {:.2f}".format(
          gamma, accuracy, auc))
    plt.plot(fpr, tpr, label="gamma={:.3f}".format(gamma))
plt.xlabel("FPR")
plt.ylabel("TPR")
plt.xlim(-0.01, 1)
plt.ylim(0, 1.02)
plt.legend(loc="best")
```

Out[66]:

```
gamma = 1.00  accuracy = 0.90  AUC = 0.50
gamma = 0.05  accuracy = 0.90  AUC = 0.90
gamma = 0.01  accuracy = 0.90  AUC = 1.00
```

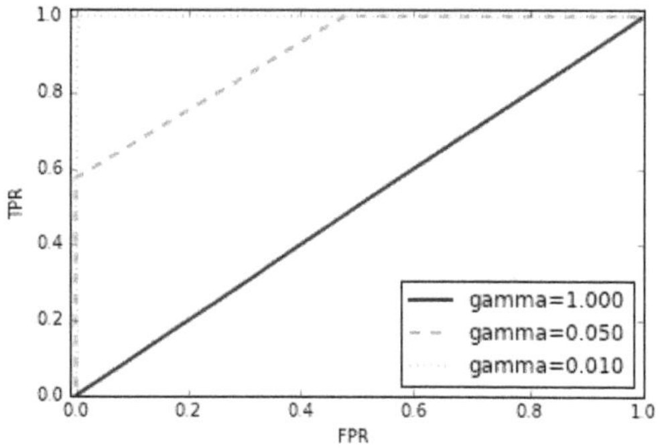

Figure 5-17. Comparing ROC curves of SVMs with different settings of gamma

The accuracy of all three settings of gamma is the same, 90%. This might be the same as chance performance, or it might not. Looking at the AUC and the corresponding curve, however, we see a clear distinction between the three models. With gamma=1.0, the AUC is actually at chance level, meaning that the output of the decision_function is as good as random. With gamma=0.05, performance drastically improves to an AUC of 0.9. Finally, with gamma=0.01, we get a perfect AUC of 1.0. That means that all positive points are ranked higher than all negative points according to the decision function. In other words, with the right threshold, this model can classify the data perfectly![5] Knowing this, we can adjust the threshold on this model and obtain great predictions. If we had only used accuracy, we would never have discovered this.

For this reason, we highly recommend using AUC when evaluating models on imbalanced data. Keep in mind that AUC does not make use of the default threshold, though, so adjusting the decision threshold might be necessary to obtain useful classification results from a model with a high AUC.

5.3.3 Metrics for Multiclass Classification

Now that we have discussed evaluation of binary classification tasks in depth, let's move on to metrics to evaluate multiclass classification. Basically, all metrics for multiclass classification are derived from binary classification metrics, but averaged over all classes. Accuracy for multiclass classification is again defined as the fraction of correctly classified examples. And again, when classes are imbalanced, accuracy is not a great evaluation measure. Imagine a three-class classification problem with 85% of points belonging to class A, 10% belonging to class B, and 5% belonging to class C. What does being 85% accurate mean on this dataset? In general, multiclass classification results are harder to understand than binary classification results. Apart from accuracy, common tools are the confusion matrix and the classification report we saw in the binary case in the previous section. Let's apply these two detailed evaluation methods on the task of classifying the 10 different handwritten digits in the digits dataset:

In[67]:

```
from sklearn.metrics import accuracy_score
X_train, X_test, y_train, y_test = train_test_split(
    digits.data, digits.target, random_state=0)
lr = LogisticRegression().fit(X_train, y_train)
pred = lr.predict(X_test)
print("Accuracy: {:.3f}".format(accuracy_score(y_test, pred)))
print("Confusion matrix:\n{}".format(confusion_matrix(y_test, pred)))
```

5 Looking at the curve for gamma=0.01 in detail, you can see a small kink close to the top left. That means that at least one point was not ranked correctly. The AUC of 1.0 is a consequence of rounding to the second decimal point.

Out[67]:

```
Accuracy: 0.953
Confusion matrix:
[[37  0  0  0  0  0  0  0  0  0]
 [ 0 39  0  0  0  0  2  0  2  0]
 [ 0  0 41  3  0  0  0  0  0  0]
 [ 0  0  1 43  0  0  0  0  0  1]
 [ 0  0  0  0 38  0  0  0  0  0]
 [ 0  1  0  0  0 47  0  0  0  0]
 [ 0  0  0  0  0  0 52  0  0  0]
 [ 0  1  0  1  1  0  0 45  0  0]
 [ 0  3  1  0  0  0  0  0 43  1]
 [ 0  0  0  1  0  1  0  0  1 44]]
```

The model has an accuracy of 95.3%, which already tells us that we are doing pretty well. The confusion matrix provides us with some more detail. As for the binary case, each row corresponds to a true label, and each column corresponds to a predicted label. You can find a visually more appealing plot in Figure 5-18:

In[68]:

```
scores_image = mglearn.tools.heatmap(
    confusion_matrix(y_test, pred), xlabel='Predicted label',
    ylabel='True label', xticklabels=digits.target_names,
    yticklabels=digits.target_names, cmap=plt.cm.gray_r, fmt="%d")
plt.title("Confusion matrix")
plt.gca().invert_yaxis()
```

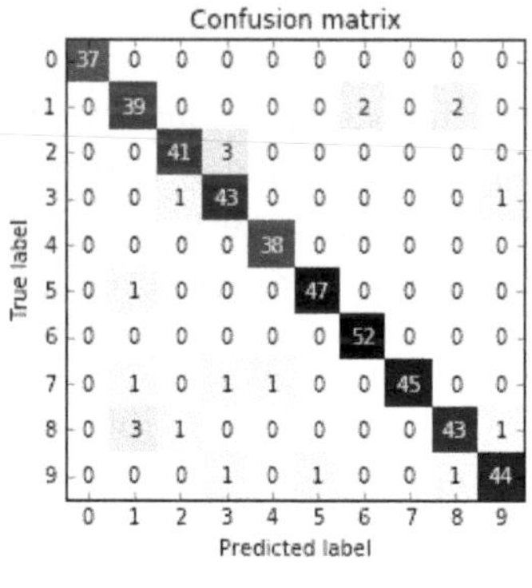

Figure 5-18. Confusion matrix for the 10-digit classification task

For the first class, the digit 0, there are 37 samples in the class, and all of these samples were classified as class 0 (there are no false negatives for class 0). We can see that because all other entries in the first row of the confusion matrix are 0. We can also see that no other digits were mistakenly classified as 0, because all other entries in the first column of the confusion matrix are 0 (there are no false positives for class 0).

Some digits were confused with others, though—for example, the digit 2 (third row), three of which were classified as the digit 3 (fourth column). There was also one digit 3 that was classified as 2 (third column, fourth row) and one digit 8 that was classified as 2 (third column, ninth row).

With the `classification_report` function, we can compute the precision, recall, and *f*-score for each class:

In[69]:

```
print(classification_report(y_test, pred))
```

Out[69]:

```
              precision    recall  f1-score   support

           0       1.00      1.00      1.00        37
           1       0.89      0.91      0.90        43
           2       0.95      0.93      0.94        44
           3       0.90      0.96      0.92        45
           4       0.97      1.00      0.99        38
           5       0.98      0.98      0.98        48
           6       0.96      1.00      0.98        52
           7       1.00      0.94      0.97        48
           8       0.93      0.90      0.91        48
           9       0.96      0.94      0.95        47

   micro avg       0.95      0.95      0.95       450
   macro avg       0.95      0.95      0.95       450
weighted avg       0.95      0.95      0.95       450
```

Unsurprisingly, precision and recall are a perfect 1 for class 0, as there are no confusions with this class. For class 7, on the other hand, precision is 1 because no other class was mistakenly classified as 7, while for class 6, there are no false negatives, so the recall is 1. We can also see that the model has particular difficulties with classes 8 and 3.

The most commonly used metric for imbalanced datasets in the multiclass setting is the multiclass version of the *f*-score. The idea behind the multiclass *f*-score is to compute one binary *f*-score per class, with that class being the positive class and the other classes making up the negative classes. Then, these per-class *f*-scores are averaged using one of the following strategies:

- `"macro"` averaging computes the unweighted per-class *f*-scores. This gives equal weight to all classes, no matter what their size is.
- `"weighted"` averaging computes the mean of the per-class *f*-scores, weighted by their support. This is what is reported in the classification report.

- "micro" averaging computes the total number of false positives, false negatives, and true positives over all classes, and then computes precision, recall, and *f*-score using these counts.

If you care about each *sample* equally much, it is recommended to use the "micro" average f_1-score; if you care about each *class* equally much, it is recommended to use the "macro" average f_1-score:

In[70]:

```
print("Micro average f1 score: {:.3f}".format(
    f1_score(y_test, pred, average="micro")))
print("Macro average f1 score: {:.3f}".format(
    f1_score(y_test, pred, average="macro")))
```

Out[70]:

```
Micro average f1 score: 0.953
Macro average f1 score: 0.954
```

5.3.4 Regression Metrics

Evaluation for regression can be done in similar detail as we did for classification—for example, by analyzing overpredicting the target versus underpredicting the target. However, in most applications we've seen, using the default R^2 used in the `score` method of all regressors is enough. Sometimes business decisions are made on the basis of mean squared error or mean absolute error, which might give incentive to tune models using these metrics. In general, though, we have found R^2 to be a more intuitive metric to evaluate regression models.

5.3.5 Using Evaluation Metrics in Model Selection

We have discussed many evaluation methods in detail, and how to apply them given the ground truth and a model. However, we often want to use metrics like AUC in model selection using `GridSearchCV` or `cross_val_score`. Luckily `scikit-learn` provides a very simple way to achieve this, via the `scoring` argument that can be used in both `GridSearchCV` and `cross_val_score`. You can simply provide a string describing the evaluation metric you want to use. Say, for example, we want to evaluate the SVM classifier on the "nine vs. rest" task on the `digits` dataset, using the average precision score. Changing the score from the default (accuracy) to average precision can be done by providing "`average_precision`" as the `scoring` parameter:

In[71]:

```
# default scoring for classification is accuracy
print("Default scoring:",
      cross_val_score(SVC(), digits.data, digits.target == 9, cv=5))
# providing scoring="accuracy" doesn't change the results
```

```
explicit_accuracy =  cross_val_score(SVC(), digits.data, digits.target == 9,
                                     scoring="accuracy", cv=5)
print("Explicit accuracy:", explicit_accuracy)
ap =  cross_val_score(SVC(), digits.data, digits.target == 9,
                      scoring="average_precision", cv=5)
print("Average precision:", ap)
```

Out[71]:

```
Default scoring: [0.9 0.9 0.9 0.9 0.9]
Explicit accuracy scoring: [0.9 0.9 0.9 0.9 0.9]
AUC scoring: [0.997 0.997 0.996 0.998 0.992]
```

Using `cross_validate`, we can even compute several metrics at once:

In[72]:

```
res = cross_validate(SVC(), digits.data, digits.target == 9,
                     scoring=["accuracy", "average_precision", "recall_macro"],
                     return_train_score=True, cv=5)
display(pd.DataFrame(res))
```

Out[72]:

```
[cols=",,,,,,,,",options="header",]
|=======================================================================
| |fit_time |score_time |test_accuracy |train_accuracy
|test_average_precision |train_average_precision |test_recall_macro
|train_recall_macro
|0 |0.34 |0.20 |0.9 |1.0 |0.98 |1.0 |0.5 |1.0

|1 |0.24 |0.16 |0.9 |1.0 |1.00 |1.0 |0.5 |1.0

|2 |0.25 |0.17 |0.9 |1.0 |1.00 |1.0 |0.5 |1.0

|3 |0.23 |0.16 |0.9 |1.0 |1.00 |1.0 |0.5 |1.0

|4 |0.24 |0.15 |0.9 |1.0 |0.99 |1.0 |0.5 |1.0
|=======================================================================
```

Similarly, we can change the metric used to pick the best parameters in `GridSearchCV`:

In[73]:

```
X_train, X_test, y_train, y_test = train_test_split(
    digits.data, digits.target == 9, random_state=0)

# we provide a somewhat bad grid to illustrate the point:
param_grid = {'gamma': [0.0001, 0.01, 0.1, 1, 10]}
# using the default scoring of accuracy:
grid = GridSearchCV(SVC(), param_grid=param_grid)
grid.fit(X_train, y_train)
print("Grid-Search with accuracy")
```

```
    print("Best parameters:", grid.best_params_)
    print("Best cross-validation score (accuracy)): {:.3f}".format(grid.best_score_))
    print("Test set average precision: {:.3f}".format(
          average_precision_score(y_test, grid.decision_function(X_test))))
    print("Test set accuracy: {:.3f}".format(
          # identical to grid.score here
          accuracy_score(y_test, grid.predict(X_test))))
```

Out[73]:

```
Grid-Search with accuracy
Best parameters: {'gamma': 0.0001}
Best cross-validation score (accuracy)): 0.970
Test set average precision: 0.966
Test set accuracy: 0.973
```

In[74]:

```
# using AUC scoring instead:
grid = GridSearchCV(SVC(), param_grid=param_grid, scoring="average_precision")
grid.fit(X_train, y_train)
print("Grid-Search with average precision")
print("Best parameters:", grid.best_params_)
print("Best cross-validation score (average precision): {:.3f}".format(grid.best_score_))
print("Test set average precision: {:.3f}".format(
      # identical to grid.score here
      average_precision_score(y_test, grid.decision_function(X_test))))
print("Test set accuracy: {:.3f}".format(
      accuracy_score(y_test, grid.predict(X_test))))
```

Out[74]:

```
Grid-Search with average precision
Best parameters: {'gamma': 0.01}
Best cross-validation score (average precision): 0.985
Test set average precision: 0.996
Test set accuracy: 0.896
```

When using accuracy, the parameter `gamma=0.0001` is selected, while `gamma=0.01` is selected when using average precision. The cross-validation score is consistent with the test set score in both cases. As might be expected, the parameters found optimizing average precision perform better on the test set in terms of average precision, while the parameters found optimizing accuracy perform better on the test set in terms of accuracy.

The most important values for the `scoring` parameter for classification are `accuracy` (the default), `roc_auc` for the area under the ROC curve, `average_precision` for the area under the precision-recall curve, `recall_macro` and `precision_macro` for (macro) averaged precision or recall, `f1`, `f1_macro`, and `f1_weighted` for the binary f_1-score and the different weighted variants. For regression, the most commonly used values are `r2` for the R^2 score, `mean_squared_error` for mean squared error, and mean_absolute_error for mean absolute error. You can find a full list of supported arguments in the documentation (*http://scikit-learn.org/stable/modules/model_evaluation.html#the-scoring-parameter-defining-model-evaluation-rules*) or by looking at the SCORER dictionary defined in the metrics.scorer module:

In[75]:

```
from sklearn.metrics.scorer import SCORERS
print("Available scorers:\n{}".format(sorted(SCORERS.keys())))
```

Out[75]:

```
Available scorers:
['accuracy', 'adjusted_mutual_info_score', 'adjusted_rand_score', 'average_precision',
 'balanced_accuracy', 'brier_score_loss', 'completeness_score', 'explained_variance',
 'f1', 'f1_macro', 'f1_micro', 'f1_samples', 'f1_weighted', 'fowlkes_mallows_score',
 'homogeneity_score', 'mutual_info_score', 'neg_log_loss', 'neg_mean_absolute_error',
 'neg_mean_squared_error', 'neg_mean_squared_log_error', 'neg_median_absolute_error',
 'normalized_mutual_info_score', 'precision', 'precision_macro', 'precision_micro',
 'precision_samples', 'precision_weighted', 'r2', 'recall', 'recall_macro',
 'recall_micro', 'recall_samples', 'recall_weighted', 'roc_auc',
 'v_measure_score']
```

5.4 Summary and Outlook

In this chapter we discussed cross-validation, grid search, and evaluation metrics, the cornerstones of evaluating and improving machine learning algorithms. The tools described in this chapter, together with the algorithms described in Chapters 2 and 3, are the bread and butter of every machine learning practitioner.

There are two particular points that we made in this chapter that warrant repeating, because they are often overlooked by new practitioners. The first has to do with cross-validation. Cross-validation or the use of a test set allow us to evaluate a machine learning model as it will perform in the future. However, if we use the test set or cross-validation to select a model or select model parameters, we "use up" the test data, and using the same data to evaluate how well our model will do in the future will lead to overly optimistic estimates. We therefore need to resort to a split into training data for model building, validation data for model and parameter selection, and test data for model evaluation. Instead of a simple split, we can replace each of these splits with cross-validation. The most commonly used form (as described earlier) is a training/test split for evaluation, and using cross-validation on the training set for model and parameter selection.

The second point has to do with the importance of the evaluation metric or scoring function used for model selection and model evaluation. The theory of how to make business decisions from the predictions of a machine learning model is somewhat beyond the scope of this book.[6] However, it is rarely the case that the end goal of a machine learning task is building a model with a high accuracy. Make sure that the metric you choose to evaluate and select a model for is a good stand-in for what the model will actually be used for. In reality, classification problems rarely have balanced classes, and often false positives and false negatives have very different consequences. Make sure you understand what these consequences are, and pick an evaluation metric accordingly.

The model evaluation and selection techniques we have described so far are the most important tools in a data scientist's toolbox. Grid search and cross-validation as we've described them in this chapter can only be applied to a single supervised model. We have seen before, however, that many models require preprocessing, and that in some applications, like the face recognition example in Chapter 3, extracting a different representation of the data can be useful. In the next chapter, we will introduce the `Pipeline` class, which allows us to use grid search and cross-validation on these complex chains of algorithms.

6 We highly recommend Foster Provost and Tom Fawcett's book *Data Science for Business* (O'Reilly) for more information on this topic.

CHAPTER 6

Algorithm Chains and Pipelines

For many machine learning algorithms, the particular representation of the data that you provide is very important, as we discussed in Chapter 4. This starts with scaling the data and combining features by hand and goes all the way to learning features using unsupervised machine learning, as we saw in Chapter 3. Consequently, most machine learning applications require not only the application of a single algorithm, but the chaining together of many different processing steps and machine learning models. In this chapter, we will cover how to use the `Pipeline` class to simplify the process of building chains of transformations and models. In particular, we will see how we can combine `Pipeline` and `GridSearchCV` to search over parameters for all processing steps at once.

As an example of the importance of chaining models, we noticed that we can greatly improve the performance of a kernel SVM on the `cancer` dataset by using the `MinMaxScaler` for preprocessing. Here's code for splitting the data, computing the minimum and maximum, scaling the data, and training the SVM:

In[1]:

```
from sklearn.svm import SVC
from sklearn.datasets import load_breast_cancer
from sklearn.model_selection import train_test_split
from sklearn.preprocessing import MinMaxScaler

# load and split the data
cancer = load_breast_cancer()
X_train, X_test, y_train, y_test = train_test_split(
    cancer.data, cancer.target, random_state=0)

# compute minimum and maximum on the training data
scaler = MinMaxScaler().fit(X_train)
```

In[2]:

```
# rescale the training data
X_train_scaled = scaler.transform(X_train)

svm = SVC()
# learn an SVM on the scaled training data
svm.fit(X_train_scaled, y_train)
# scale the test data and score the scaled data
X_test_scaled = scaler.transform(X_test)
print("Test score: {:.2f}".format(svm.score(X_test_scaled, y_test)))
```

Out[2]:

```
Test score: 0.95
```

6.1 Parameter Selection with Preprocessing

Now let's say we want to find better parameters for SVC using GridSearchCV, as discussed in Chapter 5. How should we go about doing this? A naive approach might look like this:

In[3]:

```
from sklearn.model_selection import GridSearchCV
# for illustration purposes only, don't use this code!
param_grid = {'C': [0.001, 0.01, 0.1, 1, 10, 100],
              'gamma': [0.001, 0.01, 0.1, 1, 10, 100]}
grid = GridSearchCV(SVC(), param_grid=param_grid, cv=5)
grid.fit(X_train_scaled, y_train)
print("Best cross-validation accuracy: {:.2f}".format(grid.best_score_))
print("Best parameters: ", grid.best_params_)
print("Test set accuracy: {:.2f}".format(grid.score(X_test_scaled, y_test)))
```

Out[3]:

```
Best cross-validation accuracy: 0.98
Best parameters:  {'gamma': 1, 'C': 1}
Test set accuracy: 0.97
```

Here, we ran the grid search over the parameters of SVC using the scaled data. However, there is a subtle catch in what we just did. When scaling the data, we used *all the data in the training set* to compute the minimum and maximum of the data. We then use the *scaled training data* to run our grid search using cross-validation. For each split in the cross-validation, some part of the original training set will be declared the training part of the split, and some the test part of the split. The test part is used to measure the performance of a model trained on the training part when applied to new data. However, we already used the information contained in the test part of the split, when scaling the data. Remember that the test part in each split in the cross-validation is part of the training set, and we used the information from the entire training set to find the right scaling of the data. *This is fundamentally different from how new data looks to the model.* If we observe new data (say, in form of our test set), this data will not have been used to scale the training data, and it might have a different minimum and maximum than the training data. The following example (Figure 6-1) shows how the data processing during cross-validation and the final evaluation differ:

In[4]:

```
mglearn.plots.plot_improper_processing()
```

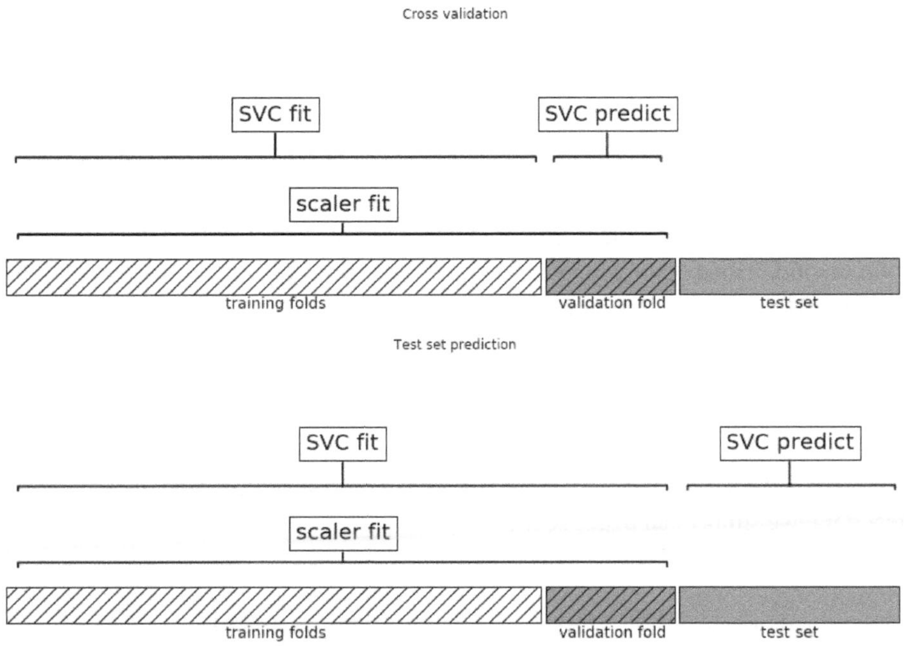

Figure 6-1. Data usage when preprocessing outside the cross-validation loop

So, the splits in the cross-validation no longer correctly mirror how new data will look to the modeling process. We already leaked information from these parts of the data into our modeling process. This will lead to overly optimistic results during cross-validation, and possibly the selection of suboptimal parameters.

To get around this problem, the splitting of the dataset during cross-validation should be done *before doing any preprocessing*. Any process that extracts knowledge from the dataset should only ever be learned from the training portion of the dataset, and therefore be contained inside the cross-validation loop.

To achieve this in scikit-learn with the `cross_val_score` function and the `GridSearchCV` function, we can use the `Pipeline` class. The `Pipeline` class is a class that allows "gluing" together multiple processing steps into a single scikit-learn estimator. The Pipeline class itself has fit, predict, and score methods and behaves just like any other model in scikit-learn. The most common use case of the Pipeline class is in chaining preprocessing steps (like scaling of the data) together with a supervised model like a classifier.

6.2 Building Pipelines

Let's look at how we can use the Pipeline class to express the workflow for training an SVM after scaling the data with MinMaxScaler (for now without the grid search). First, we build a pipeline object by providing it with a list of steps. Each step is a tuple containing a name (any string of your choosing[1]) and an instance of an estimator:

In[5]:

```
from sklearn.pipeline import Pipeline
pipe = Pipeline([("scaler", MinMaxScaler()), ("svm", SVC())])
```

Here, we created two steps: the first, called "scaler", is an instance of MinMaxScaler, and the second, called "svm", is an instance of SVC. Now, we can fit the pipeline, like any other scikit-learn estimator:

In[6]:

```
pipe.fit(X_train, y_train)
```

Here, pipe.fit first calls fit on the first step (the scaler), then transforms the training data using the scaler, and finally fits the SVM with the scaled data. To evaluate on the test data, we simply call pipe.score:

In[7]:

```
print("Test score: {:.2f}".format(pipe.score(X_test, y_test)))
```

Out[7]:

```
Test score: 0.95
```

Calling the score method on the pipeline first transforms the test data using the scaler, and then calls the score method on the SVM using the scaled test data. As you can see, the result is identical to the one we got from the code at the beginning of the chapter, when doing the transformations by hand. Using the pipeline, we reduced the code needed for our "preprocessing + classification" process. The main benefit of using the pipeline, however, is that we can now use this single estimator in cross_val_score or GridSearchCV.

1 With one exception: the name can't contain a double underscore, __.

6.3 Using Pipelines in Grid Searches

Using a pipeline in a grid search works the same way as using any other estimator. We define a parameter grid to search over, and construct a GridSearchCV from the pipeline and the parameter grid. When specifying the parameter grid, there is a slight change, though. We need to specify for each parameter which step of the pipeline it belongs to. Both parameters that we want to adjust, C and gamma, are parameters of SVC, the second step. We gave this step the name "svm". The syntax to define a parameter grid for a pipeline is to specify for each parameter the step name, followed by __ (a double underscore), followed by the parameter name. To search over the C parameter of SVC we therefore have to use "svm__C" as the key in the parameter grid dictionary, and similarly for gamma:

In[8]:

```
param_grid = {'svm__C': [0.001, 0.01, 0.1, 1, 10, 100],
              'svm__gamma': [0.001, 0.01, 0.1, 1, 10, 100]}
```

With this parameter grid we can use GridSearchCV as usual:

In[9]:

```
grid = GridSearchCV(pipe, param_grid=param_grid, cv=5)
grid.fit(X_train, y_train)
print("Best cross-validation accuracy: {:.2f}".format(grid.best_score_))
print("Test set score: {:.2f}".format(grid.score(X_test, y_test)))
print("Best parameters: {}".format(grid.best_params_))
```

Out[9]:

```
Best cross-validation accuracy: 0.98
Test set score: 0.97
Best parameters: {'svm__C': 1, 'svm__gamma': 1}
```

In contrast to the grid search we did before, now for each split in the cross-validation, the MinMaxScaler is refit with only the training splits and no information is leaked from the test split into the parameter search. Compare this (Figure 6-2) with Figure 6-1 earlier in this chapter:

In[10]:

```
mglearn.plots.plot_proper_processing()
```

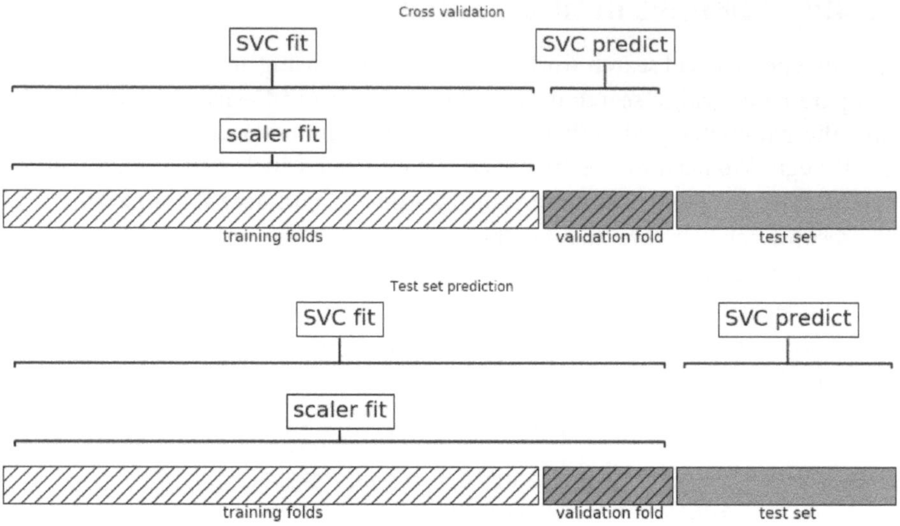

Figure 6-2. Data usage when preprocessing inside the cross-validation loop with a pipeline

The impact of leaking information in the cross-validation varies depending on the nature of the preprocessing step. Estimating the scale of the data using the test fold usually doesn't have a terrible impact, while using the test fold in feature extraction and feature selection can lead to substantial differences in outcomes.

Illustrating Information Leakage

A great example of leaking information in cross-validation is given in Hastie, Tibshirani, and Friedman's book *The Elements of Statistical Learning*, and we reproduce an adapted version here. Let's consider a synthetic regression task with 100 samples and 10,000 features that are sampled independently from a Gaussian distribution. We also sample the response from a Gaussian distribution:

In[11]:

```
rnd = np.random.RandomState(seed=0)
X = rnd.normal(size=(100, 10000))
y = rnd.normal(size=(100,))
```

Given the way we created the dataset, there is no relation between the data, `X`, and the target, `y` (they are independent), so it should not be possible to learn anything from this dataset. We will now do the following. First, select the most informative of the 10,000 features using `SelectPercentile` feature selection, and then we evaluate a `Ridge` regressor using cross-validation:

In[12]:

```
from sklearn.feature_selection import SelectPercentile, f_regression

select = SelectPercentile(score_func=f_regression, percentile=5).fit(X, y)
X_selected = select.transform(X)
print("X_selected.shape: {}".format(X_selected.shape))
```

Out[12]:

```
X_selected.shape: (100, 500)
```

In[13]:

```
from sklearn.model_selection import cross_val_score
from sklearn.linear_model import Ridge
print("Cross-validation accuracy (cv only on ridge): {:.2f}".format(
      np.mean(cross_val_score(Ridge(), X_selected, y, cv=5))))
```

Out[13]:

```
Cross-validation accuracy (cv only on ridge): 0.91
```

The mean R^2 computed by cross-validation is 0.91, indicating a very good model. This clearly cannot be right, as our data is entirely random. What happened here is that our feature selection picked out some features among the 10,000 random features that are (by chance) very well correlated with the target. Because we fit the feature selection *outside* of the cross-validation, it could find features that are correlated both on the training and the test folds. The information we leaked from the test folds was very informative, leading to highly unrealistic results. Let's compare this to a proper cross-validation using a pipeline:

In[14]:

```
pipe = Pipeline([("select", SelectPercentile(score_func=f_regression,
                                             percentile=5)),
                 ("ridge", Ridge())])
print("Cross-validation accuracy (pipeline): {:.2f}".format(
      np.mean(cross_val_score(pipe, X, y, cv=5))))
```

Out[14]:

```
Cross-validation accuracy (pipeline): -0.25
```

This time, we get a *negative* R^2 score, indicating a very poor model. Using the pipeline, the feature selection is now *inside* the cross-validation loop. This means features can only be selected using the training folds of the data, not the test fold. The feature selection finds features that are correlated with the target on the training set, but because the data is entirely random, these features are not correlated with the target on the test set. In this example, rectifying the data leakage issue in the feature selection makes the difference between concluding that a model works very well and concluding that a model works not at all.

6.4 The General Pipeline Interface

The `Pipeline` class is not restricted to preprocessing and classification, but can in fact join any number of estimators together. For example, you could build a pipeline containing feature extraction, feature selection, scaling, and classification, for a total of four steps. Similarly, the last step could be regression or clustering instead of classification.

The only requirement for estimators in a pipeline is that all but the last step need to have a `transform` method, so they can produce a new representation of the data that can be used in the next step.

Internally, during the call to `Pipeline.fit`, the pipeline calls `fit` and then `transform` on each step in turn,[2] with the input given by the output of the `transform` method of the previous step. For the last step in the pipeline, just `fit` is called.

Brushing over some finer details, this is implemented as follows. Remember that `pipeline.steps` is a list of tuples, so `pipeline.steps[0][1]` is the first estimator, `pipeline.steps[1][1]` is the second estimator, and so on:

In[15]:

```
def fit(self, X, y):
    X_transformed = X
    for name, estimator in self.steps[:-1]:
        # iterate over all but the final step
        # fit and transform the data
        X_transformed = estimator.fit_transform(X_transformed, y)
    # fit the last step
    self.steps[-1][1].fit(X_transformed, y)
    return self
```

When predicting using `Pipeline`, we similarly `transform` the data using all but the last step, and then call `predict` on the last step:

In[16]:

```
def predict(self, X):
    X_transformed = X
    for step in self.steps[:-1]:
        # iterate over all but the final step
        # transform the data
        X_transformed = step[1].transform(X_transformed)
    # predict using the last step
    return self.steps[-1][1].predict(X_transformed)
```

2 Or just `fit_transform`.

The process is illustrated in Figure 6-3 for two transformers, T1 and T2, and a classifier (called Classifier).

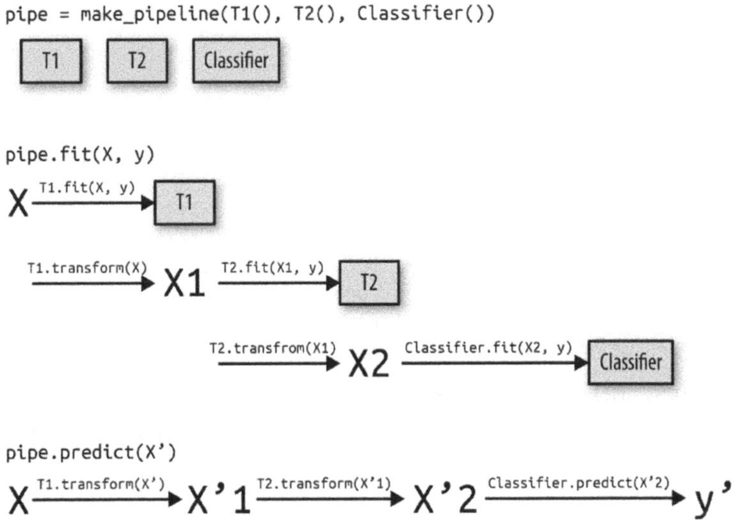

Figure 6-3. Overview of the pipeline training and prediction process

The pipeline is actually even more general than this. There is no requirement for the last step in a pipeline to have a `predict` function, and we could create a pipeline just containing, for example, a scaler and PCA. Then, because the last step (PCA) has a `transform` method, we could call `transform` on the pipeline to get the output of `PCA.transform` applied to the data that was processed by the previous step. The last step of a pipeline is only required to have a `fit` method.

6.4.1 Convenient Pipeline Creation with make_pipeline

Creating a pipeline using the syntax described earlier is sometimes a bit cumbersome, and we often don't need user-specified names for each step. There is a convenience function, `make_pipeline`, that will create a pipeline for us and automatically name each step based on its class. The syntax for `make_pipeline` is as follows:

In[17]:

```
from sklearn.pipeline import make_pipeline
# standard syntax
pipe_long = Pipeline([("scaler", MinMaxScaler()), ("svm", SVC(C=100))])
# abbreviated syntax
pipe_short = make_pipeline(MinMaxScaler(), SVC(C=100))
```

The pipeline objects pipe_long and pipe_short do exactly the same thing, but pipe_short has steps that were automatically named. We can see the names of the steps by looking at the steps attribute:

In[18]:

```
print("Pipeline steps:\n{}".format(pipe_short.steps))
```

Out[18]:

```
Pipeline steps:
[('minmaxscaler', MinMaxScaler(copy=True, feature_range=(0, 1))),
 ('svc', SVC(C=100, cache_size=200, class_weight=None, coef0=0.0,
             decision_function_shape='ovr', degree=3, gamma='auto',
             kernel='rbf', max_iter=-1, probability=False,
             random_state=None, shrinking=True, tol=0.001,
             verbose=False))]
```

The steps are named minmaxscaler and svc. In general, the step names are just lowercase versions of the class names. If multiple steps have the same class, a number is appended:

In[19]:

```
from sklearn.preprocessing import StandardScaler
from sklearn.decomposition import PCA

pipe = make_pipeline(StandardScaler(), PCA(n_components=2), StandardScaler())
print("Pipeline steps:\n{}".format(pipe.steps))
```

Out[19]:

```
Pipeline steps:
[('standardscaler-1', StandardScaler(copy=True, with_mean=True, with_std=True)),
 ('pca', PCA(copy=True, iterated_power='auto', n_components=2, random_state=None,
             svd_solver='auto', tol=0.0, whiten=False)),
 ('standardscaler-2', StandardScaler(copy=True, with_mean=True, with_std=True))]
```

As you can see, the first StandardScaler step was named standardscaler-1 and the second standardscaler-2. However, in such settings it might be better to use the Pipeline construction with explicit names, to give more semantic names to each step.

6.4.2 Accessing Step Attributes

Often you will want to inspect attributes of one of the steps of the pipeline—say, the coefficients of a linear model or the components extracted by PCA. The easiest way to access the steps in a pipeline is via the named_steps attribute, which is a dictionary from the step names to the estimators:

In[20]:

```
# fit the pipeline defined before to the cancer dataset
pipe.fit(cancer.data)
# extract the first two principal components from the "pca" step
components = pipe.named_steps["pca"].components_
print("components.shape: {}".format(components.shape))
```

Out[20]:

```
components.shape: (2, 30)
```

6.4.3 Accessing Attributes in a Pipeline inside GridSearchCV

As we discussed earlier in this chapter, one of the main reasons to use pipelines is for doing grid searches. A common task is to access some of the steps of a pipeline inside a grid search. Let's grid search a `LogisticRegression` classifier on the `cancer` dataset, using `Pipeline` and `StandardScaler` to scale the data before passing it to the `LogisticRegression` classifier. First we create a pipeline using the `make_pipeline` function:

In[21]:

```
from sklearn.linear_model import LogisticRegression

pipe = make_pipeline(StandardScaler(), LogisticRegression())
```

Next, we create a parameter grid. As explained in Chapter 2, the regularization parameter to tune for `LogisticRegression` is the parameter `C`. We use a logarithmic grid for this parameter, searching between 0.01 and 100. Because we used the `make_pipeline` function, the name of the `LogisticRegression` step in the pipeline is the lowercased class name, `logisticregression`. To tune the parameter `C`, we therefore have to specify a parameter grid for `logisticregression__C`:

In[22]:

```
param_grid = {'logisticregression__C': [0.01, 0.1, 1, 10, 100]}
```

As usual, we split the `cancer` dataset into training and test sets, and fit a grid search:

In[23]:

```
X_train, X_test, y_train, y_test = train_test_split(
    cancer.data, cancer.target, random_state=4)
grid = GridSearchCV(pipe, param_grid, cv=5)
grid.fit(X_train, y_train)
```

So how do we access the coefficients of the best `LogisticRegression` model that was found by `GridSearchCV`? From Chapter 5 we know that the best model found by `GridSearchCV`, trained on all the training data, is stored in `grid.best_estimator_`:

In[24]:

```
print("Best estimator:\n{}".format(grid.best_estimator_))
```

Out[24]:

```
Best estimator:
Pipeline(memory=None, steps=[
    ('standardscaler', StandardScaler(copy=True, with_mean=True, with_std=True)),
    ('logisticregression', LogisticRegression(C=0.1, class_weight=None,
    dual=False, fit_intercept=True, intercept_scaling=1, max_iter=100,
    multi_class='warn', n_jobs=None, penalty='l2', random_state=None,
    solver='warn', tol=0.0001, verbose=0, warm_start=False))])
```

This best_estimator_ in our case is a pipeline with two steps, standardscaler and logisticregression. To access the logisticregression step, we can use the named_steps attribute of the pipeline, as explained earlier:

In[25]:

```
print("Logistic regression step:\n{}".format(
      grid.best_estimator_.named_steps["logisticregression"]))
```

Out[25]:

```
Logistic regression step:
LogisticRegression(C=0.1, class_weight=None, dual=False, fit_intercept=True,
                  intercept_scaling=1, max_iter=100, multi_class='warn',
                  n_jobs=None, penalty='l2', random_state=None, solver='warn',
                  tol=0.0001, verbose=0, warm_start=False)
```

Now that we have the trained LogisticRegression instance, we can access the coefficients (weights) associated with each input feature:

In[26]:

```
print("Logistic regression coefficients:\n{}".format(
      grid.best_estimator_.named_steps["logisticregression"].coef_))
```

Out[26]:

```
Logistic regression coefficients:
[[-0.389 -0.375 -0.376 -0.396 -0.115  0.017 -0.355 -0.39  -0.058  0.209
  -0.495 -0.004 -0.371 -0.383 -0.045  0.198  0.004 -0.049  0.21   0.224
  -0.547 -0.525 -0.499 -0.515 -0.393 -0.123 -0.388 -0.417 -0.325 -0.139]]
```

This might be a somewhat lengthy expression, but often it comes in handy in understanding your models.

6.5 Grid-Searching Preprocessing Steps and Model Parameters

Using pipelines, we can encapsulate all the processing steps in our machine learning workflow in a single `scikit-learn` estimator. Another benefit of doing this is that we can now *adjust the parameters of the preprocessing* using the outcome of a supervised task like regression or classification. In previous chapters, we used polynomial features on the `boston` dataset before applying the ridge regressor. Let's model that using a pipeline instead. The pipeline contains three steps—scaling the data, computing polynomial features, and ridge regression:

In[27]:

```
from sklearn.datasets import load_boston
boston = load_boston()
X_train, X_test, y_train, y_test = train_test_split(boston.data, boston.target,
                                                    random_state=0)

from sklearn.preprocessing import PolynomialFeatures
pipe = make_pipeline(
    StandardScaler(),
    PolynomialFeatures(),
    Ridge())
```

How do we know which degrees of polynomials to choose, or whether to choose any polynomials or interactions at all? Ideally we want to select the `degree` parameter based on the outcome of the classification. Using our pipeline, we can search over the `degree` parameter together with the parameter `alpha` of `Ridge`. To do this, we define a `param_grid` that contains both, appropriately prefixed by the step names:

In[28]:

```
param_grid = {'polynomialfeatures__degree': [1, 2, 3],
              'ridge__alpha': [0.001, 0.01, 0.1, 1, 10, 100]}
```

Now we can run our grid search again:

In[29]:

```
grid = GridSearchCV(pipe, param_grid=param_grid, cv=5, n_jobs=-1)
grid.fit(X_train, y_train)
```

We can visualize the outcome of the cross-validation using a heat map (Figure 6-4), as we did in Chapter 5:

In[30]:

```
plt.matshow(grid.cv_results_['mean_test_score'].reshape(3, -1),
            vmin=0, cmap="viridis")
plt.xlabel("ridge__alpha")
plt.ylabel("polynomialfeatures__degree")
```

```
plt.xticks(range(len(param_grid['ridge__alpha'])), param_grid['ridge__alpha'])
plt.yticks(range(len(param_grid['polynomialfeatures__degree'])),
           param_grid['polynomialfeatures__degree'])

plt.colorbar()
```

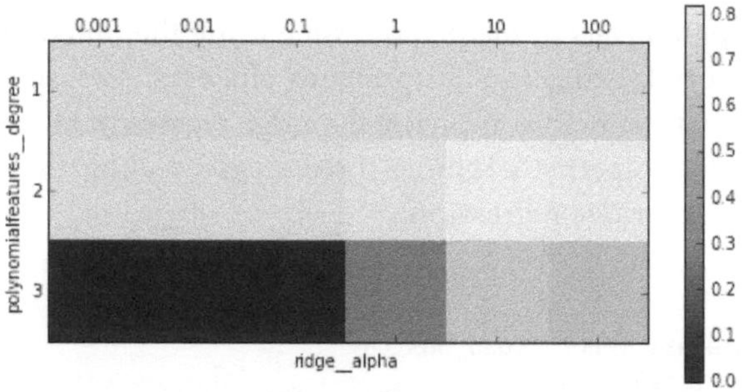

Figure 6-4. Heat map of mean cross-validation score as a function of the degree of the polynomial features and alpha parameter of Ridge

Looking at the results produced by the cross-validation, we can see that using polynomials of degree two helps, but that degree-three polynomials are much worse than either degree one or two. This is reflected in the best parameters that were found:

In[31]:

```
print("Best parameters: {}".format(grid.best_params_))
```

Out[31]:

```
Best parameters: {'polynomialfeatures__degree': 2, 'ridge__alpha': 10}
```

Which lead to the following score:

In[32]:

```
print("Test-set score: {:.2f}".format(grid.score(X_test, y_test)))
```

Out[32]:

```
Test-set score: 0.77
```

Let's run a grid search without polynomial features for comparison:

In[33]:

```
param_grid = {'ridge__alpha': [0.001, 0.01, 0.1, 1, 10, 100]}
pipe = make_pipeline(StandardScaler(), Ridge())
grid = GridSearchCV(pipe, param_grid, cv=5)
grid.fit(X_train, y_train)
print("Score without poly features: {:.2f}".format(grid.score(X_test, y_test)))
```

Out[33]:

```
Score without poly features: 0.63
```

As we would expect looking at the grid search results visualized in Figure 6-4, using no polynomial features leads to decidedly worse results.

Searching over preprocessing parameters together with model parameters is a very powerful strategy. However, keep in mind that `GridSearchCV` tries *all possible combinations* of the specified parameters. Therefore, adding more parameters to your grid exponentially increases the number of models that need to be built.

6.6 Grid-Searching Which Model To Use

You can even go further in combining `GridSearchCV` and `Pipeline`: it is also possible to search over the actual steps being performed in the pipeline (say whether to use `StandardScaler` or `MinMaxScaler`). This leads to an even bigger search space and should be considered carefully. Trying all possible solutions is usually not a viable machine learning strategy. However, here is an example comparing a `RandomForestClassifier` and an `SVC` on the `iris` dataset. We know that the `SVC` might need the data to be scaled, so we also search over whether to use `StandardScaler` or no preprocessing. For the `RandomForestClassifier`, we know that no preprocessing is necessary. We start by defining the pipeline. Here, we explicitly name the steps. We want two steps, one for the preprocessing and then a classifier. We can instantiate this using `SVC` and `StandardScaler`:

In[34]:

```
pipe = Pipeline([('preprocessing', StandardScaler()), ('classifier', SVC())])
```

Now we can define the `parameter_grid` to search over. We want the `classifier` to be either `RandomForestClassifier` or `SVC`. Because they have different parameters to tune, and need different preprocessing, we can make use of the list of search grids we discussed in "Search over spaces that are not grids" on page 278. To assign an estimator to a step, we use the name of the step as the parameter name. When we wanted to skip a step in the pipeline (for example, because we don't need preprocessing for the `RandomForest`), we can set that step to `None`:

In[35]:

```
from sklearn.ensemble import RandomForestClassifier

param_grid = [
    {'classifier': [SVC()], 'preprocessing': [StandardScaler(), None],
     'classifier__gamma': [0.001, 0.01, 0.1, 1, 10, 100],
     'classifier__C': [0.001, 0.01, 0.1, 1, 10, 100]},
    {'classifier': [RandomForestClassifier(n_estimators=100)],
     'preprocessing': [None], 'classifier__max_features': [1, 2, 3]}]
```

Now we can instantiate and run the grid search as usual, here on the `cancer` dataset:

In[36]:

```
X_train, X_test, y_train, y_test = train_test_split(
    cancer.data, cancer.target, random_state=0)

grid = GridSearchCV(pipe, param_grid, cv=5)
grid.fit(X_train, y_train)

print("Best params:\n{}\n".format(grid.best_params_))
print("Best cross-validation score: {:.2f}".format(grid.best_score_))
print("Test-set score: {:.2f}".format(grid.score(X_test, y_test)))
```

Out[36]:

```
Best params:
{'classifier':
 SVC(C=10, cache_size=200, class_weight=None, coef0=0.0,
     decision_function_shape='ovr', degree=3, gamma=0.01, kernel='rbf',
     max_iter=-1, probability=False, random_state=None, shrinking=True,
     tol=0.001, verbose=False),
 'preprocessing':
 StandardScaler(copy=True, with_mean=True, with_std=True),
 'classifier__C': 10, 'classifier__gamma': 0.01}

Best cross-validation score: 0.99
Test-set score: 0.98
```

The outcome of the grid search is that `SVC` with `StandardScaler` preprocessing, `C=10`, and `gamma=0.01` gave the best result.

6.6.1 Avoiding Redundant Computation

When performing a large grid-search like the ones described earlier, the same steps are often used several times. For example, for each setting of the `classifier`, the `StandardScaler` is built again. For the `StandardScaler` this might not be a big issue, but if you are using a more expensive transformation (say, feature extraction with PCA or NMF), this is a lot of wasted computation. The easiest solution to this problem is caching computations. This can be done with the `memory` parameter of `Pipeline`, which takes a `joblib.Memory` object—or just a path to store the cache. Enabling caching can therefore be as simple as this:

In[37]:

```
pipe = Pipeline([('preprocessing', StandardScaler()), ('classifier', SVC())],
                memory="cache_folder")
```

There are two downsides to this method. The cache is managed by writing to disk, which requires serialization and actually reading and writing from disk. This means that using `memory` will only accelerate relatively slow transformations. Just scaling the data is likely to be faster than trying to read the already scaled data from disk. For expensive transformations, this can still be a big win, though. The other disadvantage is that using `n_jobs` can interfere with the caching. Depending on the execution order of the grid search, in the worst case a computation could be performed redundantly at the same time by `n_jobs` amount of workers before it is cached.

Both of these can be avoided by using a replacement for `GridSearchCV` provided by the `dask-ml` library (*https://dask-ml.readthedocs.io/*). `dask-ml` allows you to avoid redundant computation while performing parallel computations, even distributed over a cluster. If you are using expensive pipelines and performing extensive parameter searches, you should definitely have a look at `dask-ml`.

6.7 Summary and Outlook

In this chapter we introduced the `Pipeline` class, a general-purpose tool to chain together multiple processing steps in a machine learning workflow. Real-world applications of machine learning rarely involve an isolated use of a model, and instead are a sequence of processing steps. Using pipelines allows us to encapsulate multiple steps into a single Python object that adheres to the familiar `scikit-learn` interface of `fit`, `predict`, and `transform`. In particular when doing model evaluation using cross-validation and parameter selection using grid search, using the `Pipeline` class to capture all the processing steps is essential for proper evaluation. The `Pipeline` class also allows writing more succinct code, and reduces the likelihood of mistakes that can happen when building processing chains without the `pipeline` class (like forgetting to apply all transformers on the test set, or not applying them in the right order). Choosing the right combination of feature extraction, preprocessing, and models is somewhat of an art, and often requires some trial and error. However, using pipelines, this "trying out" of many different processing steps is quite simple. When experimenting, be careful not to overcomplicate your processes, and make sure to evaluate whether every component you are including in your model is necessary.

With this chapter, we have completed our survey of general-purpose tools and algorithms provided by `scikit-learn`. You now possess all the required skills and know the necessary mechanisms to apply machine learning in practice. In the next chapter, we will dive in more detail into one particular type of data that is commonly seen in practice, and that requires some special expertise to handle correctly: text data.

CHAPTER 7

Working with Text Data

In Chapter 4, we talked about two kinds of features that can represent properties of the data: continuous features that describe a quantity, and categorical features that are items from a fixed list. There is a third kind of feature that can be found in many applications, which is text. For example, if we want to classify an email message as either a legitimate email or spam, the content of the email will certainly contain important information for this classification task. Or maybe we want to learn about the opinion of a politician on the topic of immigration. Here, that individual's speeches or tweets might provide useful information. In customer service, we often want to find out if a message is a complaint or an inquiry. We can use the subject line and content of a message to automatically determine the customer's intent, which allows us to send the message to the appropriate department, or even send a fully automatic reply.

Text data is usually represented as strings, made up of characters. In any of the examples just given, the length of the text data will vary. This feature is clearly very different from the numeric features that we've discussed so far, and we will need to process the data before we can apply our machine learning algorithms to it.

7.1 Types of Data Represented as Strings

Before we dive into the processing steps that go into representing text data for machine learning, we want to briefly discuss different kinds of text data that you might encounter. Text is usually just a string in your dataset, but not all string features should be treated as text. A string feature can sometimes represent categorical variables, as we discussed in Chapter 5. There is no way to know how to treat a string feature before looking at the data.

There are four kinds of string data you might see:

- Categorical data
- Free strings that can be semantically mapped to categories
- Structured string data
- Text data

Categorical data is data that comes from a fixed list. Say you collect data via a survey where you ask people their favorite color, with a drop-down menu that allows them to select from "red," "green," "blue," "yellow," "black," "white," "purple," and "pink." This will result in a dataset with exactly eight different possible values, which clearly encode a categorical variable. You can check whether this is the case for your data by eyeballing it (if you see very many different strings it is unlikely that this is a categorical variable) and confirm it by computing the unique values over the dataset, and possibly a histogram over how often each appears. You also might want to check whether each variable actually corresponds to a category that makes sense for your application. Maybe halfway through the existence of your survey, someone found that "black" was misspelled as "blak" and subsequently fixed the survey. As a result, your dataset contains both "blak" and "black," which correspond to the same semantic meaning and should be consolidated.

Now imagine instead of providing a drop-down menu, you provide a text field for the users to provide their own favorite colors. Many people might respond with a color name like "black" or "blue." Others might make typographical errors, use different spellings like "gray" and "grey," or use more evocative and specific names like "midnight blue." You will also have some very strange entries. Some good examples come from the xkcd Color Survey (*https://blog.xkcd.com/2010/05/03/color-survey-results/*), where people had to name colors and came up with names like "velociraptor cloaka" and "my dentist's office orange. I still remember his dandruff slowly wafting into my gaping yaw," which are hard to map to colors automatically (or at all). The responses you can obtain from a text field belong to the second category in the list, *free strings that can be semantically mapped to categories*. It will probably be best to encode this data as a categorical variable, where you can select the categories either by using the most common entries, or by defining categories that will capture responses in a way that makes sense for your application. You might then have some categories for standard colors, maybe a category "multicolored" for people that gave answers like "green and red stripes," and an "other" category for things that cannot be encoded otherwise. This kind of preprocessing of strings can take a lot of manual effort and is not easily automated. If you are in a position where you can influence data collection, we highly recommend avoiding manually entered values for concepts that are better captured using categorical variables.

Often, manually entered values do not correspond to fixed categories, but still have some underlying *structure*, like addresses, names of places or people, dates, telephone numbers, or other identifiers. These kinds of strings are often very hard to parse, and their treatment is highly dependent on context and domain. A systematic treatment of these cases is beyond the scope of this book.

The final category of string data is freeform *text data* that consists of phrases or sentences. Examples include tweets, chat logs, and hotel reviews, as well as the collected works of Shakespeare, the content of Wikipedia, or the Project Gutenberg collection of 50,000 ebooks. All of these collections contain information mostly as sentences composed of words.[1] For simplicity's sake, let's assume all our documents are in one language, English.[2] In the context of text analysis, the dataset is often called the *corpus*, and each data point, represented as a single text, is called a *document*. These terms come from the *information retrieval* (IR) and *natural language processing* (NLP) community, which both deal mostly in text data.

7.2 Example Application: Sentiment Analysis of Movie Reviews

As a running example in this chapter, we will use a dataset of movie reviews from the IMDb (Internet Movie Database) website collected by Stanford researcher Andrew Maas.[3] This dataset contains the text of the reviews, together with a label that indicates whether a review is "positive" or "negative." The IMDb website itself contains ratings from 1 to 10. To simplify the modeling, this annotation is summarized as a two-class classification dataset where reviews with a score of 7 or higher are labeled as positive, and a score 4 or lower is labeled as negative (neutral reviews are not included in the dataset). We will leave the question of whether this is a good representation of the data open, and simply use the data as provided by Andrew Maas. If you're on OS X or Linux, you can download and unpack the data using:[4]

1 Arguably, the content of websites linked to in tweets contains more information than the text of the tweets themselves.

2 Most of what we will talk about in the rest of the chapter also applies to other languages that use the Roman alphabet, and partially to other languages with word boundary delimiters. Chinese, for example, does not delimit word boundaries, and has other challenges that make applying the techniques in this chapter difficult.

3 The dataset is available at *http://ai.stanford.edu/~amaas/data/sentiment/*.

4 The "!" indicates running a command on the command line. Here we are using command-line syntax for OS X and Linux. On Windows, you can download the file using your browser, and unpack it and remove the folder using the explorer.

In[1]:

```
! wget -nc http://ai.stanford.edu/~amaas/data/sentiment/aclImdb_v1.tar.gz -P data
! tar xzf data/aclImdb_v1.tar.gz --skip-old-files -C data
```

After unpacking the data, the data set is provided as text files in two separate folders, one for the training data, and one for the test data. Each of these in turn has two subfolders, one called "positive" and one called "negative":

In[2]:

```
!tree -dL 2 data/aclImdb
```

Out[2]:

```
data/aclImdb
├── test
│   ├── neg
│   └── pos
└── train
    ├── neg
    ├── pos
    └── unsup
7 directories
```

The pos folder contains all the positive reviews, each as a separate text file, and similarly for the neg folder. The *unsup* folder contains unlabeled data, which we won't use, and therefore remove:

In[3]:

```
!rm -r data/aclImdb/train/unsup
```

There is a helper function in scikit-learn to load files stored in such a folder structure, where each subfolder corresponds to a label, called load_files. We apply the load_files function first to the training data:

In[3]:

```
from sklearn.datasets import load_files

reviews_train = load_files("data/aclImdb/train/")
# load_files returns a bunch, containing training texts and training labels
text_train, y_train = reviews_train.data, reviews_train.target
print("type of text_train: {}".format(type(text_train)))
print("length of text_train: {}".format(len(text_train)))
print("text_train[6]:\n{}".format(text_train[6]))
```

Out[3]:

```
type of text_train: <class 'list'>
length of text_train: 25000
text_train[6]:
b"This movie has a special way of telling the story, at first i found
```

```
it rather odd as it jumped through time and I had no idea whats
happening.<br /><br />Anyway the story line was although simple, but
still very real and touching. You met someone the first time, you fell
in love completely, but broke up at last and promoted a deadly agony.
Who hasn't go through this? but we will never forget this kind of pain
in our life. <br /><br />I would say i am rather touched as two actor
has shown great performance in showing the love between the characters.
I just wish that the story could be a happy ending."
```

You can see that text_train is a list of length 25,000, where each entry is a string containing a review. We printed the review with index 1. You can also see that the review contains some HTML line breaks (<br />). While these are unlikely to have a large impact on our machine learning models, it is better to clean the data and remove this formatting before we proceed:

In[4]:

```
text_train = [doc.replace(b"<br />", b" ") for doc in text_train]
```

The type of the entries of text_train will depend on your Python version. In Python 3, they will be of type bytes which represents a binary encoding of the string data. In Python 2, text_train contains strings. We won't go into the details of the different string types in Python here, but we recommend that you read the Python 2 (*https://docs.python.org/2/howto/unicode.html*) and/or Python 3 documentation (*https://docs.python.org/3/howto/unicode.html*) regarding strings and Unicode.

The dataset was collected such that the positive class and the negative class balanced, so that there are as many positive as negative strings:

In[5]:

```
print("Samples per class (training): {}".format(np.bincount(y_train)))
```

Out[5]:

```
Samples per class (training): [12500 12500]
```

We load the test dataset in the same manner:

In[6]:

```
reviews_test = load_files("data/aclImdb/test/")
text_test, y_test = reviews_test.data, reviews_test.target
print("Number of documents in test data: {}".format(len(text_test)))
print("Samples per class (test): {}".format(np.bincount(y_test)))
text_test = [doc.replace(b"<br />", b" ") for doc in text_test]
```

Out[6]:

```
Number of documents in test data: 25000
Samples per class (test): [12500 12500]
```

The task we want to solve is as follows: given a review, we want to assign the label "positive" or "negative" based on the text content of the review. This is a standard binary classification task. However, the text data is not in a format that a machine learning model can handle. We need to convert the string representation of the text into a numeric representation that we can apply our machine learning algorithms to.

7.3 Representing Text Data as a Bag of Words

One of the most simple but effective and commonly used ways to represent text for machine learning is using the *bag-of-words* representation. When using this representation, we discard most of the structure of the input text, like chapters, paragraphs, sentences, and formatting, and only count *how often each word appears in each text* in the corpus. Discarding the structure and counting only word occurrences leads to the mental image of representing text as a "bag."

Computing the bag-of-words representation for a corpus of documents consists of the following three steps:

1. *Tokenization*. Split each document into the words that appear in it (called *tokens*), for example by splitting them on whitespace and punctuation.
2. *Vocabulary building*. Collect a vocabulary of all words that appear in any of the documents, and number them (say, in alphabetical order).
3. *Encoding*. For each document, count how often each of the words in the vocabulary appear in this document.

There are some subtleties involved in step 1 and step 2, which we will discuss in more detail later in this chapter. For now, let's look at how we can apply the bag-of-words processing using `scikit-learn`. Figure 7-1 illustrates the process on the string `"This is how you get ants."`.

The output is one vector of word counts for each document. For each word in the vocabulary, we have a count of how often it appears in each document. That means our numeric representation has one feature for each unique word in the whole dataset. Note how the order of the words in the original string is completely irrelevant to the bag-of-words feature representation.

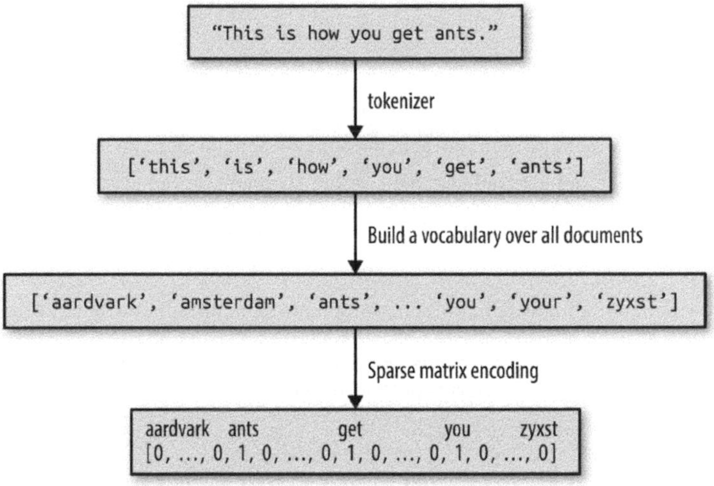

Figure 7-1. Bag-of-words processing

7.3.1 Applying Bag-of-Words to a Toy Dataset

The bag-of-words representation is implemented in `CountVectorizer`, which is a transformer. Let's first apply it to a toy dataset, consisting of two samples, to see it working:

In[7]:

```
bards_words =["The fool doth think he is wise,",
              "but the wise man knows himself to be a fool"]
```

We import and instantiate the `CountVectorizer` and `fit` it to our toy data as follows:

In[8]:

```
from sklearn.feature_extraction.text import CountVectorizer
vect = CountVectorizer()
vect.fit(bards_words)
```

Fitting the `CountVectorizer` consists of the tokenization of the training data and building of the vocabulary, which we can access as the `vocabulary_` attribute:

In[9]:

```
print("Vocabulary size: {}".format(len(vect.vocabulary_)))
print("Vocabulary content:\n {}".format(vect.vocabulary_))
```

Out[9]:

```
Vocabulary size: 13
Vocabulary content:
 {'the': 9, 'himself': 5, 'wise': 12, 'he': 4, 'doth': 2, 'to': 11, 'knows': 7,
  'man': 8, 'fool': 3, 'is': 6, 'be': 0, 'think': 10, 'but': 1}
```

The vocabulary consists of 13 words, from "`be`" to "`wise`".

To create the bag-of-words representation for the training data, we call the `transform` method:

In[10]:

```
bag_of_words = vect.transform(bards_words)
print("bag_of_words: {}".format(repr(bag_of_words)))
```

Out[10]:

```
bag_of_words: <2x13 sparse matrix of type '<class 'numpy.int64'>'
    with 16 stored elements in Compressed Sparse Row format>
```

The bag-of-words representation is stored in a SciPy sparse matrix that only stores the entries that are nonzero (see Chapter 1). The matrix is of shape 2×13, with one row for each of the two data points and one feature for each of the words in the vocabulary. A sparse matrix is used as most documents only contain a small subset of the words in the vocabulary, meaning most entries in the feature array are 0. Think about how many different words might appear in a movie review compared to all the words in the English language (which is what the vocabulary models). Storing all those zeros would be prohibitive, and a waste of memory. To look at the actual content of the sparse matrix, we can convert it to a "dense" NumPy array (that also stores all the 0 entries) using the `toarray` method:[5]

In[11]:

```
print("Dense representation of bag_of_words:\n{}".format(
    bag_of_words.toarray()))
```

Out[11]:

```
Dense representation of bag_of_words:
[[0 0 1 1 1 0 1 0 0 1 1 0 1]
 [1 1 0 1 0 1 0 1 1 1 0 1 1]]
```

We can see that the word counts for each word are either 0 or 1; neither of the two strings in `bards_words` contains a word twice. Let's take a look at how to read these feature vectors. The first string (`"The fool doth think he is wise,"`) is repre-

5 This is possible because we are using a small toy dataset that contains only 13 words. For any real dataset, this would result in a `MemoryError`.

sented as the first row in, and it contains the first word in the vocabulary, "be", zero times. It also contains the second word in the vocabulary, "but", zero times. It contains the third word, "doth", once, and so on. Looking at both rows, we can see that the fourth word, "fool", the tenth word, "the", and the thirteenth word, "wise", appear in both strings.

7.3.2 Bag-of-Words for Movie Reviews

Now that we've gone through the bag-of-words process in detail, let's apply it to our task of sentiment analysis for movie reviews. Earlier, we loaded our training and test data from the IMDb reviews into lists of strings (text_train and text_test), which we will now process:

In[12]:

```
vect = CountVectorizer().fit(text_train)
X_train = vect.transform(text_train)
print("X_train:\n{}".format(repr(X_train)))
```

Out[12]:

```
X_train:
<25000x74849 sparse matrix of type '<class 'numpy.int64'>'
    with 3431196 stored elements in Compressed Sparse Row format>
```

The shape of X_train, the bag-of-words representation of the training data, is 25,000×74,849, indicating that the vocabulary contains 74,849 entries. Again, the data is stored as a SciPy sparse matrix. Let's look at the vocabulary in a bit more detail. Another way to access the vocabulary is using the get_feature_name method of the vectorizer, which returns a convenient list where each entry corresponds to one feature:

In[13]:

```
feature_names = vect.get_feature_names()
print("Number of features: {}".format(len(feature_names)))
print("First 20 features:\n{}".format(feature_names[:20]))
print("Features 20010 to 20030:\n{}".format(feature_names[20010:20030]))
print("Every 2000th feature:\n{}".format(feature_names[::2000]))
```

Out[13]:

```
Number of features: 74849
First 20 features:
['00', '000', '0000000000001', '00001', '00015', '000s', '001', '003830',
 '006', '007', '0079', '0080', '0083', '0093638', '00am', '00pm', '00s',
 '01', '01pm', '02']
Features 20010 to 20030:
['dratted', 'draub', 'draught', 'draughts', 'draughtswoman', 'draw', 'drawback',
 'drawbacks', 'drawer', 'drawers', 'drawing', 'drawings', 'drawl',
 'drawled', 'drawling', 'drawn', 'draws', 'draza', 'dre', 'drea']
```

```
Every 2000th feature:
['00', 'aesir', 'aquarian', 'barking', 'blustering', 'bête', 'chicanery',
 'condensing', 'cunning', 'detox', 'draper', 'enshrined', 'favorit', 'freezer',
 'goldman', 'hasan', 'huitieme', 'intelligible', 'kantrowitz', 'lawful',
 'maars', 'megalunged', 'mostey', 'norrland', 'padilla', 'pincher',
 'promisingly', 'receptionist', 'rivals', 'schnaas', 'shunning', 'sparse',
 'subset', 'temptations', 'treatises', 'unproven', 'walkman', 'xylophonist']
```

As you can see, possibly a bit surprisingly, the first 10 entries in the vocabulary are all numbers. All these numbers appear somewhere in the reviews, and are therefore extracted as words. Most of these numbers don't have any immediate semantic meaning—apart from "007", which in the particular context of movies is likely to refer to the James Bond character.[6] Weeding out the meaningful from the nonmeaningful "words" is sometimes tricky. Looking further along in the vocabulary, we find a collection of English words starting with "dra". You might notice that for "draught", "drawback", and "drawer" both the singular and plural forms are contained in the vocabulary as distinct words. These words have very closely related semantic meanings, and counting them as different words, corresponding to different features, might not be ideal.

Before we try to improve our feature extraction, let's obtain a quantitative measure of performance by actually building a classifier. We have the training labels stored in y_train and the bag-of-words representation of the training data in X_train, so we can train a classifier on this data. For high-dimensional, sparse data like this, linear models like LogisticRegression often work best.

Let's start by evaluating LogisticRegression using cross-validation:[7]

In[14]:

```
from sklearn.model_selection import cross_val_score
from sklearn.linear_model import LogisticRegression
scores = cross_val_score(LogisticRegression(), X_train, y_train, cv=5)
print("Mean cross-validation accuracy: {:.2f}".format(np.mean(scores)))
```

Out[14]:

```
Mean cross-validation accuracy: 0.88
```

We obtain a mean cross-validation score of 88%, which indicates reasonable performance for a balanced binary classification task. We know that LogisticRegression has a regularization parameter, C, which we can tune via cross-validation:

6 A quick analysis of the data confirms that this is indeed the case. Try confirming it yourself.

7 The attentive reader might notice that we violate our lesson from Chapter 6 on cross-validation with preprocessing here. Using the default settings of CountVectorizer, it actually does not collect any statistics, so our results are valid. Using Pipeline from the start would be a better choice for applications, but we defer it for ease of exposure.

In[15]:

```
from sklearn.model_selection import GridSearchCV
param_grid = {'C': [0.001, 0.01, 0.1, 1, 10]}
grid = GridSearchCV(LogisticRegression(), param_grid, cv=5)
grid.fit(X_train, y_train)
print("Best cross-validation score: {:.2f}".format(grid.best_score_))
print("Best parameters: ", grid.best_params_)
```

Out[15]:

```
Best cross-validation score: 0.89
Best parameters:  {'C': 0.1}
```

We obtain a cross-validation score of 89% using `C=0.1`. We can now assess the generalization performance of this parameter setting on the test set:

In[16]:

```
X_test = vect.transform(text_test)
print("Test score: {:.2f}".format(grid.score(X_test, y_test)))
```

Out[16]:

```
Test score: 0.88
```

Now, let's see if we can improve the extraction of words. The `CountVectorizer` extracts tokens using a regular expression. By default, the regular expression that is used is `"\b\w\w+\b"`. If you are not familiar with regular expressions, this means it finds all sequences of characters that consist of at least two letters or numbers (`\w`) and that are separated by word boundaries (`\b`). It does not find single-letter words, and it splits up contractions like "doesn't" or "bit.ly", but it matches "h8ter" as a single word. The `CountVectorizer` then converts all words to lowercase characters, so that "soon", "Soon", and "sOon" all correspond to the same token (and therefore feature). This simple mechanism works quite well in practice, but as we saw earlier, we get many uninformative features (like the numbers). One way to cut back on these is to only use tokens that appear in at least two documents (or at least five documents, and so on). A token that appears only in a single document is unlikely to appear in the test set and is therefore not helpful. We can set the minimum number of documents a token needs to appear in with the `min_df` parameter:

In[17]:

```
vect = CountVectorizer(min_df=5).fit(text_train)
X_train = vect.transform(text_train)
print("X_train with min_df: {}".format(repr(X_train)))
```

Out[17]:

```
X_train with min_df: <25000x27271 sparse matrix of type '<class 'numpy.int64'>'
    with 3354014 stored elements in Compressed Sparse Row format>
```

By requiring at least five appearances of each token, we can bring down the number of features to 27,271, as seen in the preceding output—only about a third of the original features. Let's look at some tokens again:

In[18]:

```
feature_names = vect.get_feature_names()

print("First 50 features:\n{}".format(feature_names[:50]))
print("Features 20010 to 20030:\n{}".format(feature_names[20010:20030]))
print("Every 700th feature:\n{}".format(feature_names[::700]))
```

Out[18]:

```
First 50 features:
['00', '000', '007', '00s', '01', '02', '03', '04', '05', '06', '07', '08',
 '09', '10', '100', '1000', '100th', '101', '102', '103', '104', '105', '107',
 '108', '10s', '10th', '11', '110', '112', '116', '117', '11th', '12', '120',
 '12th', '13', '135', '13th', '14', '140', '14th', '15', '150', '15th', '16',
 '160', '1600', '16mm', '16s', '16th']
Features 20010 to 20030:
['repentance', 'repercussions', 'repertoire', 'repetition', 'repetitions',
 'repetitious', 'repetitive', 'rephrase', 'replace', 'replaced', 'replacement',
 'replaces', 'replacing', 'replay', 'replayable', 'replayed', 'replaying',
 'replays', 'replete', 'replica']
Every 700th feature:
['00', 'affections', 'appropriately', 'barbra', 'blurbs', 'butchered',
 'cheese', 'commitment', 'courts', 'deconstructed', 'disgraceful', 'dvds',
 'eschews', 'fell', 'freezer', 'goriest', 'hauser', 'hungary', 'insinuate',
 'juggle', 'leering', 'maelstrom', 'messiah', 'music', 'occasional', 'parking',
 'pleasantville', 'pronunciation', 'recipient', 'reviews', 'sas', 'shea',
 'sneers', 'steiger', 'swastika', 'thrusting', 'tvs', 'vampyre', 'westerns']
```

There are clearly many fewer numbers, and some of the more obscure words or misspellings seem to have vanished. Let's see how well our model performs by doing a grid search again:

In[19]:

```
grid = GridSearchCV(LogisticRegression(), param_grid, cv=5)
grid.fit(X_train, y_train)
print("Best cross-validation score: {:.2f}".format(grid.best_score_))
```

Out[19]:

```
Best cross-validation score: 0.89
```

The best validation accuracy of the grid search is still 89%, unchanged from before. We didn't improve our model, but having fewer features to deal with speeds up processing and throwing away useless features might make the model more interpretable.

If the `transform` method of `CountVectorizer` is called on a document that contains words that were not contained in the training data, these words will be ignored as they are not part of the dictionary. This is usually not really an issue for classification, as it's not possible to learn anything about words that are not in the training data. For some applications, like spam detection, it might be helpful to add a feature that encodes how many so-called "out of vocabulary" words there are in a particular document, though. This is not implemented in `scikit-learn` for now, but it's not that hard to write yourself. You need to be sure to restrict the vocabulary in some way; otherwise, no words will be "out of vocabulary" during training.

7.4 Stopwords

Another way that we can get rid of uninformative words is by discarding words that are too frequent to be informative. There are two main approaches: using a language-specific list of stopwords, or discarding words that appear too frequently. `scikit-learn` has a built-in list of English stopwords in the `feature_extraction.text` module:

In[20]:

```
from sklearn.feature_extraction.text import ENGLISH_STOP_WORDS
print("Number of stop words: {}".format(len(ENGLISH_STOP_WORDS)))
print("Every 10th stopword:\n{}".format(list(ENGLISH_STOP_WORDS)[::10]))
```

Out[20]:

```
Number of stop words: 318
Every 10th stopword:
['above', 'elsewhere', 'into', 'well', 'rather', 'fifteen', 'had', 'enough',
 'herein', 'should', 'third', 'although', 'more', 'this', 'none', 'seemed',
 'nobody', 'seems', 'he', 'also', 'fill', 'anyone', 'anything', 'me', 'the',
 'yet', 'go', 'seeming', 'front', 'beforehand', 'forty', 'i']
```

Clearly, removing the stopwords in the list can only decrease the number of features by the length of the list—here, 318—but it might lead to an improvement in performance. Let's give it a try:

In[21]:

```
# Specifying stop_words="english" uses the built-in list.
# We could also augment it and pass our own.
vect = CountVectorizer(min_df=5, stop_words="english").fit(text_train)
X_train = vect.transform(text_train)
print("X_train with stop words:\n{}".format(repr(X_train)))
```

Out[21]:

```
X_train with stop words:
<25000x26966 sparse matrix of type '<class 'numpy.int64'>'
    with 2149958 stored elements in Compressed Sparse Row format>
```

There are now 305 (27,271–26,966) fewer features in the dataset, which means that most, but not all, of the stopwords appeared. Let's run the grid search again:

In[22]:

```
grid = GridSearchCV(LogisticRegression(), param_grid, cv=5)
grid.fit(X_train, y_train)
print("Best cross-validation score: {:.2f}".format(grid.best_score_))
```

Out[22]:

```
Best cross-validation score: 0.88
```

The grid search performance decreased slightly using the stopwords—not enough to worry about, but given that excluding 305 features out of over 27,000 is unlikely to change performance or interpretability a lot, it doesn't seem worth using this list. Fixed lists are mostly helpful for small datasets, which might not contain enough information for the model to determine which words are stopwords from the data itself. As an exercise, you can try out the other approach, discarding frequently appearing words, by setting the `max_df` option of `CountVectorizer` and see how it influences the number of features and the performance.

7.5 Rescaling the Data with tf–idf

Instead of dropping features that are deemed unimportant, another approach is to rescale features by how informative we expect them to be. One of the most common ways to do this is using the *term frequency–inverse document frequency* (tf–idf) method. The intuition of this method is to give high weight to any term that appears often in a particular document, but not in many documents in the corpus. If a word appears often in a particular document, but not in very many documents, it is likely to be very descriptive of the content of that document. `scikit-learn` implements the tf–idf method in two classes: `TfidfTransformer`, which takes in the sparse matrix output produced by `CountVectorizer` and transforms it, and `TfidfVectorizer`, which takes in the text data and does both the bag-of-words feature extraction and the tf–idf transformation. There are several variants of the tf–idf rescaling scheme, which you can read about on Wikipedia (*https://en.wikipedia.org/wiki/Tf-idf*). The tf–

idf score for word w in document d as implemented in both the `TfidfTransformer` and `TfidfVectorizer` classes is given by:[8]

$$\text{tfidf}(w, d) = \text{tf} * \log\left(\frac{N+1}{N_w+1}\right) + 1$$

where N is the number of documents in the training set, N_w is the number of documents in the training set that the word w appears in, and *tf* (the term frequency) is the number of times that the word w appears in the query document d (the document you want to transform or encode). Both classes also apply L2 normalization after computing the tf–idf representation; in other words, they rescale the representation of each document to have Euclidean length 1.[9] Rescaling in this way means that the length of a document (the number of words) does not change the vectorized representation.

Because tf–idf actually makes use of the statistical properties of the training data, we will use a pipeline, as described in Chapter 6, to ensure the results of our grid search are valid. This leads to the following code:

In[23]:

```
from sklearn.feature_extraction.text import TfidfVectorizer
from sklearn.pipeline import make_pipeline
pipe = make_pipeline(TfidfVectorizer(min_df=5),
                     LogisticRegression())
param_grid = {'logisticregression__C': [0.001, 0.01, 0.1, 1, 10]}

grid = GridSearchCV(pipe, param_grid, cv=5)
grid.fit(text_train, y_train)
print("Best cross-validation score: {:.2f}".format(grid.best_score_))
```

Out[23]:

```
Best cross-validation score: 0.89
```

In this case, tf–idf had no impact. We can also inspect which words tf–idf found most important. Keep in mind that the tf–idf scaling is meant to find words that distinguish documents, but it is a purely unsupervised technique. So, "important" here does not necessarily relate to the "positive review" and "negative review" labels we are interested in. First, we extract the `TfidfVectorizer` from the pipeline:

8 We provide this formula here mostly for completeness; you don't need to remember it to use the tf–idf encoding.

9 This simply means each row is divided by its sum of squared entries.

In[24]:

```
vectorizer = grid.best_estimator_.named_steps["tfidfvectorizer"]
# transform the training dataset
X_train = vectorizer.transform(text_train)
# find maximum value for each of the features over the dataset
max_value = X_train.max(axis=0).toarray().ravel()
sorted_by_tfidf = max_value.argsort()
# get feature names
feature_names = np.array(vectorizer.get_feature_names())

print("Features with lowest tfidf:\n{}".format(
    feature_names[sorted_by_tfidf[:20]]))

print("Features with highest tfidf: \n{}".format(
    feature_names[sorted_by_tfidf[-20:]]))
```

Out[24]:

```
Features with lowest tfidf:
['poignant' 'disagree' 'instantly' 'importantly' 'lacked' 'occurred'
 'currently' 'altogether' 'nearby' 'undoubtedly' 'directs' 'fond' 'stinker'
 'avoided' 'emphasis' 'commented' 'disappoint' 'realizing' 'downhill'
 'inane']
Features with highest tfidf:
['coop' 'homer' 'dillinger' 'hackenstein' 'gadget' 'taker' 'macarthur'
 'vargas' 'jesse' 'basket' 'dominick' 'the' 'victor' 'bridget' 'victoria'
 'khouri' 'zizek' 'rob' 'timon' 'titanic']
```

Features with low tf–idf are those that either are very commonly used across documents or are only used sparingly, and only in very long documents. Interestingly, many of the high-tf–idf features actually identify certain shows or movies. These terms only appear in reviews for this particular show or franchise, but tend to appear very often in these particular reviews. This is very clear, for example, for `"homer"`, `"timon"`, and `"titanic"`. These words are unlikely to help us in our sentiment classification task (unless maybe some franchises are universally reviewed positively or negatively) but certainly contain a lot of specific information about the reviews.

We can also find the words that have low inverse document frequency—that is, those that appear frequently and are therefore deemed less important. The inverse document frequency values found on the training set are stored in the `idf_` attribute:

In[25]:

```
sorted_by_idf = np.argsort(vectorizer.idf_)
print("Features with lowest idf:\n{}".format(
    feature_names[sorted_by_idf[:100]]))
```

Out[25]:

```
Features with lowest idf:
['the' 'and' 'of' 'to' 'this' 'is' 'it' 'in' 'that' 'but' 'for' 'with'
 'was' 'as' 'on' 'movie' 'not' 'have' 'one' 'be' 'film' 'are' 'you' 'all'
 'at' 'an' 'by' 'so' 'from' 'like' 'who' 'they' 'there' 'if' 'his' 'out'
```

```
 'just' 'about' 'he' 'or' 'has' 'what' 'some' 'good' 'can' 'more' 'when'
 'time' 'up' 'very' 'even' 'only' 'no' 'would' 'my' 'see' 'really' 'story'
 'which' 'well' 'had' 'me' 'than' 'much' 'their' 'get' 'were' 'other'
 'been' 'do' 'most' 'don' 'her' 'also' 'into' 'first' 'made' 'how' 'great'
 'because' 'will' 'people' 'make' 'way' 'could' 'we' 'bad' 'after' 'any'
 'too' 'then' 'them' 'she' 'watch' 'think' 'acting' 'movies' 'seen' 'its'
 'him']
```

As expected, these are mostly English stopwords like "the" and "no". But some are clearly domain-specific to the movie reviews, like "movie", "film", "time", "story", and so on. Interestingly, "good", "great", and "bad" are also among the most frequent and therefore "least relevant" words according to the tf–idf measure, even though we might expect these to be very important for our sentiment analysis task.

7.6 Investigating Model Coefficients

Finally, let's look in a bit more detail into what our logistic regression model actually learned from the data. Because there are so many features—27,271 after removing the infrequent ones—we clearly cannot look at all of the coefficients at the same time. However, we can look at the largest coefficients, and see which words these correspond to. We will use the last model that we trained, based on the tf–idf features.

The following bar chart (Figure 7-2) shows the 25 largest and 25 smallest coefficients of the logistic regression model, with the bars showing the size of each coefficient:

In[26]:

```
mglearn.tools.visualize_coefficients(
    grid.best_estimator_.named_steps["logisticregression"].coef_,
    feature_names, n_top_features=40)
```

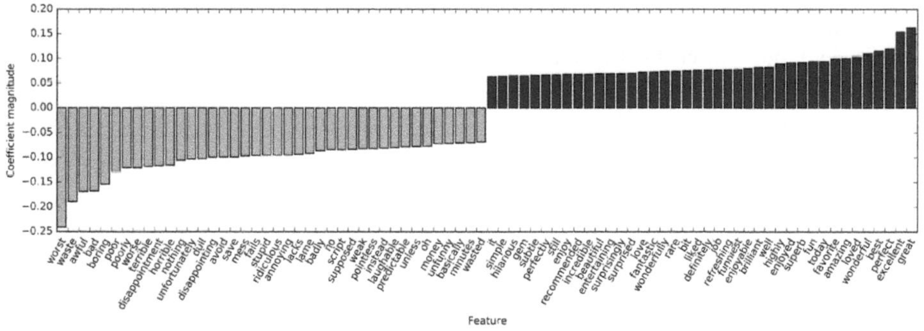

Figure 7-2. Largest and smallest coefficients of logistic regression trained on tf–idf features

The negative coefficients on the left belong to words that according to the model are indicative of negative reviews, while the positive coefficients on the right belong to words that according to the model indicate positive reviews. Most of the terms are quite intuitive, like "worst", "waste", "disappointment", and "laughable" indicating bad movie reviews, while "excellent", "wonderful", "enjoyable", and "refreshing" indicate positive movie reviews. Some words are slightly less clear, like "bit", "job", and "today", but these might be part of phrases like "good job" or "best today."

7.7 Bag-of-Words with More Than One Word (n-Grams)

One of the main disadvantages of using a bag-of-words representation is that word order is completely discarded. Therefore, the two strings "it's bad, not good at all" and "it's good, not bad at all" have exactly the same representation, even though the meanings are inverted. Putting "not" in front of a word is only one example (if an extreme one) of how context matters. Fortunately, there is a way of capturing context when using a bag-of-words representation, by not only considering the counts of single tokens, but also the counts of pairs or triplets of tokens that appear next to each other. Pairs of tokens are known as *bigrams*, triplets of tokens are known as *trigrams*, and more generally sequences of tokens are known as *n-grams*. We can change the range of tokens that are considered as features by changing the `ngram_range` parameter of `CountVectorizer` or `TfidfVectorizer`. The `ngram_range` parameter is a tuple, consisting of the minimum length and the maximum length of the sequences of tokens that are considered. Here is an example on the toy data we used earlier:

In[27]:

```
print("bards_words:\n{}".format(bards_words))
```

Out[27]:

```
bards_words:
['The fool doth think he is wise,',
 'but the wise man knows himself to be a fool']
```

The default is to create one feature per sequence of tokens that is at least one token long and at most one token long, or in other words exactly one token long (single tokens are also called *unigrams*):

In[28]:

```
cv = CountVectorizer(ngram_range=(1, 1)).fit(bards_words)
print("Vocabulary size: {}".format(len(cv.vocabulary_)))
print("Vocabulary:\n{}".format(cv.get_feature_names()))
```

Out[28]:

```
Vocabulary size: 13
Vocabulary:
['be', 'but', 'doth', 'fool', 'he', 'himself', 'is', 'knows', 'man', 'the',
 'think', 'to', 'wise']
```

To look only at bigrams—that is, only at sequences of two tokens following each other—we can set `ngram_range` to `(2, 2)`:

In[29]:

```
cv = CountVectorizer(ngram_range=(2, 2)).fit(bards_words)
print("Vocabulary size: {}".format(len(cv.vocabulary_)))
print("Vocabulary:\n{}".format(cv.get_feature_names()))
```

Out[29]:

```
Vocabulary size: 14
Vocabulary:
['be fool', 'but the', 'doth think', 'fool doth', 'he is', 'himself to',
 'is wise', 'knows himself', 'man knows', 'the fool', 'the wise',
 'think he', 'to be', 'wise man']
```

Using longer sequences of tokens usually results in many more features, and in more specific features. There is no common bigram between the two phrases in `bard_words`:

In[30]:

```
print("Transformed data (dense):\n{}".format(cv.transform(bards_words).toarray()))
```

Out[30]:

```
Transformed data (dense):
[[0 0 1 1 1 0 1 0 0 1 0 1 0 0]
 [1 1 0 0 0 1 0 1 1 0 1 0 1 1]]
```

For most applications, the minimum number of tokens should be one, as single words often capture a lot of meaning. Adding bigrams helps in most cases. Adding longer sequences—up to 5-grams—might help too, but this will lead to an explosion of the number of features and might lead to overfitting, as there will be many very specific features. In principle, the number of bigrams could be the number of unigrams squared and the number of trigrams could be the number of unigrams to the power of three, leading to very large feature spaces. In practice, the number of higher *n*-grams that actually appear in the data is much smaller, because of the structure of the (English) language, though it is still large.

Here is what using unigrams, bigrams, and trigrams on `bards_words` looks like:

In[31]:

```
cv = CountVectorizer(ngram_range=(1, 3)).fit(bards_words)
print("Vocabulary size: {}".format(len(cv.vocabulary_)))
print("Vocabulary:\n{}".format(cv.get_feature_names()))
```

Out[31]:

```
Vocabulary size: 39
Vocabulary:
['be', 'be fool', 'but', 'but the', 'but the wise', 'doth', 'doth think',
 'doth think he', 'fool', 'fool doth', 'fool doth think', 'he', 'he is',
 'he is wise', 'himself', 'himself to', 'himself to be', 'is', 'is wise',
 'knows', 'knows himself', 'knows himself to', 'man', 'man knows',
 'man knows himself', 'the', 'the fool', 'the fool doth', 'the wise',
 'the wise man', 'think', 'think he', 'think he is', 'to', 'to be',
 'to be fool', 'wise', 'wise man', 'wise man knows']
```

Let's try out the `TfidfVectorizer` on the IMDb movie review data and find the best setting of *n*-gram range using a grid search:

In[32]:

```
pipe = make_pipeline(TfidfVectorizer(min_df=5), LogisticRegression())
# running the grid search takes a long time because of the
# relatively large grid and the inclusion of trigrams
param_grid = {"logisticregression__C": [0.001, 0.01, 0.1, 1, 10, 100],
              "tfidfvectorizer__ngram_range": [(1, 1), (1, 2), (1, 3)]}

grid = GridSearchCV(pipe, param_grid, cv=5)
grid.fit(text_train, y_train)
print("Best cross-validation score: {:.2f}".format(grid.best_score_))
print("Best parameters:\n{}".format(grid.best_params_))
```

Out[32]:

```
Best cross-validation score: 0.91
Best parameters:
{'tfidfvectorizer__ngram_range': (1, 3), 'logisticregression__C': 100}
```

As you can see from the results, we improved performance by a bit more than a percent by adding bigram and trigram features. We can visualize the cross-validation accuracy as a function of the `ngram_range` and `C` parameter as a heat map, as we did in Chapter 5 (see Figure 7-3):

In[33]:

```
# extract scores from grid_search
scores = grid.cv_results_['mean_test_score'].reshape(-1, 3).T
# visualize heat map
heatmap = mglearn.tools.heatmap(
    scores, xlabel="C", ylabel="ngram_range", cmap="viridis", fmt="%.3f",
    xticklabels=param_grid['logisticregression__C'],
    yticklabels=param_grid['tfidfvectorizer__ngram_range'])
plt.colorbar(heatmap)
```

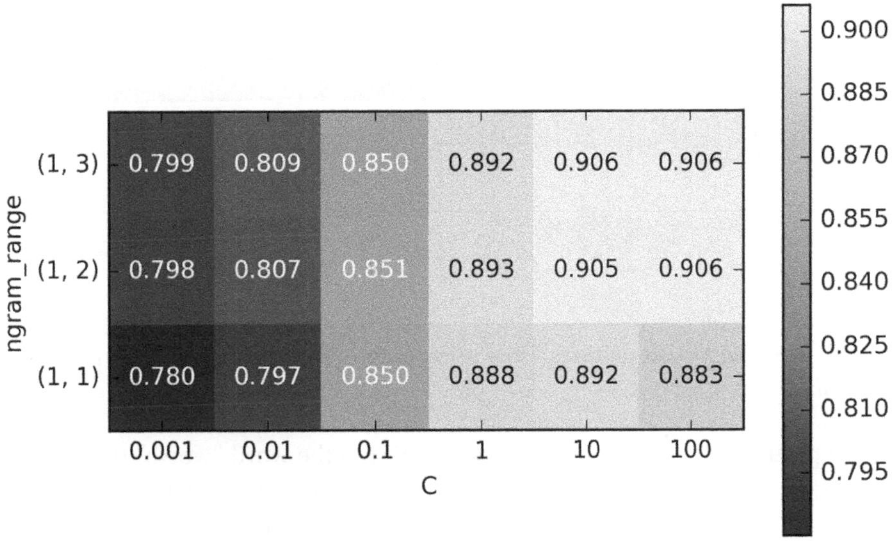

Figure 7-3. Heat map visualization of mean cross-validation accuracy as a function of the parameters ngram_range and C

From the heat map we can see that using bigrams increases performance quite a bit, while adding trigrams only provides a very small benefit in terms of accuracy. To understand better how the model improved, we can visualize the important coefficient for the best model, which includes unigrams, bigrams, and trigrams (see Figure 7-4):

In[34]:

```
# extract feature names and coefficients
vect = grid.best_estimator_.named_steps['tfidfvectorizer']
feature_names = np.array(vect.get_feature_names())
coef = grid.best_estimator_.named_steps['logisticregression'].coef_
mglearn.tools.visualize_coefficients(coef, feature_names, n_top_features=40)
```

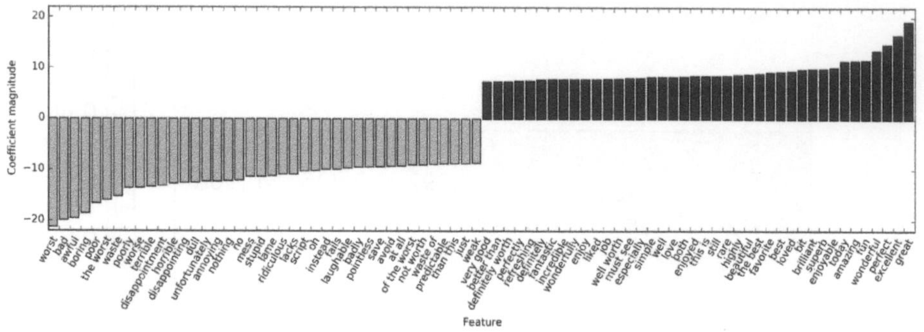

Figure 7-4. Most important features when using unigrams, bigrams, and trigrams with tf-idf rescaling

There are particularly interesting features containing the word "worth" that were not present in the unigram model: `"not worth"` is indicative of a negative review, while `"definitely worth"` and `"well worth"` are indicative of a positive review. This is a prime example of context influencing the meaning of the word "worth."

Next, we'll visualize only trigrams, to provide further insight into why these features are helpful. Many of the useful bigrams and trigrams consist of common words that would not be informative on their own, as in the phrases `"none of the"`, `"the only good"`, `"on and on"`, `"this is one"`, `"of the most"`, and so on. However, the impact of these features is quite limited compared to the importance of the unigram features, as you can see in Figure 7-5:

In[35]:

```
# find 3-gram features
mask = np.array([len(feature.split(" ")) for feature in feature_names]) == 3
# visualize only 3-gram features
mglearn.tools.visualize_coefficients(coef.ravel()[mask],
                                     feature_names[mask], n_top_features=40)
```

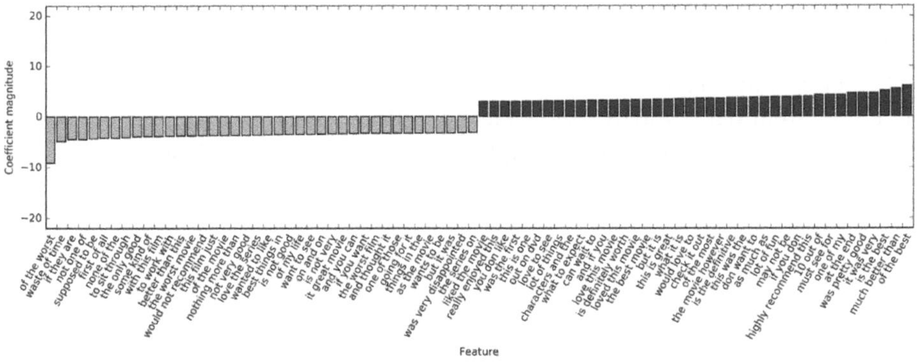

Figure 7-5. Visualization of only the important trigram features of the model

7.8 Advanced Tokenization, Stemming, and Lemmatization

As mentioned previously, the feature extraction in the `CountVectorizer` and `TfidfVectorizer` is relatively simple, and much more elaborate methods are possible. One particular step that is often improved in more sophisticated text-processing applications is the first step in the bag-of-words model: tokenization. This step defines what constitutes a word for the purpose of feature extraction.

We saw earlier that the vocabulary often contains singular and plural versions of some words, as in `"drawback"` and `"drawbacks"`, `"drawer"` and `"drawers"`, and `"drawing"` and `"drawings"`. For the purposes of a bag-of-words model, the semantics of `"drawback"` and `"drawbacks"` are so close that distinguishing them will only increase overfitting, and not allow the model to fully exploit the training data. Similarly, we found the vocabulary includes words like `"replace"`, `"replaced"`, `"replacement"`, `"replaces"`, and `"replacing"`, which are different verb forms and a noun relating to the verb "to replace." Similarly to having singular and plural forms of a noun, treating different verb forms and related words as distinct tokens is disadvantageous for building a model that generalizes well.

This problem can be overcome by representing each word using its *word stem*, which involves identifying (or *conflating*) all the words that have the same word stem. If this is done by using a rule-based heuristic, like dropping common suffixes, it is usually referred to as *stemming*. If instead a dictionary of known word forms is used (an explicit and human-verified system), and the role of the word in the sentence is taken into account, the process is referred to as *lemmatization* and the standardized form of the word is referred to as the *lemma*. Both processing methods, lemmatization and stemming, are forms of *normalization* that try to extract some normal form of a word. Another interesting case of normalization is spelling correction, which can be helpful in practice but is outside of the scope of this book.

To get a better understanding of normalization, let's compare a method for stemming —the Porter stemmer, a widely used collection of heuristics (here imported from the `nltk` package)—to lemmatization as implemented in the `spacy` package:[10]

To run this code, you need to install both `nltk` and `spacy`, by running the following on the command line:

```
conda install nltk spacy
```

You also need to download the English language support for `spacy` by executing

```
python -m spacy download en
```

on the command line. We are using the following versions of the two libraries:

In[36]:

```
import spacy
print("SpaCy version: {}".format(spacy.__version__))
import sklearn
print("nltk version: {}".format(nltk.__version__))
```

In[37]:

```
import spacy
import nltk

# load spacy's English-language models
en_nlp = spacy.load('en')
# instantiate nltk's Porter stemmer
stemmer = nltk.stem.PorterStemmer()

# define function to compare lemmatization in spacy with stemming in nltk
def compare_normalization(doc):
    # tokenize document in spacy
    doc_spacy = en_nlp(doc)
    # print lemmas found by spacy
    print("Lemmatization:")
    print([token.lemma_ for token in doc_spacy])
    # print tokens found by Porter stemmer
    print("Stemming:")
    print([stemmer.stem(token.norm_.lower()) for token in doc_spacy])
```

We will compare lemmatization and the Porter stemmer on a sentence designed to show some of the differences:

10 For details of the interface, consult the `nltk` (*http://www.nltk.org/*) and `spacy` (*https://spacy.io/docs/*) documentation. We are more interested in the general principles here.

In[38]:

```
compare_normalization(u"Our meeting today was worse than yesterday, "
                      "I'm scared of meeting the clients tomorrow.")
```

Out[38]:

```
Lemmatization:
['our', 'meeting', 'today', 'be', 'bad', 'than', 'yesterday', ',', 'i', 'be',
 'scared', 'of', 'meet', 'the', 'client', 'tomorrow', '.']
Stemming:
['our', 'meet', 'today', 'wa', 'wors', 'than', 'yesterday', ',', 'i', "'m",
 'scare', 'of', 'meet', 'the', 'client', 'tomorrow', '.']
```

Stemming is always restricted to trimming the word to a stem, so `"was"` becomes `"wa"`, while lemmatization can retrieve the correct base verb form, `"be"`. Similarly, lemmatization can normalize `"worse"` to `"bad"`, while stemming produces `"wors"`. Another major difference is that stemming reduces both occurrences of `"meeting"` to `"meet"`. Using lemmatization, the first occurrence of `"meeting"` is recognized as a noun and left as is, while the second occurrence is recognized as a verb and reduced to `"meet"`. In general, lemmatization is a much more involved process than stemming, but it usually produces better results than stemming when used for normalizing tokens for machine learning.

While `scikit-learn` implements neither form of normalization, `CountVectorizer` allows specifying your own tokenizer to convert each document into a list of tokens using the `tokenizer` parameter. We can use the lemmatization from `spacy` to create a callable that will take a string and produce a list of lemmas:

In[39]:

```
# Technicality: we want to use the regexp-based tokenizer
# that is used by CountVectorizer and only use the lemmatization
# from spacy. To this end, we replace en_nlp.tokenizer (the spacy tokenizer)
# with the regexp-based tokenization.
import re
# regexp used in CountVectorizer
regexp = re.compile('(?u)\\b\\w\\w+\\b')

# load spacy language model
en_nlp = spacy.load('en', disable=['parser', 'ner'])
old_tokenizer = en_nlp.tokenizer
# replace the tokenizer with the preceding regexp
en_nlp.tokenizer = lambda string: old_tokenizer.tokens_from_list(
    regexp.findall(string))

# create a custom tokenizer using the spacy document processing pipeline
# (now using our own tokenizer)
def custom_tokenizer(document):
    doc_spacy = en_nlp(document)
    return [token.lemma_ for token in doc_spacy]
```

```
# define a count vectorizer with the custom tokenizer
lemma_vect = CountVectorizer(tokenizer=custom_tokenizer, min_df=5)
```

Let's transform the data and inspect the vocabulary size:

In[40]:

```
# transform text_train using CountVectorizer with lemmatization
X_train_lemma = lemma_vect.fit_transform(text_train)
print("X_train_lemma.shape: {}".format(X_train_lemma.shape))

# standard CountVectorizer for reference
vect = CountVectorizer(min_df=5).fit(text_train)
X_train = vect.transform(text_train)
print("X_train.shape: {}".format(X_train.shape))
```

Out[40]:

```
X_train_lemma.shape:  (25000, 21596)
X_train.shape:  (25000, 27271)
```

As you can see from the output, lemmatization reduced the number of features from 27,271 (with the standard `CountVectorizer` processing) to 21,596. Lemmatization can be seen as a kind of regularization, as it conflates certain features. Therefore, we expect lemmatization to improve performance most when the dataset is small. To illustrate how lemmatization can help, we will use `StratifiedShuffleSplit` for cross-validation, using only 1% of the data as training data and the rest as test data:

In[41]:

```
# build a grid search using only 1% of the data as the training set
from sklearn.model_selection import StratifiedShuffleSplit

param_grid = {'C': [0.001, 0.01, 0.1, 1, 10]}
cv = StratifiedShuffleSplit(n_splits=5, test_size=0.99,
                            train_size=0.01, random_state=0)
grid = GridSearchCV(LogisticRegression(), param_grid, cv=cv)
# perform grid search with standard CountVectorizer
grid.fit(X_train, y_train)
print("Best cross-validation score "
      "(standard CountVectorizer): {:.3f}".format(grid.best_score_))
# perform grid search with lemmatization
grid.fit(X_train_lemma, y_train)
print("Best cross-validation score "
      "(lemmatization): {:.3f}".format(grid.best_score_))
```

Out[41]:

```
Best cross-validation score (standard CountVectorizer): 0.721
Best cross-validation score (lemmatization): 0.731
```

In this case, lemmatization provided a modest improvement in performance. As with many of the different feature extraction techniques, the result varies depending on the dataset. Lemmatization and stemming can sometimes help in building better (or at least more compact) models, so we suggest you give these techniques a try when trying to squeeze out the last bit of performance on a particular task.

7.9 Topic Modeling and Document Clustering

One particular technique that is often applied to text data is *topic modeling*, which is an umbrella term describing the task of assigning each document to one or multiple *topics*, usually without supervision. A good example for this is news data, which might be categorized into topics like "politics," "sports," "finance," and so on. If each document is assigned a single topic, this is the task of clustering the documents, as discussed in Chapter 3. If each document can have more than one topic, the task relates to the decomposition methods from Chapter 3. Each of the components we learn then corresponds to one topic, and the coefficients of the components in the representation of a document tell us how strongly related that document is to a particular topic. Often, when people talk about topic modeling, they refer to one particular decomposition method called *Latent Dirichlet Allocation* (often LDA for short).[11]

7.9.1 Latent Dirichlet Allocation

Intuitively, the LDA model tries to find groups of words (the topics) that appear together frequently. LDA also requires that each document can be understood as a "mixture" of a subset of the topics. It is important to understand that for the machine learning model a "topic" might not be what we would normally call a topic in everyday speech, but that it resembles more the components extracted by PCA or NMF (which we discussed in Chapter 3), which might or might not have a semantic meaning. Even if there is a semantic meaning for an LDA "topic", it might not be something we'd usually call a topic. Going back to the example of news articles, we might have a collection of articles about sports, politics, and finance, written by two specific authors. In a politics article, we might expect to see words like "governor," "vote," "party," etc., while in a sports article we might expect words like "team," "score," and "season." Words in each of these groups will likely appear together, while it's less likely that, for example, "team" and "governor" will appear together. However, these are not the only groups of words we might expect to appear together. The two reporters might prefer different phrases or different choices of words. Maybe one of them likes to use the word "demarcate" and one likes the word "polarize." Other "topics" would

11 There is another machine learning model that is also often abbreviated LDA: Linear Discriminant Analysis, a linear classification model. This leads to quite some confusion. In this book, LDA refers to Latent Dirichlet Allocation.

then be "words often used by reporter A" and "words often used by reporter B," though these are not topics in the usual sense of the word.

Let's apply LDA to our movie review dataset to see how it works in practice. For unsupervised text document models, it is often good to remove very common words, as they might otherwise dominate the analysis. We'll remove words that appear in at least 15 percent of the documents, and we'll limit the bag-of-words model to the 10,000 words that are most common after removing the top 15 percent:

In[42]:

```
vect = CountVectorizer(max_features=10000, max_df=.15)
X = vect.fit_transform(text_train)
```

We will learn a topic model with 10 topics, which is few enough that we can look at all of them. Similarly to the components in NMF, topics don't have an inherent ordering, and changing the number of topics will change all of the topics.[12] We'll use the "batch" learning method, which is somewhat slower than the default ("online") but usually provides better results, and increase "max_iter", which can also lead to better models:

In[43]:

```
from sklearn.decomposition import LatentDirichletAllocation
lda = LatentDirichletAllocation(n_topics=10, learning_method="batch",
                                max_iter=25, random_state=0)
# We build the model and transform the data in one step
# Computing transform takes some time,
# and we can save time by doing both at once
document_topics = lda.fit_transform(X)
```

Like the decomposition methods we saw in Chapter 3, `LatentDirichletAllocation` has a `components_` attribute that stores how important each word is for each topic. The size of `components_` is `(n_topics, n_words)`:

In[44]:

```
print("lda.components_.shape: {}".format(lda.components_.shape))
```

Out[44]:

```
lda.components_.shape: (10, 10000)
```

To understand better what the different topics mean, we will look at the most important words for each of the topics. The `print_topics` function provides a nice formatting for these features:

12 In fact, NMF and LDA solve quite related problems, and we could also use NMF to extract topics.

In[45]:

```
# For each topic (a row in the components_), sort the features (ascending)
# Invert rows with [:, ::-1] to make sorting descending
sorting = np.argsort(lda.components_, axis=1)[:, ::-1]
# Get the feature names from the vectorizer
feature_names = np.array(vect.get_feature_names())
```

In[46]:

```
# Print out the 10 topics:
mglearn.tools.print_topics(topics=range(10), feature_names=feature_names,
                           sorting=sorting, topics_per_chunk=5, n_words=10)
```

Out[46]:

```
topic 0       topic 1       topic 2       topic 3       topic 4
--------      --------      --------      --------      --------
between       war           funny         show          didn
young         world         worst         series        saw
family        us            comedy        episode       am
real          our           thing         tv            thought
performance   american      guy           episodes      years
beautiful     documentary   re            shows         book
work          history       stupid        season        watched
each          new           actually      new           now
both          own           nothing       television    dvd
director      point         want          years         got


topic 5       topic 6       topic 7       topic 8       topic 9
--------      --------      --------      --------      --------
horror        kids          cast          performance   house
action        action        role          role          woman
effects       animation     john          john          gets
budget        game          version       actor         killer
nothing       fun           novel         oscar         girl
original      disney        both          cast          wife
director      children      director      plays         horror
minutes       10            played        jack          young
pretty        kid           performance   joe           goes
doesn         old           mr            performances  around
```

Judging from the important words, topic 1 seems to be about historical and war movies, topic 2 might be about bad comedies, topic 3 might be about TV series. Topic 4 seems to capture some very common words, while topic 6 appears to be about children's movies and topic 8 seems to capture award-related reviews. Using only 10 topics, each of the topics needs to be very broad, so that they can together cover all the different kinds of reviews in our dataset.

Next, we will learn another model, this time with 100 topics. Using more topics makes the analysis much harder, but makes it more likely that topics can specialize to interesting subsets of the data:

In[47]:

```
lda100 = LatentDirichletAllocation(n_topics=100, learning_method="batch",
                                   max_iter=25, random_state=0)
document_topics100 = lda100.fit_transform(X)
```

Looking at all 100 topics would be a bit overwhelming, so we selected some interesting and representative topics:

In[48]:

```
topics = np.array([7, 16, 24, 25, 28, 36, 37, 45, 51, 53, 54, 63, 89, 97])

sorting = np.argsort(lda100.components_, axis=1)[:, ::-1]
feature_names = np.array(vect.get_feature_names())
mglearn.tools.print_topics(topics=topics, feature_names=feature_names,
                           sorting=sorting, topics_per_chunk=5, n_words=20)
```

Out[48]:

```
topic 7       topic 16      topic 24      topic 25      topic 28
--------      --------      --------      --------      --------
thriller      worst         german        car           beautiful
suspense      awful         hitler        gets          young
horror        boring        nazi          guy           old
atmosphere    horrible      midnight      around        romantic
mystery       stupid        joe           down          between
house         thing         germany       kill          romance
director      terrible      years         goes          wonderful
quite         script        history       killed        heart
bit           nothing       new           going         feel
de            worse         modesty       house         year
performances  waste         cowboy        away          each
dark          pretty        jewish        head          french
twist         minutes       past          take          sweet
hitchcock     didn          kirk          another       boy
tension       actors        young         getting       loved
interesting   actually      spanish       doesn         girl
mysterious    re            enterprise    now           relationship
murder        supposed      von           night         saw
ending        mean          nazis         right         both
creepy        want          spock         woman         simple


topic 36      topic 37      topic 41      topic 45      topic 51
--------      --------      --------      --------      --------
performance   excellent     war           music         earth
role          highly        american      song          space
actor         amazing       world         songs         planet
cast          wonderful     soldiers      rock          superman
play          truly         military      band          alien
actors        superb        army          soundtrack    world
performances  actors        tarzan        singing       evil
played        brilliant     soldier       voice         humans
supporting    recommend     america       singer        aliens
director      quite         country       sing          human
oscar         performance   americans     musical       creatures
```

```
roles          performances  during        roll          mike
actress        perfect       men           fan           monsters
excellent      drama         us            metal         apes
screen         without       government    concert       clark
plays          beautiful     jungle        playing       burton
award          human         vietnam       hear          tim
work           moving        ii            fans          outer
playing        world         political     prince        men
gives          recommended   against       especially    moon


topic 53       topic 54      topic 63      topic 89      topic 97
--------       --------      --------      --------      --------
scott          money         funny         dead          didn
gary           budget        comedy        zombie        thought
streisand      actors        laugh         gore          wasn
star           low           jokes         zombies       ending
hart           worst         humor         blood         minutes
lundgren       waste         hilarious     horror        got
dolph          10            laughs        flesh         felt
career         give          fun           minutes       part
sabrina        want          re            body          going
role           nothing       funniest      living        seemed
temple         terrible      laughing      eating        bit
phantom        crap          joke          flick         found
judy           must          few           budget        though
melissa        reviews       moments       head          nothing
zorro          imdb          guy           gory          lot
gets           director      unfunny       evil          saw
barbra         thing         times         shot          long
cast           believe       laughed       low           interesting
short          am            comedies      fulci         few
serial         actually      isn           re            half
```

The topics we extracted this time seem to be more specific, though many are hard to interpret. Topic 7 seems to be about horror movies and thrillers; topics 16 and 54 seem to capture bad reviews, while topic 63 mostly seems to be capturing positive reviews of comedies. If we want to make further inferences using the topics that were discovered, we should confirm the intuition we gained from looking at the highest-ranking words for each topic by looking at the documents that are assigned to these topics. For example, topic 45 seems to be about music. Let's check which kinds of reviews are assigned to this topic:

In[49]:

```
# sort by weight of "music" topic 45
music = np.argsort(document_topics100[:, 45])[::-1]
# print the five documents where the topic is most important
for i in music[:10]:
    # show first two sentences
    print(b".".join(text_train[i].split(b".")[:2]) + b".\n")
```

Out[49]:

```
b'I love this movie and never get tired of watching. The music in it is great.\n'
b"I enjoyed Still Crazy more than any film I have seen in years. A successful
  band from the 70's decide to give it another try.\n"
b'Hollywood Hotel was the last movie musical that Busby Berkeley directed for
  Warner Bros. His directing style had changed or evolved to the point that
  this film does not contain his signature overhead shots or huge production
  numbers with thousands of extras.\n'
b"What happens to washed up rock-n-roll stars in the late 1990's?
  They launch a comeback / reunion tour. At least, that's what the members of
  Strange Fruit, a (fictional) 70's stadium rock group do.\n"
b'As a big-time Prince fan of the last three to four years, I really can\'t
  believe I\'ve only just got round to watching "Purple Rain". The brand new
  2-disc anniversary Special Edition led me to buy it.\n'
b"This film is worth seeing alone for Jared Harris' outstanding portrayal
  of John Lennon. It doesn't matter that Harris doesn't exactly resemble
  Lennon; his mannerisms, expressions, posture, accent and attitude are
  pure Lennon.\n"
b"The funky, yet strictly second-tier British glam-rock band Strange Fruit
  breaks up at the end of the wild'n'wacky excess-ridden 70's. The individual
  band members go their separate ways and uncomfortably settle into lackluster
  middle age in the dull and uneventful 90's: morose keyboardist Stephen Rea
  winds up penniless and down on his luck, vain, neurotic, pretentious lead
  singer Bill Nighy tries (and fails) to pursue a floundering solo career,
  paranoid drummer Timothy Spall resides in obscurity on a remote farm so he
  can avoid paying a hefty back taxes debt, and surly bass player Jimmy Nail
  installs roofs for a living.\n"
b"I just finished reading a book on Anita Loos' work and the photo in TCM
  Magazine of MacDonald in her angel costume looked great (impressive wings),
  so I thought I'd watch this movie. I'd never heard of the film before, so I
  had no preconceived notions about it whatsoever.\n"
b'I love this movie!!! Purple Rain came out the year I was born and it has had
  my heart since I can remember. Prince is so tight in this movie.\n'
b"This movie is sort of a Carrie meets Heavy Metal. It's about a highschool
  guy who gets picked on alot and he totally gets revenge with the help of a
  Heavy Metal ghost.\n"
```

As we can see, this topic covers a wide variety of music-centered reviews, from musicals, to biographical movies, to some hard-to-specify genre in the last review. Another interesting way to inspect the topics is to see how much weight each topic gets overall, by summing the `document_topics` over all reviews. We name each topic by the two most common words. Figure 7-6 shows the topic weights learned:

In[50]:

```
fig, ax = plt.subplots(1, 2, figsize=(10, 10))
topic_names = ["{:>2} ".format(i) + " ".join(words)
               for i, words in enumerate(feature_names[sorting[:, :2]])]
# two column bar chart:
for col in [0, 1]:
    start = col * 50
```

```
    end = (col + 1) * 50
    ax[col].barh(np.arange(50), np.sum(document_topics100, axis=0)[start:end])
    ax[col].set_yticks(np.arange(50))
    ax[col].set_yticklabels(topic_names[start:end], ha="left", va="top")
    ax[col].invert_yaxis()
    ax[col].set_xlim(0, 2000)
    yax = ax[col].get_yaxis()
    yax.set_tick_params(pad=130)
plt.tight_layout()
```

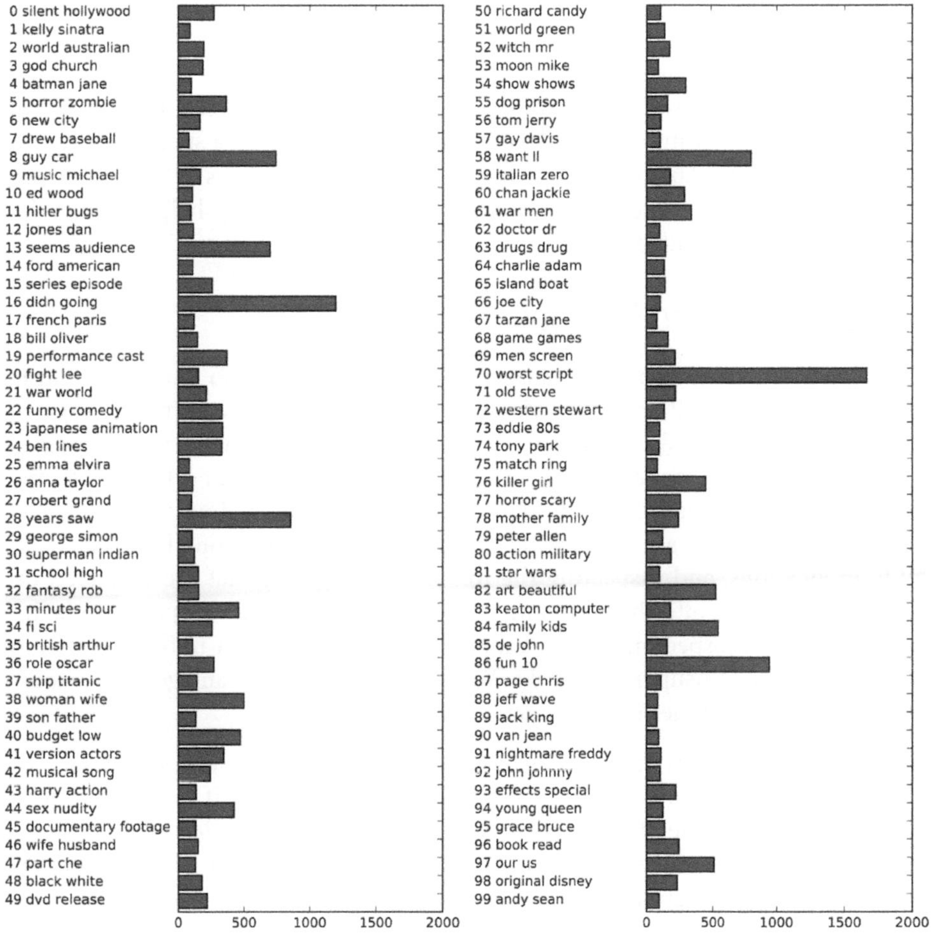

Figure 7-6. Topic weights learned by LDA

The most important topics are 70, which seems to correspond to a negative sentiment; 16, 13 and 58, which seem to contain stop words; and 86, which is associated with positive reviews. The "10" in 86 likely corresponds to a 10 out of 10 rating mentioned in the comment. These main topics are followed by more genre-specific topics like 8, 38, 40, 44, 76, 82, and 84.

It seems like LDA mostly discovered two kind of topics, genre-specific and rating-specific, in addition to several more unspecific topics. This is an interesting discovery, as most reviews are made up of some movie-specific comments and some comments that justify or emphasize the rating.

Topic models like LDA are interesting methods to understand large text corpora in the absence of labels—or, as here, even if labels are available. The LDA algorithm is randomized, though, and changing the `random_state` parameter can lead to quite different outcomes. While identifying topics can be helpful, any conclusions you draw from an unsupervised model should be taken with a grain of salt, and we recommend verifying your intuition by looking at the documents in a specific topic. The topics produced by the `LDA.transform` method can also sometimes be used as a compact representation for supervised learning. This is particularly helpful when few training examples are available.

7.10 Summary and Outlook

In this chapter we talked about the basics of processing text, also known as *natural language processing* (NLP), with an example application classifying movie reviews. The tools discussed here should serve as a great starting point when trying to process text data. In particular for text classification tasks such as spam and fraud detection or sentiment analysis, bag-of-words representations provide a simple and powerful solution. As is often the case in machine learning, the representation of the data is key in NLP applications, and inspecting the tokens and *n*-grams that are extracted can give powerful insights into the modeling process. In text-processing applications, it is often possible to introspect models in a meaningful way, as we saw in this chapter, for both supervised and unsupervised tasks. You should take full advantage of this ability when using NLP-based methods in practice.

Natural language and text processing is a large research field, and discussing the details of advanced methods is far beyond the scope of this book. If you want to learn more, we recommend the O'Reilly book *Natural Language Processing with Python* by Steven Bird, Ewan Klein, and Edward Loper, which provides an overview of NLP together with an introduction to the `nltk` Python package for NLP. Another great and more conceptual book is the standard reference *Introduction to Information Retrieval* (*http://nlp.stanford.edu/IR-book/*) by Christopher Manning, Prabhakar Raghavan, and Hinrich Schütze, which describes fundamental algorithms in information retrieval, NLP, and machine learning. Both books have online versions that can be accessed free of charge. As we discussed earlier, the classes `CountVectorizer` and `TfidfVectorizer` only implement relatively simple text-processing methods. For more advanced text-processing methods, we recommend the Python packages `spacy` (a relatively new but very efficient and well-designed package), `nltk` (a very well-established and complete but somewhat dated library), and `gensim` (an NLP package with an emphasis on topic modeling).

There have been several very exciting new developments in text processing in recent years, which are outside of the scope of this book and relate to neural networks. The first is the use of continuous vector representations, also known as word vectors or distributed word representations, as implemented in the `word2vec` library. The original paper "Distributed Representations of Words and Phrases and Their Compositionality" (*https://papers.nips.cc/paper/5021-distributed-representations-of-words-and-phrases-and-their-compositionality.pdf*) by Thomas Mikolov et al. is a great introduction to the subject. Both `spacy` and `gensim` provide functionality for the techniques discussed in this paper and its follow-ups.

Another direction in NLP that has picked up momentum in recent years is the use of *recurrent neural networks* (RNNs) for text processing. RNNs are a particularly powerful type of neural network that can produce output that is again text, in contrast to classification models that can only assign class labels. The ability to produce text as output makes RNNs well suited for automatic translation and summarization. An introduction to the topic can be found in the relatively technical paper "Sequence to Sequence Learning with Neural Networks" (*http://papers.nips.cc/paper/5346-sequence-to-sequence-learning-with-neural-networks.pdf*) by Ilya Suskever, Oriol Vinyals, and Quoc Le. A more practical tutorial using the `tensorflow` framework can be found on the TensorFlow website (*https://www.tensorflow.org/versions/r0.8/tutorials/seq2seq/index.html*).

CHAPTER 8

Wrapping Up

You now know how to apply the important machine learning algorithms for supervised and unsupervised learning, which allow you to solve a wide variety of machine learning problems. Before we leave you to explore all the possibilities that machine learning offers, we want to give you some final words of advice, point you toward some additional resources, and give you suggestions on how you can further improve your machine learning and data science skills.

8.1 Approaching a Machine Learning Problem

With all the great methods that we introduced in this book now at your fingertips, it may be tempting to jump in and start solving your data-related problem by just running your favorite algorithm. However, this is not usually a good way to begin your analysis. The machine learning algorithm is usually only a small part of a larger data analysis and decision-making process. To make effective use of machine learning, we need to take a step back and consider the problem at large. First, you should think about what kind of question you want to answer. Do you want to do exploratory analysis and just see if you find something interesting in the data? Or do you already have a particular goal in mind? Often you will start with a goal, like detecting fraudulent user transactions, making movie recommendations, or finding unknown planets. If you have such a goal, before building a system to achieve it, you should first think about how to define and measure success, and what the impact of a successful solution would be to your overall business or research goals. Let's say your goal is fraud detection.

Then the following questions open up:

- How do I measure if my fraud prediction is actually working?
- Do I have the right data to evaluate an algorithm?
- If I am successful, what will be the business impact of my solution?

As we discussed in Chapter 5, it is best if you can measure the performance of your algorithm directly using a business metric, like increased profit or decreased losses. This is often hard to do, though. A question that can be easier to answer is "What if I built the perfect model?" If perfectly detecting any fraud will save your company $100 a month, these possible savings will probably not be enough to warrant the effort of you even starting to develop an algorithm. On the other hand, if the model might save your company tens of thousands of dollars every month, the problem might be worth exploring.

Say you've defined the problem to solve, you know a solution might have a significant impact for your project, and you've ensured that you have the right information to evaluate success. The next steps are usually acquiring the data and building a working prototype. In this book we have talked about many models you can employ, and how to properly evaluate and tune these models. While trying out models, though, keep in mind that this is only a small part of a larger data science workflow, and model building is often part of a feedback circle of collecting new data, cleaning data, building models, and analyzing the models. Analyzing the mistakes a model makes can often be informative about what is missing in the data, what additional data could be collected, or how the task could be reformulated to make machine learning more effective. Collecting more or different data or changing the task formulation slightly might provide a much higher payoff than running endless grid searches to tune parameters.

8.1.1 Humans in the Loop

You should also consider if and how you should have humans in the loop. Some processes (like pedestrian detection in a self-driving car) need to make immediate decisions. Others might not need immediate responses, and so it can be possible to have humans confirm uncertain decisions. Medical applications, for example, might need very high levels of precision that possibly cannot be achieved by a machine learning algorithm alone. But if an algorithm can make 90 percent, 50 percent, or maybe even just 10 percent of decisions automatically, that might already decrease response time or reduce cost. Many applications are dominated by "simple cases," for which an algorithm can make a decision, with relatively few "complicated cases," which can be rerouted to a human.

8.2 From Prototype to Production

The tools we've discussed in this book are great for many machine learning applications, and allow very quick analysis and prototyping. Python and `scikit-learn` are also used in production systems in many organizations—even very large ones like international banks and global social media companies. However, many companies have complex infrastructure, and it is not always easy to include Python in these systems. That is not necessarily a problem. In many companies, the data analytics teams work with languages like Python and R that allow the quick testing of ideas, while production teams work with languages like Go, Scala, C++, and Java to build robust, scalable systems. Data analysis has different requirements from building live services, and so using different languages for these tasks makes sense. A relatively common solution is to reimplement the solution that was found by the analytics team inside the larger framework, using a high-performance language. This can be easier than embedding a whole library or programming language and converting from and to the different data formats.

Regardless of whether you can use `scikit-learn` in a production system or not, it is important to keep in mind that production systems have different requirements from one-off analysis scripts. If an algorithm is deployed into a larger system, software engineering aspects like reliability, predictability, runtime, and memory requirements gain relevance. Simplicity is key in providing machine learning systems that perform well in these areas. Critically inspect each part of your data processing and prediction pipeline and ask yourself how much complexity each step creates, how robust each component is to changes in the data or compute infrastructure, and if the benefit of each component warrants the complexity. If you are building involved machine learning systems, we highly recommend reading the paper "Machine Learning: The High Interest Credit Card of Technical Debt" (*http://research.google.com/pubs/pub43146.html*), published by researchers in Google's machine learning team. The paper highlights the trade-off in creating and maintaining machine learning software in production at a large scale. While the issue of technical debt *is* particularly pressing in large-scale and long-term projects, the lessons learned can help us build better software even for short-lived and smaller systems.

8.3 Testing Production Systems

In this book, we covered how to evaluate algorithmic predictions based on a test set that we collected beforehand. This is known as *offline evaluation*. If your machine learning system is user-facing, this is only the first step in evaluating an algorithm, though. The next step is usually *online testing* or *live testing*, where the consequences of employing the algorithm in the overall system are evaluated. Changing the recommendations or search results users are shown by a website can drastically change their behavior and lead to unexpected consequences. To protect against these surprises, most user-facing services employ *A/B testing*, a form of blind user study. In A/B testing, without their knowledge a selected portion of users will be provided with a website or service using algorithm A, while the rest of the users will be provided with algorithm B. For both groups, relevant success metrics will be recorded for a set period of time. Then, the metrics of algorithm A and algorithm B will be compared, and a selection between the two approaches will be made according to these metrics. Using A/B testing enables us to evaluate the algorithms "in the wild," which might help us to discover unexpected consequences when users are interacting with our model. Often A is a new model, while B is the established system. There are more elaborate mechanisms for online testing that go beyond A/B testing, such as *bandit algorithms*. A great introduction to this subject can be found in the book *Bandit Algorithms for Website Optimization* by John Myles White (O'Reilly).

8.4 Building Your Own Estimator

This book has covered a variety of tools and algorithms implemented in `scikit-learn` that can be used on a wide range of tasks. However, often there will be some particular processing you need to do for your data that is not implemented in `scikit-learn`. It may be enough to just preprocess your data before passing it to your `scikit-learn` model or pipeline. However, if your preprocessing is data dependent, and you want to apply a grid search or cross-validation, things become trickier.

In Chapter 6 we discussed the importance of putting all data-dependent processing inside the cross-validation loop. So how can you use your own processing together with the `scikit-learn` tools? There is a simple solution: build your own estimator! Implementing an estimator that is compatible with the `scikit-learn` interface, so that it can be used with `Pipeline`, `GridSearchCV`, and `cross_val_score`, is quite easy. You can find detailed instructions in the `scikit-learn` documentation (*http://scikit-learn.org/stable/developers/contributing.html#rolling-your-own-estimator*), but here is the gist. The simplest way to implement a transformer class is by inheriting from `BaseEstimator` and `TransformerMixin`, and then implementing the `__init__`, `fit`, and `predict` functions like this:

In[1]:

```
from sklearn.base import BaseEstimator, TransformerMixin

class MyTransformer(BaseEstimator, TransformerMixin):
    def __init__(self, first_parameter=1, second_parameter=2):
        # All parameters must be specified in the __init__ function
        self.first_parameter = 1
        self.second_parameter = 2

    def fit(self, X, y=None):
        # fit should only take X and y as parameters
        # Even if your model is unsupervised, you need to accept a y argument!

        # Model fitting code goes here
        print("fitting the model right here")
        # fit returns self
        return self

    def transform(self, X):
        # transform takes as parameter only X

        # Apply some transformation to X
        X_transformed = X + 1
        return X_transformed
```

Implementing a classifier or regressor works similarly, only instead of `TransformerMixin` you need to inherit from `ClassifierMixin` or `RegressorMixin`. Also, instead of implementing `transform`, you would implement `predict`.

As you can see from the example given here, implementing your own estimator requires very little code, and most `scikit-learn` users build up a collection of custom models over time.

8.5 Where to Go from Here

This book provides an introduction to machine learning and will make you an effective practitioner. However, if you want to further your machine learning skills, here are some suggestions of books and more specialized resources to investigate to dive deeper.

8.5.1 Theory

In this book, we tried to provide an intuition of how the most common machine learning algorithms work, without requiring a strong foundation in mathematics or computer science. However, many of the models we discussed use principles from probability theory, linear algebra, and optimization. While it is not necessary to understand all the details of how these algorithms are implemented, we think that knowing some of the theory behind the algorithms will make you a better data scientist. There have been many good books written about the theory of machine learning, and if we were able to excite you about the possibilities that machine learning opens up, we suggest you pick up at least one of them and dig deeper. We already mentioned Hastie, Tibshirani, and Friedman's book *The Elements of Statistical Learning* in the Preface, but it is worth repeating this recommendation here. Another quite accessible book, with accompanying Python code, is *Machine Learning: An Algorithmic Perspective* by Stephen Marsland (Chapman and Hall/CRC). Two other highly recommended classics are *Pattern Recognition and Machine Learning* by Christopher Bishop (Springer), a book that emphasizes a probabilistic framework, and *Machine Learning: A Probabilistic Perspective* by Kevin Murphy (MIT Press), a comprehensive (read: 1,000+ pages) dissertation on machine learning methods featuring in-depth discussions of state-of-the-art approaches, far beyond what we could cover in this book.

8.5.2 Other Machine Learning Frameworks and Packages

While `scikit-learn` is our favorite package for machine learning[1] and Python is our favorite language for machine learning, there are many other options out there. Depending on your needs, Python and `scikit-learn` might not be the best fit for your particular situation. Often using Python is great for trying out and evaluating models, but larger web services and applications are more commonly written in Java or C++, and integrating into these systems might be necessary for your model to be deployed. Another reason you might want to look beyond `scikit-learn` is if you are more interested in statistical modeling and inference than prediction. In this case, you should consider the `statsmodels` package for Python, which implements several linear models with a more statistically minded interface. If you are not married to Python, you might also consider using R, another lingua franca of data scientists. R is a language designed specifically for statistical analysis and is famous for its excellent visualization capabilities and the availability of many (often highly specialized) statistical modeling packages.

Another popular machine learning package is `vowpal wabbit` (often called `vw` to avoid possible tongue twisting), a highly optimized machine learning package written in C++ with a command-line interface. `vw` is particularly useful for large datasets and for streaming data. For running machine learning algorithms distributed on a cluster, one of the most popular solutions at the time of writing is `mllib`, a Scala library built on top of the `spark` distributed computing environment.

1 Andreas might not be entirely objective in this matter.

8.5.3 Ranking, Recommender Systems, and Other Kinds of Learning

Because this is an introductory book, we focused on the most common machine learning tasks: classification and regression in supervised learning, and clustering and signal decomposition in unsupervised learning. There are many more kinds of machine learning out there, with many important applications. There are two particularly important topics that we did not cover in this book. The first is *ranking*, in which we want to retrieve answers to a particular query, ordered by their relevance. You've probably already used a ranking system today; this is how search engines operate. You input a search query and obtain a sorted list of answers, ranked by how relevant they are. A great introduction to ranking is provided in Manning, Raghavan, and Schütze's book *Introduction to Information Retrieval*. The second topic is *recommender systems*, which provide suggestions to users based on their preferences. You've probably encountered recommender systems under headings like "People You May Know," "Customers Who Bought This Item Also Bought," or "Top Picks for You." There is plenty of literature on the topic, and if you want to dive right in you might be interested in the now classic "Netflix prize challenge" (*http://www.netflixprize.com/*), in which the Netflix video streaming site released a large dataset of movie preferences and offered a prize of $1 million to the team that could provide the best recommendations. Another common application is prediction of time series (like stock prices), which also has a whole body of literature devoted to it. There are many more machine learning tasks out there—much more than we can list here—and we encourage you to seek out information from books, research papers, and online communities to find the paradigms that best apply to your situation.

8.5.4 Probabilistic Modeling, Inference, and Probabilistic Programming

Most machine learning packages provide predefined machine learning models that apply one particular algorithm. However, many real-world problems have a particular structure that, when properly incorporated into the model, can yield much better-performing predictions. Often, the structure of a particular problem can be expressed using the language of probability theory. Such structure commonly arises from having a mathematical model of the situation for which you want to predict. To understand what we mean by a structured problem, consider the following example.

Let's say you want to build a mobile application that provides a very detailed position estimate in an outdoor space, to help users navigate a historical site. A mobile phone provides many sensors to help you get precise location measurements, like the GPS, accelerometer, and compass. You also have an exact map of the area. This problem is highly structured. You know where the paths and points of interest are from your map. You also have rough positions from the GPS, and the accelerometer and compass in the user's device provide you with very precise relative measurements. But throwing these all together into a black-box machine learning system to predict positions might not be the best idea. This would throw away all the information you already know about how the real world works. If the compass and accelerometer tell you a user is going north, and the GPS is telling you the user is going south, you probably can't trust the GPS. If your position estimate tells you the user just walked through a wall, you should also be highly skeptical. It's possible to express this situation using a probabilistic model, and then use machine learning or probabilistic inference to find out how much you should trust each measurement, and to reason about what the best guess for the location of a user is.

Once you've expressed the situation and your model of how the different factors work together in the right way, there are methods to compute the predictions using these custom models directly. The most general of these methods are called probabilistic programming languages, and they provide a very elegant and compact way to express a learning problem. Examples of popular probabilistic programming languages are `PyMC` (which can be used in Python) and `Stan` (a framework that can be used from several languages, including Python). While these packages require some understanding of probability theory, they simplify the creation of new models significantly.

8.5.5 Neural Networks

While we touched on the subject of neural networks briefly in Chapters 2 and 7, this is a rapidly evolving area of machine learning, with innovations and new applications being announced on a weekly basis. Recent breakthroughs in machine learning and artificial intelligence, such as the victory of the Alpha Go program against human champions in the game of Go, the constantly improving performance of speech understanding, and the availability of near-instantaneous speech translation, have all been driven by these advances. While the progress in this field is so fast-paced that any current reference to the state of the art will soon be outdated, the recent book *Deep Learning* by Ian Goodfellow, Yoshua Bengio, and Aaron Courville (MIT Press) is a comprehensive introduction into the subject.[2]

8.5.6 Scaling to Larger Datasets

In this book, we always assumed that the data we were working with could be stored in a NumPy array or SciPy sparse matrix in memory (RAM). Even though modern servers often have hundreds of gigabytes (GB) of RAM, this is a fundamental restriction on the size of data you can work with. Not everybody can afford to buy such a large machine, or even to rent one from a cloud provider. In most applications, the data that is used to build a machine learning system is relatively small, though, and few machine learning datasets consist of hundreds of gigabites of data or more. This

2 A preprint of *Deep Learning* can be viewed at *http://www.deeplearningbook.org/*.

makes expanding your RAM or renting a machine from a cloud provider a viable solution in many cases. If you need to work with terabytes of data, however, or you need to process large amounts of data on a budget, there are two basic strategies: *out-of-core learning* and *parallelization over a cluster*.

Out-of-core learning describes learning from data that cannot be stored in main memory, but where the learning takes place on a single computer (or even a single processor within a computer). The data is read from a source like the hard disk or the network either one sample at a time or in chunks of multiple samples, so that each chunk fits into RAM. This subset of the data is then processed and the model is updated to reflect what was learned from the data. Then, this chunk of the data is discarded and the next bit of data is read. Out-of-core learning is implemented for some of the models in `scikit-learn`, and you can find details on it in the online user guide (*http://scikit-learn.org/stable/modules/scaling_strategies.html#scaling-with-instances-using-out-of-core-learning*). Because out-of-core learning requires all of the data to be processed by a single computer, this can lead to long runtimes on very large datasets. Also, not all machine learning algorithms can be implemented in this way.

The other strategy for scaling is distributing the data over multiple machines in a compute cluster, and letting each computer process part of the data. This can be much faster for some models, and the size of the data that can be processed is only limited by the size of the cluster. However, such computations often require relatively complex infrastructure. One of the most popular distributed computing platforms at the moment is the `spark` platform built on top of Hadoop. `spark` includes some machine learning functionality within the `MLLib` package. If your data is already on a Hadoop filesystem, or you are already using `spark` to preprocess your data, this might be the easiest option. If you don't already have such infrastructure in place, establishing and integrating a `spark` cluster might be too large an effort, however. The `vw` package mentioned earlier provides some distributed features and might be a better solution in this case.

8.5.7 Honing Your Skills

As with many things in life, only practice will allow you to become an expert in the topics we covered in this book. Feature extraction, preprocessing, visualization, and model building can vary widely between different tasks and different datasets. Maybe you are lucky enough to already have access to a variety of datasets and tasks. If you don't already have a task in mind, a good place to start is machine learning competitions, in which a dataset with a given task is published, and teams compete in creating the best possible predictions. Many companies, nonprofit organizations, and universities host these competitions. One of the most popular places to find them is Kaggle (*https://www.kaggle.com/*), a website that regularly holds data science competitions, some of which have substantial prize money attached.

The Kaggle forums are also a good source of information about the latest tools and tricks in machine learning, and a wide range of datasets are available on the site. Even more datasets with associated tasks can be found on the OpenML platform (*http://www.openml.org/*), which hosts over 20,000 datasets with over 50,000 associated machine learning tasks. Working with these datasets can provide a great opportunity to practice your machine learning skills. A disadvantage of competitions is that they already provide a particular metric to optimize, and usually a fixed, preprocessed dataset. Keep in mind that defining the problem and collecting the data are also important aspects of real-world problems, and that representing the problem in the right way might be much more important than squeezing the last percent of accuracy out of a classifier.

8.6 Conclusion

We hope we have convinced you of the usefulness of machine learning in a wide variety of applications, and how easily machine learning can be implemented in practice. Keep digging into the data, and don't lose sight of the larger picture.

Index

A

L

M

N

O

P

R

S

T

U

About the Authors

Andreas Müller received his PhD in machine learning from the University of Bonn. After working as a machine learning researcher on computer vision applications at Amazon for a year, he joined the Center for Data Science at New York University. For the last four years, he has been a maintainer of and one of the core contributors to `scikit-learn`, a machine learning toolkit widely used in industry and academia, and has authored and contributed to several other widely used machine learning packages. His mission is to create open tools to lower the barrier of entry for machine learning applications, promote reproducible science, and democratize the access to high-quality machine learning algorithms.

Sarah Guido is a data scientist who has spent a lot of time working in start-ups. She loves Python, machine learning, large quantities of data, and the tech world. An accomplished conference speaker, Sarah attended the University of Michigan for grad school and currently resides in New York City.

Colophon

The animal on the cover of *Introduction to Machine Learning with Python* is a hellbender salamander (*Cryptobranchus alleganiensis*), an amphibian native to the eastern United States (ranging from New York to Georgia). It has many colorful nicknames, including "Allegheny alligator," "snot otter," and "mud-devil." The origin of the name "hellbender" is unclear: one theory is that early settlers found the salamander's appearance unsettling and supposed it to be a demonic creature trying to return to hell.

The hellbender salamander is a member of the giant salamander family, and can grow as large as 29 inches long. This is the third-largest aquatic salamander species in the world. Their bodies are rather flat, with thick folds of skin along their sides. While they do have a single gill on each side of the neck, hellbenders largely rely on their skin folds to breathe: gas flows in and out through capillaries near the surface of the skin.

Because of this, their ideal habitat is in clear, fast-moving, shallow streams, which provide plenty of oxygen. The hellbender shelters under rocks and hunts primarily by sense of smell, though it is also able to detect vibrations in the water. Its diet is made up of crayfish, small fish, and occasionally the eggs of its own species. The hellbender is also a key member of its ecosystem as prey: predators include various fish, snakes, and turtles.

Hellbender salamander populations have decreased significantly in the last few decades. Water quality is the largest issue, as their respiratory system makes them very sensitive to polluted or murky water. An increase in agriculture and other human activity near their habitat means greater amounts of sediment and chemicals in the water. In an effort to save this endangered species, biologists have begun to raise the amphibians in captivity and release them when they reach a less vulnerable age.

Many of the animals on O'Reilly covers are endangered; all of them are important to the world. To learn more about how you can help, go to *animals.oreilly.com*.

The cover image is from *Wood's Animate Creation*. The cover fonts are URW Typewriter and Guardian Sans. The text font is Adobe Minion Pro; the heading font is Adobe Myriad Condensed; and the code font is Dalton Maag's Ubuntu Mono.

Milton Keynes UK
Ingram Content Group UK Ltd.
UKHW051302191024
449883UK00003B/5

9 781449 369415